Study Guide for

Psychology Today:
An Introduction

Fifth Edition

Study Guide for | Psychology Today: An Introduction

Fifth Edition

Richard R. Bootzin / **Elizabeth F. Loftus** / **Robert B. Zajonc**
Northwestern University   University of Washington   University of Michigan

Prepared by

Richard B. Stalling / **Ronald E. Wasden**
Bradley University

Chris Hunter, Consultant

Random House  New York

Fourth Edition

9 8 7 6 5 4 3 2

Copyright © 1973 by Richard B. Stalling and Ronald E. Wasden
Copyright © 1975, 1979, 1983 by Random House, Inc.

ISBN 0-394-33182-6

Manufactured in the United States of America

Preface to the Student

Often students overlook introductions to Study Guides, but we feel there are ways of studying with this book which will optimize its usefulness. Here are some suggestions:

1. The programmed review (fill-in) questions in the study guide are designed to be answered only *after* a particular portion of the text has been read. We have cross-referenced and labeled each section of the study guide to correspond with the text, so it will be fairly easy to read as much of the text as you feel you can digest comfortably and then turn to the comparable study guide section.

2. We have devised a special instrument for revealing answers to the programmed review questions: it's called a *hand*. Simply place your hand over the left side of the page and slide it down as you answer the questions. (We find that special pens and cardboard masks tend to get lost but hands don't.)

3. If the answer doesn't occur to you right away, *don't* look at the answer immediately. Stop and think about it, review the text, and if you are still puzzled then check the answer. We have tried to devise questions that are relatively unambiguous *if* the text is read concurrently.

4. After responding to the programmed review, answer the *learning objectives* that follow. While *objectives* traditionally precede corresponding material, one cannot understand the objectives until one has read the material. So, we chose to put them after. We recommend that you write your answers in a notebook and then review this material just prior to examinations. In all cases, answers to the learning objectives are found in the immediately preceding programmed section.

Note also the *general objectives* which appear at the beginning of chapters. These provide a brief summary of the major concepts in each chapter, and may be useful in preparing for essay tests.

5. The study guide is designed to be used in either a conventional lecture course or in a PSI procedure. In the latter case, your instructor will provide you with appropriate instructions. We have also written a set of test questions for use with a PSI course which are keyed exclusively to the learning objectives in this study guide. For example, if an objective indicates that you should know something about the burial of Ulysses S. Grant, then a multiple choice question could well ask "Who is buried in Grant's tomb?" For this set of test questions, the learning objectives take the guesswork out of studying; if the concept is not in the learning, it won't be on a test composed from this set of items.

There are several other things we could say about using a study guide, such as the fact that it provides an opportunity for active responding and hence better learning, but you probably already know that—or will soon find out.

R. B. S.
R. E. W.

Contents

Study Guide for

Psychology Today:
An Introduction
Fifth Edition

Chapter One
Understanding Psychology: An Introduction

General Objectives

1. Compare the common-sense and scientific approaches to human behavior.

2. Define the term *psychology*, and discuss how the definition has changed across the history of psychology.

3. Name the founder of psychoanalysis, the discoverer of the conditioned reflex, and the founder of the first psychology laboratory.

4. Name the founder of behaviorism, discuss the main tenet of early behaviorism, and name the foremost proponent of modern behaviorism.

5. Be aware of the breadth and diversity of the field of psychology, and be able to recognize some of the major subfields.

6. Explain the difference between applied and basic science; illustrate the difference with examples from psychology.

7. Describe the requirements for obtaining the various professional degrees in psychology.

Understanding Psychology: An Introduction

Learning Objectives appear at
the end of each major section.

contradictory

1. Both psychology and common-sense sayings offer explanations for human behavior, and in some cases the two approaches agree. For example, psychologists have found that people who are similar to one another also tend to like one another; or, as the common saying indicates, "birds of a feather flock together." The trouble with the common-sense approach, however, is that its predictions are frequently (consistent/contradictory). Another proverb tells us that opposites attract.

scientific

2. While psychology and common sense may not always differ in conclusions, they do differ in method. Psychology, which may be defined as the study of behavior, uses the _Scientific_ method.

1

behavior

3. Psychology is the study of <u>behavior</u>. Your text defines behavior broadly—to include not only observable action but more subjective events, including thoughts, feelings, and dreams.

THE GROWTH OF PSYCHOLOGY

Psychology as the Study of Conscious Experience

4. Psychologists have not always assumed that behavior is the proper subject matter

Wundt

of psychology. For example, Wilhelm <u>Wundt</u>, who founded the first psychological laboratory in 1879, considered psychology to be the study of

conscious

<u>conscious</u> experience.

5. Wundt assumed that consciousness was made up of sensations, much like matter is composed of atoms. The method he used in an attempt to determine how

sensations/consciousness

<u>sensations</u> might combine to produce <u>consciousness</u> was

introspection

the technique of <u>introspection</u>.

6. Wundt's theories are of little importance to modern psychology, but his place in

psychologist

history as the first true <u>psychologist</u> and founder of the first psycho-

laboratory

logical <u>laboratory</u> is assured.

Psychology as the Study of Unconscious Processes

small

7. For Sigmund Freud, consciousness comprised a (small/large) part of the mind.

unconscious

Freud believed that most of our behaviors are directed by <u>unconscious</u> urges and conflicts.

8. Since unconscious processes could not be studied by introspection, Freud devel-

free association

oped a procedure termed <u>free</u> <u>association</u> in which patients were instructed to say everything that came to mind. Freud also developed dream analysis, another method he used for exploring

unconscious

<u>unconscious</u> processes.

9. From extensive notes made during sessions with his patients, Freud developed a general theory of personality and a method of treatment. Freud's theory and

are still

treatment (are still/are no longer) an influence in psychology today.

Psychology as the Study of Individual Differences

Galton

differences

individual

10. Another approach to psychology was pioneered by Sir Francis

    Galton. While Wundt and Freud were largely interested in find-
    ing commonalities in human behavior, Galton was interested in individual

    differences. Thus, Galton is associated with the founding of

    individual psychology.

11. Galton traced the ancestry of famous people and found that greatness tends to
    run in families. From this he concluded that genius was a(n)

hereditary (inherited, genetic)

    hereditary trait. This conclusion was not warranted from his data,
    but it foreshadowed the current heredity-versus-environment debate in this area.

statistical

12. Galton also devised testing procedures and _statistical_ techniques,
    such as the correlation coefficient, which are still in use today.

Learning Objectives

1. What is a major drawback of the common-sense approach in comparison with the approach of scientific psychology?

2. What is the definition of *psychology?* What is meant by the term *behavior* in this definition?

3. Who did the following? Place the correct names next to the descriptions below.
   a. Developed the theory and technique known as psychoanalysis. _Freud_
   b. The first true psychologist, founded the first psychology laboratory. _Wundt_
   c. Pioneered the study of individual differences, devised the correlation coefficient and other statistics. _Galton_

4. For Wundt, what was the subject matter of psychology, and of what smaller units was it comprised? What method of investigation did he use?

5. Wundt emphasized consciousness. What did Freud emphasize in his description of the mind?

6. Name two treatment methods developed by Freud.

Psychology as the Study of Observable Behavior

Pavlov

13. Another landmark in the history of psychology was the discovery of the condi-

    tioned reflex by the Russian physiologist Ivan _Pavlov_.

14. In a now famous experiment, Pavlov noted that dogs, which would originally
    salivate when meat powder was presented, began to salivate at the sound of a
    metronome present just before the meat powder. He termed this acquired re-

conditioned reflex

    sponse a _conditioned reflex_.

15. An important aspect of Pavlov's discovery was that it pioneered the investigation of learning, the study of changes in behavior resulting from experience. One of the early learning theorists influenced by Pavlov's discovery was the *founder* of behaviorism, an American psychologist by the name of John B.

Watson   _Watson_.

introspection   16. Like Pavlov, Watson rejected the method of _Introspection_ favored by Wundt and Freud. Watson contended that psychology should deal only with

observable (objective)   _observable_ aspects of behavior and not with mental processes. Wat-

conditioning   son also asserted that all behavior is the result of the _conditioning_ processes discovered by Pavlov.

17. While Watson may be said to be the *founder* of behaviorism, modern behavior-

Skinner   ism is represented by B. F. _Skinner_, who considerably refined and popularized the approach.

18. Among Skinner's well-known contributions are his development of the

teaching   _teaching_ machine (and the programmed learning approach used here); his books, including the novel *Walden Two;* and techniques of reinforcement, extended by others for use in toilet training, weight loss, control of smoking, and a number of other treatments. Clearly, the procedures Skinner developed with lower animals have found extensive use with

human beings   _human   beings_.

Learning Objectives

7. Who did the following? Place the correct names next to the descriptions below.
   a. Founded behaviorism. _Watson_
   b. Is the modern proponent of behaviorism. _B.F. Skinner_
   c. Discovered the conditioned reflex. _Pavlov_

8. What did Watson consider to be the subject matter of psychology? That is, what should psychologists study, according to Watson? _observable things_

9. Name two contributions for which B. F. Skinner is well known. _Walden Two, Teaching Machine_

The next section lists more than twenty separate specialties within the field of psychology (twenty-one if you include consumer psychology), and it is difficult not only for undergraduates but for psychologists to distinguish clearly between them. What we hope to do in this section is simply to give you an appreciation of the diversity of the field of psychology and a rough recognition of some of the activities involved in each field.

Before attempting to answer the programmed section, reread the text carefully.

PSYCHOLOGY TODAY

the United

States

19. While people in various nations have contributed to the field of psychology, and especially its origins, it is in _____ the United _____ States _____

_____ that modern psychology has the greatest diversity and public support.

Fields of Specialization

forty

20. The diversity of the field of psychology is easily illustrated by the number of specialized divisions in the American Psychological Association (APA). In 1982 there were _____ forty _____ divisions of the APA.

21. *Experimental and Physiological Psychology.* Since most fields of psychology involve experimental research, it may strike you as strange that one field is designated as "experimental" psychology. Such a reaction is reasonable; the field of experimental psychology has come to refer not only to a method of study,

experiments (research)

namely, the use of controlled laboratory _____ Experiments _____ , but to the topics or areas of study.

22. The topics studied in the field of experimental psychology include sensation, perception, learning, memory, and so on—many of the topics to which chapters are devoted in this text. Experimental psychologists use primarily controlled

experiments

_____ experiments _____ in their research.

23. Those experimental psychologists who focus on the physiological bases of be-

physiological

havior are called _____ physiological _____ psychologists or *neuropsychologists*.

academic

24. While most experimental psychologists work in (academic/applied) settings, some, because of their training in mathematics and computer sciences, work in the computer industry.

25. Experimental psychologists who study the relationship between drugs and behav-

psychopharmacologists

ior are known as _____ psychopharmacologists _____

26. *Developmental Psychology.* Is the thinking of children really qualitatively different from that of adults, or is there simply less of it? This is the type of question

developmental

with which people in the field of _____ developmental _____ psychology might be concerned.

27. Developmental psychologists study changes in human behavior across the life

death (old age)

span, from birth to _____ death _____ .

academic (university)

28. While some developmental psychologists may work in school or industrial settings, most work in _academic_ settings.

29. *Personality Psychology.* If an individual is described as aggressive, independent, compassionate, and sociable, we have a description of that person's

personality

personality. Personality psychology may be defined as the study of an individual's traits or characteristics.

characteristics

30. Personality theorists and researchers study the traits or _characteristics_ of people; they look for both differences among individuals and consistencies within individuals.

31. *Social Psychology.* While personality psychologists may concentrate on traits of

social

individuals, _social_ psychologists are interested in behavior resulting from *relationships* between people.

32. One of the major areas studied by social psychologists is that of attitude formation and change, including the related areas of attraction between people (a positive attitude), prejudice (a negative attitude), and persuasion (how to change

social

people's attitudes). These and other areas studied by the _social_ psychologist involve interactions or relationships between people.

33. While most social psychologists probably work in academic settings, not all are found in psychology departments; some work in schools of

business

business.

34. *Educational and School Psychology.* *Educational* psychologists study all aspects of the learning process as it relates to education. *School* psychologists generally work in elementary and secondary schools, where they assess children with learning or emotional problems and attempt to remedy these problems. Thus, a psychologist interested in research on gender differences in math would probably

educational

be a(n) _educational_ psychologist; a psychologist concerned with the learning difficulty of a particular fifth grader would probably be a

school

school psychologist.

35. *Industrial and Organizational Psychology.* Both of these specialties study the re-

jobs (work)

lationship between people and their _jobs_, including employee morale, conditions of employment, and so forth.

personnel

36. Industrial or organizational psychologists who specialize in screening job applicants or evaluating job performance are called ___personnel___ psychologists, while those primarily concerned with designing machinery or environments which match the capabilities of their human operators are called

human-factors

___human-factors___ psychologists.

37. *Clinical Psychology*. Clinical psychologists engage in the study, diagnosis, and

abnormal (disordered, maladaptive)

treatment of ___abnormal___ behavior.

38. While a large number of clinical psychologists work in universities, about half of

clinics

them are employed in hospitals or ___clinics___ or else have private practices.

39. A specialty within the area of clinical psychology, with an emphasis on preven-

community

tion of mental disorders, is the field of ___community___ psychology. The ultimate goal of this specialty is to change aspects of the environment which may lead to disorder. Community psychologists frequently staff community mental health clinics, halfway houses, and so forth.

40. Along with findings concerning the role of stress in such physical illnesses as heart disease, stress may also be a factor in a large number of other illnesses. Clinical psychologists concerned with helping people change their life styles and deal with stress in the attempt to reduce physical illness are known as

health

___health___ psychologists.

41. *Emerging Specialties*. A relatively new field concerned with such problems as crowding and noise and how to change social behavior through building design is

environmental

known as ___enviormental___ psychology.

42. Psychologists who may provide expert legal testimony in courts, aid law-enforcement procedures, or provide counseling to inmates are referred to as

forensic

___forensic___ psychologists.

43. Psychologists with a specialty in statistics or measurement are termed

quantitative

___quantitative___ psychologists. These individuals may work in the area of

program

___program___ evaluation in which they assess the cost of governmental or educational programs.

Learning Objectives

10. Provide the names of each of the fields in psychology indicated by the following activities or descriptions. (Note: Because this area is apt to be confusing, answers are given below.)
    a. Includes study of attitude change, relationships between people. _Social_
    b. Study of changes in children as they grow, in adults as they age. _Develop_
    c. Specialty in the study of the effect of drugs on behavior. _Psychopharmacology_
    d. The field concerned with the physiological bases of behavior, including the nervous and endocrine systems. (Either of two answers.) _physiological_
    e. Research likely to be in the areas of sensation, perception, learning, and memory. _experimental_
    f. Study of learning processes associated with primary and secondary schools. _educational_
    g. Screening job applicants, evaluating job performance. _personnel_
    h. Meshing man and machine—designing machinery to fit the capabilities of human beings. _human factors_
    i. Concern with law and courts. _forensic_
    j. Study of the relationship between people and their jobs, including employee morale. (Either of two answers.) _industrial_
    k. Work with children in school settings. _School_
    l. Evaluating governmental or educational programs. (Either of two answers.) _Program_
    m. Study and treatment of abnormal behavior. _clinical_
    n. Branch of clinical psychology largely concerned with prevention. (Either of two answers.) _health_
    o. Concern with building design, noise, crowding. _Enviormental_

Answers: (a) social (b) developmental (c) psychopharmacology (d) physiological psychology or neuropsychology (e) experimental (f) educational (g) personnel (h) human-factors (i) forensic (j) industrial or organizational (k) school (l) program evaluation or quantitative (m) clinical (n) health or community (o) environmental

Psychology: Basic and Applied Science

44. Some research in psychology is done simply to acquire knowledge and understanding about the nature of things, and in this respect psychology is a

    basic   _basic_ science. Other aspects of psychological research are directed toward solving practical problems, so psychology is also an

    applied   _applied_ science.

45. For example, a clinical psychologist who does research primarily to understand the essential nature of psychological disturbances, rather than because of the po-

    basic   tential usefulness of the findings, is practicing _basic_ psychology. Psychologists who use these findings to help remedy behavioral problems

    applied   are primarily interested in _applied_ psychology.

46. Some students in the introductory psychology course are initially disappointed to learn that much of what they are studying cannot immediately be applied to their own lives. The textbook suggests that an interest in applications may lead to an

    basic   interest in the _basic_-science aspects of psychology as well.

Psychology as a Vocation

Ph.D.

47. The majority of psychologists earn the _____Ph.D._____ degree in one of the fields of psychology such as those discussed earlier. Study for the Ph.D. typ-

four/six

ically involves between _____four_____ and _____six_____ years of graduate work at a university.

48. While most clinical psychologists hold the Ph.D. degree, some attend so-called

Psy.D.

professional schools where they earn a _____Psy D_____ degree. The main difference between the training for these degrees is that the Psy.D. places less emphasis on research and may not be associated with a university.

49. After meeting all the requirements for either the Ph.D. or Psy.D. degree, those

clinical

specializing in _____clinical_____ psychology must complete an additional

internship

year of training in an _____internship_____ program.

Learning Objectives

11. Briefly define *basic science* and *applied science*, and provide an example of each from the field of psychology.

12. What degree is held by most doctoral-level psychologists? Ph D

13. Most clinical psychologists hold the Ph.D. degree. What other degree may be held by doctoral-level clinical psychologists? Psy D

14. Approximately how many years past the bachelor's degree are required for completion of the Ph.D.? four to six

15. What specialty in psychology requires one year of internship? clinical

Chapter Two
Doing Psychology: Methodology

General Objectives

1. Describe the major components of an experiment.

2. Explain why one cannot make causal conclusions from correlational data.

3. Describe the research done with surveys, naturalistic observation, and case studies.

4. Explain the difference between descriptive and inferential statistics.

5. List and describe the measures of central tendency and variability, and indicate their use in summarizing data.

6. Give examples of positive and negative, high and low correlation coefficients.

7. Describe and compare experimenter bias, demand characteristics, and the Hawthorne effect.

8. List some of the major ethical principles used to guide research with human subjects.

Doing Psychology: Methodology

Learning Objectives appear at
the end of each major section.

Gathering the Data

1. The factors that may change or vary in an experiment are called

variables

variables. The variable that is *altered* or *manipulated* by the experimenter is termed the *independent* variable.

2. For example, if researchers wished to determine whether a particular type of music helps or hinders learning, they might "manipulate" the music by playing it for one group of subjects and not playing it for a second group. The presence or

independent

absence of music would be the altered or _independent_ variable.

3. Learning in this experiment could be defined in terms of a test score on the words studied. *If* music influences learning, *then* differences in test scores *depend on* the prior manipulation of music. Thus, test scores in this example would

dependent   be the ___dependent___ variable.

4. The independent variable is the variable that is manipulated (or altered or

dependent   changed) by the experimenter. The ___dependent___ variable is the one that depends on this previous manipulation.

5. As a review, place the abbreviations IV (independent variable) or DV (dependent variable) next to the appropriate descriptions below:

IV   ___IV___ Follows the "if" part of "if/then" statements.

IV   ___IV___ Is altered or manipulated by the experimenter.

DV   ___DV___ Results from the prior manipulation.

IV   ___IV___ Refers to different treatments given to different groups.

6. In almost any type of study, the data gathered are from a limited part, or

sample   ___sample___, of the population about which the researcher wishes to make a general statement. To be unbiased, a sample must

represent   ___represent___ the population from which it is derived.

7. Two methods of sampling are discussed in the text. One involves deliberate inclusion of known and proportionate *subsections* of a population; this is known as

representative   a ___representative___ sample. The other involves selecting cases at

random   ___random___ from a population.

8. A sample is random if every datum in a population has a(n)

equal   ___equal___ chance of being selected. For example, if the population of a particular school is 5,723 students, then for the sample to be random each of these 5,723 students must have an equal chance of being selected.

The Experiment

9. More than any of the other methods to be discussed, the true experiment permits

cause-effect (causal)   researchers to infer ___cause___-___effect___ relationships.

10. The simplest experiment contains two groups of subjects, an *experimental* group

control   and a ___control___ group.

11. To insure that the two groups are as comparable as possible, subjects are generally randomly assigned to the groups. In addition, researchers attempt to treat subjects in the groups identically in all ways except one, which is that subjects in

experimental

the ~~experimental~~ group are exposed to the independent variable while those in the control group are not.

12. The terms *dependent* and *independent variable* are generally used in connection with a true experiment. The treatment or manipulated variable, you will recall, is

independent

known as the ~~independent~~ variable; the outcome variable, the one that

dependent

depends on the treatment, is termed the ~~dependent~~ variable.

13. The group that receives the experimental treatment is known as the

experimental

~~experimental~~ group. The group that does not receive the treatment is

control

known as the ~~control~~ group.

14. To review, suppose a researcher examines the effect of a drug on the running speed of rats. The presence or absence of the drug would be the

independent

~~independent~~ variable, and the running speed would be the

dependent

~~dependent~~ variable. The rats that receive the drug comprise the

experimental

~~experimental~~ group, and the rats that do not receive it comprise the

control

~~control~~ group.

15. If there are differences between groups as measured by the dependent variable, it is reasonable to conclude that these differences are caused by the

independent

~~independent~~ variable. Thus, differences in running speed would be attributed to the drug and not to differences in the animals (since rats were assigned randomly).

16. It is not necessary for research to be conducted in a laboratory for it to qualify as

independent

an experiment. As long as the ~~independent~~ variable is truly manipulated, experiments may be done at street corners, schools, airports, and so on. If done in such locations rather than a laboratory, the studies are known as

field

~~field~~ studies.

Learning Objectives

1. Define or give an example of each of the following:
   independent variable – *variable manipulated by researcher*
   dependent variable – *shows the outcome of independent variable*
   random sample – *every person in the population has a fair chance of being picked*
   experimental group – *group that the experiment is performed on*
   control group – *nothing is done to them*

2. Must a study be conducted in a laboratory to qualify as a true experiment? What is the essential characteristic of the
   False
   true experiment? *As long as indep. variable is truly manipulated*

Correlation Research

17. The best way to determine whether one thing causes another is to perform an

experiment   *experiment* . In some research with human beings, however, it is impractical or unethical to do an experiment, and one must resort to

correlational   *correlational* methods, which examine the relationship between variables.

18. The relationship shown by a correlation may be either *positive* or *negative*. For example, one study has found a positive correlation between income and reported happiness—the greater the income, the happier people said they were. Had an increase in income been associated with *decreases* in reported happiness, then

negative   the relationship would have been a *negative* correlation.

do not 19. By themselves, correlations (do/do not) permit one to make *cause-effect* conclusions. For example, from the positive correlation above it would not be correct

causes   to infer that income *causes* happiness—or, for that matter, that happiness causes income.

20. In our example it would be possible to conclude that money causes happiness, or that happiness causes one to make money, or that both happiness and money are

third   caused by a *third* variable which has not been measured (e.g., that education causes both happiness and success at making money).

21. Because the treatment is not manipulated by the experimenter, there is more than
cannot   one possible causal explanation in a correlation study. Thus, one (can/cannot) make a cause-effect conclusion from a correlation.

22. While one cannot make causal conclusions from correlations, one can use corre-

predict

lational data to ___predict___ one event from a knowledge of the other. For example, since there tends to be a positive correlation between IQ and grades, one could predict that, on the average, those who obtain low IQ scores

low (poor)

would also tend to obtain ___low___ grades in school.

Learning Objectives

3. Give an example of a positive correlation and a negative correlation.

4. In terms of the type of conclusion justified, what is the disadvantage of correlational studies in comparison with experimental studies?

5. Explain, or give an example of, the way in which a correlational relationship may be used to predict.

The Survey

23. To assess people's attitudes, opinions, and other characteristics, researchers gen-

surveys

erally use ___surveys___.

24. Surveys may be either oral or written. Oral surveys involve face-to-face

interviews

___interviews___ with subjects; written surveys use

questionnaires

___questionnaires___

25. The advantage of the oral or interview survey method over the written or

questionnaire

___questionnaire___ method is that the former permits the investigator to interact with subjects and modify the questions if needed.

questionnaire

26. Written or ___questionnaire___ surveys, however, have the advantage of taking less time than interviews.

representative

27. Survey data must be truly ___representative___ of the group being studied.
For example, the results of an opinion survey taken at a college student union

would not

(would/would not) be considered representative of student opinion at the college as a whole.

The Case Study

28. Case studies provide descriptive information and, occasionally, brilliant insights into a phenomenon. For example, Freud's theory of personality development is

case studies

in large part based on ___case studies___ of patients who came to him for treatment.

cannot

29. While case studies may suggest testable hypotheses about a phenomenon, they generally do not qualify as experiments and (can/cannot) provide evidence of cause-effect relationships.

30. There is a type of case study, however, in which variables are manipulated and repeated observations are made on a single person. While results from a single individual may not generalize to other people, such studies are considered to be a

experiment

      form of an ___experiment___.

Naturalistic Observation

31. If researchers wish to study the behavior of people or lower animals under natural conditions, without the somewhat artificial changes that may occur in labora-

naturalistic

observation

      tory settings, they may use the method of ___nautralistic___ ___observation___.

32. The primary requirement in using naturalistic observation is that the observations

disturb (interfere with, disrupt)

      be unobtrusive—that is, that they do not ___disturb___ the organism's normally occurring behavior.

33. If members of a research team actually join a group they wish to observe, the

participant observation

      method is termed ___participant observation___. When using this type of naturalistic observation, it is essential, of course, that the other group members do not know that they are being observed.

Learning Objectives

6. Define or give an example of each of the following:
   survey – _it asseses peoples attitudes, opinions and other characteristics_
   interview – _face to face survey with subjecs_
   questionnaire – _written method for a survey_
   naturalistic observation – _observing things in their natural Enviorment_
   participant observation – _joining a group to observe people while also participating in their group_

7. List the advantages and disadvantages associated with the following methods:
   a. Interview versus questionnaire methods of survey research.
   b. Case study versus experimental research.

8. Is it possible for a case study to qualify also as an experiment? _Yes_

ANALYZING THE DATA: STATISTICAL TOOLS

Descriptive Statistics

summarize (describe)

34. Statistics are of two types: descriptive or inferential. Descriptive statistics are used to ___Summarize___ the data.

frequency

35. *Describing Distributions of Scores*. One method of summarizing or describing involves displaying the data in a ___Frequency___ distribution such as shown in Figure 2.1 in your text.

central tendency

36. To further describe these data, one could use a single number, one of the measures of ___central tendency___. For example, adding all the scores and dividing by the total number of scores produces the

mean

___mean___ or arithmetic average.

4

37. Suppose five subjects in an experiment obtain the following scores: 2, 2, 3, 4, and 9. What is the mean? ___4___

central tendency

38. In addition to the mean there are two other commonly used measures of ___central tendency___: the *median* and the *mode*. The median is simply the most central score.

39. Although the mean takes into account the size of each score, the median does not. It is simply the most central score, the one that falls in the middle of the distribution. What is the median score in the following numbers: 2, 2, 3, 4, 9?

3

___3___

40. The mode is the *most frequently occurring* score. What is the mode of the above

2

scores? ___2___

41. Determine the mean, median, and mode of the following set of scores. (The scores have been placed in rank order.)

5

___5___ mean   1
                        2
                        4
                        4

5

___5___ median   5
                        5
                        5
                        9

5

___5___ mode   10

42. Determine the mean, median, and mode of the following set of scores. To determine the median, first place the scores in rank order.

	UNRANKED ORDER	RANK ORDER
		1
_____7_____ mean	2	2
	4	2
	3	3
	1	4
_____3_____ median	5	5
	2	32
	32	
_____2_____ mode		

7

3

2

43. In the preceding example the mean is a misleading measure of central tendency: all the scores except one are below the mean. With such skewed sets of data, the

median

_____median_____ is usually considered a better indication of central tendency than the mean.

44. By plotting scores on graphs (like those in Figure 2.1 in your text), psychologists

normal

can show how the scores, or data, are distributed. In a _____normal_____ distribution, the curve produced by the scores is bell-shaped. In a normal distri-

identical

bution the mean, median, and mode are (different/identical).

45. *Variability and Standard Deviation.* The variability of a distribution is simply the extent to which it is dispersed or spread out. Which of the following sets of data has greater variability?

a

(a)   1, 5, 7, 9, 13   12   35   7 mean
b.   4, 6, 7, 8, 10   6   35   7 mean

46. The mean alone provides an incomplete description of data. While the above sets of data are obviously different, both have a mean of 7. To help complete the

variability

description, a measure of _____variability_____ is used to indicate dispersion.

47. Two measures of variability are discussed in your text: the

range

_____range_____ and the standard deviation. The range is determined by subtracting the lowest score from the highest score. For example, in question 45, data set *a*, above, the highest score was 13 and the lowest was 1. The range is

12

_____12_____.

48. The range is determined by using only two numbers in a distribution. The

standard deviation

<u>standard deviation</u> is a more precise measure of variability than the range because it takes into account the difference between

normal

each score and the mean. In fact any <u>normal</u> distribution is adequately described by the mean and standard deviation.

Learning Objectives

9. What is the function of *descriptive* statistics? Give an example.

10. List the three measures of central tendency, and define each. mean, median, mode

11. Under what conditions are the three measures of central tendency the same? When are they not the same?
Normal distribution

12. Nine subjects obtain the following scores on a test of anxiety: 1, 2, 2, 2, 3, 3, 4, 6, and 22. Determine the mean, median, mode, and range of this set of data. Which is probably the better measure of central tendency for these data, the mean or median? Why? median   mean 5
3 median
3 mode

13. Describe or illustrate the following terms:
range
standard deviation

49. *Correlation Coefficients.* As discussed earlier, correlations indicate the degree of relationship between variables. The descriptive statistic used to summarize a cor-

coefficient

relation is termed the correlation <u>coefficient</u>.

50. Correlation coefficients range between -1 and $+1$. A correlation approaching

negative

-1 indicates a strong <u>negative</u> relationship, and one approaching

positive

$+1$ a strong <u>positive</u> relationship.

51. For example, there is a correlation between intoxication and reflexes: the greater the intoxication, the slower the reflexes. In this case intoxication and speed of

negatively

reaction are (negatively/positively) correlated.

52. If the relationship between drunkenness and speed of reaction were perfect, the

-1
0

correlation coefficient would be (-1, $+1$, or 0). If there were no relationship between these variables, the correlation coefficient would be (-1, $+1$, or 0).

53. It is important to note that correlations found in psychological studies are rarely, if ever, perfect (that is, $+1$ or -1). In addition correlations (are/are not) like

are not
does not

percentages: a coefficient of .35, for example, (does/does not) indicate a relationship half as strong as .70.

54. Which of the following would indicate the strongest correlation between two variables?

d (not c, because correlations range between −1 and +1)

  a. + .72
  b. + .40
  c. + 1.25
  (d.) − .82

Learning Objectives

14. Consider this hypothesis: The *more* surgeons practice their craft, the *fewer* mishaps occur. What kind of statistic could be used to relate amount of practice to number of failures? *correlational*

15. What correlation coefficient represents a perfect positive relationship? A perfect negative one? What coefficient represents the absence of a relationship?

Inferential Statistics

55. After the data in an experiment have been described or summarized, the researchers make *inferences* from them to support or modify the original hy-

inferential

  potheses. To do this _inferential_ statistics are used.

56. Suppose, for example, the researchers test the effect of relaxation training on test anxiety. The experimental group is given the relaxation treatment, and the control group is given a placebo treatment (which has no true effects other than those resulting from subjects' expectations). The results indicate that the mean test score of the experimental group is 70 and of the control group, 65. The question the researchers must then decide is this: Is the difference between 70 and 65 the result of the *treatment,* or is it likely that such a difference occurred

chance

  simply on the basis of _chance_ alone?

57. The so-called null hypothesis states that any difference between groups is due to chance. Thus, if the experimenters conclude that the treatment did produce a dif-

reject

  ference between groups, they must (reject/accept) the null hypothesis.

58. Using various statistical methods, the researchers indicate how likely it is that such a difference as the one obtained would have occurred on a chance basis. If the probability of such a chance difference is small—say, less than five times out of one hundred—then they may decide against chance and against the

null

  null hypothesis. In this case, the researchers would reject the

.05

  null at the _.05_ level of significance.

59. Sometimes researchers choose a more stringent level of significance, such as the

.01

_____.01_____ level (or 1 out of 100). In any case, the probability of the results occurring on a chance basis is computed, and only if that probability is quite low does the experimenter reject the null hypothesis and

accept

_____accept_____ the experimental hypothesis.

Learning Objectives

16. What is the difference between descriptive and inferential statistics? Give examples to illustrate each type.

17. What is the null hypothesis? How is it related to the experimental hypothesis?

18. What does it mean to say that a finding is statistically significant at the .01 level? What levels are most frequently used as cutoff points for deciding whether to accept or reject a hypothesis?

SELECTED METHODOLOGICAL PROBLEMS

Experimenter Bias

60. In conducting an experiment researchers attempt to control all variables except

independent

the one intentionally manipulated, the _independent_ variable.

61. Robert Rosenthal has reported, however, that an experimenter's *expectations* may unintentionally influence the results. He has termed this phenomenon

experimenter bias

experimenter bias.

62. For example, in one study some students were told that the rats they were to train were "maze bright" and others were told that they were "maze dull." Ac-

no difference

tually, there was (no difference/a large difference) between the two groups of rats, but those students who expected bright performance in the maze obtained

bright

(bright/dull) performance; and students who expected dull performance obtained dull performance.

63. Similar results may also occur for human beings. First graders whose teachers

gained

were told to expect them to do well (to "bloom" in IQ) actually (gained/lost) in IQ over those not associated with such expectations. Unknown to the teachers,

at random

the students described as "bloomers" were picked (according to IQ/at random) and were not different from the rest of the children.

64. In an attempt to avoid experimenter bias, researchers use a procedure in which neither the experimenter nor the subject knows which treatment group the subject is in—that is, they are both "blind" to the condition of the subject. This proce-

double-blind

dure is known as the _double_-_blind_ technique.

Demand Characteristics

demand characteristics

65. If subjects' responses are determined by factors "demanded" by the research setting rather than by the independent variable, psychologists say that

_demand___ _characteristic_are operating.

demand characteristics

66. Demand characteristics and experimenter bias are similar concepts; in fact, experimenter bias is really one form of demand characteristics. All aspects of the experimental situation that influence subjects' responses—including the instructions, the equipment, the setting, and the demeanor of the experimenter—are included in the concept of _demand___ _characteristics_

Hawthorne effect

67. The so-called _Hawthorne___ _effect____ is also a form of demand characteristics. This effect refers to the finding that almost any changes in the working environment, including ones that would logically seem related to work decrement, resulted in an increase in workers' productivity.

attention

68. Subjects in an experiment, like the workers at Hawthorne, behave differently when they feel that special _attention____ is being paid to them. Thus, research must be designed to minimize this effect.

Learning Objectives

19. Define or give examples of the following:
    experimenter bias
    demand characteristics
    Hawthorne effect

20. Briefly describe the results of the following studies:
    the "maze bright" and "maze dull" rats
    the "IQ bloomers"

21. What is the double-blind procedure?

Problems of Measurement

independent

69. In an experiment a researcher first manipulates the _independent___ variable and then measures the effect on the _dependent___ variable. Problems are encountered both through failure to vary truly the independent variable and through use of an insensitive dependent measure.

dependent

70. For example, some studies had reported that subjects were able to learn while they were asleep. Later studies, which used the electroencephalogram (EEG) to define sleep, found that learning occurred only while subjects were dozing lightly or awake. (In fact, the more awake the subjects were, the better they learned.) The problem in the earlier studies had been the researchers' assumption that because subjects' eyes were closed they were asleep. The researchers had failed to

manipulate (vary)   _manipulate_ truly the independent variable. Their

experimental/control   _experimental_ and _control_ groups were not really different.

Replications

71. The attempt to repeat or duplicate a study is referred to as

replication   _replication_ . Research must be replicated before it is accepted by the scientific community.

72. Replications that produce essentially the same results as the original study are
a different   most convincing if done by ((the same)/a different) scientist in
a different   (the same/(a different)) laboratory.

73. Replications are of two general types. Some attempt to reproduce exactly the

modify (change)   conditions of the previous study, while others _modify_ one or more of the conditions in an attempt to test another explanation for the hypothesis about the results.

74. A study by Lee Salk, for example, was modified by other researchers to test Salk's conclusion that the sound of the human heartbeat has a unique and beneficial effect on newborn infants. Salk believed this occurred because infants be-

imprinted   come _imprinted_ on the heartbeat before birth.

75. In his study, Salk played an amplified human heartbeat in one nursery and not in
were   a second. He found that the infants who ((were)/were not) exposed to the heartbeat cried less, gained weight faster, and slept more than babies in the other nursery.

76. In a later study, however, Brackbill compared three different types of rhythmic sounds—a heartbeat, the ticking of a metronome, and a lullaby—to test whether the crucial factor was the specific quality of the heartbeat sound or simply its

rhythmicity (rhythm)   _rhythmicity_ .

77. In this study, all three rhythmic sounds produced quieter infants. Thus, some

imprinting   doubt was cast on Salk's idea that _imprinting_ was responsible for the soothing effect of heartbeat sounds. It appeared, in fact, that any type of rhythmic sound would have the same effect.

78. Brackbill hypothesized, however, that the characteristic of the sounds most responsible for the soothing effect was neither imprinting nor

rhythmicity   ___rhythmicity___ , but the fact that the sounds were

constant/monotonous   ___constant___ and ___monotonous___ stimuli. In a further study, Brackbill used a number of other constant and monotonous stimuli to test this hypothesis: heartbeat, constant light, increased heat, and swaddling.

79. The results of this later study showed that the crucial factor seemed to be

constant stimulation   (rhythm/constant stimulation). Furthermore, the most effective single stimulus

swaddling   was ___swaddling___ , and a combination of all the stimuli produced an even greater calming effect.

80. While replications are directed toward clarifying or correcting the findings of research, occasionally they do not do so. For example, despite many attempts at

eye   replication, the relationship between ___eye___ movements and
is not   brain activity (is/is not) clear.

Learning Objectives

22. Give an example of a "problem of measurement" involving failure to manipulate the independent variable.

23. What is a replication? Under what conditions is replication most convincing?

24. Describe the Salk study and the two studies by Brackbill, indicating the change in conclusions that accompanied the changes in procedure.

25. What single stimulus was found to have the greatest calming effect on newborns? What was the effect of adding other constant or monotonous stimuli?

26. Replication may not always clarify an issue. Give an example of such a situation.

ETHICAL PRINCIPLES IN PSYCHOLOGICAL RESEARCH

No programmed review is provided for this portion of the chapter, but the principles discussed in it are of immense importance to the conduct of psychological research. They should also be of interest to you—in all likelihood a potential experimental subject. The learning objectives which follow are designed to reflect questions that anyone considering participation in an experiment would probably wish to know.

Learning Objectives

27. The American Psychological Association has developed a set of principles to guide the conduct of research involving human subjects. The four basic conditions required in research with human subjects are given below. To be sure you understand what these concepts refer to, match them to the descriptions or examples which follow.

_____b_____ privacy   _____d_____ informed consent
_____a_____ voluntary participation   _____c_____ freedom from harm

    a. Subjects must be informed that they do not have to participate and that they are free to drop out of an experiment.
    b. Data must be kept in such a way that the identity of participants cannot be determined.
    c. No lasting harm should come to subjects from participating in an experiment.
    d. Subjects must be told what they are to do in an experiment and the extent of possible risk involved, if any.

28. Who reviews planned research involving human subjects in an attempt to determine whether or not subjects will be adequately protected? APA

29. Deception in psychological studies is undesirable and should be avoided if at all possible. What two situations were discussed in which deception seems either necessary for the conduct of a study or less harmful to subjects than full disclosure?

30. When should subjects be informed about the deception? Most of the time before but alot of the times After

31. What are the ethical procedures and standards that apply to animal care?

Chapter Three
The Brain and Behavior

General Objectives

1. Name and describe the three kinds of specialized cells in the central nervous system.

2. Name the divisions of the nervous system, and describe the function of each of these divisions.

3. Tell how neural signals are transmitted.

4. Name some of the more important glands that make up the endocrine system, and describe their functions.

5. Locate the major areas of the cerebral cortex, and describe their general functions.

6. Describe some of the important functions of the limbic system.

7. Name the structures located in the central core, and describe a major function of each structure.

8. Name and define some of the common disorders of the brain.

9. Name and describe the major methods for studying brain-behavior relationships.

The Brain and Behavior

Learning Objectives appear at
the end of each major section.

1. Persons who specialize in the study of the intimate relationship between the brain

neuropsychologists   and behavior are called *neuro psychologists*

2. Their primary goal is to discover how the brain changes various kinds of external and internal stimuli into feelings, thoughts, and actions. In other words, they

information   view the brain as a system for *processing* _information_ .

THE NERVOUS SYSTEM

3. Complex organisms such as human beings have three types of specialized cells. Identify each of these specialized cells from the following descriptions:

a. Cells that are tuned to receive specialized information from the environment

receptor

are called _receptor_ cells.

b. Cells that control movement in muscles and secretion in glands are called

motor

motor cells.

c. Cells specialized for conducting neural messages are called

neurons

neurons.

d. Neurons carry messages between the receptor cells and the

motor

motor cells and thereby coordinate their activity.

Learning Objectives

1. What are neuropsychologists, and what is their primary goal?

2. Describe the function of receptor cells, motor cells, and neurons.

Divisions of the Nervous System

4. The brain and the spinal cord together form a huge clump of neurons called the

central

central *nervous system*. This system is the ultimate control center for all forms of behavior.

5. The network of nerves that carries messages from the central nervous system to the various muscles and organs in the periphery of the body and back is called

peripheral

the _peripheral_ *nervous system*. The peripheral nervous system has two major divisions. The division that controls the voluntary movements of the

somatic

muscles is called the _somatic_ *nervous system*. The other division, which controls involuntary biological functions such as the beating of the heart

autonomic

and glandular secretion, is called the _autonomic_ *nervous system*.

6. The autonomic nervous system is in turn composed of two general divisions

parasympathetic

called the *sympathetic* and the _parasympathetic_ *nervous systems*. Each of these divisions supplies nerves to the same muscles and glands.

7. The sympathetic division is usually most active during emergency or stress con-

expend (use)

ditions and thus serves to _expend_ energy. On the other hand, the parasympathetic system dominates during times of calmness and relaxation, thus

conserve

helping to _conserve_ energy.

8. While these two systems oppose each other in some actions, they work together

parasympathetic

in others. For example, sexual arousal is mediated by the _parasympathetic_

sympathetic

nervous system, but sexual orgasm depends on the _sympathetic_ nervous system.

Learning Objectives

3. What are the two parts of the central nervous system? What is the major role of the central nervous system?

4. Describe the following systems:
   peripheral nervous system
   somatic nervous system
   autonomic nervous system

5. Name the two divisions of the autonomic nervous system, and describe the general function of each.

Neurons

9. Some neurons carry information from the sense organs to the brain, some carry information from the brain to the muscles and glands, and some carry informa-

neurons

tion *between* the _neurons_. Our thoughts, feelings, memories, etc., result from the translation of information carried by these three kinds of

neurons

neurons.

10. Neurons are surrounded by more numerous and smaller cells called

glia/unclear

glia ("glue"). The exact nature of glia cells is (clear/unclear), but they appear to provide nutrients and structural support to the neurons as well as filter certain substances from the bloodstream. The major role in behavior,

neurons

however, results from the interaction of (glia/neurons).

11. The neuron has three major parts. Identify each of these parts from their description, and point them out in the figure on page 28.

dendrite

a. The _dendrite_ receives messages from other neurons and passes them to the cell body.

cell body

b. The _cell body_ provides the energy for neuronal activities.

axon

c. The _axon_ carries the impulses from the cell body to the dendrites of other neurons.

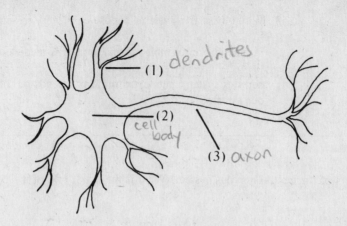

12. Signals in the neuron generally travel in only one direction. The signal from an-

dendrites

other neuron is received by the _dendrites_. It then passes through

axon

the cell body and down the _axon_ to perhaps fire another neuron.

Learning Objectives

6. Draw a simple neuron, label its three major parts, and describe the function of each part.

7. Describe the sequence of events in the firing of a single neuron.

Transmission of Neural Signals

13. The electrically charged atoms and molecules that pass in and out of the neuron

ions/membrane

are called _ions_. The cell _membrane_ regulates the flow of these ions in and out of the neuron.

14. When the neuron is in its normal resting state, the exterior of the cell is posi-

negatively

tively charged and the interior of the cell is _negatively_ charged. When this electrical imbalance across the cell membrane is in effect, the cell is

polarized

said to be _polarized_.

15. When a stimulus of sufficient intensity is applied to a neuron in its polarized state, the cell membrane opens and permits an exchange of

ions

ions that reverses the normal polarity; that is, for only an in-stant the exterior of the cell becomes negatively charged and the interior becomes

positively

positively charged.

refractory

16. As soon as a charge of electrical impulses has traveled through the cell body and down the axon, the neuron enters a brief _refractory_ _period_ in which it will not transmit an impulse. The neuron quickly restores itself to fire again,

1,000

however, and some neurons can repeat this up to _1000_ times per second.

17. Some neural axons are enclosed in a white fatty substance which insulates the axon and provides for more rapid transmission of the neural impulse. This fatty

myelin sheath

enclosure is known as _myelin sheath_ .

white

18. Myelinated axons form the _white_ _matter_ of the nervous system, whereas nonmyelinated axons, cell bodies, and dendrites form the

gray

gray _matter_.

19. Information as to the intensity of a stimulus stimulating a neuron is conveyed by

firing
higher

the _firing_ _rate_ of the neuron. Strong stimuli produce (higher/lower) firing rates than do weak stimuli.

20. In addition, information about the nature of the message is also conveyed by the particular pathway a neural message follows. For example, stimulating the visual

visual

nerves by pressing against the eyeball results in _visual_ sensations being transmitted to the brain. Pressure against the ear results in

auditory

auditory information being sent to the brain.

21. When a nerve impulse reaches the end of an axon, it causes the release of chemicals (_neurotransmitters_) stored in the tip of the axon into the gap separating it from other neurons. This gap between neurons is called a

synapse

synapse .

neurotransmitter

22. The release of the _Neurotransmitter_ in turn stimulates the dendrites of other neurons. Neurotransmitters can, in some cases, also stimulate the cell body and axon of a neuron, but the majority of chemical stimulation is received

dendrites

through the _dendrites_ .

23. Messages transferred from one neuron to another may be either _excitatory_ or

inhibitory

inhibitory , depending on the chemical structure of the neurotransmitter. If the neurotransmitter is excitatory, it causes the receiving neuron to

begin

(begin/cease) firing; if it is inhibitory, it causes the receiving neuron to

cease

cease firing.

different

24. There are many kinds of neurotransmitters, and different neural pathways apparently use (the same/different) neurotransmitters. For example, serotonin, norepinephrine, and dopamine, three of the most common neurotransmitters, affect different pathways and produce (similar/different) behavioral effects.

different

25. One kind of neurotransmitter acts very much in the manner of opiates and blocks the neural pathways that transmit the perception of pain. This particular group of

endorphins

neurotransmitters is called ___endorphins___.

26. There are numerous disorders, including schizophrenia, Parkinson's disease, and some forms of depression, that appear to be related to deficiencies in

neurotransmitters

___neurotransmitters___

Learning Objectives

8. What mechanism controls the flow of ions, in and out of the neuron?

9. Describe the electrical state of a neuron in its polarized state. Describe what occurs with respect to the ions when a signal passes through a neuron.

10. What is the refractory period?

11. How do neurons indicate the intensity of a particular stimulus? What other means do they have for providing information about the nature of a message?

12. Identify and describe the following:
    myelin sheath
    neurotransmitter
    synapse

13. Describe how a neuron transmits a signal to another neuron.

14. What are the two general effects of neurotransmitters?

15. What are endorphins?

16. Name three disorders that may be related to deficiencies in neurotransmitters.

Reflex Arcs and the Spinal Cord

reflex

27. The knee-jerk reflex illustrates a simple two-neuron ___reflex___

arc

___arc___. Hitting the tendon just below the knee sends an impulse through a sensory neuron which has a synaptic junction with a motor neuron in

spinal
does not

the ___spinal___ cord. The resulting reflexive jerk of the leg (does/does not) actively involve the brain.

28. Most reflexes, however, involve more than two neurons and often actively involve the brain. Moreover, the brain can exert some control even over simple

inhibit

reflex arcs. This can be demonstrated by our ability to ___inhibit___ the knee-jerking reflex.

Learning Objectives

17. Describe how a two-neuron reflex arc works.

18. How can one demonstrate that the brain can exert control over reflex arcs?

THE ENDOCRINE SYSTEM

29. The endocrine system delivers messages to all parts of the body by means of

hormones

chemical substances called ___hormones___. However, each of the hormones circulating in the bloodstream affects only particular

target

___target___ organs.

30. In comparison to the speed of neural impulses, these chemical messages travel

slowly

much more ___slowly___.

31. The tendency of the body to maintain a stable internal environment is called

homeostasis

___homeostasis___. Any significant deviation from a stable state will elicit

equilibrium

actions that return the system to ___equilibrium___.

32. The pituitary and thyroid glands are an example of a homeostatic system. The amount of thyroxin produced by the thyroid is controlled by the amount of thy-

pituitary

roid-stimulating hormone produced by the ___pituitary___ gland, and vice versa. When the level of thyroxin becomes low, the pituitary secretes

more

(more/less) thyroid-stimulating hormone and the thyroid begins to produce more thyroxin. When the thyroxin level becomes high, the pituitary secretes

less

(more/less) thyroid-stimulating hormone, which causes the thyroid to produce less thyroxin.

33. Each of these glands thus controls the output of the other, and the levels of thy-

equilibrium

roxin and thyroid-stimulating hormone remain in ___equilibrium___ (balance).

master

34. The pituitary gland actually secretes many hormones, which have controlling effects similar to that of the thyroid-stimulating hormone on other hormone-producing glands. For this reason it is sometimes called the _master_ gland of the endocrine system. The pituitary gland is in turn controlled by the

brain

brain, which therefore controls (and monitors) the amount of various hormones circulating in the blood through its neural connections with the pituitary gland.

35. When one is faced with a stressful situation, hormones that prepare the body for

adrenal

fleeing or fighting are secreted by the _adrenal_ *glands*. The ad-

sympathetic

renal glands are activated by the _sympathetic_ *nervous system*.

36. Phenomena such as voodoo death can be caused by the continuous flow of hormones from the adrenal glands. In these situations the overproduction of adrenal

heart

hormones results in _heart_ failure.

gonads

37. The sex glands, or _gonads_, work in conjunction with the *pituitary gland* to control sex characteristics. In females these glands are called the

testes

ovaries; in males they are called the _testes_.

is not

38. Sexual behavior in adult human beings (is/is not) directly controlled by sex hor-

psychological

mones. The more important role here is played by _psychological_ factors. This can be shown by the fact that men and women generally experience little decline in their sexual responsiveness following removal of the gonads.

Learning Objectives

19. What does the endocrine system do, and how does it do it?

20. How does the endocrine message system differ from that of the nervous system?

21. What does *homeostasis* mean?

22. Describe how the pituitary and thyroid glands interact to maintain *equilibrium*.

23. Why is the pituitary gland called the master gland of the endocrine system?

24. How does the brain exert its control over the endocrine system?

25. What is the role of the adrenal glands? How might they be implicated in phenomena such as voodoo death?

26. Identify the following glands:
    gonads _sex glands_
    ovaries _female sex organs_
    testes _male sex organs_

27. How do we know that sexual responsiveness in adult human beings is not under the direct control of sex hormones?

THE BRAIN

39. The three overlapping layers of the brain are the cerebral cortex, the limbic system, and the central core. In the brain's evolutionary development, the

central core   _central_   _core_   came first, the

limbic system   _limbic_   _system_   came next, and the final

cerebral cortex   development was the _cerebral_   _cortex_ .

The Cerebral Hemispheres

40. The cerebral hemispheres include the cerebral cortex and the

limbic   _limbic_   system. There are two such hemispheres, the *right* and

left/different   the _left_ . Each hemisphere controls (the same/(different))
                functions.

41. The two cerebral hemispheres account for about 85 percent of the brain's weight.
unknown   It is (known/(unknown)) how much of this tissue is required for normal
                functioning.

hydrocephalics   42. Studies of _hydrocephalics_ (persons with excessive fluid trapped in the
                cranium) have shown that in spite of excessive compression of the brain tissue,
                normal functioning is still possible. The explanation for this remains a puzzle.

43. The convoluted (folded) outer surface of the cerebral hemispheres is called the

cortex   cerebral _cortex_ . Each of the two hemispheres of the cerebral

four   cortex is divided into _4_ lobes. In some cases, the bounda-

fissures   ries are formed by crevices called _fissures_ .

44. Look at Figure 3.7 in the text. Then, on the figure below, identify the four lobes and the two major fissures.

(a) parietal

(b) frontal

(c) central

(d) lateral

(e) temporal

(f) occipital

(a) _parietal_ lobe

(c) _central_ fissure

(d) _lateral_ fissure

(b) _frontal_ lobe

(e) _temporal_ lobe

(f) _Occipital_ lobe

45. Identify each of the four lobes on the basis of their functions as listed below:

frontal

occipital

parietal

temporal

central

a. The _frontal_ lobe controls fine voluntary movements and speech in the dominant hemisphere.

b. The _occipital_ lobe is the center for the reception and analysis of visual information.

c. The _parietal_ lobe is the main receiving area for sensory information from the skin; it is also responsible for the sense of bodily position.

d. The _temporal_ lobe is the main receiving area for auditory information; it also processes some visual information.

46. The area known as the *motor cortex* forms a band directly in front of the

central fissure and is responsible for the integration of bodily movements.

47. Immediately behind the central fissure lies another band of cortex that receives touch and positional information from various parts of the body. This area is

sensory

known as the _____ *cortex*.

48. It has been demonstrated that specific sensory and motor functions have specific locations in the brain; the same (is/is not) true of more general and abstract functions such as emotions, intelligence, and consciousness. Approximately 75 percent of the cortex consists of areas that do not have a specific sensory or motor

is not

associative

function. These areas, called the _____ *cortex,* are thought to play a major role in the more abstract brain processes.

49. The right side of the body is controlled by the _____ hemisphere, and the left side of the body is controlled by the

left

right

_____ hemisphere. Each hemisphere also tends to specialize in the kind of information it processes and stores. This is called

lateralization

_____ .

50. Information exchange between the two hemispheres takes place primarily through

corpus callosum

a large neural tract called the _____ _____ . If

independently

the corpus callosum is severed, each hemisphere operates _____ of the other.

51. Evidence continues to accumulate that the dominant hemisphere in most persons

left

is the _____ cerebral hemisphere. Behavior involving language and logical thought is apparently under the general control of this hemisphere.

52. On the other hand, behavior involving spatial abilities, musical abilities, and visual imagery appears to be under the general control of the

right

_____ cerebral hemisphere.

53. There is some evidence that right-handed persons do better than left-handed per-

left

sons at language-related tasks and that _____-handed persons are superior in artistic abilities and recognition of tones.

54. There are also some sex differences related to hemispheric lateralization. With respect to language-related skills, (women/men) tend to do better, while (women/men) are more proficient at spatial and mathematical skills. The difference between the sexes in this respect is (small/large).

women
men
small

Learning Objectives

28. Name the three overlapping areas of the brain, and describe their evolutionary sequence of development.

29. What two major structures are included in the cerebral hemispheres? In what way do the two cerebral hemispheres differ?

30. What is puzzling about the mental functioning of many hydrocephalics?

31. Name the four lobes of the cerebral cortex, and list the major functions of each lobe.

32. What areas of the cerebral cortex are divided by the central fissure? What areas are divided by the lateral fissure?

33. Identify and describe the following:
    motor cortex
    sensory cortex
    corpus callosum
    associative cortex
    lateralization of function

34. Which of the two cerebral hemispheres has primary control over the following functions or areas?
    language
    musical ability
    right side of the body
    critical thought
    spatial ability
    visual imagery
    left side of the body

35. In what way do right-handed persons differ from left-handed persons with respect to mental abilities? In what way do men and women differ? Are these differences large or small?

The Limbic System

55. Although the limbic system first evolved as a center for olfactory (smell) information, it now plays a major role in regulating such behaviors as eating, drinking,

mating

    ing, fleeing, fighting, and _mating_. Damage to the limbic system has been observed to produce marked changes in these behaviors.

56. A common feature in behaviors regulated by the limbic system is that they have

emotional

    a *motivational* or _emotional_ component and involve an animal in

avoid

    making a decision as to whether to *approach* or _avoid_ a particular object or event. The limbic system does not have complete control over these emotionally tinged behaviors. Rather it shares this control with the

cerebral

    cerebral *cortex.*

57. It has also been discovered that direct electrical stimulation to some parts of the limbic system appears to be highly pleasurable, since rats will run mazes or press levers to receive this stimulation. These limbic areas have been named

pleasure   "___pleasure___ centers." Other areas in the limbic system, however,

avoid (stop)
have   appear to be *aversive*. Rats will perform work to ___avoid___ electrical stimulation of these areas. Similar pleasure centers (have/have not) been found in human beings.

Learning Objectives

36. What was the earlier role of the limbic system, and what is its current role? With what other structure does it share this role?

37. What are "pleasure centers"? In what general area of the brain are they located? Can stimulation of this general area produce other emotional behavior?

The Central Core

58. The central core was the first layer of the brain to evolve, and thus it is not surprising that the structures within it carry out functions necessary for

survival   ___survival___.

59. The following structures are the most important components of the central core. Identify them from the descriptions given below.

a.   This is a control center for breathing and circulation and for controlling

medulla   chewing, salivation, and facial expressions. ___medulla___

b.   This area relays motor information from higher brain centers to the cerebellum and also integrates movements between the right and left sides of the

pons   body. ___pons___

c.   This is primarily a center for visual and auditory reflexes.

midbrain   ___midbrain___

d.   This system alerts the brain to important incoming information and maintains

reticular   a normal sleep-waking cycle. ___reticular___

activating system   ___activating___ ___system___ (RAS)

e.   This area coordinates the voluntary muscles and is necessary for maintaining

cerebellum   physical balance. ___cerebellum___

f.   This center is primarily a relay station that routes incoming sensory informa-

thalamus   tion to appropriate regions in the higher brain. ___thalamus___

g.   This is an especially important area that plays a major role in regulating the body's internal environment, including temperature regulation and regulation

hypothalamus   of hunger and thirst, to name a few of its functions. ___hypothalamus___

Learning Objectives

38. Describe the major functions of the following structures that make up the central core:
    medulla
    pons
    midbrain
    reticular activating system (RAS)
    cerebellum
    thalamus
    hypothalamus

Disorders of the Brain

aphasia

60. Damage to the brain by disease or injury can result in many kinds of abnormal behavior. For example, brain damage can result in an inability to speak or understand spoken language, a condition known as _aphasia_.

amnesia

agnosia

61. Brain damage can also result in a general loss of memory, a condition known as _amnesia_. Or it might result in the loss of ability to recognize common sounds, a condition known as _agnosia_.

scar

neurotransmitter

62. Some forms of epilepsy can result from the _scar_ *tissue* left on the brain surface following an injury or infection. Other forms of epilepsy appear to result from deficiencies or abnormalities in a _neurotransmitter_

decreased

63. Chronic alcoholism, perhaps combined with vitamin deficiencies, may lead to an irreversible impairment of judgment and memory. A study of young alcoholic men and women found that their left cerebral hemispheres had (increased/~~decreased~~) in density compared to the left cerebral hemispheres of nonalcoholic controls.

Learning Objectives

39. Identify the following disorders that may result from damage to the brain:
    aphasia _inability to speak_
    amnesia _- loss of memory_
    agnosia _- can't recognize things_

40. What are two major causes of epilepsy?

41. What change has been found in the brains of chronic alcoholic persons?

STUDYING BRAIN-BEHAVIOR RELATIONSHIPS

Clinical Observations

specific

64. Clinical observations, in which the brains of stroke victims were examined following their deaths, have shown that specific behavioral deficits previously exhibited by the victims involved (specific/general) areas of the brain. For example, when a patient suffered some loss of motor ability on the right side of the body following a stroke, an autopsy later revealed damage to the

left

_____left_____ side of the cerebral cortex.

65. Accumulation of this kind of clinical evidence has allowed for a mapping of brain-behavior relationships in which specific sensory and motor deficits have

localized (located)

been _____localized_____ in specific areas of the brain.

Stimulation

66. Penfield observed that he could map similar brain-behavior relationships by the

stimulation

direct _____stimulation_____ of specific brain areas using a mild electric current. For example, stimulation of the sensory cortex caused patients to feel as

touched

though they had been _____touched_____ on a particular area of the body.

67. Direct stimulation of the brain has also been achieved by the application of

chemicals

_____chemicals_____ through a small tube inserted into the brain. It has been observed that different chemicals applied directly to various areas in the

hypothalamus

_____hypothalamus_____ can affect feeding, drinking, and sexual behavior in animals.

68. The information gained from direct electrical and chemical stimulation

has

(has/has not) proven useful for clinical application with human beings. For example, it is possible to provide temporary relief from severe pain by implanting electrodes into the "pleasure centers" of patients suffering from terminal cancer.

69. Another method for studying the brain-behavior relationships is to surgically remove a small selected area of the brain and then observe the resulting behavior when the animal recovers from the operation. The small area removed is called a

lesion

_____lesion_____.

opposite

70. Observation of animal behavior following selected brain lesions has shown that the lesions generally produce (similar/opposite) effects on behavior as compared to direct stimulation. For example, while lesions in a particular area in the hypothalamus cause animals to stop eating, direct electrical stimulation of this same

begin

area in unoperated animals causes them to ___begin___ eating, even though they may be well fed.

71. The reverse has been found for a different area of the hypothalamus. Direct electrical stimulation causes the animal to stop eating, even though previously deprived of food, while lesioning of this area causes the animal to

overeat

___overeat___.

Evoked Potentials

72. The nervous systems of all animals are constantly producing bioelectrical activity that can be monitored by appropriate instruments. Changes in this ongoing bioelectrical activity caused by stimulating some other part of the animal are called

evoked potentials

___evoked___ ___potentials___.

73. For example, when electrodes are attached to the scalp of a human being and he

evoked

or she is presented with a sudden sound, ___evoked___

potentials

___potentials___ will occur. The evoked potentials will be greatest over

temporal

the auditory cortex located in the ___temporal___ lobe. In this instance the evoked potentials being monitored through the scalp electrodes are the result

group of

of bioelectrical activity in a (group of/single) neuron(s).

74. By using an extremely small electrode (called a microelectrode) it is also possi-

neuron
are

ble to monitor the bioelectrical activity in a single ___neuron___. This method has demonstrated that individual neurons in the brain (are/are not) selective as to the stimuli to which they respond.

cortical

75. This selectivity found in ___cortical___ neurons (specific cortical neurons respond only to specific stimuli) is thought to be the foundation of the fine-grained perceptual and behavioral capabilities found in human beings and other animals as well. In other words, people can make exceptionally fine perceptual discriminations (size, shape, color, and so on) because of the

selectivity

___selectivity___ found in the cortical neurons.

Learning Objectives

42. Explain how each of the following techniques has allowed for the mapping of brain-behavior relationships:
    clinical observation
    direct electrical stimulation
    direct chemical stimulation
    brain lesion techniques
    evoked potential (both group and single-neuron recordings)

43. What difference has been noted when comparing lesioning techniques with direct electrical stimulation of brain areas? (Be able to identify the area of the brain and the resulting behavior when answering this question.)

44. What is one clinical application made possible by the information gained from direct electrical stimulation of specific brain areas?

45. What brain-behavior relationship has been found that indicates why human beings and other higher animals can respond to extremely fine gradations of stimuli?

The Debate over Mind Control

76. Research on the functioning of the brain has presented new opportunities for putting some of the findings to use in treating persons suffering from various disorders. Two such techniques are electrical stimulation of the brain and the removal of brain tissue for the purpose of altering behavior, known as

psychosurgery
controversial

psychosurgery . Both of these treatment techniques, and especially psychosurgery, have become very (well accepted/controversial).

Complex Behavioral Functions of the Brain

77. While many specific sensory and motor abilities are found to be localized in specific areas of the brain, more complex behaviors, such as intellectual functioning,

most (all)

appear to involve activity in _____ most _____ of the brain.

78. If complex behaviors, such as intellectual activity, are likely to involve many areas of the brain, then it must also be true that specific areas of the brain are

likely

(likely/unlikely) to be involved in many different behaviors. Thus a complex behavior is likely to be under the multiple control of several areas of the

brain

_____ brain _____.

79. Multiple control extends to all areas of the brain and not just to the cerebral cortex. For example, destruction of feeding areas in the hypothalamus of rats not only impaired their eating behavior, but also caused them to exhibit certain

learning

_____ learning _____ deficits.

80. It is apparent that a full understanding of the brain-behavior relationships must

individual

involve both a knowledge of how _individual_ neurons respond to specific stimuli and a knowledge of how these individual neurons are organized

unit (whole)

into an integrated system that generally functions as a _unit_.

Learning Objectives

46. What two treatment techniques that have evolved out of brain-behavior research have become very controversial?

47. What is the general conclusion as to how the brain performs complex intellectual activity?

48. What information indicates that a complex task such as learning is not only a function of the cerebral cortex?

Chapter Four
Sensation and the Senses

General Objectives

1. Describe the concept of threshold, and explain why signal detection theory rejects the notion of true threshold.

2. Illustrate Weber's law; describe the major features of Fechner's law and Stevens's power law.

3. Explain how adaptation level influences sensory judgments.

4. Identify the main anatomical characteristics of the eye.

5. Describe the functions of the rods and the cones.

6. Explain how the two major theories of color vision have become united.

7. Identify the major anatomical characteristics of the ear.

8. Describe the physical characteristics of sound waves and their relationship to sensory experience.

9. Describe the place and volley theories and the way in which they have both been incorporated in our modern understanding of pitch perception.

10. Name and describe the four skin senses; the two chemical senses; and the senses for balance, posture, and movement.

Sensation and the Senses

Learning Objectives appear at
the end of each major section.

1. Our only source for acquiring information about the world around us comes from the specialized receptor and nervous-system structures known as the

senses
Senses.

2. The sensory structures of human beings, like those of all animals, respond to (all/a limited range) of environmental events. For example, we cannot hear the higher-frequency sounds that dogs can hear, and dogs do not see the colors that we see.

a limited range

43

psychophysics

3. Historically, the study of sensory processes has consisted of two major branches:

sensory physiology and _psychophysics_. We will cover the area of psychophysics first.

STIMULI AND SENSATIONS: PSYCHOPHYSICS

psychologically

4. Stimuli may be defined both physically and _psychologically_. For example, light may be defined physically in terms of wavelength and psychologically in terms of reported color.

5. Psychological responses fall along two principal dimensions:

quality

quality and quantity. For example, the perceived color of light

quality

involves the dimension of _quality_.

The Limits of Sensation

6. There are clear limits concerning what we are able to perceive, and in discussing such limits psychologists use the concept of *threshold*. There are two types of

absolute/difference

threshold: the _absolute_ threshold and the _difference_ threshold.

7. The *weakest stimulus* that produces a detectable sensation is known as the

absolute

absolute threshold. The *smallest change* in a stimulus that pro-

difference

duces a noticeable change in sensation is known as the _difference_

noticeable

threshold or *just* _noticeable_ difference (jnd).

8. For example, if a psychologist alternately increases and then decreases light intensity and asks a person to report when it appears and disappears, the psychologist is attempting to determine the

absolute

absolute threshold of light.

9. The absolute threshold is the lowest intensity of a stimulus that an individual

50 percent (half)

reports noticing _50%_ of the time. The difference threshold is the lowest change in the intensity that an individual reports noticing

50 percent (half)

_50%_ of the time.

10. The difference threshold is established in a manner similar to that of the absolute

two

difference in intensity

threshold except that (one/two) stimulus(li) is (are) involved and the psychologist gradually increases and then decreases the (intensity/difference in intensity) between the stimuli.

11. The reported detection of a stimulus varies as a function of several extraneous factors, some internal and some external, which may interfere with the detection.

noise
internal

Such extraneous factors are referred to as "___noise___." Spontaneous neural activity, for example, is a type of (internal/external) *noise*.

12. Since no situation is actually free of noise, researchers who advocate *signal*

detection/is not

___detection___ *theory* assume that there (is/is not) a single, true absolute threshold. Instead, they assume that a stimulus, called a signal, is always de-

noise

tected in the presence of ___noise___, which can interfere with detection of the signal.

Learning Objectives

1. The study of the senses or sensory processes has consisted of two major branches. What are they?

2. Give an example of both the *physical* and *psychological* dimensions of a stimulus.

3. What are the two major categories in which sensations are experienced psychologically? Give an example of each.

4. Define or give an example of the following:
   absolute threshold
   difference threshold
   jnd

5. Why does signal detection theory assume that there is no such thing as an absolute threshold?

Sensory Scaling

13. According to Weber's law, the amount of a stimulus necessary to produce a

just noticeable

___just___ ___noticeable___ *difference (jnd)* in sensation is a constant fraction of the intensity of that stimulus.

14. For example, if you can barely detect the difference between 50 and 51 ounces, your difference threshold for weight is one-fiftieth the intensity of the first stimulus. According to Weber's law, you should also just be able to notice the differ-

102

ence between 100 ounces and ___102___ ounces.

15. Similarly, you should just be able to notice the difference between 200 ounces

204

and ___204___ ounces.

16. Weber's law describes only our ability to detect differences in *physical stimuli*. Fechner attempted to carry this further by relating physical changes to *sensation*, to the subjective experience of stimuli. Fechner assumed, for example, that a change from 50 to 51 ounces would produce the same change in

sensation   _____sensation_____ as a change from 200 to 204 ounces. He assumed, in other words, that in terms of sensation *all just noticeable differences are equal*.

17. S. S. Stevens provided methods by which people could directly estimate the magnitude of a sensation, and by using such scaling techniques he found that the

power   relationship between physical intensity and sensation was a (logarithmic/power) function.

18. Thus, while Fechner had said that units of sensation are a direct function of the

logarithm   _____logarithm_____ of a stimulus, Stevens said sensation was a function of

power   the stimulus raised to some _____power_____. While modern psychologists probably favor Stevens's law, debate over the correct form of the true "psycho-physical law" continues.

Sensory Adaptation

19. After prolonged exposure to a stimulus, a person's sensory capacity will undergo

adaptation   change or _____adaptation_____. For example, our eyes undergo adaptation as we adjust to light and again as we adjust to darkness.

20. An individual's perception of a stimulus is influenced not only by its magnitude

adaptation   but also by the person's level of _____adaptation_____. For example, a dim light in a dark room will appear brighter after the person has

adapted   _____adapted_____ to the darkness.

21. Similarly, how heavy a weight is judged to be will depend on whether or not an individual has just lifted other weights and how heavy these other weights were. Judgment of stimuli, in other words, depends on the frame of reference or *adap-*

level   *tation* _____level_____ under which the judgments were made.

Learning Objectives

In the space of a few pages it would be very difficult to explain the details of Fechner's and Stevens's laws. These are complicated concepts, and in the following you are expected to provide only highly general descriptions of these laws.

6. What is Weber's law? Give an example to illustrate it.

7. How did Fechner extend Weber's law and relate it to sensation?

8. Provide a rough description of Stevens's power law.

9. Define or give examples of the following:
   adaptation
   adaptation level

THE SENSES: SENSORY PHYSIOLOGY

more than five

22. There are five obvious sense organs, and there are actually (five/~~more than five~~) senses. The text restricts its coverage to the classic five senses and the senses of balance and movement, but it notes that all sense organs operate according to similar principles.

23. Each sense organ contains special receptors that transform environmental stimuli

transduction

into neural impulses. This process is referred to as _transduction_.

Vision

light

24. The basic stimulus for vision is ___light___, a range of wavelengths that makes up only a small part of the electromagnetic spectrum. The human eye

middle

is most sensitive to the (lower/~~middle~~/higher) wavelengths of the visible spectrum; that is, dim light from this portion of the spectrum is easier to see.

25. *Structure of the Eye.* Identify the four major structures of the eye in the figure below.

a. iris

a. ___iris___

b. cornea

b. ___cornea___

c. lens

c. ___lens___

d. retina

d. ___retina___

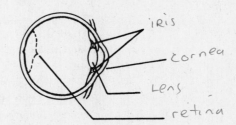

26. The opening just behind the cornea, which appears black as we look at the eye,

pupil

is known as the ___pupil___.

27. Complete the following sentences to identify the functions of the structures you labeled above.

iris

a. The structure known as the ___iris___ regulates the

amount

___amount___ of light that enters the eye through the pupil.

b. The transparent window covering the eye, called the

cornea/focusing

___cornea___, is sharply curved to aid in ___focusing___ the light entering the eye.

lens

c. The muscles of the _lens_ change its shape to _focus_ the light on the retina.

focus

retina

d. The _retina_, located at the back of the eye, contains the receptors (rods and cones).

Learning Objectives

10. What is the name of the process by which environmental stimuli are transformed into neural impulses?

transduction

11. Do we see all of the electromagnetic spectrum or only a limited range? In what area of the spectrum are our eyes most sensitive?

12. Locate the four structures of the eye in the figure below, and briefly describe the function of each.

cornea

iris

lens

retina

13. Where is the pupil of the eye?

28. _The Retina and the Receptor Cells._ There are two types of receptor cells in the

rods

retina: the _rods_, which are receptive to dim light, and the

cones

cones, which are receptive to brighter light.

color
do not

29. Cones are responsible for detailed vision and for _color_ vision; rods (do/do not) signal information about color.

rods

30. In terms of sheer number, there are many more _rods_ in the retina than there are cones, but at the very center of the _fovea_, which is at the

cones

center of the retina, there are only _cones_.

31. All rods contain _rhodopsin_, a _photopigment_ that is very sensitive to light. The

photopigment

cones contain three varieties of _photopigment_, each sensitive to different wavelengths, which contribute to our perception of color. Thus, the rods can operate in very dim light, which the cones cannot; and the cones are receptive to

color

color, which the rods are not.

32. We see most clearly when the image is focused directly on the central area of the

fovea

retina, an area known as the ___Fovea___. One reason this area has such superior visual acuity is because each cone in it is connected to

a single

(a single/many) ganglion cell(s).

more
a single

33. Rods are (more/less) sensitive than cones at low levels of illumination. In part this is true because many rods converge on (many/a single) ganglion cell(s).

34. After light energy is transduced by the receptor cells, the impulses are passed to

ganglion

the *bipolar* cells and then to the ___ganglion___ cells. The axons of the

nerve

ganglion cells in each eye form the optic ___Nerve___, which leaves

blind

the eye through an area known as the ___blind___

spot

___spot___ or optic disk (see Figure 4.4A).

35. At a point behind and between the eyes the optic nerves join. At this point,

chiasm

called the optic ___chiasm___, the two nerves divide and are rerouted, with the fibers from the *right* side of the retina of each eye going to the *right* hemisphere of the brain and fibers from the *left* side of each eye going to the

left

___left___ hemisphere of the brain.

Learning Objectives

14. Name the two receptor cells in the retina. ___rods&cones___

15. Compare the rods and cones with regard to the following:
    a. The type of light to which they are responsive. ___rods-b/w cones-color___
    b. The quantity of cells of each type in the retina. ___more rods less cone___
    c. The type of cells in the fovea. ___cones___
    d. The special function of each type of cell.

16. In terms of connections with the ganglion cells, why are the rods more sensitive to dim light and why do the cones at the fovea produce greater visual acuity?

17. What causes the blind spot? ___optic disk___

18. What is the optic chiasm? ___whare optic nesves join behind eyes___

36. *Color Vision*. There are two major theories that have been developed to explain color vision: the *trichromatic theory* and the *opponent-process theory*. Most investigators now accept:
    a. the trichromatic theory.
    b. the opponent-process theory.
    c. a dual-process theory, incorporating both.

c

37. According to the *trichromatic theory* of color vision, human beings possess

three

_____3_____ types of cones, each type maximally sensitive to a different color (wavelength). One type of cone is particularly sensitive to red light,

green

another to blue light, and still another to ___green___ light.

38. When we see colors other than red, blue, or green, it is because

more than one

(one/more than one) type of cone is being stimulated. If an equal number of red-sensitive and green-sensitive cones are being stimulated, for example, then we

yellow

would report seeing ___yellow___, which is between red and green in the color spectrum.

39. A person who lacks one type of color-sensitive cone is called a

dichromat

___dichromat___, referring to the fact that only two types of cones are functioning. The rarest and most extreme form of color blindness is

monochromacy

___monochromacy___, in which all the cones are either missing or malfunctioning. People with this type of color blindness see only in shades of gray.

40. The opponent-process theory assumes the existence of three pairs of opposing color processors. For example, some cells in the visual area are excited by red and inhibited by green, while the opponent in this pair is excited by

green/red

___green___ and inhibited by ___red___. The second opponent system involves blue/yellow, and the third involves

light/dark

___light , dark___.

41. Experimental evidence has led to acceptance of the involvement of both the trichromatic and opponent-process systems in color vision. At the level of the ret-

three

ina, research has demonstrated the existence of ___3___ different

trichromatic

cone photopigments, in support of the ___trichromatic___ theory.

42. Beyond the retina, along the pathway to the cerebral cortex, color processing

opponent-

seems to be carried out in accordance with the ___opponent___-

process

___process___ theory.

Learning Objectives

19. Briefly describe the two theories of color vision:
    trichromatic theory
    opponent-process theory

20. What is a dichromat? A monochromat?

21. Modern explanations of color vision incorporate both the trichromatic and opponent-process theories by indicating that they operate at different levels. Explain.

Hearing

43. The ear, like the eye, is an energy-transducing device. It changes air waves into

neural (nerve) _____neural_____ signals, which, as they are transmitted to the brain, are

sound perceived as _____sound_____.

44. The physical stimulus for sound is waves of compressed and

expanded _____expanded_____ (made less dense) air particles that strike the eardrum. Sound waves have two main characteristics important for hearing:

frequency/intensity _____frequency_____ and _____intensity_____.

45. *Frequency* is determined by the number of peaks and valleys (or compression-expansion cycles) that pass a given point in one second, expressed in a unit

Hertz known as a _____Hertz_____ (Hz). The frequency of sound produces what we subjectively experience as pitch. The higher the frequency, the higher the

pitch _____pitch_____.

46. The other physical attribute of sound waves is *intensity,* which can be thought of as the amplitude (size) of the air-pressure waves, measured in terms of

decibels _____decibels_____ (dB). Thus, the two sound waves represented below dif-

intensity/frequency fer in _____intensity_____ but not in _____frequency_____.

amplitude

47. The intensity of sound waves is represented by the _amplitude_ of the
waves. Intensity is subjectively experienced as loudness. Thus, the sound wave

louder
on the left, on page 51, will sound (louder/higher) than the one on the right.

48. The sound waves represented in the illustration below differ in

frequency/intensity
Frequency but not in _intensity_ . The one on the left

higher
will sound _higher_ .

49. The physical characteristic of *frequency* is largely responsible for producing the

pitch
subjective, sensory experience of _pitch_ . *Intensity* produces the

loudness
experience of _loudness_ .

intensity (amplitude)
50. The louder a sound, the greater is its _am intensity_; the higher the

frequency
tone, the greater is the _Frequency_ of its sound waves and the higher

pitch
the subjectively experienced _pitch_ .

Learning Objectives

22. What is a sound wave?

23. Name and define the main two characteristics of sound waves important for hearing. Also list the names of the units
in which these characteristics are measured.

24. What is the name of the subjective or sensory experience produced by frequency? By intensity?

Note: The following section contains several anatomical terms that are difficult to remember, so the best plan of
attack would probably be to review the text carefully before attempting this section. The terms are repeated in several of
the frames, so if you miss some concepts during the earlier frames you can review them in ones that follow.

51. *Structure of the Ear*. The ear has three major divisions: (1) the outer ear, which

pinna

includes the external projection known as the ___pinna___ and the

auditory

___auditory___ canal; (2) the middle ear, which contains the

ossicles

___ossicle___; and (3) the inner ear, comprised of the

cochlea

___cochlea___.

52. Open your text to Figure 4.11 and compare the drawing there to the one presented below. As you can see, the drawing here distorts the structure a bit to make it easier to see; the cochlea has been unrolled and greatly enlarged. After rereading the section on structure, identify the parts of the ear indicated in the figure below.

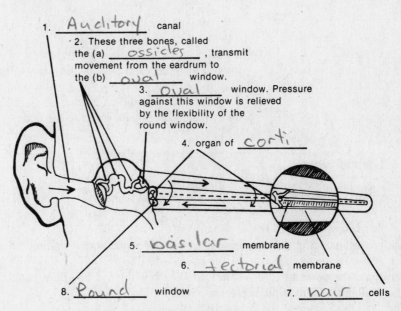

1. ___Auditory___ canal
2. These three bones, called the (a) ___ossicles___, transmit movement from the eardrum to the (b) ___oval___ window.
3. ___Oval___ window. Pressure against this window is relieved by the flexibility of the round window.
4. organ of ___corti___
5. ___basilar___ membrane
6. ___tectorial___ membrane
7. ___hair___ cells
8. ___Round___ window

9. The entire structure which begins at the middle of the figure and extends to the right is known as the ___cochlea___ (shown here unrolled and greatly enlarged).

53. After a sound wave enters the auditory canal, it pushes against the tympanic

eardrum

membrane, or ___eardrum___, and causes it to vibrate. The vibration is

ossicles

then amplified by the three small bones known as the ___ossicles___

oval

(the *hammer, anvil,* and *stirrup*) and transmitted to the ___oval___ window at the *beginning* of the vestibular canal.

54. Vibrations of the oval window travel up one side of the cochlea (along the *vestibular* canal) and return down the other side (along the *tympanic* canal) to the

round
the opposite

round window. Thus, sound-wave vibrations are continuously moving in (the opposite/the same) direction on opposite sides of the cochlea.

55. The central or cochleal canal, which lies between the vestibular and tympanic

organ

canals, contains the main organ of hearing, the _organ_ of

Corti

Corti.

56. The organ of Corti consists of two membranes, the basilar and tectorial mem-

hair cells

branes, and receptors called _hair_ _cells_.

basilar

57. The hair cells are embedded in the _basilar_ membrane but touch

tectorial

the _tectorial_ membrane, so that as the fluids in the canals vibrate the two membranes in opposite directions, the hair cells between them are bent.

hair cells

It is the bending of the _hair_ _cells_ that produces the neural impulses sent to the brain.

Learning Objectives

25. Name the structures that comprise the *outer, middle,* and *inner ear*.

26. Name the structures described below:
    a. The general name for the three bones that amplify sound waves striking the eardrum. Ossicles
    b. The names of the ossicles. hammer ranvil, stirrup
    c. The spiral-shaped and fluid-filled structure which is divided into three parallel canals. cochlea
    d. The flexible structure at the beginning of the vestibular canal. eardrum
    e. The flexible structure at the end of the tympanic canal.
    f. The membrane in which the hair cells are embedded. Basilar
    g. The structure consisting of the basilar and tectorial membranes and the hair cells. organ of Corti

27. What actions initiate the neural impulses that are sent to the brain, signaling sound? hair cells

Neural Coding by the Ear

58. The way in which the brain distinguishes between high and low tones is not fully understood. Part of the explanation involves the *place* on the

basilar

basilar membrane affected by sound waves. High-frequency sounds vibrate the basilar membrane near the oval window, while low-frequency waves have a greater effect near the top of the cochlea.

59. Our capacity to distinguish between high and low tones may be explained in part

place

by the ___place___ theory of pitch. According to this theory it is the

basilar

particular location of maximum displacement on the ___basilar___

membrane

___membrane___ that signals the frequency of sound.

60. While the place theory accounts successfully for higher frequencies, it cannot explain how we distinguish low tones, since there is a great deal of overlap in the areas of maximum displacement at low frequencies. A second theory, the

volley

___volley___ theory, explains our perception of pitch in terms of the *frequency* at which volleys or groups of neurons fire. The frequency at which

frequency

neurons fire would match the ___frequency___ of the tone stimulus.

61. Contemporary researchers believe that both theories are needed to explain hear-

volley

ing. At low frequencies the ___volley___ theory is particularly impor-

place

tant, while at higher frequencies the ___place___ theory comes into play.

hair

62. Our hearing depends on the condition of the ___hair___ cells on the

intensity

basilar membrane. Sounds of high ___intensity___, such as jets, loud music, or jackhammers, may tear these hairs and cause irreversible hearing loss.

Learning Objectives

28. How do the *place theory* and *volley theory* account for our capacity to distinguish between sound frequencies? How have these two theories been incorporated in the contemporary explanation of the perception of pitch?

29. If someone's hearing has been impaired by listening, for example, to very *high-frequency* sounds, what specific portion of the basilar membrane would probably be damaged? ___hair cells___

The Skin Senses

touch

63. There are four basic skin sensations: ___touch___,

warmth/cold/pain

___warmth___, ___cold___, and ___pain___.

physiological

64. *Warmth and Cold.* The temperature at which an object applied to the skin produces a sensation of neither warmth nor cold is called _physiological_ zero. Temperatures above physiological zero are experienced as

warm

warm and temperatures below physiological zero as

cold

cold.

in specific spots
more

65. Warm and cold receptors are located (everywhere/in specific spots) on the skin. There are (more/fewer) cold receptors than warm receptors.

66. If a cold spot is stimulated with a hot stimulus, a person often reports that the

paradoxical

stimulus is cold. This phenomenon is called _paradoxical_ cold, and its occurrence supports the notion that there are separate receptors for warmth and cold.

67. The sensation of *hot* appears to result from a mixing of information from both

warm/cold

warm and _cold_ receptors in a particular area of the skin.

68. *Touch.* Some areas of the body are more sensitive to touch than others, the most

fingers

sensitive parts of the body being the _fingers_, the

lips/tongue

lips, and the tip of the _tongue_.

69. *Pain.* The sensation of pain arises not only from the skin, but also from the

interior (inside)

interior of the body, although little is known about this latter type of pain.

70. Pain thresholds, the lowest amount of stimulation needed to produce a report of pain, vary across people, time, occupation, sex, and so on. For example, women

lower/lower

have (lower/higher) thresholds than men, and clerks have (lower/higher) thresholds than laborers.

little

71. Under ordinary circumstances there is (little/much) adaptation to pain. This is fortunate, since pain alerts us to real or potential bodily injury.

72. For many years it was assumed that, as is the case with other senses, specialized nerve cells operated to carry pain signals to specific regions of the brain. In the

is not

late 1950s, however, research demonstrated that pain (is/is not) associated with one specialized nerve.

gate

73. In 1965, Melzack and Wall set forth their _gate_ *control theory* of pain, which asserts that the sensation of pain depends not on a single nerve type but on the balance of activity between large- and small-diameter nerve

fibers

fibers within the spinal cord.

small

74. In brief, this theory proposes that activity in the ___small___ nerve fibers opens the gate, permitting pain to pass, while activity in the

large

___Large___ nerve fibers closes the gate, thus preventing the experience of pain. While evidence concerning the theory is mixed, some chronic pain

large

patients have been treated by electrical stimulation of the ___large___ fibers in an attempt to block pain.

Learning Objectives

30. Name the four skin senses. *touch, warmth, cold, pain*

31. Define physiological zero and paradoxical cold.

32. Which are more numerous, receptors for warmth or receptors for cold? *cold receptors*

33. Are some parts of the body more sensitive to touch or pressure than others? Give some examples. *Yes*

34. In what respect is pain *not* a skin sense? *It can be interior to. Inside our body*

35. What factors or variables have been found to be related to pain threshold? Give examples.

36. Do people adapt very readily to pain? What is the advantage of this? *Know No*

37. What is the name of Melzack and Wall's theory of pain? Briefly describe the theory, especially in terms of the way in which the "gate" operates. *Gate* *small nerve fibers lets pain go through* *large " " block pain*

The Chemical Senses

taste

75. Because the receptors for the chemical senses of ___taste___ and

smell
often confused

___smell___ are located close to one another in the mouth, throat, and nasal cavity, these senses are (quite distinct/often confused). In fact, without a sense of smell we would have difficulty discriminating among many foods.

76. *Smell.* In terms of survival value, a principal function of smell among human

dangerous (toxic)

beings is to alert us to ___dangerous___ stimuli that we might otherwise eat or inhale.

77. The major sense organ for smell (olfaction) is the olfactory

epithelium/nasal (nose)

___epithelium___, located at the top of the ___nasal___ passages and connected to the base of the brain.

hair

78. Projecting from the olfactory epithelium are millions of ___hair___ cells, which are sensitive to volatile (gaseous) substances and which transduce this information into neural impulses.

is not

79. While there have been several theoretical attempts to understand how our sense of smell operates, the exact physical basis of odor sensation (is/is not) known.

80. A number of animal species, ranging from spiders to monkeys, release chemicals

pheromones

called _pheremones_ which trigger behavioral reactions in other animals of the same species. A major function of pheromones is to attract the opposite sex.

81. The odor of fatty acids in the vaginal secretions of female monkeys stimulates sexual behavior in male monkeys; thus, these fatty acids function as

pheromones

pheremones. The same fatty acids have been found in young women, but the effect of these on human behavior is unknown.

82. *Taste*. As suggested earlier, much of what we attribute to taste actually involves smell. We can discriminate hundreds of odors. But when odor is eliminated,

sweet

there appear to be only four basic categories of taste: _Sweet_,

sour/salty/bitter

Sour, _Salty_, and _bitter_.

taste

83. The receptors for taste are contained in the _taste_

buds

buds, structures that are grouped in projections from the

papillae

tongue termed *papillae*. There are about 10,000 _papillae_ on the surface of the human tongue.

Learning Objectives

38. Name the two chemical senses. Why are sensations from these often confused? _Taste & Smell_

39. In terms of survival value, what is a principal function of smell? _identify toxic substances_

40. What is the major sense organ for smell, and where is it located? To what form of matter is it responsive?

41. What are pheromones, and what is their major function?

42. Of what substance are the pheromones in monkeys composed? What is the significance of this finding with regard to human beings?

43. Name the four basic categories of taste.

44. What is the name of the receptors for taste? What is the name of the structures in which they are grouped?

Balance, Posture, and Movement

84. *The Vestibular Sense*. The vestibular sense contributes to our sense of

balance

_____ balance _____. The main organ for this sense is located in the inner

semicircular

ear, largely in the three fluid-filled __semicircular__ canals located above the cochlea of the ear.

85. When the head shifts or rotates, the fluid within the semicircular canals bends

hair

receptor _____ hair _____ cells that connect with the vestibular nerve leading to the brain. This process contributes to the sense of balance.

86. *The Kinesthetic Sense*. If you close your eyes, you will still be aware of the position of your arms or legs and you will still perceive any movement you may make. Our sense of body position and movement involves the

kinesthetic

_____ Kinesthetic _____ sense.

joints

87. The receptors for the kinesthetic sense are located in the __joints__, muscles, and tendons.

88. The kinesthetic sense acts in cooperation with both vision and the

vestibular

_____ vestibular _____ sense to produce balance and coordinate movement.

89. *Homing Sense*. Several animals, ranging from lobsters and snails to birds and

homing

bats, have an internal sense of navigation referred to as a __homing__ sense. When taken from their homes and released, they are able to find their way home.

90. A recent study in England examined the question of whether or not some aspects of the homing sense may also exist in human beings. Two separate groups of students, blindfolded and driven to a point far from their point of origin,

were

(were)/were not) able to indicate the direction of "home" even before the blindfolds were removed.

91. Whether or not there is a homing sense in human beings is

controversial

(well established/(controversial)). Attempts to replicate these experiments in this country so far have failed.

Learning Objectives

45. What is the function of the vestibular sense? What is the main organ for this sense?
balance   *semicircular canals*

46. What is the function of the kinesthetic sense, and where are its receptors? *position joints muscles, tendons*

47. What other major sense works with the vestibular and kinesthetic senses to help maintain balance and coordinate movement?

48. What is the homing sense, and what evidence suggests that it may or may not operate in human beings?

Chapter Five
Perception

General Objectives

1. Distinguish between sensation and perception, and give examples of each process.

2. Provide examples of how brain processes operate in perception to fill in missing details, to compensate for misleading distortion, and to create perceptions in the absence of appropriate sensory input.

3. List and describe the gestalt principles of perceptual organization.

4. Tell what is meant by perceptual constancy, and provide examples of this phenomenon.

5. Tell what is meant by resolution of ambiguity and by feature analysis.

6. Name and describe the various cues for depth perception.

7. Name and describe the various cues for the perception of motion.

8. Describe the various factors that give rise to illusions.

9. Explain how both experience and culture can influence perception.

Perception

Learning Objectives appear at
the end of each major section.

FROM SENSATION TO PERCEPTION

1. The process by which stimulation of the sense organs is converted into an organized awareness of objects and events in the environment is called

perception   perception.

more

2. While the distinction between perception and sensation is not always clear, perception is the (more/less) complex of the two processes; it must make sense or meaning out of the raw sensory data. For example, the inference that a particular

perception

object is an apple would be termed _perception_ . The basic sensory data that would help in this inference, such as "redness" or "roundness," would

sensation

be termed _sensation_ .

3. Both sensation and perception are largely a function of processes in the

brain

brain . In many cases where the sensory information being received is limited or incomplete, the brain processes operate so as to

fill in

"_fill in_" the missing details. Thus, people perceive a complete and detailed object or event, as illustrated by the

subjective

subjective contours that they add when they view drawings such as shown in Figure 5.2 in the text.

can

4. When confronted with misleading distortions in incoming sensory information, the brain (can/cannot) compensate for it. For example, Stratton wore lenses that inverted the retinal image, which in turn caused him to see the world upside

great

down. At first he experienced (little/great) difficulty in moving about, but after about a week he could walk around somewhat normally, sometimes even forgetting he was living in an inverted world.

5. This "compensation" phenomenon was also studied by Kohler, who used prism goggles that produced moderate distortion of the environment by making straight

curved

lines appear _curved_ . Subjects who wore these goggles were at

compensate

first bothered by the distortion, but they soon learned to _compensate_ for the distortion and their environment began to look normal. However, upon removing the goggles after weeks or months of use, the environment

did not

(did/did not) appear normal; the natural environment without the goggles appeared to be distorted.

6. The compensation or adaptation phenomena observed in these two experiments do not occur unless the subjects actively

move about (interact with)

move _about_ their distorted environment.

7. In addition to filling in missing details and compensating for misleading distor-

perceptions

tions, the brain processes can also create _perceptions_ even in the absence of sensory information. For example, direct electrical stimulation of partic-

brain

ular areas in the _brain_ was found to produce clear perceptions of nonexistent sights, sounds, and feelings.

is not

8. It can be concluded that the perceptual process (is/is not) simply the detection of stimuli by sensory receptors. Rather it is a more complex process of the brain

meaning

which organizes these stimuli so as to create ___meaning___.

Learning Objectives

1. Define perception, and tell how it is related to sensation.

2. In what way is the perceptual process more complex than the sensation process?

3. Give an example of how brain processes operate in perception to:
   a. fill in missing details.
   b. compensate for misleading distortions.
   c. create perceptions in the absence of appropriate sensory stimulation.

4. What is necessary in order for persons to learn to compensate for misleading distortions in their visual field? adaptation

5. What is the end goal of perceptual processing by the brain? create meaning

---

PERCEPTUAL ORGANIZATION

Gestalt Principles

9. According to gestalt psychologists, we do not see bits and pieces of information as we look about our environment. Rather these bits and pieces of information

gestalts

are organized into meaningful *whole* patterns called ___gestalts___.

whole

Thus, to perceive a gestalt is to perceive a perceptual ___whole___.

10. *Grouping.* Gestalt psychologists attempted to identify the principles that underlie pattern perception. For example, elements (or stimuli) in a field that are close to one another (or proximate) tend to be perceived as belonging together. Thus, one of the principles of perceptual organization involves closeness, or

proximity

___proximity___.

11. Another important factor in organizing perceptions, which in some cases may override proximity, involves certain aspects of the direction or pattern of the elements. Thus, while the X indicated by the arrow in the figure on page 64 has

proximity

more ___proximity___ to an X in the top row, it has more

continuity

___continuity___ with the diagonal row of X's.

```
        X    X    X   ↓X    X
        B    Q    w    X         u

             v    T    X    Y    E

             p    C    X    o    Z

             R    X    w    N    i
```

12. A third factor involves the *similarity* of elements. For example, we tend to read-

similar   ily group the X's in the above figure because they are _Similar_.

are also   13. These three factors (are also/are not) important in the perception of sounds. For example, the fact that we tend to group sounds played by the same instrument

similarity   illustrates the principle of _Similarity_.

14. The tendency to perceive the notes in a melody as a pattern illustrates the princi-

continuity   ple of _continuity_. A third factor in organizing perception of sounds

proximity   involves the _proximity_ in time, or closeness, of the sounds.

15. It has been pointed out that all three of these gestalt principles can be integrated

simplicity   under the concept of _simplicity_. We tend to see the simplest patterns that exist in nature, whether the simplicity results from proximity, continuity, or similarity.

16. *Figure and Ground*. In organizing our perceptions we separate the object, or

figure/ground   _Figure_, from the space, or _ground_.

does not   17. The ability to separate figure and ground (does/does not) seem to depend on past
experience. Research by Senden has shown that people blind from birth

are   (are/are not) able to distinguish objects from their background immediately following an operation that has given them sight.

18. Although the capacity to distinguish between figure and ground seems to be innate, the difficulty in seeing a Dalmatian dog in Figure 5.4 in the text illustrates

experience   that _experience_ may also affect our perception of figure and ground.

19. The distinction between figure and ground is also apparent in organizing perceptions of sound stimuli. If you ignore the whispering of students and attend to
what a lecturer is saying in a classroom, the lecturer's voice becomes the

figure   _Figure_; but if you attend to what a classmate is saying, the lec-

ground   turer's voice becomes the _ground_.

Learning Objectives

6. What is a gestalt? *Bits and pieces in enviornment are organized into a meaningful whole*

7. Describe what is meant by each of the following principles of perceptual organization:
   proximity
   continuity
   similarity
   simplicity *encompasses all of them*

8. What is meant by the distinction between figure and ground in perception? What evidence indicates that the ability to separate figure from ground is innate? What evidence indicates that experience has some influence on this ability?

Perceptual Constancy

increases

20. Suppose that you are walking across campus and spot a friend approaching in the distance. As the distance between the two of you diminishes, the size of the retinal image cast by the friend (increases/decreases). Your friend, however, remains the same size. This tendency to perceive objects as having constant or stable

constancy

properties is called *perceptual* ___Constancy___.

21. As in the previous example, the size of images projected onto the retina of the eye varies with distance, yet objects generally appear to remain the same size.

size

This particular kind of perceptual constancy is called ___size___

constancy

___constancy___.

22. The visual system is able to maintain size constancy because of the exact, in-

distance

verse relationship between the size of an object and its ___distance___ from an observer. The farther an object is from an observer, the

smaller

___smaller___ is the size of the image projected onto the retina of the eye.

more

23. When objects are viewed against a vague background (the open sky, for example), size and distance judgments are (less/more) difficult to make. This was illustrated by the World War II anecdote in which the Germans were fooled by dummy paratroopers dropped by the Allies. While the dummies were actually only two feet high, the Germans perceived them as being normal-sized human

great

beings at a ___great___ distance.

24. The moon illusion provides a similar example of how perceptual judgments become less accurate or change with the decrease in supporting background information. Less supporting background information is the reason that the moon

smaller   looks much _____smaller_____ at its zenith than when it is on the horizon.

distance   The horizon provides additional _____distance_____ cues that are not present when the moon reaches higher elevations.

25. Size constancy is only one of several perceptual constancies. The fact that a coin always looks round regardless of one's viewing angle illustrates

shape   _____shape_____ constancy; the fact that a white sweater looks white in

color   sunshine and shadow illustrates _____color_____ constancy; and finally, the fact that a picture on a wall does not seem to move about even though head movement may cause a rapid movement of the retinal image illustrates

location   _____location_____ constancy.

Learning Objectives

9. What is meant by perceptual constancy? Use the example of size constancy to illustrate this principle.

10. Why does the moon look smaller at its zenith than when it is on the horizon?

Resolution of Ambiguity

26. The ambiguity referred to in this section has to do with the fact that occasionally.

two   a single set of stimuli may be interpreted in _____two_____ or more different ways. The tendency to see either a vase or two profiles in Figure 5.1 in the text illustrates this point, as does the depth reversal that occurs when viewing the Necker cube illustrated in Figure 5.8.

is not   27. In resolving the ambiguity in these two instances, there (is/is not) a correct an-

resolves   swer. Thus, the brain _____resolves_____ the ambiguity by alternating back and forth between the two equally likely possibilities.

28. When perceptual ambiguity is encountered, we generally go beyond the immedi-

context   ate sensory information and use the _____context_____ of the situation for additional clues. For example, we are easily able to fill in the missing letters in the sentence "She _roke her _eg while skiing" because of the

context   _____context_____ provided by the other letters and words.

Learning Objectives

11. Explain what is meant by ambiguity resolution, using the figure of the vase (or two profiles) and the Necker cube to illustrate your answer.

12. Explain how context may help in resolving perceptual ambiguity.

Feature Analysis

feature analysis

29. Identifying objects according to distinctive characteristics or features is called _feature analysis_. For example, we can easily distinguish an *A* from an *F* on a course grade because these two letters have

features

features that distinguish them from each other and all other letters as well.

have not

30. Computers have been programmed to recognize the letters of the alphabet by analyzing their distinctive features, but they (have/have not) been able to surpass human beings at this task. Unlike human beings, computers cannot recognize letters that are not printed in a prescheduled manner.

Learning Objectives

13. What is meant by feature analysis? How do human beings and computers compare in this ability? _Identifying objects according to distinctive characteristics_

Depth Perception

localize

31. The fact that our ears are on opposite sides of the head helps us to determine the direction from which a sound is coming. In other words, our two ears help us to _localize_ sounds. Similarly, our two eyes help us to localize an

depth

object in space and to perceive _depth_.

binocular disparity

32. The separation of our eyes provides two slightly different views of any given object in our line of sight. Although our perception is of a single object, our eyes actually receive disparate views of the object. This cue to depth is called _binocular disparity_. We can use this cue to judge

distance

the _distance_ of an object from us.

more

33. As we move about our environment or move our heads back and forth while remaining stationary, objects that are closer to us seem to move (less/more) quickly than objects farther away. This cue to depth is called

motion parallax

motion parallax.

two (both)

34. Binocular disparity obviously depends on ___two___ eyes for cues to depth perception, whereas motion parallax provides both binocular and

monocular

___monocular___ cues to depth perception.

35. There are also several other monocular cues that augment depth perception. Identify these cues from the descriptions given below.
    a. Objects that are closer to us partially block the view of subjects farther

interposition

away. ___interposition___
    b. Parallel lines, such as railroad tracks, appear to converge as they recede into

linear perspective

the distance. ___linear___ ___perspective___
    c. As an object moves closer to an observer, it casts a larger retinal image.

relative size

___relative   size___
    d. The grain and texture of objects become harder to distinguish as they recede

texture

into the distance. ___texture___ *gradient*

Learning Objectives

14. Describe how each of the following principles provides cues for the perception of depth, and indicate whether they are binocular or monocular cues:
    binocular disparity
    motion parallax
    interposition
    linear perspective
    relative size
    texture gradient

Perception of Motion

36. Movement of an image across the retina can result from movement of the eyes,

movement

from movement of the head or body, or from the actual ___movement___ of an object one is observing. The issue here is how an individual knows which of these possibilities is operating.

37. Thus, as *we* move about in our environment, everything we see moves constantly, but we are able to interpret the movement we perceive as being in our

bodies

___bodies___ rather than in the objects in the environment. When we are stationary and looking about a room, the retinal image changes rapidly, giving a notion of movement. In this case we interpret the movement as being in

eyes

our ___eyes___.

38. We can still perceive motion when we are completely stationary and riding in a moving vehicle. The constant flow of objects past the visual field, called

global

_____global_____ *motion parallax,* produces a perception of moving through space.

39. In addition to the perception of actual movement of objects, rapid movement in motionless stimuli, such as the successive frames in a motion picture, may result

apparent

in the perception of _____apparent_____ motion. This same apparent motion can be produced by switching lights on and off sequentially, as occurs in many neon advertising signs. These forms of apparent motion are called the

phi

_____phi_____ *phenomenon.*

40. Another form of apparent movement occurs when one stares at a waterfall for long periods of time and then looks at the riverbank. In this case the riverbank

opposite

will appear to move in the (opposite/same) direction of (as) the falling water. The waterfall illusion probably results from the adaptation activity of *direction-*

selective

_____selective_____ cells in the visual cortex.

Learning Objectives

15. Define the following terms:
    global motion parallax   moving through space
    apparent movement   movie or neon sign
    phi phenomenon –

16. What is the waterfall illusion, and what accounts for it?

Illusions

41. A perception that does not correspond to a real object or event is called an

illusion

_____illusion_____. Illusions can result from physical distortions present in the environment, such as the mirages frequently encountered in desert or arctic regions. These illusions can be explained by the physical principles of

light

_____light_____ refraction.

psychological

42. Illusions can also result from _____psychological_____ sources of distortion, such as the illusions produced by the Muller-Lyer and Ponzo figures (Figures 5.14A-B and 5.14C-D in the text).

43. The lengths of lines in the Muller-Lyer and Ponzo illusions are actually the same, even though they appear to be different. These illusions seem to occur because our brain and visual system misapply the principle of

size

_____size_____ constancy. In the Ponzo illusion, for example, we tend to judge the upper line as larger because in a three-dimensional world it would

farther away

be (closer/farther away).

44. Another example of an illusion resulting from psychological distortion is the Ames room illusion. This illusion is created by distorting the dimensions of a chamber so that when viewed from a peephole in one of the walls, it appears

rectangular

_____rectangular_____; actually, the walls are trapezoidal in shape. The illusion remains even when people are inside the room and appear to be giants or midgets. Like the Muller-Lyer and Ponzo illusions, this is also a misapplication of the

size

principle of _____size_____ constancy by the brain and visual system.

Learning Objectives

17. What is an illusion?   does not correspond to a real object or event

18. What is the cause of the following illusions?
    a desert mirage
    the Muller-Lyer illusion
    the Ponzo illusion
    the Ames room illusion

THE INFLUENCE OF EXPERIENCE ON PERCEPTION

45. A readiness to attend to and perceive certain stimuli in a specific way and to

set

ignore other stimuli is called a _perceptual_ _____set_____. For example, the hungry traveler will be highly susceptible to signs or cues that signal the

food

availability of _____food_____, even misleading ones.

46. The text mentions three major factors that affect perceptual set as well as perceptions in general. One of these factors was illustrated by the ambiguous figure that could be interpreted as either an old woman or a young woman. In this illustra-

experience

tion, the _____experience_____ of viewing one of the figures influenced perception when viewing another one. Thus, one of the factors that affects perceptual

experience

set is _previous_ _____experience_____.

47. Another factor that affects perceptual set is illustrated by the tendency for missing letters in a printed sentence to go unnoticed. People tend to see what they

expectations

expect to see. Thus, _expectations_ can play a major role in perceptual set.

48. The previous example of the hungry traveler who is searching for road signs that signal the availability of food illustrates the third factor, in this case

motivation

motivation, that can affect perceptual set.

Early Life Experiences

49. There is a good deal of evidence to suggest that some perceptual processes may fail to develop properly unless an individual has adequate exposure to a

normal

normal visual environment at an early age.

50. For example, it was found that kittens reared without light showed deficits in

depth

their ability to perceive _depth_. When these light-deprived kittens were later allowed to freely explore a lighted environment, they

were

(were/were not) able to overcome this deficit. Light-deprived kittens who were not allowed to move freely about in a lighted environment but who were moved

not

about mechanically were (also/not) able to overcome this deficit.

Learning Objectives

19. What is a perceptual set? What are three major factors that influence perceptual set? _experience_ _expectations_ _motivations_

20. What deficits were found in kittens reared in the absence of light? Was this deficit later overcome? _depth_ _yes & no_

Cultural Influences

51. Anthropologists have observed that cultural learning can influence perceptual processes and produce perceptual biases. This phenomenon, called *cultural*

relativism

relativism, is illustrated by the difficulty a Bushwoman was found to have in perceiving a photograph of her son.

52. Psychologists have speculated that cultural factors can have a great influence on the ways people from different societies view the world. The Bushwoman's culture, for example, had provided her with little experience in translating

two

two-dimensional pictorial representations of the world into three-dimensional objects.

53. It has also been suggested that it is our special cultural influences that make us susceptible to the Muller-Lyer illusion. The Zulu people were found to be much **(more/less)** susceptible to this illusion than Westerners. This difference was attributed to the **(absence/presence)** of straight lines, corners, and right angles in Zulu architecture.

less
absence

54. A similar kind of study compared the susceptibility of Ugandan university students with Ugandan villagers to the Ponzo illusion. It was found that the **(villagers/students)** were much more likely to see the illusion. In fact, they were as likely to see it as Pennsylvania university students.

students

55. The above study concluded that the difference in susceptibility to the illusion resulted from the more extensive experience of the students with two-dimensional pictorial representations of ___three___-dimensional space. Lacking this experience, the villagers were unable to see the two-dimensional ___depth___ cues in the Ponzo illusion.

three

depth

Learning Objectives

21. What do anthropologists mean by cultural relativism? Cite an example to illustrate your answer.

22. What difference was found between the Zulu people and Westerners with respect to the Muller-Lyer illusion? To what was the difference attributed?

23. What difference was found between Ugandan students and Ugandan villagers with respect to the Ponzo illusion? To what was this difference attributed?

Chapter Six
Varieties of Consciousness

General Objectives

1. Describe what is meant by consciousness, and discuss its three basic characteristics.

2. Name and define the four stages of non-REM sleep, and describe the sleep pattern during a typical night.

3. Discuss the various phenomena associated with REM sleep and dreams.

4. Know why the hypnotic state is difficult to define, and describe some of the phenomena associated with this state.

5. Discuss some of the uses and abuses of hypnosis.

6. Describe some of the techniques that can be used for the self-regulation of consciousness.

7. Define what is meant by sensory deprivation, and describe some of the important findings associated with this phenomenon.

8. Identify the major classes of psychoactive drugs, and describe their effects on behavior.

9. Discuss some of the phenomena and problems associated with extrasensory perception.

Varieties of Consciousness

Learning Objectives appear at
the end of each major section.

THE NATURE OF CONSCIOUSNESS

is not

1. While consciousness may be defined loosely as the personal *awareness* of one's own thoughts and feelings, it should be realized that there (is/is not) a specific and completely satisfactory definition of consciousness.

2. Although psychologists do not agree on one specific definition of consciousness, there is general agreement that it has three basic characteristics: consciousness is

brain

limited, it is related to activity in the ___brain___, and it has various

modes

___modes___ (forms or states).

The Limits of Consciousness

3. There are many stimuli, such as X-rays and high-frequency sounds, that we are unable to perceive. Thus, one limitation on consciousness is the relatively narrow

perceptual (sensory)

range of our ___perceptual___ capacities. The other limitation is also physical in nature and involves the difficulty we encounter in doing two or more things at the same time, such as watching television while reading a book. Thus, the other limitation on consciousness is our limited capacity to deal with different

simultaneously

events ___simultaneously___.

The Relation of Consciousness to Brain Activity

4. Although the exact nature of the relationship remains vague, there is evidence of

brain

a relationship between consciousness and ___brain___ activity. For example, stimulating particular areas in the cerebral cortex elicits specific conscious experiences of past and present events. That is, when particular areas of

consciousness

the brain are stimulated, experiences come rushing into ___consciousness___ automatically.

The Modes of Consciousness

5. *The Split Brain.* Some psychologists have suggested that there are *two* modes of

cerebral (brain)

consciousness based on the different functions of the two ___cerebral___ hemispheres. One hemisphere is said to handle the logical and analytic mode of

intuitive

consciousness, while the other hemisphere handles the ___intuitive___

artistic

and ___artistic___ mode.

are not

6. These two different modes of consciousness (are/are not) noticeable in normal persons since the two cerebral hemispheres coordinate their separate functions by means of a large neural tract connecting them. However, these two separate functions are evident in epileptic patients who have had the connecting neural tract surgically severed. The two cerebral hemispheres can be made to operate

split-brain

independently in these "___split___-___brain___" patients.

do not   7. The two separate consciousnesses found in split-brain patients (do/do not) demonstrate unequivocally that the lateral specialization of each of the hemispheres is related to various states of consciousness among normal persons.

will   8. *The Continuum of Consciousness*. Throughout a typical day an individual (will/will not) experience natural changes in his or her state of consciousness. The text lists four different states of consciousness that lie on a *continuum* (meaning one stage merges with the next without any distinct boundary line) be-

dreaming   tween normal waking consciousness and ___dreaming___. As one proceeds from normal waking to dreaming across these states of consciousness,

decreases   objective reality (increases/decreases).

9. Changes in states of consciousness that are deliberately, rather than naturally, induced can be placed on a different continuum, according to the level of

arousal   ___arousal___. In this case, states of consciousness associated with

high   ecstasy and irrationality are accompanied by ___high___ levels of arousal, while tranquility and meditation are associated with

low   ___low___ levels of arousal. The level of arousal during daily waking activity lies between these two extremes.

Learning Objectives

1. Give a "loose" definition of consciousness.

2. List the three basic characteristics of consciousness.

3. What are the two basic limitations of consciousness?

4. How do we know that consciousness is related to brain activity?

5. What do split-brain studies show about the nature of consciousness?

6. What mode of consciousness is thought to be a function of the left cerebral hemisphere? What mode of consciousness is thought to be a function of the right cerebral hemisphere?

7. What two states make up the end points on the natural continuum of consciousness? What happens to objective reality as one progresses along this continuum?

8. What states lie at the end points of the deliberately induced states of consciousness? What are changes on this continuum associated with?

SLEEP AND DREAMS

Brain Activity from Wakefulness to Deep Sleep

10. Through the use of the electroencephalograph (EEG), psychologists have been able to identify *four* distinct stages of sleep in addition to the dream stage, or rapid eye movement (REM) sleep. They have named these stages of sleep stages

2/3   1, _____2_____, _____3_____, and 4.

11. Each stage of sleep is distinguished by a change in the frequency of the brain

waves   _____waves_____ being monitored by the EEG. The following designations have been given to four brain-wave patterns on the basis of their frequency as measured in cycles per second (cps):

BRAIN-WAVE PATTERN	CPS
beta	14 or more
alpha	8–13
theta	5–7
delta	1–4

slower   12. As one progresses from stage 1 sleep to stage 4 sleep, the frequency of the EEG waves becomes (slower/faster). Thus the lowest frequency is found in stage 4

delta   sleep in which the _____delta_____ waves dominate.

4   13. People are very difficult to awaken during stage _____4_____ sleep. In fact, they appear to be in a comalike state. It is difficult to determine what mental activity is occurring during this stage of sleep since, when subjects are awakened, any mental activity they report may have occurred during the

wakening   _____wakening_____ process. Yet it is clear that some mental activity does occur, since most episodes of sleepwalking, sleeptalking, and intense nightmares occur during stage 4.

Learning Objectives

9. Name the four stages of non-REM sleep, and describe the changes that occur as one progresses through these stages.

beta Alpha theta delta

10. Describe the pattern of sleep that occurs during a typical night.

REM Sleep

14. During a typical night of sleep people do not sink progressively into deeper and

cyclical   deeper sleep. Rather, they show a _____cyclical_____ pattern; they go through various stages of sleep several times a night.

REM

15. All people show periods of rapid eye movement, or _____REM_____, sleep, in addition to the other four stages of sleep. The other four stages of sleep are collectively called non-REM (or NREM) sleep.

16. When persons are awakened during REM sleep, they often report that they have

dreaming

been ___dreaming___. Although mental activity occurs during all stages of sleep, the mental activity that occurs during REM sleep (dreaming) is much

more

(less/more) vivid and structured than during the other stages of sleep.

17. It has been suggested that the rapid eye movement occurs during dreams because

watching (scanning)

the sleeper is ___watching___ the dream as it unfolds. This is called the *scanning hypothesis*. Although conclusive evidence has not been found to sup-

scanning
do not

port the ___scanning___ *hypothesis,* it has been observed that persons blind from birth (do/do not) generally show rapid eye movement during sleep.

18. REM sleep is also peculiar in other ways. The EEG pattern resembles that of a

waking

___waking___ state, as do other physiological measures, such as heart rate, breathing, and blood pressure. These are all patterns associated with

waking (arousal)

___waking___.

19. Yet during REM sleep, people behave as if they were in a very deep sleep simi-

4

lar to the sleep in stage ___4___. They are often difficult to awaken, and they do not respond to external stimuli as readily as they do in stages 2 and 3 sleep.

20. Thus, persons show physiological signs of arousal during REM sleep, and, at the same time, they behave as if they were in deep sleep. This has led researchers to

paradoxical

describe REM sleep as ___paradoxical___ sleep.

21. Another physiological change that occurs during REM sleep is that most of the

tone

major body muscles lose their normal ___tone___. It has been shown that a particular area in the brain *inhibits* the muscles from being activated during REM sleep. When this particular area was removed from cats, they *moved about* whenever REM sleep occurred. This finding suggests that the loss of muscle tone during REM sleep prevents human beings from acting out their

dreams

___dreams___.

22. It has been found that persons deprived of REM sleep spend a longer than normal time in REM sleep when given the opportunity to make up the loss. Thus, we apparently have a need for REM sleep since we automatically

compensate (make up)   _compensate_ for its loss. While deprivation of any of the stages of sleep results in tiredness and irritability, it appears that strenuous physical activity increases the need for deep (NREM/REM) sleep, while intellectual activity

NREM
REM   and emotional stress increase the need for (NREM/REM) sleep.

23. Some researchers have suggested that REM sleep helps maintain the responsiveness of the brain by allowing sensory and motor areas to prepare for handling the

waking   mass of stimulation during _waking_ hours. The need for such preparation and the need for REM sleep are greatest among newborns and

decrease/less   (increase/decrease) with age. Older people spend much (less/more) time in REM sleep than do younger people.

Learning Objectives

11. Why is REM sleep frequently called "paradoxical" sleep?

12. What is the scanning hypothesis? What evidence has been found to support this tentative hypothesis?

13. What was found with respect to REM sleep in cats when a particular portion of their brains was removed? What does this tell us about the loss of muscle tone during REM sleep?

14. What hypothesis has been suggested to explain the purpose of REM sleep? What evidence supports this hypothesis?

15. In what way does strenuous physical activity make different demands upon our sleep patterns than does intellectual activity and/or emotional stress?

The Content of Dreams

is not   24. The average person may have as many as 150,000 dreams during his or her lifetime but (is/is not) able to recall most of them. Rather, people tend to remember only the most exciting or disturbing dreams.

25. It was found that when water was sprayed on the faces of some volunteers sleep-

water   ing in a laboratory, they reported more dreams about _water_ than did unsprayed subjects. This indicates that some of the content of our

stimuli   dreams arises from the _stimuli_ in the immediate environment, such as sounds, touches, and so on.

26. Sigmund Freud (the founder of psychoanalysis) claimed that there is an unconscious meaning to our dreams (which he called the *latent* content) that is hidden
by the obvious or evident meaning (which he called the *manifest* content). According to Freud, a psychoanalyst could interpret the symbolic meaning found in

latent

the *manifest* content and thus discover the _____latent_____ content of the

no longer

dream. Most present-day psychoanalysts and psychologists (still/no longer) subscribe to this theory.

Learning Objectives

16. What evidence supports the idea that to some extent the content of dreams is influenced by immediate environmental
stimuli?

17. Describe what Freud meant by the *latent* and *manifest* content of dreams. Does this view have wide support today?

Recalling and Controlling Dreams

27. Persons who daydream frequently and who are good at creating visual imagery

more

are (more/less) likely to recall dreams than persons who do not show these characteristics. Moreover, dream recallers usually have a better

visual

_____visual_____ memory than nonrecallers, but not a better *auditory*
memory.

28. It has been found that mood can affect dream recall: going to sleep in an un-

increases

pleasant mood _____increases_____ the ability to recall dreams.

slowly

29. Poor dream recall is likely to occur if one awakens (slowly/rapidly) or if one is
distracted upon awakening. Persons who were requested to call the weather

less

bureau immediately after waking were (less/more) likely to recall their dreams,
because their attention was distracted.

30. The ability to recall dreams may result from an interest in them and

practice

_____practice_____ in recalling them. Learning to control dreams is

more

(more/less) difficult than learning to recall them.

Learning Objectives

18. List three characteristics that persons who are good at recalling dreams appear to have.

19. In what way can one's mood affect dream recall?

20. What two factors can affect dream recall upon awakening?

HYPNOSIS

is not   31. There is conclusive evidence that the hypnotic state (is/is not) similar to sleepwalking.

32. Four important differences have been observed that distinguish the hypnotic state from sleepwalking. First, the EEG pattern of the sleepwalker shows waves typical of stages 3 and 4 sleep, while the EEG pattern of the hypnotic subject shows

waking   the pattern of a normal ___waking___ state.

does   33. Second, unlike the sleepwalker, the hypnotic subject (does/does not) respond to instructions and pays attention to persons around him or her.

34. Third, the sleepwalker does not remember the experience, whereas the

hypnotized   ___hypnotized___ subject does, unless specifically instructed not to remember it.

35. Finally, oxygen consumption gradually decreases during sleep, but there is no

hypnosis   change in oxygen consumption during ___hypnosis___ .

Hypnotic Susceptibility

nine   36. Approximately ___9___ out of ten persons can be hypnotized if they *want* to be and if they *trust* the hypnotist. Some persons, however, are much more susceptible to hypnosis than others.

37. The stage hypnotist ensures the success of his or her act by picking out persons

high   who have ___high___ susceptibility to some of the easier hypnotic suggestions. Psychologists have devised several tests to measure hypnotic susceptibility. Among more than 500 students who took one of these tests, about

10   ___10___ percent scored as highly susceptible to hypnosis.

38. Persons who score high on hypnotic susceptibility scales tend to become deeply

absorbed   ___absorbed___ when reading novels, listening to music, watching movies, etc. This ability to become deeply absorbed may develop in early

childhood   ___childhood___ . These persons are more likely to engage in daydreaming and to have had imaginary friends as young children.

Learning Objectives

21. List four differences that have been observed to distinguish sleepwalking from a hypnotic trance.

22. What percentage of persons can be hypnotized? What two conditions must be present?

23. How do stage hypnotists ensure their success?

24. What percentage of college students were found to be highly susceptible to hypnotic suggestion? In what way did the highly susceptible persons differ from less susceptible persons? Where and how did this ability arise?

The Hypnotic State

39. While hypnosis has been widely researched, many questions remain to be answered. One problem is that psychologists have been unable to define the hyp-

behavior

notic state other than by simply describing the ___behavior___ of hypnotized subjects. There is no physiological pattern of responses—such as the brain-wave patterns found in the four different stages of sleep—that is peculiar only to the hypnotic state. This has led some psychologists to doubt that hypno-

unique (separate)

sis even represents a ___unique___ state of consciousness.

40. While hypnotized subjects do exhibit some unusual behavior, such as arm levitation or body rigidity, it has been observed that all of these unusual behaviors can

hypnotized

also be performed by non-___hypnotized___ subjects when instructed to do so under appropriate conditions.

was

41. Frank Pattie was able to demonstrate that one woman (was/was not) faking when she claimed that she could not see out of one eye after being given a hypnotic suggestion that she was blind in this particular eye. However, the subject appar-

did not

ently (did/did not) believe she was cheating.

42. *Two Explanations: Neodissociation Theory and Role Enactment Theory.* Two explanations have been offered to explain instances like the woman's denial of cheating. One explanation is that consciousness depends on multiple systems, such as a visual system, an emotional system, and an awareness system, which are coordinated through a hierarchy of controls that can shift during hypnosis. In the case of this woman, her awareness system was not coordinated with her visual system; she was simply *unaware* that she was actually seeing with her

neodissociation

"blind" eye according to the ___neodissociation___ theory.

43. The other explanation assumes that the woman's denial of cheating only represents a special case of a person playing a role that she had been specifically instructed to play. In this case the woman was playing the role of a

hypnotized

"___hypnotized___" person who had been told she was blind in one eye.

enactment

Thus, the *role* ___enactment___ theory denies the idea that hypnosis is a special state of consciousness.

cannot

44. At the present time we (can/cannot) say which of these two theories is correct. One prominent researcher has suggested that both may be correct and has distinguished between two groups of "susceptible" people. One group is highly hypno-

neodissociation

tizable and thus would be subject to _Neodissociation_. The other group is

role

highly suggestible and thus would be subject to _role_

enactment

enactment.

Learning Objectives

25. How is the hypnotic state defined at the present time?

26. Why do some psychologists doubt that hypnosis represents a unique state of consciousness?

27. What two theories have been offered to explain the case of Pattie's subject who claimed she was blind? Which of the theories is correct?

Uses and Abuses of Hypnosis

45. Hypnosis has been used in psychotherapy, in medicine, and in the courtroom. While if used properly it can prove useful in all three areas, its greatest abuse

courtroom

can occur when used in the _courtroom_.

46. Courtroom applications of hypnosis are usually for the purpose of enhancing the

memory

memory of an individual who may possess pertinent information. The problem here is that the information these individuals recall under hypnosis

true (correct)

may not be _true_.

47. A hypnotized person is uncritical and compliant and will obligingly fill in re-

imagined

quested details. These details, however, may be _imagined_. Moreover, these imagined details then become merged into the subject's memory, and he or she becomes convinced that they are real.

48. Four proposals have been suggested to make the courtroom use of hypnosis more

without

reliable. The first is that only a specially trained professional (with/without) verbal information about the case be used.

49. The second proposal is that all encounters between the hypnotist and the subject

videotaped

be _videotaped_.

no

50. The third proposal is that (few/no) observers be present during the sessions; the reactions of observers can influence the subject's responses.

videotaped

51. The fourth proposal is that all interrogations be _videotaped_. This allows for checking to see that information brought out under hypnosis was not implanted by earlier interrogations.

Learning Objectives

28. List three general areas which have employed hypnosis. In which of these areas is hypnosis most likely to be abused?   _psychotherapy medicine, courtroom - most abused_

29. What is the predominant reason for employing hypnosis in the courtroom? What might inadvertently happen here?

30. List the four precautions that have been proposed to insure the reliability of hypnosis as a courtroom tool.

THE SELF-REGULATION OF CONSCIOUSNESS

52. Unlike other altered states of consciousness that we regularly and automatically experience, such as sleep, or altered states that are induced by other persons,

hypnosis

such as _hypnosis_, the altered states of consciousness resulting from techniques such as meditation and biofeedback are under the full control of

individual

the _individual_.

Meditation

53. Meditation is a technique that induces an altered state of consciousness through

attention
a different

the retraining of _attention_. There are two major paths to the meditative retraining of attention. Each leads to (the same/(a different)) state of consciousness.

54. *Learning to Meditate.* One method of meditative retraining calls for the subject to focus his or her attention upon a single object or sound, such as a *mantra,* a sound that the meditator repeatedly chants. This form of meditation is called

concentrative

concentrative meditation.

55. The other method has the subject focus his or her attention on the body, concentrating on internal sensations or mental states. This form of meditation is called

mindful

mindful meditation.

56. *Physiological Changes during Meditation.* Research evidence has shown that there ((are)/are not) distinct physiological changes associated with meditation.

are

57. Many of the physiological changes found with meditation, such as lowered metabolism, lowered heart rate, and lowered blood pressure, are (also/(not)) found with other altered states such as sleep and hypnosis.

not

58. Instead, the physiological changes produced by meditation resemble those found

relaxation

in _relaxation_. However, meditation differs from relaxation in that

brain-

forms of meditation have been found to produce unique _brain_-

wave

wave patterns.

59. For example, one study of Zen meditators found that they produced alpha and even theta brain waves, although they still had their eyes

open

open. These particular brain waves are not usually observed when the eyes are open.

Learning Objectives

31. What distinguishes the altered states of consciousness produced by meditation and biofeedback from other states of altered consciousness?

32. What are the two basic meditation techniques? By what process do both of these techniques accomplish their goal?

33. What physiological changes are common to meditation as well as relaxation? What unique physiological changes have been found with some forms of meditation?

Biofeedback

60. Biofeedback is a technique whereby electronic monitoring devices are employed to provide an individual with *immediate* and continuous information about a par-

bodily (physiological)

ticular _bodily_ response, such as heart rate or skin temperature.

immediate

Since the feedback information is _immediate_, the individual can experiment with various efforts to control a specific bodily response. By trial and error, some people gradually learn to influence the desired response.

has

61. Biofeedback (has/has not) been found to be an effective treatment technique for stress-related disorders such as high blood pressure and chronic headaches due to excessive muscle tension.

62. Some early claims about the benefits of biofeedback have failed to hold up under closer scrutiny, however. One claim was that persons could achieve a blissful state of deep relaxation by using biofeedback to train themselves to produce

alpha
was not

alpha brain waves. Further research showed that the blissful state (was/was not) a reliable result of alpha wave production. Moreover, it has been found that persons can increase their alpha wave production just as readily

eyes

by simply relaxing and closing their _eyes_. Biofeedback does not speed up this process.

Learning Objectives

34. How does biofeedback work?   *electronic devices used*

35. Biofeedback has been found to be an effective treatment for what disorders?   *stress related*

36. What was wrong with early claims that biofeedback could produce a blissful state by training a person to produce alpha waves?

Sensory Deprivation

63. Depriving an individual of normal visual, auditory, and tactual

stimulation (stimuli)   *stimulation* can lead to a hypnogogic state that may include hallucinations. This hypnogogic state that results from sensory deprivation is commonly found among certain occupational groups such as sailors and long-distance

truck drivers   *truck drivers*, who are exposed to a monotonous, unchanging environment for long periods of time.

64. While early research on sensory deprivation found its effects to be only

negative   *negative*, later and better-controlled research showed that it could have negative, positive, or neutral effects, depending on the

expectations   *expectations* of the subjects. Subjects who had been previously told to
more   expect pleasant effects were (more/less) likely to experience the situation as positive than subjects who had been told to expect unpleasant effects.

65. It has also been found that sensory deprivation increases a person's acceptance of

persuasion   *persuasion*. Thus sensory deprivation has been included in some forms of psychotherapy as an aid in gaining the patient's acceptance of the treatment package.

is not   66. Sensory deprivation (is/is not) the same as brainwashing. Sensory deprivation is achieved by reducing the sensory load on an individual, while brainwashing is

increasing   achieved by *increasing* the sensory load on an individual, even to the point of overload.

Learning Objectives

37. What is sensory deprivation, and what are some of its possible effects on an individual?   *Depriving an individual of normal visual, auditory stimulation*

38. Under what kind of circumstances might sensory deprivation occur outside of the laboratory?   *people with monotonous jobs*

39. In what manner did the expectations of subjects affect the outcomes of sensory deprivation studies?

40. What effect commonly found with sensory deprivation has proven useful in psychotherapy?

41. In what way does sensory deprivation differ from brainwashing?

reduces sensory load — increases sensory load

DRUG-ALTERED CONSCIOUSNESS

67. Drugs that interact with the central nervous system so as to change a person's

psychoactive   mood, perceptions, and behavior are called _psychoactive_ drugs.

The Effects of Certain Drugs on Consciousness

68. *Marijuana.* The active ingredient in marijuana (cannabis) is a complex molecule

THC   with the initials _THC_. Both marijuana and hashish contain

hashish   THC, but it is far more concentrated in _hashish_.

heighten
both

69. The general effect of marijuana is to (lower/heighten) sensory experiences. These heightened experiences may be accompanied by (pleasant/unpleasant/both) feelings, depending primarily upon the circumstances or setting in which the drug is taken.

70. One of the first well-controlled studies of the effect of marijuana on human beings was conducted with both experienced and inexperienced marijuana users. "Highs" from inhaling the marijuana were more frequently reported by the

experienced   _experienced_ group.

71. Impairment in both intellectual and motor skills as a result of inhaling marijuana

inexperienced
not

was found with the _inexperienced_ group. This impairment was (also/not) found with the experienced group.

72. However, later studies have found that impairment in both intellectual and motor tasks occurred equally among both experienced and inexperienced users, but the

experienced   _experienced_ users were better able to "come down" when necessary to carry out a task.

73. One consistent finding is that marijuana appears to interfere with some aspects of

memory   _memory_ in all groups.

can

74. Further research has shown that a frequent user (can/cannot) overcome the memory problems caused by marijuana. One study found that the memories of people who smoked marijuana over a thirty-day period in a laboratory first

decreased/increased   _decreased_ and then _increased_.

no

75. The first study of long-term heavy users of marijuana has found (some/no) intellectual deficits in this group.

Learning Objectives

42. What is a psychoactive drug? *affects CNS*

43. What general results were found in the studies that compared the effects of marijuana on experienced and inexperienced users? What contrary results were found by later studies?

44. What is the one consistent finding with respect to the use of marijuana? Does this finding apply to long-term users of marijuana?

45. In what two ways are marijuana and hashish alike? In what way are they different?

---

76. *Stimulants*. Drugs that arouse the central nervous system, increasing heart rate,

stimulants
blood pressure, muscle tension, etc., are called ___Stimulants___ .

nicotine
77. One of the most widely used stimulants is the ___Nicotine___ found in cigarettes. In addition to the other physiological arousal patterns found with stim-

decrease
ulants, cigarette smoking has also been found to ___decrease___ alpha

increase
opposite
wave production and to ___increase___ the production of the faster beta waves. This is the (same/opposite) change that is found with meditation.

78. Studies in sleep laboratories have shown that chronic smokers take longer than

asleep
do
nonsmokers to fall ___asleep___ . Smokers who give up nicotine (do/do not) immediately begin to sleep better, but they still experience other unpleasant withdrawal symptoms.

79. Another commonly used stimulant is found in many soft drinks, chocolate, tea,

caffeine
and coffee. This stimulant is called ___caffeine___ .

80. Unlike most drugs, which are associated with recreational uses, caffeine is asso-

work
ciated with ___work___ . While moderate doses of caffeine can increase alertness and reaction time, excessive doses can lead to restlessness and
does
sleep disturbance. Abrupt withdrawal (does/does not) lead to unpleasant symptoms such as depression and headaches.

81. Another commonly used stimulant comes from the leaves of certain coca plants.

cocaine
This stimulant, ___cocaine___ , is usually taken in the form of a white powder.

little

82. There has been (little/much) systematic laboratory research on the effects of cocaine. Users have reported that moderate doses of cocaine improve attention, reaction time, and speed in simple mental tasks. Moderate doses also produce feel-

euphoria

ings of _euphoria_ that can last more than thirty minutes.

83. Stimulant drugs such as cocaine trigger the central nervous system into burning up bodily energy at an accelerated rate. But these drugs (do/do not) supply this energy. Consequently, once the euphoric state passes, the body is left

do not

exhausted

exhausted until it once again replaces the consumed energy.

84. Large or repeated doses of cocaine can have much harsher effects. One of the common effects from long-term inhalation is irreversible damage to the mucous

nasal septum

membranes of the _nasal_ _septum_ (the structure that separates the nostrils).

85. Cocaine taken in large doses can also produce false perceptions, such as the feeling that bugs are crawling under the skin. These false perceptions are called

hallucinations

hallucinations. When taken in excessive doses, especially by injection, cocaine can produce headaches, nausea, convulsions, coma, and sometimes

death

death.

86. Another group of stimulants, generally called "speed," are the

amphetamines

amphetamines. In moderate doses, amphetamines can increase general alertness and produce a state of euphoria. Large and frequent doses can result in a condition that highly resembles schizophrenia, a condition called *amphetamine*

psychosis

psychosis.

Learning Objectives

46. What is the general effect of the stimulant drugs?

47. Describe the short-term effects from moderate doses of the following four stimulant drugs:
    nicotine
    caffeine
    cocaine
    amphetamine

48. In what way do smokers and nonsmokers differ with respect to sleep patterns? What results from abrupt cessation of smoking?

49. What physiological damage has been found to result from the long-term use of cocaine? What psychological effects can result from heavy doses or long-term use of this drug?

50. What is amphetamine psychosis?

87. *Depressants*. The general effect of the depressant drugs is to

retard (slow)
decrease

retard the action of the central nervous system. In small doses depressants produce intoxication and euphoria. They also (increase/(decrease)) alertness and motor coordination. In large doses they can produce a loss of consciousness.

88. Some of the most widely used depressants are tranquilizers, barbiturates, and the

alcohol

most widely used of all, _alcohol_. When two depressants are taken together, the general effect is greater than the sum of the two individual effects of each drug. It is for this reason that depressants are called

synergistic

synergistic.

recent

89. The use of alcohol has been shown to impair the ability to recall ((recent)/old) information from memory. This deficit in memory is most pronounced

prior to

((prior to)/following) the peak period of intoxication.

concentration

90. The effects of long-term use of alcohol on memory appear to depend on the ((concentration)/total amount) of alcohol that has been consumed. Thus memory is less likely to be affected when a person consumes a given amount of alcohol,

one can per day for six days

say a six-pack of beer, at the rate of ((one can per day for six days)/six cans in one day and resting the next five days). This prevents concentration of large amounts of alcohol in the body at any one time.

Learning Objectives

51. What is the general effect of the depressant drugs when taken in small doses? When taken in large doses?

52. List three of the most widely used depressant drugs. Which of these is the most popular?

53. Why are depressants referred to as being synergistic?

54. What has been found with respect to the short-term effects of alcohol on memory? What has been found with respect to the long-term effects on memory?

91. *Hallucinogens*. Hallucinogens come in both natural and synthetic forms, and, as

hallucinations

their name implies, all are capable of producing _hallucination._ This

psychedelic

group of drugs is also commonly referred to as _psychedelic_ (mind-manifesting) drugs.

92. One of the hallucinogenic drugs is derived from the peyote cactus and has been used for years by the Native American Church of North America for religious

mescaline

purposes. The name of this drug is _mescaline._

PCP

93. Often called "angel dust," _____PCP_____ is a synthetic hallucinogen. In low doses it produces hallucinations, but in large doses it can result in coma or

death

even _____death_____.

LSD

94. The most powerful of the hallucinogens is _____LSD_____ (lysergic acid diethylamide). Common reactions to this drug are perceptual distortions and

hallucinations

_____hallucinations_____ (false perceptions), the exact form and intensity depending on the user's expectancies and surroundings.

panic

95. The most common side effect of LSD is a _____panic_____ reaction in which the user becomes frightened that he or she may not recover from the illusory world and panic state.

Learning Objectives

55. Why are mescaline, PCP, and LSD called hallucinogens? Which is by far the most powerful of these drugs? By what other name are they known? psychedelic   LSD

56. What effects can result from large doses of PCP? Death coma

57. What are some of the common reactions found with LSD? What is the most common side effect found with this drug?   Panic

EXTRASENSORY PERCEPTION

96. The reception of knowledge about the environment that does not arrive through a

extrasensory

known sensory channel is referred to as _____extrasensory_____ perception (ESP). The study of ESP and related psychological events that go beyond what is

parapsychology

considered possible is called _____parapsychology_____

97. There are several kinds of parapsychology phenomena that have been investigated. Identify four of these different kinds of phenomena from the descriptions given below:
    a. The transference of thought from one person to another is called

telepathy

_____telepathy_____.

precognition

    b. The ability to see future events is called _____precognition_____

    c. Obtaining knowledge about events without using normal sensory channels is

clairvoyance

called _____clairvoyance_____.

    d. The ability to move objects without touching them is called

psychokinesis

_____psychokinesis_____ (PK).

is not

98. At the present time it (is/is not) clear that ESP and PK do exist.

Explanations of ESP

frequently

99. Unusual events that are reported to be examples of ESP can (frequently/seldom) be explained without resorting to ESP. This is a major problem for proponents of parapsychology.

100. For example, a husband and wife may simultaneously think about a mutual friend. While proponents of ESP might attribute this simultaneous thought to

telepathy (ESP)

telepathy, it is also quite possible that it was triggered by common

stimulus (event)

memories and some barely noticed _stimulus_ in their environment.

The Problem of Scientific Validation

have not
does not

101. Scientific investigations into ESP phenomena (have not/have) shown that ESP events can repeatedly and reliably be demonstrated. This (does/does not) prove the nonexistence of ESP, only that if it does exist, it is a very fleeting and fragile thing.

102. Thus proponents of ESP are faced with two problems. One is that it is

difficult (hard)

difficult to verify occurrences of ESP which occur outside of the

difficult (hard)

laboratory, and the other is that it is equally _difficult_ to replicate instances of ESP in the laboratory.

103. It has been suggested by some researchers that a common link among all the various forms of altered consciousness is that they are all dependent on the

right

right hemisphere of the brain. In other words it is this _lateralization_ of the brain that makes many different states of consciousness possible.

104. Another common feature is that all of these various states of consciousness are accompanied by relaxation, an absence of logical information processing, and the

alpha/theta

production of _alpha_ or _beta_ waves. Whether or not these common features are important remains to be demonstrated.

Learning Objectives

58. Define the following terms:
   extrasensory perception _ESP - Reception of knowledge that does not arrive through a known sensory channel_
   parapsychology - _going beyond thing in psychological world considered possible_
   telepathy - _transfering thought from one person to next_
   precognition - _seeing future events_
   clairvoyance - _knowledge about events_
   psychokinesis - _moving objects without touching them_

59. Why cannot unusual events that are attributed to ESP be used as hard evidence that such phenomena do exist?

60. What are the two major problems faced by proponents of parapsychology?

Chapter Seven
Perspectives on Behavior

General Objectives

1. Explain how the study of animal behavior is related to understanding human behavior. Describe some of the more important reasons for studying animal behavior in order to better understand human beings.

2. Describe the "nature versus nurture" issue and its resolution in psychology today.

3. Explain what was wrong with the term *instinct,* and indicate what terminology has replaced it.

4. Describe and provide illustrations of how both heredity and environment influence behavior.

5. Explain what is meant by the adaptive significance of a trait.

6. Define the principle of parsimony, and use an illustration to demonstrate the significance of this principle.

7. Describe what sociobiologists do and why there are difficulties in accepting some of their explanations for human behavior.

Perspectives on Behavior

Learning Objectives appear at
the end of each major section.

1. There are several reasons for studying the behavior of lower animals in order to gain a better understanding of human behavior. One reason is that it allows us to

simplest   look at behavior in its _simplest_ form. Another reason is that it
greater   allows for (greater/lesser) control over extraneous factors, such as previous experience, than is possible with human beings. A final reason is that it allows for

studies (experiments)   _studies_ that would be considered too extreme for human beings.

2. A basic concept derived from studies of animals is that their behavior results from a combination of two factors *working together*. These factors are heredity

environment (experience)   and _enviorment_.

93

ANIMAL STUDIES: THE HISTORICAL BACKGROUND

Ethology and Comparative Psychology

ethology

3. The study of animal behavior from an evolutionary and physiological viewpoint is called _Ethology_. The early ethologists were highly influenced by such works as *On the Origin of Species* and *The Expression of Emotion in Man and Animal*, by Charles _Darwin_.

Darwin

form

4. Ethologists came to believe that evolutionary principles not only accounted for the body structure and physiology or _form_ of animals, but also that these principles were applicable to the patterns of behavior or

function

function as well. In other words, form and function are interde-

environment

pendent and inherited adaptations to the _environment_.

adaptive

5. The influence of evolutionary principles thus led ethologists to concentrate on how an animal's behavior allows it to survive and reproduce or, to put it another way, to concentrate on the _adaptive_ significance of animal behavior.

little

6. While the ethologists paid (little/much) attention to the manner in which experience (learning) affected patterns of animal behavior, the opposite was true of

comparative

comparative psychologists.

7. In fact, the comparative psychologists largely ignored the behavior of animals in their natural habitats, which was the focus of the ethologists, and instead concen-

laboratory

trated on more controlled experiments in the _laboratory_. Their

learning

general focus was on the role of _learning_ in the determination of behavior.

Learning Objectives

1. List three reasons for studying animal behavior in order to gain a better understanding of human behavior.

2. Define ethology. Who strongly influenced the thinking of early ethologists?

3. What did ethologists mean when they said that form and function are adaptations to the environment? What was the ultimate purpose of both form and function?

4. How did the comparative psychologists differ from the ethologists in their approach to understanding animal behavior?

The "Nature versus Nurture" Issue

learning (experience)

8. The "nature versus nurture" controversy was an argument over the relative importance of instinct versus _____learning_____ in determining a given pattern of behavior.

unlearned

9. The concept of instinctive behavior was meant to describe organized patterns of (learned/unlearned) behavior which had to occur in its complete form at the earli-

universal

est opportunity. Moreover, instinctive behavior had to be _____universal_____ among all members of a species and be identified with specific neurophysiological processes.

components (parts)

10. Simple reflexes were regarded as only _____components_____ of an instinctive behavior pattern, much like the musical notes that are the components of a melody.

McDougall

11. The champion of the instinctive view was William _____McDougall_____. On the opposite side, arguing for an extreme learning explanation for most behavior,

Watson

was John B. _____Watson_____.

neither

12. Continuing investigation over the years began to make it clear that _____neither_____ view was correct, but neither was completely wrong either. Complex behavior patterns contained both instinctive and learned compo-

nest

nents, as was illustrated by studying _____nest_____

building

_____building_____ in pregnant female rats.

Learning Objectives

5. What were the two opposing views in the "nature versus nurture" argument? Who championed an extreme "nature" view? Who championed an extreme "nurture" view? _____instinct vs. learning_____

6. List the four components that were said to comprise instinctive behavior. What role did simple reflexes play here?

7. How was the "nature versus nurture" issue finally resolved? What did nest building in pregnant female rats have to do with this issue?

Species-Specific Behavior

13. The concept of instinctive behavior thus came to be replaced by the term

species-specific

_____species_____ - _____specific_____ behavior. Species-specific behavior is defined as behavior that is typical of a given species, the members of

environment

which have shared a common *inheritance* and a common _____environment_____ that has provided them with similar influences and experiences.

14. Thus, rather than viewing behavior as the result of either heredity or environment, the concept of _species_ - _specific_ behavior acknowledges both of these influences.

species-specific

15. The interdependence of heredity and environment on the development of a given species-specific behavior is exemplified in the laboratory and field studies of the development of singing in the chaffinch. For example, the chaffinch (will/~~will not~~) develop a normal song without exposure to the songs of a normal mature chaffinch (either live birds or tape recordings).

will not

16. If the taped song of a typical mature chaffinch is electronically rearranged and played to young developing chaffinches who have never heard the normal songs, they will later reproduce the rearranged version. If exposed to the songs of a very different species, the young chaffinches (will/~~will not~~) later reproduce them. Thus the form of the song is flexible within certain limits and is determined by the experience of hearing other chaffinches sing during what is called the

will not

sensitive period. It is during the sensitive period that an animal is particularly sensitive to special influences that may produce enduring changes in behavior.

sensitive

Learning Objectives

8. What term was used to replace the term _instinctive_ behavior? _species - specific_

9. What two components must exist before a behavior can be said to be species-specific? _common environmenta inheritance_

10. How does the concept of species-specific behavior deal with the heredity-versus-environment issue?

11. Use the example of the chaffinch to describe how heredity and environment interact in the development of species-specific behavior.

12. What is the sensitive period? _Time when a animal can be greatly influenced_

INFLUENCES ON BEHAVIOR

Inheritance

17. *Sensory Capacities*. The use of sight, sound, and smell by various animals in finding their way—honeybees use polarized light, bats use high-frequency echoes, and salmon use odors in the water—demonstrates that much of the be-

sensory
how

havior of animals depends on their ___sensory___ capacities. By knowing the sensory capacities of a particular species we can usually tell (how)why) they perform a particular behavior. Having this information, however, does not

why

tell us ___why___ the behavior pattern originally developed. Perhaps the best guess as to why a behavior pattern occurs is that it has adaptive value, or perhaps it is merely accidental.

18. *Fixed-Action Patterns*. A good deal of species-specific behavior in any animal consists of frequent and consistent patterns of movements called

fixed-action

___fixed___-___Action___ patterns. The grooming, eating, and courtship behavior of animals are examples of fixed-action patterns.

19. As demonstrated by direct electrical stimulation of the brain in chickens, the basis of fixed-action patterns appears to be contained in the characteristic patterns

brain

of ___brain___ organization. That is, the stimulation of a specific

fixed-

area in a chicken's brain elicits a specific ___Fixed___-

action

___action___ pattern.

20. Similar fixed-action patterns have also been observed when stimulating the brains of other animals. Cats without any experience outside of a laboratory would immediately kill a rat when a particular area of the brain was

electrically

___electrically___ stimulated.

21. *Selective Breeding Experiments*. The selective breeding of animals for specific behavioral traits provides some of the most compelling evidence of the role of

heredity

___heredity___ in the development of those traits.

22. It is possible not only to breed for particular behavior tendencies, such as phototaxis in fruit flies or retrieving ability in dogs, but also for the capacity to

learn

___learn___, as shown by breeding "maze bright" and "maze dull" rats.

23. In the case of "maze bright" rats, selective breeding increased their capacity to learn their way through mazes. Thus, a specific learning ability was shown to be

heritable
cannot

heritable. The actual inherited biological change that allowed for this increased ability (can/cannot) be identified.

24. A genetic difference that may be of small consequence to an individual may be

population

of significant consequence when it occurs in an entire _population_.

minor

25. For example, raising the IQ of one individual by five points would be of (minor/major) consequence to that particular person. Raising the IQ of an entire popula-

major

tion by five points, however, would be of _major_ consequence

extreme

to the population as a whole. This is because such an increase would substantially affect the (extreme/middle) segment(s) of a population.

26. *Sign Stimuli.* Highly specific stimuli that serve as automatic signals for certain

sign

fixed-action patterns of behavior are called _Sign_

stimuli

Stimuli. For example, the odor of butyric acid from animal skin glands leads the female tick to drop on a mammal passing beneath her. The key element in a sign stimulus may be odor, size, shape, color, and so on.

27. *Innate Releasers or Novelty?* At first it was believed that the male stickleback

red

fish would attack another stickleback with a _red_ belly be-

innate

cause the red belly served as an _innate_ *releaser* for aggressive behavior.

28. A similar explanation was given for the tendency of young chicks and ducklings to react fearfully to the suspended cardboard figures of birds of prey. These card-

innate

board figures were said to constitute _innate_

releasers

releasers for the fear response in the young birds.

29. Further research revealed, however, that both the sticklebacks and the young

were not

birds (were/were not) responding to innate-releasing stimuli, but rather to the

novelty

novelty of the stimuli. Male sticklebacks will attack most

novel

novel objects, and young birds will show fear of most

novel

Novel objects.

30. *Sequential Stimuli.* In many cases, patterns of behavior, such as the seasonal migration of birds, depend on ___sequential patterns___ (a chain of environmental stimuli) to trigger the behavior. Thus the *sequential stimuli* that trigger the snowbird's northward migration in the spring are gradually increasing amounts of ___daylight___.

sequential stimuli

daylight

31. Studies of ring doves have shown that there is a sequence of stimuli leading to reproduction. Each step in the process—courting, mating, nest building, etc.— requires distinctive and ___sequential___ stimuli.

sequential

Learning Objectives

13. Give three illustrations to demonstrate that much of the behavior of animals depends on their sensory capacities.

14. Define and give examples of fixed-action patterns.

15. What does direct electrical stimulation of the brains of chickens tell us about the basis of fixed-action patterns?

16. What do selective breeding experiments tell us about the heritability of specific behavioral traits, such as phototaxis and retrieving ability, as well as more general behavioral traits, such as the ability to learn?

17. What remains unknown about the difference between "maze bright" and "maze dull" rats?

18. Explain why a genetic difference that may be of small consequence to an individual may be of significant difference to a population.

19. Define and give an example of a sign stimulus.

20. Red bellies and cardboard figures of birds of prey were said to be innate releasers for stickleback fish and young birds, respectively. What was meant by this? What is a better explanation?

21. Describe the sequential series of stimuli that leads the snowbird to migrate.

Learning

32. There are two general conclusions to be drawn from studies of species-specific behavior in young animals. The first is that to some degree the ability to learn is itself ___species-specific___. For example, the hunting wasp finds it relatively easy to learn ___landmarks___ that guide its return to the nest, and rats are very quick to learn ___taste___ aversions, even though many hours may elapse between the ingestion of the distinctively flavored food and the subsequent illness.

species-specific

landmarks

taste (food)

less

33. Among rats, learning this relationship between taste and illness is (more/less) difficult than learning relationships between other kinds of sensory events. This

novel

ability, however, is limited to _____novel_____ foods.

34. Perhaps the tendency of human beings to become nauseous and vomit when

visual

confronted with an unstable _____visual_____ field is related to the taste aversion in rats. Many toxic substances can produce this visual instability and subsequent vomiting in human beings.

35. Thus motion sickness may be a result of this genetic predisposition we carry; it

visual

mimics the same _____visual_____ instability produced by many toxic substances.

36. *Imprinting.* Many species of birds are quick to learn to follow the first moving

imprinting

object they see after hatching, a phenomenon called _____imprinting_____.

sensitive

37. Imprinting occurs only during the _____sensitive_____ period and makes possible the young bird's later participation in the social system. Thus imprinting appears to be a primary mechanism for the development of

social

_____social_____ bonds among many birds.

is not

38. The restricted sensitive period in which imprinting occurs (is/is not) directly controlled by the passage of time. The sensitive period can be extended, even to the period before birth, by arranging for particular experiences to occur. Thus chicks

tones

that were exposed to particular _____tones_____ before hatching would follow in the direction of these particular tones after hatching.

39. The relationship between imprinting and experience illustrates the second general conclusion regarding species-specific behavior: species-specific behavior must it-

learned

self be _____learned_____.

40. *Life Experiences.* This relationship between species-specific behavior and learning is also illustrated by studies that demonstrated that a cat's response to a rat

learned

depends primarily on what the cat has _____learned_____ about rats as a kitten.

41. Moreover, it has been shown that a mouse raised by a foster rat mother will later

rat

prefer a (mouse/rat) as a companion. A mouse raised by a mouse mother will

mouse

prefer to associate with a _____mouse_____, while a mouse raised in isola-

mouse

tion without any mother will prefer a _____mouse_____.

42. Thus while the tendency to seek affiliation is a species-specific behavior among many animals, the object of this affiliation is to a large extent

learned   _learned_.

Learning Objectives

22. What are the two general conclusions to be drawn from species-specific behavior in young animals? Provide two examples to illustrate each of the conclusions.

23. In what way might the tendency of human beings to become nauseous when confronted with an unstable visual environment be related to taste aversion in rats?

24. What is imprinting? Describe how the sensitive period was extended even to the period before hatching.

INTERPRETING BEHAVIOR

What Is the Adaptive Significance of a Trait?

43. A major assumption about a trait that an animal consistently exhibits in its natu-

adaptive   ral habitat is that the trait must have some kind of _adaptive_ signif-
                   icance for the animal.

44. Adaptive significance means that the trait allows the animal to

survive   _survive_ in its particular part of the environment.

is not   45. It (is/is not) always easy to see the adaptive significance of a particular trait in an animal. In some cases laboratory experiments must be performed, as in the case of the Io moth's sudden exposure of its wing pattern to frighten potential predators. This particular behavior also illustrates the fact that the behavior of one

animal   animal may be dependent upon the behavior of another _animal_.

Learning Objectives

25. What is meant when it is said that consistent traits found in animals have adaptive significance?

26. What does the example of the Io moth illustrate?

How Purposive Is Behavior?

does not

46. The example of nest building in pregnant female rats illustrates that in many cases an animal (does/does not) perform a behavior for the same purpose as would a human being. The rat's nest building is merely a reaction to

lowered

lowered body temperature; the female rat is not preparing a warm place for her future offspring.

47. The scientific approach in situations where there are two equally reasonable explanations, such as why a female rat constructs a nest, is to choose the

simpler

simpler explanation. This is known as the *principle of*

parsimony

parsimony.

48. It was Lloyd Morgan who first suggested that comparative psychologists adopt

Morgan's

the principle of parsimony. Thus it is also known as "_Morgan's_ Canon." Morgan believed that making overly complex explanations for animal behavior often interfered with understanding the behavior.

Learning Objectives

27. Define the principle of parsimony, and illustrate its use in the problem of why pregnant female rats build nests. By whom and why was this principle first suggested?

Generalizing to Human Behavior

49. It is also possible to err in an opposite direction and ascribe animal characteris-

beastopomorphic

tics to the behavior of human beings. Edney calls this a _beastopomorphic_ interpretation.

50. For example, some writers have said that human beings have a drive to claim, defend, and compete for territory and that the explanation for this territorial drive

animals

is the same as for lower _animals_.

some

51. There are (no/some) similarities between human beings and animals in this respect. There are also significant differences. For example, the use of territorial

lower

space is much more stereotyped and less variable in _lower_

animals

animals.

is not
52. Evidence also supports the contention that aggression (is/is not) an inescapable part of our animal inheritance. Moreover, even if human beings do inherit aggressive tendencies, they can learn to control the aggression or redirect it into more appropriate behavior, just as cats learn to control their predatory behavior

rats
toward ___rats___ .

53. The systematic study of the biological basis of all social behavior is called

sociobiology
___sociobiology___ . This approach to the study of behavior attempts to iden-

genetic
tify a ___genetic___ origin for many forms of social behavior in human beings, such as aggression and altruism.

54. Thus sociobiologists have proposed that altruism exists in animals (and human

inherited (genetic)
beings) because of a(n) ___inherited___ tendency to protect their own gene pools. This also includes their own lives.

55. The altruistic behavior observed in animals in which they sacrifice their own lives to protect others is thus said to arise from a genetic basis for the concept of

inclusive
___inclusive___ *fitness:* one's own fitness to survive may be sacrificed for one's relative's fitness to survive.

is
56. There (is/is not) some evidence that both animals and human beings are most likely to risk their own lives for their closest relatives rather than for more distant relatives or strangers. However, there is also evidence to the contrary.

cannot
57. At this time it (can/cannot) be said that sociobiologists have identified the genetic origins for social behavior in human beings. While genes may be an important component of human social behavior, they cannot determine it without the inclu-

experiences
sion of appropriate ___experiences___ .

is not
58. It (is/is not) appropriate to make direct analogies between the behavior of animals and that of human beings. However, some of the concepts borrowed from animal studies, such as species-specific behavior, are useful in analyzing human behavior.

59. One of the species-specific behaviors of human beings is their ability to use

language
___language___ . In order to speak, a child must inherit the necessary vocal apparatus and brain organization, something unique to the human species. But the ability to use language is also determined by one's

environment (experience)
___enviornmment___ .

60. Thus the use of language by human beings involves both experience and

heredity
___heredity___ , just as the species-specific behavior of other animals involves both.

Learning Objectives

28. What did Edney mean by beastopomorphic interpretations of human behavior (use the example of a territorial drive to explain your answer)? Is this a correct explanation?

29. Give a definition of sociobiology.

30. How do sociobiologists explain the presence of altruism in animals and human beings? Is this a correct explanation?

31. In addition to genetic foundations, what else must be included in order to explain the social behavior of human beings?

32. Give an example of how the concept of species-specific behavior has proven useful in the study of human beings.

Chapter Eight
Learning

General Objectives

1. Define the term *learning*.

2. Describe classical conditioning, and distinguish it from operant conditioning.

3. Describe the concepts of generalization, discrimination, and extinction as they apply both to classical conditioning and to operant conditioning.

4. Define or give examples of these concepts from operant conditioning: reinforcement, positive discriminative stimulus, negative discriminative stimulus, punishment, negative reinforcement, superstitious behavior, and shaping.

5. Provide examples of the four major schedules of reinforcement.

6. Discuss some practical applications of operant principles.

7. Present the major tenets of social learning theory.

Learning

Learning Objectives appear at
the end of each major section.

LEARNING AND PERFORMANCE

learning

performance (behavior)

has

practice

1. Learning involves a change in behavior or performance. Not all changes in performance may be considered to be learning, however. This is the main point being made in the first section: one cannot necessarily infer _learning_ from a change in _performance_.

2. If a rat consistently turns left in a T-shaped maze following *practice*, it is reasonable to infer that learning (has/has not) occurred. Learning may be defined as (a) a *relatively enduring* change in behavior caused by (b) *experience* or _practice_.

3. There are two main points to remember in distinguishing learning from other changes in performance: a change in behavior due to learning is (a) relatively

enduring/practice (experience)   _enduring_, and it is caused by (b) _practice_.

4. If a well-trained rat stops pressing a lever after one hundred responses, its behavior or performance has clearly changed, perhaps because it is full. But this

enduring   change is not relatively _enduring_, since it will change again once the rat is food-deprived, and the change is not caused by

experience (practice)   _experience_. Thus, the rat's performance change cannot be classified

learning   as _learning_.

5. Which of the following changes in behavior are probably the result of learning? In the blanks at the left place an *L* for learning and a *P* for performance changes not due to learning. (For each item ask yourself whether or not the behavior change is due to *practice* and whether or not it is *relatively enduring*.)

L   _L_ Ralph practices a new golf swing daily, and his distance gradually improves.

P   _P_ After taking a few drinks, Ralph is unable to hit the ball.

P   _P_ A rat's performance in a swimming maze begins to deteriorate after about twenty trials, due to fatigue.

P   _P_ A rat runs a maze much faster when hungry and when there is food at the end of the maze.

6. To have answered "learning" in the above, one would have to know that the

practice (experience)   change in behavior is the result of _practice_ and that it is a rela-

enduring   tively _enduring_ or permanent change.

Learning Objectives

1. What is the definition of learning presented in your text? List the two main components of this definition.
   Enduring change in behavior due to experience or practice   practice & enduring

2. Provide examples that illustrate performance changes that *are due to learning* and performance changes that *are not due to learning.*   _practice_   _maturation_

CLASSICAL CONDITIONING

The Conditioned Response

Pavlovian

7. Classical conditioning, also called ___Pavlovian___ conditioning after its discoverer, involves reflexive behavior. A reflexive response is generally elicited

stimulus

    by a specific ___stimulus___.

does not

8. The procedure of classical conditioning involves repeatedly associating a "neutral" stimulus, which at first (does/*does not*) elicit a particular response, with a stimulus that does elicit the response. For example, the sound of a bell might be paired with food.

9. After repeated pairing of the two stimuli, the neutral stimulus will also begin to elicit the response. For example, after repeated pairing of a bell with food, a dog

bell (sound, tone)

    will begin to salivate to the ___bell___ as well as the food.

10. *Pavlov's Experiments.* In a series of studies Pavlov used the salivary reflex in dogs as the behavior to be conditioned. Since salivating in response to food placed in the mouth usually does not depend on experience, Pavlov referred to it

unconditioned

    as the "unlearned" or ___unconditioned___ response.

unconditioned

11. The food in the dog's mouth is referred to as the ___unconditioned___ stimulus.

before
food

12. The procedure followed in conditioning the salivary reflex is to present a neutral stimulus, such as a light or bell, during or just (*before*/after) the presentation of the unconditioned stimulus, which in this case is the (*food*/bell).

13. After several trials in which a bell is paired with food, the bell will elicit a response much like that elicited by the food. The response to the bell is learned or

conditioned

    conditioned, so the bell is termed the ___conditioned___ stimulus and the

conditioned

    salivating response to it the ___conditioned___ response.

14. Describe the components of classical conditioning of the salivary reflex by placing the appropriate abbreviations in the blanks below: CS (conditioned stimulus), UCS (unconditioned stimulus), CR (conditioned response), UCR (unconditioned response).

CS/CR

    bell ___CS___ salivation to bell ___CR___

UCS/UCR

    meat ___UCS___ salivation to meat ___UCR___

15. Pavlov conditioned other reflexes as well, including a dog's response of withdrawing its forepaws. At first, the dog withdrew its paws in response to electric

unconditioned

shock, which would be considered the unlearned or _unconditioned_ stimulus. The dog's reflex response to shock would be termed the

unconditioned response   _unconditioned   response_ .

16. Following training, the dog would respond to the tick of a metronome as well as to the shock. The tick of the metronome would be the

conditioned stimulus   _conditioned   stimulus_ and the shock would be the

unconditioned stimulus   _unconditioned stimulus_ .

17. The *unconditioned* response in the above example would be the response to the

shock   _shock_ ; the *conditioned* response would be the response to the

metronome (tick)   _metronome_ .

18. In classical conditioning the dog learned to respond to the metronome as if it were the same as the shock. To some extent, it seemed that one stimulus had been *substituted* for another. Hence, Pavlov called this tendency *stimulus*

substitution   _substitution_ .

Learning Objectives

3. Who discovered and performed the early research on classical conditioning? _Pavlov_

4. Read the following passage. Then match the items below with one of the following abbreviations: CS (conditioned stimulus), CR (conditioned response), UCS (unconditioned stimulus), UCR (unconditioned response).
A young woman is allergic to dog and cat hair and sneezes when she comes in contact with these stimuli. Her new boyfriend has a dog which leaves hair on his clothing which causes the woman to sneeze. After several meetings she notices that she begins to sneeze whenever she sees her boyfriend, even when he is at a distance.
animal hair _UCS_
sneezing caused by animal hair _UCR_
sight of boyfriend _CS_
sneezing at the sight of boyfriend _CR_

5. Using the example involving a bell and food and the abbreviations listed above, describe the procedure of classical conditioning.

6. Explain what Pavlov meant by *stimulus substitution*. _you use a substitute in place of the real_
   stimulus like a bell in place of the food,

19. *The Garcia Effect.* For nearly half a century after Pavlov, psychologists believed that responses could be conditioned with equal ease to almost any "neutral" stim-

were not   ulus. It turned out, however, that the conditioned stimuli (were/were not) as neutral as had been thought.

20. Garcia found that animals readily connected some types of "neutral" stimuli with some unconditioned responses but not with others. For example, in one study *sweetened water* was followed either by *foot shock* or a *nausea*-producing treatment as the unconditioned stimuli. Aversion to the sweet taste was conditioned only for those rats which had been (shocked/nauseated).

nauseated

21. Other rats were presented with a different type of water, water accompanied not by a sweet taste but by flashing lights and loud noise. For half of these rats drinking was followed by *nausea* and for half by *shock*. Afterward, water accompanied by lights and noise was avoided by those rats for which drinking was

shock

followed by ___shock___.

22. The main point of Garcia's findings is that some conditioned stimuli seem to fit more naturally with specific unconditioned stimuli. Taste is more easily con-

nausea (illness)

nected to ___nausea___, and noise and light to

shock (pain)

___shock___.

taste

23. Human beings, like rats, seem prepared to connect ___taste___ with illness. In one study, for example, cancer patients who were served a distinctively flavored ice cream (Mapletoff) just prior to chemotherapy later tended to

reject

(reject/accept) that flavor.

24. There is one other point made with regard to these conditioned aversions: while psychologists previously thought that the CS must be presented *with* or *immediately following* the UCS, these studies indicate that in some cases delays between

twelve

CS and UCS for as long as ___twelve___ hours will still produce the aversion.

Learning Objectives

UCS and CS do not have to follow each other   *light*

7. What is the main point of Garcia's findings? Which conditioned stimulus conditions more easily to shock and which to nausea? Do the findings seem to generalize to human beings?—*Yes*

taste

8. Generally, the UCS must immediately follow the CS. Give an example of a situation in which this seems not to be the case. *Chemotherapy patients and ice cream*

Generalization and Discrimination

25. The more similar a stimulus is to a conditioned stimulus, the more likely it is for

generalize
would

a response to ___generalize___ to it. For example, if a dog is conditioned to respond to a tone of 1,000 cps, it probably (would/would not) salivate to a tone of 600 cps, although not nearly as much.

26. A response learned in one situation, or to one stimulus, will also tend to occur in

similar

other situations which are _____similar_____ to it. This is the process called

generalization

_____generalization_____

27. The curve produced by the tendency of the response to increase in strength as the new stimulus becomes more similar to the CS and decrease in strength as it be-

gradient

comes less similar is referred to as a generalization _____gradient_____.

28. If the UCS regularly follows one stimulus and not another, however, the animal

discriminate

will learn to _____discriminate_____. For example, if food were presented only after the 1,000 cps sound and not after the 600 cps sound, the animal would

1,000

learn to respond only to the _____1000_____ cps sound.

29. Organisms can be trained not to respond to similar stimuli. This process is re-

discrimination

ferred to as _____discrimination_____

Extinction of a Classically Conditioned Response

30. If the UCS no longer occurs after the CS, the CR (the conditioned response) will

extinction

gradually disappear. This process is referred to as _____extinction_____.

31. The procedure of extinction simply involves presentation of the

CS/UCS

_____CS_____ without the _____UCS_____. Unless the CS is at

CR (conditioned response)

least occasionally followed by the UCS, the _____CR_____ will gradu-ally disappear.

Learning Objectives

9. What is stimulus generalization, and to what types of stimuli do animals tend to generalize? What is a generalization gradient? What is the name of the procedure by which animals are trained not to respond to similar stimuli? _discrimination_

10. What procedure does one follow to produce extinction of a classically conditioned response? _Don't give the UCS after the c.s. is given_

Classical Conditioning and Human Behavior

Watson

32. Pavlov's findings led John B. _____Watson_____, the founder of American

behaviorism

_____Behaviorism_____, to the conclusion that all learning could be explained in terms of classical conditioning.

33. In his demonstration with Albert, for example, Watson showed how fear could be acquired through classical conditioning. While Albert showed no initial fear of a white rat, after the rat was paired with a loud noise on several occasions

fear (phobia)   Albert developed a ___fear___ of the rat.

generalize   34. Albert's fear also began to ___generalize___ to other similar stimuli, including a rabbit, dog, and fur coat.

35. Watson also explored ways of removing conditioned fears. For example, in one study by Jones, a caged rabbit was gradually brought closer to the table where the child was eating a snack. Through the process of gradually associating pleasant things with the feared object, the child's fears were greatly

reduced ("unconditioned")   ___reduced___.

36. While most psychologists acknowledge the importance of classical conditioning in many types of learning, including the development of phobias, modern behaviorists generally (do/do not) believe that classical conditioning can explain all learning.

do not

Learning Objectives

11. What was the name of the *founder* of American behaviorism? What was his belief concerning classical conditioning and human behavior?   _John B. Watson_   _He believed humans could be conditioned to do anything also unconditioned_   _show rat - loud noise_

12. How did Watson condition fear in Albert? How did Jones remove fear in Peter?   _snacks - bring rabbit closer_

OPERANT CONDITIONING

Thorndike   37. Another early psychologist, Edward ___Thorndike___, formulated a

Effect   principle which he called the Law of ___Effect___.

38. According to the Law of Effect, responses followed by satisfying consequences tend to be repeated, while responses followed by annoying

consequences   ___consequences___ tend to disappear.

Skinner   39. Thorndike's Law of Effect was elaborated by B. F. ___Skinner___, and "satisfying consequences" became known as reinforcement.

40. To differentiate these reinforcement procedures from classical conditioning, Skinner referred to classically conditioned reflexes as *respondent* behavior and to behavior that operates on the environment to produce consequences as

operant   ___operant___ behavior.

respondent (Pavlovian)

operant

41. Understanding the differences between classical or _respondent_ con-

ditioning and instrumental or _operant_ conditioning is not a simple matter. As an aid to understanding these concepts, reread the last two paragraphs in this section. Then label the descriptions below by filling in the blanks with either C (for classical) or O (for operant).

O   _O_ applies to "voluntary" behavior

C   _C_ responses elicited by particular stimuli

C   _C_ generally involves reflexive behavior

O   _O_ depends on consequences—rewards and punishments

O   _O_ also termed "instrumental conditioning"

C   _C_ behavior termed "respondent"

42. Label the procedures described below with either C (for classical) or O (for operant).

O   _O_ Polly speaks; she receives a cracker.

C   _C_ A tone and food are paired; the animal salivates to both.

C   _C_ A dog flexes its leg to light and to an electric shock that follows it.

O   _O_ A child stops fingering an electrical outlet when shocked.

Learning Objectives

13. What is the Law of Effect, and who formulated this principle?

14. What is Skinner's name for classical conditioning? What is Skinner's name for the type of conditioning that stresses the consequences of behavior?

15. List two major differences between classical and operant conditioning.

Reinforcement and Punishment

after

43. Operant responses are strengthened or weakened as a result of their *consequences,* the events that occur (before/after) a response is made.

44. The procedure in which a consequence *increases* the frequency of behavior is

reinforcement (reward)

called _reinforcement_ and the procedure in which a consequence *de-*

punishment

creases response frequency is called _punishment_ .

reinforcement

punishment

45. Behavior that is followed by _reinforcement_ tends to be repeated (or to increase in frequency). Behavior followed by _punishment_ tends *not* to be repeated (or to decrease in frequency).

46. There are two main types of reinforcement. *Positive* reinforcement involves presentation of a stimulus (such as food or praise). *Negative* reinforcement involves

removal (termination, delay)
increase

removal of a stimulus (such as shock). Both positive and negative reinforcement result in a(n) (increase/decrease) *in responding*.

47. Under one procedure a rat can turn off an electric shock to its feet for a period

negative

increase

of time by pressing a bar. This procedure would involve _negative_ reinforcement, and the response of pressing the bar when shock came on would (increase/decrease) in frequency.

increase

decreases

48. Both positive and negative reinforcement _increase_ response strength or frequency. *Punishment*, on the other hand, _decrease_ response strength or frequency.

49. If an unpleasant event, such as shock, is *presented* following a response and the response *decreases* in frequency, the procedure referred to as

punishment

punishment is involved. If an unpleasant event is *removed* following a response and the response *increases* in frequency, then the procedure known as

negative reinforcement

negative _reinforcement_ is involved.

temporarily suppresses

50. While some psychologists disagree, Skinner believes that punishment (permanently eliminates/temporarily suppresses) behavior. For this reason Skinner feels that punishment is not an effective procedure.

51. When punishment immediately follows behavior, it does work to suppress behavior, and sometimes the suppression may last for a long time. There are disadvantages to the use of punishment, however, including the fact that the punished

avoid (dislike, fear)

animal or person may _avoid_ the individual who did the punishing.

52. Reinforcement that happens to follow a particular behavior by chance—as when a baseball player hits a home run immediately after spitting on his shoe—may

superstitious

is not

lead to the development of _superstitious_ behavior. The ball player is likely to spit on his shoe whenever he comes up to bat, even though the reinforcement of a home run (is/is not) actually contingent on spitting.

53. Pigeons and other lower animals may also develop what B. F. Skinner called superstitious behavior. For example, if a pigeon receives a food reward that is not intentionally contingent on its behavior, once every minute for example, the pigeon will tend to:

a. turn around.
b. peck a disk.
c. bob its head.
d.) any of the above or whatever other behavior happens to occur just before reinforcement.

d

Learning Objectives

16. What is the effect of positive reinforcement on behavior? What is the effect of negative reinforcement?
increases the frequency of something desireable   increase response to do something

17. Explain or give an example of the way in which negative reinforcement increases the frequency of a response.
shock a cat until it opens a door to stop the shock

18. What is punishment, and what is its major effect on behavior? *It generally inhibits that behavior for a while decreasing a consequence*

19. Name one disadvantage of using punishment. *— Person or animal may avoid or hate person doing the Punishing*

20. Explain the reinforcement procedure that produces *superstitious behavior* in animals and human beings.

Stop

Establishing and Maintaining Operantly Conditioned Responses

54. *Shaping*. Training a dog to jump a hurdle would involve reinforcing the dog after it jumped. But how would you get the dog to jump in the first place? For training such new behaviors, psychologists generally use the procedure called

shaping   _____Shaping_____.

55. To train a dog to jump a hurdle you might simply wait for it to jump and then reinforce it. You would probably have a long wait, however, since it is unlikely that the dog would emit this particular response very quickly, if at all. Thus, you

shaping   would use the procedure of _____Shaping_____, which involves reinforcing closer and closer *approximations* to the desired response.

56. The trainer might first reinforce the dog for merely coming near the hurdle. This

approximation   would be the first _____approximation_____ of the final response.

57. As a second approximation, the trainer might reinforce the dog for running to-
small   ward the hurdle. Thus, shaping proceeds in (small/large) increments, or steps,

approximation   with each step representing a closer _____approximation_____ of the final response.

58. In which of the following has shaping been used?
a. teaching pigeons to play Ping-Pong
b. teaching dolphins to "hula"
c. toilet training children
d   d.) all of the above

59. *Schedules of Reinforcement.* Once a response has been shaped, it may be maintained by various schedules of reinforcement. For example, reinforcement of a

continuous

response each time it occurs would be a _continuous_ reinforcement schedule.

60. Continuous reinforcement is the best schedule to use for establishing behavior initially, but once behavior is well established it may be maintained with one of

partial

the _partial_ schedules of reinforcement.

61. The text describes four basic schedules of partial reinforcement: fixed-ratio (FR), fixed-interval (FI), variable-ratio (VR), and variable-interval (VI) schedules. *Reread the section on schedules,* and then place the appropriate abbreviations next to the examples below.

FI

_FI_ A rat is reinforced for the first bar press following a two-minute period.

FR

_FR_ A pigeon receives a food pellet for each one hundred pecks on a lighted disk.

VR

_VR_ A dolphin is given a fish, on the average, for every fifth jump it makes.

VI

_VI_ A fish is given a synthetic worm for each sucking response it makes following, on the average, a one-minute period.

number (frequency)

62. The fixed- and variable-ratio schedules are based on the _number_ of responses an animal must emit to obtain reinforcement. The fixed- and

time

variable-interval schedules are based on the amount of _time_ that must elapse before a response is reinforced.

interval

63. The irregular schedules of reinforcement, the variable-_interval_

ratio/higher

and variable-_ratio_ schedules, tend to produce (higher/lower) *rates of responding and greater persistence* in behavior than do the comparable fixed schedules.

64. In the spaces below, place the appropriate abbreviations (FR, FI, VR, or VI) next to the examples.

VR

_VR_ A rat is first reinforced for making fifty-two responses, then twelve responses, then sixty-six responses, and so on.

VI

_VI_ A peacock is reinforced for its first peck after 39 seconds elapse, then after 102 seconds, then after 12 seconds.

Learning Objectives

21. What is shaping, and when is it used? What is meant by the term *approximation*?

22. List and describe the four partial reinforcement schedules discussed in the text. FI VI VR FR

Conditioned Reinforcers

conditioned (secondary)

65. Reinforcing stimuli that occur immediately after a response and that precede primary reinforcing stimuli are called Conditioned reinforcers.

after

66. For example, the click of a food apparatus in a Skinner box occurs immediately (after/before) the response and before delivery of food. Food is the

primary/secondary

primary reinforcer, and the click is the secondary or conditioned reinforcer.

conditioned

67. Secondary or conditioned reinforcers may be used to bridge delays between the response and delivery of the primary reinforcer. For example, the

tokens

conditioned reinforcers used in the Chimp-O-Mat, the tokens which chimps collected to exchange for fruit, permitted the chimps to tolerate long delays between the response and the primary reinforcer.

Generalization and Discrimination

68. A pigeon trained to peck a yellow light for a food reward may also peck a green light. As with classical conditioning, a phenomenon known as stimulus

generalization

generalization occurs in which an animal trained to respond in a stimulus situation may also respond to other similar stimuli.

69. An animal can be trained *not* to generalize. For example, if a pigeon is reinforced when it pecks a yellow light and not reinforced when it pecks any other

yellow

color, it will gradually learn to peck only when the yellow light

discrimination

is on. This procedure is called discrimination training.

discriminative

70. The lights in the above example are referred to as discriminative stimuli. A stimulus, such as a light, that regularly precedes rewarded behavior is

positive

referred to as a positive discriminative stimulus, and one that precedes a response not followed by reward is referred to as a

negative

negative discriminative stimulus.

Learning Objectives

23. What are conditioned or secondary reinforcers? What importance do they have relative to the effect of primary reinforcers?

24. Give an example of *generalization* and *discrimination* in an operant training procedure.

25. What is a positive discriminative stimulus? A negative discriminative stimulus?

Aversive Conditioning

aversive

71. In addition to control of behavior with reinforcement, there are other procedures that use subjectively unpleasant, or _aversive_, stimuli. The two procedures discussed are *negative reinforcement* and *punishment*.

negative

reinforcement

72. Removal of an aversive stimulus following a response results in an *increase* in response frequency and is referred to as _negative reinforcement_. Presentation of an aversive stimulus following a response results in a decrease in response frequency and is known as

punishment

punishment.

decrease

punishment

73. For example, if a rat is shocked each time it presses a bar, the frequency of its bar pressing will (increase/decrease). Thus, the procedure involved is called _punishment_.

punishment

74. If a child touches a hot stove, his touching response will probably be effectively suppressed. The procedure that stopped his stove touching would be called _punishment_, even though it was not "intentionally" applied by anyone.

increase

negative reinforcement

75. Use of an alarm clock will probably (increase/decrease) the likelihood that one will arise early and turn off the alarm. Thus, use of an alarm clock involves the procedure known as _negative_ _reinforcement_.

positive

76. Punishment is probably most effective when used in combination with _positive_ reinforcement. For example, if a child is punished for running into the street, she could also be *rewarded* for behaviors that compete with this, such as going to a parent when she wants to cross.

Learning Objectives

26. What are the differences between *punishment* and *negative reinforcement* with regard to (a) the effect of each on behavior strength or frequency and (b) the way in which the aversive stimulus is used?

27. Punishment is probably most effective when used in conjunction with what other operant procedure?

positive reinforcement

Practical Applications of Operant Conditioning

77. *Computer-Assisted Instruction.* This form of instruction uses immediate feed-

reinforcement

back. Feedback may be described as a type of *reinforcement* which includes information about past performance used to alter future behavior.

computer-

78. The feedback principle is the basis of *computer*-

assisted

assisted instruction. In a course of this type students move ahead
at their own pace while the computer adjusts to the students' abilities, branching
off into remedial programs if needed or perhaps skipping sections for a particularly fast learner.

wide variety

79. Computers have been used in a (wide variety/limited range) of college courses
with promising results, including evidence that in some cases computer-assisted
instruction may be better than conventional instruction.

80. *Behavior Modification.* Behavior modification involves the application of

operant

operant techniques to human behavior. Your text describes the
use of these procedures in a situation involving incorrigible junior high school

students

students. In this case instruction and techniques of using behavior modification
were taught to the (students/teachers).

81. In learning to shape the teachers to be more pleasant to them, the students used

reinforcement

reinforcement for positive comments and actions and extinction or mild

punishment
verbal

punishment for negative ones. The reinforcers and punishers used
were (verbal/monetary).

82. Reinforcement was also used to help keep an area clear of litter. In that study

twenty-five cents

people were paid either _*25¢*_ or a chance on a weekly lottery
for turning in a bag of litter. The money or chance functioned as positive

reinforcement

reinforcement for picking up litter.

Learning Objectives

28. How does feedback differ from other forms of reinforcement? Describe the use of feedback in computer-assisted
    courses. Have computers been used in a wide variety of courses or is their use fairly restricted?

29. In terms of the principles or techniques it tends to use, what is behavior modification? Present an example that
    illustrates the use of behavior modification in an applied setting.

COMPARISON OF CLASSICAL AND OPERANT CONDITIONING

elicited

83. While psychologists may debate differences between these two forms of learning, some terminology is agreed upon. For example, classically conditioned responses are said to be (elicited/emitted) by a *specific* stimulus.

autonomic

84. In addition, classical conditioning usually involves the (autonomic/somatic) nervous system. For example, such autonomic activities as salivation may be classi-

somatic (skeletal)

cally conditioned, while such ___Somatic___ activities as walking,

operantly

jumping, bar pressing, and so on are ___operantly___ conditioned.

85. Your text makes the point that classical conditioning is more likely to involve emotions, attitudes, and expectations, while operant conditioning is more likely

goal

to involve responses directed toward a ___goal___.
(*As a review, look back at frames 41 and 42 in the preceding section.*)

Learning Objectives

Don't be discouraged by this section. As we indicated earlier, it is not easy to understand the differences between classical and operant conditioning, and psychologists still debate the more theoretical points. What you should be able to do, however, is to recognize examples of each procedure. If a response involves primarily autonomic activity (glandular and "gut" activities) and is "drawn out" or elicited by a stimulus, then classical conditioning is probably involved. If the food or other reinforcement is presented *only if* the response occurs, and if the response involves skeletal muscles (running, bar pressing, pecking, etc.), then the procedure is probably operant conditioning.

30. Know whether the following examples illustrate *classical* conditioning or *operant* conditioning.
    a. A pigeon pecks a lighted disk and receives food. operant
    b. A rat runs a maze for a food pellet at the end. operant
    c. A human being blinks when a puff of air is blown into her eyes. After the air puff is preceded several times by light, she also blinks to the light. classical
    d. When a light is turned on, a dog jumps a hurdle and avoids shock to its feet. classical
    e. A dog withdraws its paws to an electric shock and eventually to a light that precedes the shock. classical

31. Know whether the following describe *classical* or *operant* conditioning.
    a. Usually autonomic responses. classical
    b. Somatic or skeletal responses. operant
    c. Is elicited. classical
    d. Is emitted. operant
    e. A specific stimulus precedes and produces the response. classical

SOCIAL LEARNING THEORY

86. It has become clear that classical and operant conditioning do not account for a major process by which human beings learn, the process of

observational

___observational___ learning in which we learn by watching others.

87. While some of our behaviors are gradually shaped, human beings acquire a number of behavior patterns by observing the consequences of other people's behavior. We tend to model those behaviors of others which we see

reinforced   _reinforced_ and avoid those we see punished.

social   88. Observational learning is a major component of _social_

learning   _learning_ theory, a conceptualization developed in part by Bandura.

89. Social learning theory emphasizes the fact that the interpretations of stimuli, not just the stimuli themselves, are important determinants of human behavior. In other words, the theory stresses the importance of thinking or

cognitive   _cognitive_ processes.

Learning Objectives

32. Name a major determinant, other than classical and operant conditioning, of human learning.

33. Under what circumstances do we tend to model the behavior we observe?

34. What is the name of the theoretical system that emphasizes cognitive processes and observational learning?
social learning theory

Chapter Nine
Memory

General Objectives

1. Name and describe the three basic memory processes.

2. Name and describe the three kinds of memory stores.

3. Distinguish between episodic and semantic memory.

4. Describe two theories for the mental representation of information in the brain.

5. Distinguish between recognition, recall, and relearning.

6. Explain what is meant by state-dependent memory, and point out the common feature in its many forms.

7. Explain what is meant by remembering as reconstructing.

8. Explain what is meant by confabulation, and indicate how it is related to motivational states.

9. Describe several mnemonic devices, and indicate how they and other techniques can be used to improve memory.

10. List some of the important factors associated with forgetting.

Memory

Learning Objectives appear at
the end of each major section.

WHAT IS MEMORY?

1. The human capacity to register, retain, and remember information is how the text

memory

defines _memory_. As the definition implies, memory can be
divided into three basic processes: *acquisition, retention,* and

retrieval

retrieval.

2. Transforming raw information into the form in which it will be stored comprises

    acquisition/do not

    the ___acquisition___ or *encoding* process. We (do/do not) encode all aspects of information we wish to remember.

3. Once new information has been encoded for storage, the next process,

    retention

    ___retention___, comes into the act. Failure at this stage means that information is forgotten.

4. The process of getting encoded information out of storage and back into aware-

    retrieval
    variety of strategies

    ness is called ___retrieval___ and makes up the final stage of memory. Retrieval is an active process that employs a (single strategy/variety of strategies).

5. Psychologists have identified at least three kinds of memory stores. One type refers to the momentary persistence of sensory information after stimulation has

    sensory

    ceased and is called ___sensory___ memory. Sensory memory is found with all of the senses—sight, taste, sound, etc.—and only lasts for approximately

    second

    one (second/minute). Sensory memory has no meaning because it is

    unprocessed

    ___unprocessed___.

6. Another memory store that holds information for only about fifteen seconds is

    short-term
    limited

    appropriately called ___short___-___term___ memory. The short-term memory can hold a (limited/vast) amount of information.

7. The third type of memory store can retain an unlimited amount of information

    long-

    over long periods of time and is appropriately called ___long___-

    term

    ___term___ memory. Our ability to recognize old friends and famil-

    long-term

    iar foods are examples of ___long___-___term___ memory.

8. Although most psychologists view the memory process as an exchange of information among these three memory stores or *structures*, other psychologists have proposed an alternative view. In this approach, called *levels of processing*, the

    depth

    ability to retain information in memory depends upon the ___depth___ of the processing. Thus information that is processed at greater depths is

    less

    (less/more) easily forgotten than information processed at shallower depths.

9. Both the *structural* and the *levels-of-processing* approaches have proven useful to

    neither

    researchers; (both/neither) can supply all the answers to every aspect of human memory.

Learning Objectives

1. Give a definition of memory. *ability to register, retain retrieve information*

2. Name the three basic processes of memory, and describe what occurs in each of these processes. *sensory short long*
   acquisition, retention & retrieval

3. Name the three kinds of memory stores or structures, and tell which of these stores is identified with the following functions:
   a. where the memory of language is stored *long term*
   b. only lasts for a second *sensory*
   c. lasts for approximately fifteen seconds *short*
   d. contains unprocessed information without meaning *sensory*
   e. virtually unlimited in its storage capacity *long*
   f. quite limited in its storage capacity *short*

4. How does the levels-of-processing approach differ from the structural approach with respect to how the memory process works?

TYPES OF MEMORY

Sensory Memory

sensory

10. All of the information registered by the various sense organs is held for about one second in the ___*sensory*___ memory.

iconic

11. The sensory information coming from the eyes is held in ___*iconic*___ *memory*, the visual portion of sensory memory.

12. Sperling found that when his subjects were shown lists of ten or more numbers

four (five)
all of the

or letters, they could remember no more than ___*four*___. However, careful research revealed that the iconic memory contained (only this/(all of the)) information from the lists. The inability to remember more than four or five numbers or letters resulted not from failure to record all of the information in

forgetting

iconic memory, but rather from ___*forgetting*___.

13. The sensory memory that temporarily stores auditory information is called the

echoic
longer
not

___*echoic*___ *memory*. The duration of echoic memory is somewhat ((longer)/shorter), lasting up to approximately four seconds. Without this longer duration conversation with another person would ((not)/still) be possible. One would forget the first word of a spoken sentence before hearing the last one.

14. *Selective Attention.* The ability of human beings to concentrate on only selective parts of the sensory information being sent to the central nervous system is due

selective attention

to a control process called ___*selective attention*___.

also

15. For example, if you are listening intently to an old friend at a crowded cocktail party, you will (also/not) hear other sounds in the room. The extraneous sounds will be somewhat dampened by the brain, and you will be unable to describe much of their content. However, unusual sounds or the sound of your own name mentioned in another conversation will get your immediate

attention

attention. Thus, some processing of this background information must be occurring at all times.

16. Many well-practiced skills (such as walking, riding a bicycle, playing a piano, etc.) do not require selective attention, a phenomenon called

automaticity

automaticity

17. Automaticity can also occur while processing visual information. Research has shown that subjects can easily pick out target letters when they are surrounded by (numbers/letters), but this task becomes much more difficult when the target letter is surrounded by other letters. Thus the process of discriminating numbers

numbers

automaticity

from letters is *automatic* and is an example of visual _automaticity_.

Learning Objectives

5. What is the sensory memory that temporarily stores visual information? Auditory information? _echoic_
   iconic

6. Which of these two sensory memories has the longer duration, and why is this important? _echoic so you_
   can carry on a conversation with someone

7. About how many items can a person temporarily store in iconic memory? Is this the limit of this system? _No_
   four to five

8. Use the example of a person at a cocktail party to explain the concept of selective attention. _Name_

9. Describe how one can illustrate the principle of visual automaticity by the use of figures and numbers.

Short-Term Memory

18. In order to become useful the unprocessed information in the sensory memory

short-term

must be transferred into _Short - term_ memory. Material in short-term memory is meaningful but limited by two basic characteristics of short-term memory: it can hold information for only a short time,

limited

and it has a(n) (limited/unlimited) capacity.

19. While information can be held in short-term memory for about fifteen seconds, it is possible to keep information there indefinitely through

rehearsal

rehearsal.

20. There are two kinds of rehearsal that can be used for this purpose. In the first kind of rehearsal one continues to verbally repeat items to be remembered, such as those which might be found on a grocery list. This kind of rehearsal is called

maintenance ___maintenance___ rehearsal.

21. Another kind of rehearsal transfers information into long-term memory for later retrieval by organizing or *elaborating* upon it. This kind of rehearsal is called

elaborative ___elaborative___ rehearsal.

22. The amount of material that can be maintained through rehearsal is limited by the capacity of short-term memory, which for most people is about

seven ___seven___ items at one time.

23. Although it is not possible to directly increase the number of items that can be retained in short-term storage much beyond seven, additional information can be

chunks handled by combining items into ___chunks___. When chunks are employed, the amount of information that can be stored in short-term memory is

virtually unlimited (limited/virtually unlimited), but the number of chunks that can be handled at one time remains at seven.

24. Chunks are often constructed through the use of verbal labels. The word *coed*, for example, provides information about the sex, occupation, and approximate

visual age of an individual. But chunks are also used with ___visual___ information, such as the arrangement of pieces on a chess board.

Learning Objectives

10. What are the two basic limitations of short-term memory?

11. Describe the two rehearsal methods that can be used to hold information in short-term memory for long periods of time.

12. What is the capacity of the short-term memory? In what way does "chunking" increase this capacity?

seven   *handle more items*

Long-Term Memory

long- 25. The repository of permanent knowledge is found in the ___long___-

term ___term___ memory. The amount of information that can be stored in long-term memory is virtually unlimited.

26. *Rationale for a Dichotomous Memory.* Free-recall experiments indicate that

dichotomous short-term and long-term memories are two distinct (___dichotomous___) entities, each having characteristics of its own.

27. Subjects who were read lists of words and then immediately asked to recall them usually best remembered words from the (beginning/middle/end) of the list.

These words were most likely retrieved from ___*short*___-___*term*___ memory. The subjects were next best at recalling words from the (beginning/middle/end) of the list. These words were most likely stored in ___*long*___-___*term*___ memory. Fewest words were recalled from the (beginning/middle/end) of the list.

28. On the other hand, when subjects were asked to count backward by threes immediately after the last word on the list was read, their subsequent recall of words from the end of the list dropped substantially. The counting interfered with information in ___*short*___-___*term*___ memory.

29. The results from these free-recall experiments are generally plotted in the form of serial ___*position*___ curves. For example, in a list of twenty words the first word is in serial position number 1 and the last word is in serial position number ___*20*___.

30. Injuries to the brain in the area of the *hippocampus* have been found to impair the transfer of *new* information to long-term memory. In this case the person is unable to remember information encountered (before/after) the damage to the brain.

31. Cases of damage to the hippocampus, such as the one described in the text, give additional support to the notion of a dichotomous memory. Short-term memory remained unimpaired, as did long-term memory. What was missing was the mechanism for transferring information from ___*short*___-___*term*___ memory to ___*long*___-___*term*___ memory.

32. *Semantic and Episodic Memory.* Human beings appear to have two kinds of long-term memory. One kind is virtually an autobiographical record of one's experiences and is called ___*Episodic*___ *memory*. The other kind contains an organized knowledge about the rules and meanings of words and symbols and is called ___*Semantic*___ *memory*.

33. Recalling what occurred during the first week of college would depend upon ___*episodic*___ memory, while classifying numbers as to odd or even would depend upon ___*semantic*___ memory.

end

short-

term
beginning

long-term
middle

short-term

position

20

after

short-

term/long-

term

episodic

semantic

episodic

semantic

34. Of these two kinds of long-term memory stores, information in the

episodic   _episodic_ memory is more likely to be changed or forgotten. This is because retrieval of information from either semantic or episodic memory leaves the semantic information unaffected, but the act of retrieval is an episode

episodic   in itself and thus must be stored in the _episodic_ memory.

35. *Representation of Information in Memory*. Two major theories have been advanced to account for the mental representation of information in the memory stores. One theory proposes that information is stored in the form of images and

dual   words and is known as the _dual_ -*code* theory.

36. The other theory proposes that information is stored in an abstract manner in the

propositional   form of rule-governed propositions and is known as the _propositional_-*code* theory.

37. Research showing that words and events are represented in different ways sup-

dual-code   ports the _dual_ - _code_ theory and is difficult for the propositional-code theory to explain.

38. Research showing that when meaningful labels are attached to drawings it is eas-

propositional-   ier to recall the drawings at a later date supports the _propositional_-

code   _code_ theory. At the present time it appears that neither theory can explain all of the phenomena associated with the representation of memory in the brain.

Learning Objectives

13. Explain how serial position curves demonstrate a distinction between short-term and long-term memory. What other evidence supports this dichotomy?

14. Distinguish between episodic and semantic long-term memory. Which of these is more easily changed or forgotten, and why?

15. Name the two theories that have been advanced to account for the mental representation of information in the brain, and cite evidence that supports each theory. _dual and propositional theory_ _code_ _code_

MEMORY RETRIEVAL

all
is not   39. When persons are seeking information stored in short-term memory, they apparently make a search of (selected parts/all) of the information currently in the memory store. This (is/is not) true for long-term memory.

Retrieval Cues

40. Since the amount of information in the long-term memory store is so vast, an exhaustive search would be impossible. However, the information is stored in an

retrieval   orderly fashion, and retrieving it can be greatly aided by _retrieval_ cues.

41. Retrieval cues are simply pieces of information that aid in the recovery of infor-

can   mation from long-term memory. They (can/cannot) arise from all of the senses. Sights, sounds, odors, etc., may all serve as retrieval cues.

42. *Recognition and Recall.* The two basic methods for retrieving information from

recognition/recall   memory storage are _recognition_ and _recall_.

43. If called upon to identify a person in a police line-up, one would employ

recognition   _recognition_ as the method of retrieval. Recognition involves a decision based on information already present. One need only indicate that one

recognizes   _recognizes_ it.

44. When asked to provide one's telephone number or the name of an individual,

recall   however, one employs _recall_ as the method of retrieval. In this case the appropriate information is not presented to the individual, and he or she

long-   must make an active search of the _long_-

term/more   _term_ memory. For this reason recall is (more/less) difficult than recognition.

Learning Objectives

16. In what way does retrieval from short-term memory differ from retrieval from long-term memory?

17. What is a retrieval cue? _something that helps you get information out of long term memory_

18. Name and give examples of the two methods we use to retrieve information from memory. Which of these two is the more difficult to do?
recognition/recall   recall is harder

45. *Relearning.* Even when information can no longer be recalled or recognized, it is still possible to demonstrate that some trace of the material remains. This can be

relearning   done by _relearning_ the forgotten material and comparing the speed of relearning with the time required for initial learning. Studies have shown that

faster   learning forgotten material (such as a list of words) a second time is (slower/faster) than learning it originally.

46. This difference in the number of trials (or in the time) it takes to learn a list perfectly between the original and subsequent learning sessions is called a

savings (relearning)

___savings___ score.

47. *State-Dependent Memory.* Information learned in one physiological state becomes

more

(less/more) difficult to recall when in a different physiological state. This phe-

state-dependent

nomenon is called ___State___-___Dependent___ memory.

48. State-dependent memory effects have been found with both drug-induced and emotionally induced physiological states. Thus one is more likely to recall a sad

sad

experience from a summer ago when in a (sad/happy) emotional mood. Simi-

intoxicated

larly, information acquired while intoxicated will be best recalled when one is (sober/intoxicated).

49. The common feature in the many kinds of state-dependent memory is that the

retrieval

internal physiological state acts as a ___retrieval___ cue. Restoring the

context

internal state to its original condition creates the original ___context___ or setting, and it is this context that acts as the retrieval cue.

50. A similar situation is found when one restores the original physical context that accompanied an experience that one wants to recall. Thus the forgotten name of an individual can often be coaxed from memory by recalling the original

context

___context___ that accompanied previous meetings with this individual.

51. *"Tip of the Tongue" Phenomenon.* When people strive to recall a word, number, etc., that is on the tip of the tongue but cannot quite be remembered, they usu-

retrieval cues

ally generate their own internal ___retrieval cues___ to aid in the search. They do this by generating images, sounds, meanings, etc., that may be associated with the missing information.

Learning Objectives

19. How can a researcher demonstrate that previously learned material is still in the memory even though recall and recognition have failed? by relearning

20. What is a savings score? # of times it takes you to relearn something

21. What is meant by "state-dependent" memory? What is the common feature in the many kinds of state-dependent memory?

22. What does "context" have to do with the retrieval of information? If you are in a similar context as when you learn the information it is easier to recall

23. What do people usually do when faced with "tip of the tongue" situations? Try to generate images or sounds that will help them recall things

Remembering as Reconstructing

52. When one attempts to recall a particular event, such as the details of an automobile accident, one frequently does so by constructing a total picture out of bits and pieces of stored information. This is what is meant by remembering as

reconstructing   *reconstructing*

53. Since preconceptions, which may not be correct, help to guide the search for relevant pieces of information in the reconstructing process, the reconstructed

accurate (correct)   memory of an event is not always ___*accurate*___. Moreover, informa-

after   tion received ___*after*___ an event can also contribute to the faulty reconstruction of an event.

54. When a person who is unable to retrieve a particular event from memory instead reconstructs an appropriate recollection that is actually incorrect, the phenomenon

confabulation   is called ___*Confabulation*___. In confabulation, the individual often combines several memories of other events in reconstructing the original event.

high   55. Confabulation is more likely to occur under (low/high) motivational states. For example, it is possible to induce a high state of motivation in most people

hypnosis   through the use of ___*hypnosis*___. While under hypnotic induction, most people provide the hypnotist with the information requested, but they often

confabulation   resort to ___*confabulation*___ in order to do so.

Learning Objectives

24. What is meant by "remembering as reconstructing"? What factors may contribute to faulty reconstructed memories?
we reconstruct things from similar situations to remember things

25. What is confabulation? How is it related to motivational states?
incorrect recollection of events   Occurs under high motivational states - to make   hypnosis

Aiding Retrieval

56. Systems for organizing material into some scheme for aiding later recall are

mnemonic   called ___*mnemonic*___ systems. Mnemonics (the first "m" is silent) can
do not   prove very effective for later retrieval of information. They (also/do not) result in a photographic memory.

57. A small percentage of the population has the ability to recall a visual scene with

eidetic   photographic clarity. This ability is called ___*eidetic*___ imagery. Re-
does not   search with children who have this ability has shown that it (does/does not) aid in storing verbal information, nor does it seem to aid long-term memory processes.

58. *Method of Loci.* One of the most common mnemonic schemes has one visualize placing items to be remembered along a familiar route. This scheme is called the

loci

    method of ___loci___ (locations).

59. A similar scheme also based on loci requires one to first memorize twenty simple words that can later be used as pegs upon which to hang items one desires to

peg-word

    remember. This is called the ___peg___-___word___ system.

60. *Imagery.* Research has shown that people can aid their memory of verbal mate-

image
concrete

    rial when they can picture an ___image___ of some kind. Images are most helpful when the materials to be learned are ((concrete)/abstract).

61. Memory for visual images improves further if the images are entwined into some

emotional

    sort of *scene,* especially if the scene has a strong ___emotional___ impact. Thus if you wanted to remember to pick up sugar and oranges later in the day you would imagine something like walking through a large pile of sugar while

oranges

    someone was throwing ___oranges___ at you.

62. It has been suggested that the reason imagery can greatly facilitate memory is

two

    that the words and images used are stored in ___two___ different locations. This is analogous to having two reminders instead of one.

63. Research with people totally blind from birth shows that their memories can also be aided by imagery, thus indicating that imagery effects do not rely on

vision

    ___vision___.

64. *The Key-Word System.* A mnemonic scheme that has been found useful for learning foreign languages requires linking key English words with foreign words

key-

    that have similar sounds. This is known as the ___key___-

word

    ___word___ system.

65. *Rhymes and Acronyms.* The saying "*i* before *e* except after *c*" is a mnemonic that

rhyme

    makes use of the ___rhyme___ system. A somewhat similar mnemonic scheme constructs a word from the first letter (or letters) of the several items to be remembered together. This kind of mnemonic word is called an

acronym

    ___acronym___.

66. Unlike the previous mnemonic schemes, rhymes and acronyms are specific and

once

    can be used only ___once___.

Learning Objectives

26. What is eidetic imagery? Does it benefit other memory processes? *NO*
Like a photographic memory   You remember practically everything

27. List four different mnemonic schemes, and illustrate how each is used.
peg word, image, key-word system & method of loci

28. Describe how images can prove useful as a mnemonic device. What is one suggested reason for this facilitative effect? *They can cause emotional things to happen*

29. What evidence demonstrates that the use of images for improving memory does not depend on vision?
Blind people can do it

FORGETTING

Retrieval Failure

67. Some forgetting may simply be an instance of the inability to remember information that is quite definitely in the memory store. This would be an example of

retrieval   _____*retrieval*_____ failure.

68. Sometimes traumatic injury to the brain causes persons to forget information ac-

retrograde   quired prior to the injury, a condition known as ___*retrograde*___ amnesia. Since these people often begin to regain their memories of past events, this would indicate that the information was there all the time. Their problem was

retrieval   due to ___*retrieval*___ *failure*.

Decay

69. According to the decay theory of forgetting, all learning experiences result in

trace   some form of *memory* ___*trace*___ in the brain. The more frequently
stronger   a given experience is repeated, the (weaker/(stronger)) will become the memory trace.

70. This theory further assumes that forgetting occurs because the memory trace

decays   ___*decays*___. While this idea appears to account for the fragility of sensory and short-term memory, it encounters much more difficulty in explaining

long-term   ___*long*___-___*term*___ *memory*.

71. For example, decay theory has difficulty explaining the fact that (pick the correct answer):
    a. motor skills, like riding a bicycle, seem not to be forgotten even after many years of not riding.
    b. senile persons who cannot remember what they had for breakfast can still remember childhood experiences.
    c. people forget substantially less if they sleep for several hours after learning something than if they stay awake.
    d. all of the above.

d

Learning Objectives

30. How do cases of retrograde amnesia demonstrate that some forgetting may be the result of retrieval failure?

31. How does the decay theory explain forgetting? To what two kinds of memory does this theory seem most applicable? *sensory – short term*

32. What evidence argues against the decay theory with respect to long-term memory? *It doesn't explain a lot of things*

Interference

less

72. There is substantial evidence that forgetting is (less/more) rapid if one goes to sleep immediately after a learning experience than if one remains awake per-

interference

forming other activities. This evidence supports the _interference_ theory of forgetting.

73. According to the interference theory, the ongoing activities during waking

interfere

interfere with the storage or retrieval of new information. This is prevented during sleep because no interfering activities take place.

74. There are two general kinds of interference. One kind of interference occurs when material previously learned interferes with the retrieval of information

proactive

learned more recently. This is called _proactive_ interference. The

before

source of interference occurs _before_ the material to be retrieved is learned.

75. The other kind of interference occurs when material more recently learned interferes with the retrieval of information previously learned. This is called

retroactive

retroactive interference. The source of interference occurs

after

after the material to be retrieved is learned.

76. It has also been found that both kinds of interference are more likely to occur

similar

when the materials to be learned are (similar/dissimilar). The practical implications of this finding for study behavior are obvious.

Motivated Forgetting

is

motivated

77. In many cases the failure to retrieve information may occur because of conscious (suppression) or unconscious (repression) desires to forget unpleasant memories. In this case the material (is/is not) still in storage. The person is simply

    motivated not to retrieve it.

anxiety (stress)

78. Some evidence of this motivated blocking is found when persons exhibit fumbling and physiological signs of _anxiety_ when attempting to retrieve the material.

more

over

79. Motivation may also be responsible for the finding that people tend to remember themselves in a (more/less) favorable manner than deserved. A study of men in Iowa, for example, found that they tended to (over/under)-estimate the incomes they had received ten years ago.

reconstructed

80. It is probable that these self-serving recollections are not attempts to deceive others, but rather are _reconstructed_ memories that have been colored to bolster self-esteem.

reconstruction

81. It is important to realize that any memory of an original event is a _reconstruction_ built out of bits and pieces of the original event and combined with many other preconceptions and related experiences that followed.

Learning Objectives

33. Differentiate between proactive and retroactive interference. What condition increases both of these kinds of interference? _proactive comes before learning material : similar condition / interference retroactive comes after learning material_

34. What is the point of the experiment that had some subjects go to sleep right after learning and others remain awake? _To see if other information interfered after learning something_

35. What is meant by "motivated forgetting"? What physical signs can suggest this kind of forgetting is taking place? _Trying to forget something bad that happened to you — anxiety and fumbling_

36. In what way do people's memories of their past experiences change? What accounts for this change? _People reconstruct their memories   Helps bolster self-esteem / From this that happend in the past_

Chapter Ten
Cognition

General Objectives

1. Provide a brief history of the fall and subsequent rise of cognitive psychology.

2. Distinguish between reductive and creative thinking.

3. Describe some of the more important problem-solving strategies.

4. Explain what is meant by categorization and why it is important in problem solving.

5. Describe some of the important impediments to problem solving.

6. Describe how employing various kinds of heuristics can lead to biases in judgment.

7. Define framing and anchoring, and describe how they interact.

8. List the key elements in the creative process, and name the stages that lead to the creative solutions of problems.

9. List some of the important characteristics of creative persons.

Cognition

Learning Objectives appear at
the end of each major section.

1. The process of knowing, which encompasses all of the higher processes (think-ing, decision making, judging, etc.), is what psychologists call

cognition

____cognition____. All of these various cognitive processes have two com-mon underlying elements: they depend upon *memory* and

learning

____learning____.

2. The earliest attempts at studying cognitive processes used trained observers to report their own mental activities under controlled conditions, an approach

introspection
subjective

known as ___introspection___. Unfortunately, introspection was found to be a very (subjective/objective) technique—one laboratory could not duplicate an-other laboratory's results.

135

3. Psychologists abandoned the study of cognitive processes, and the dominant

behaviorism   force that arose to replace cognitive psychology was _behaviorism_.
While behaviorists were willing to admit that cognitive processes did exist, they

objective   resisted studying these processes because there were no _objective_
methods for doing so.

4. The study of cognitive processes, using more objective techniques, returned fol-

II   lowing World War _II_ . The major influence in this return

processing   was the *information-* _processing_ approach to handling information,
an outgrowth of communications and computer technology.

5. While cognitive psychologists and behaviorists both employ objective techniques
in their research, a major difference between them is that behaviorists are interested in thought processes to the extent that they help to explain

behavior   _behavior_ ; cognitive psychologists are interested in behavior to the

thought processes   extent that it helps to explain _thought_ _processes_ .

Learning Objectives

1. What are the two common elements that can be found in all of the higher mental (cognitive) processes?
   memory a learning
2. What is introspection? Why was it abandoned as a research technique? _Because it was subjective_
   subjective approach to learning about the mind
3. What was the dominant force that arose to replace cognitive psychology? How did this new force view cognitive
   processes? _Behaviorism_
4. What was the major influence that sparked the return of cognitive psychology? _information processing_

5. What distinguishes the behavioral and cognitive approaches to psychology?
   study behavior   _study thought processes_

PROBLEM SOLVING

6. Although there is an almost unlimited number of problems that require different
kinds of solutions, all problems have two common elements. The first element is

barrier   that a _barrier_ prevents reaching a goal. The second element is

path (way)   that a _path_ around the barrier must be found.

Importance of Past Experience

past

experience

7. Solving a problem requires the use of knowledge specific to the problem as well as general knowledge. This illustrates the importance of _past_ _experiences_ in problem solving.

cued (retrieved)

reductive

8. When a problem that has been previously experienced and solved arises, the previous experience is _cued_, and the problem is solved. When a similar past experience is lacking, the problem frequently cannot be solved. The direct application of previous knowledge to solving problems in this manner is called _reductive_ thinking.

creative

9. When a problem cannot be solved because an identical past experience is lacking, new rules must be generated from other stores of information, and _creative_ thinking is required.

Learning Objectives

6. What are the two elements common to all problems? barrier, path or way to get around barrier

7. Why is past experience important with respect to problem-solving ability? What does this have to do with reductive thinking? Helps you solve problems easier It helps you deal with same problem that has arisen in the past

8. What is creative thinking? New ways to deal with New problems

Problem-Solving Strategies

hypothesis

testing

10. *Hypothesis Testing.* Retrieving past information and using it to imagine possible solutions to a problem is the basis of _hypothesis_ _testing_.

hypothesis/test

results

1

11. Hypothesis testing involves four steps. The first step is to generate a _hypothesis_. The second step is to devise a _test_ of the hypothesis. The third step is to evaluate the _results_ of the test. If step 3 fails to generate a correct answer, then step 4 is to return to step _1_ and generate a new hypothesis.

12. *Algorithms.* An orderly set of rules that specifies the sequence of all possible

algorithm
operations that might solve a problem is called an _algorith_. Although the application of an algorithm will eventually solve a problem, the major inadequacy of this method is that with some problems—chess, for example—an algorithm may specify more solutions than can be practically

tested
tested.

13. *Heuristics.* An alternative method for problem solving calls for the use of a few of the most probable solutions so as to allow for a quick, if not altogether per-

heuristic
fect, solution to a problem. This is called the _heuristic_ method.

14. A very common heuristic used by many chess players calls for dividing into several smaller goals the major goal of making an appropriate move. This particular

subgoal
heuristic is called _subgoal_ *analysis.*

15. Frequently, the solution to a problem, such as why a car will not start, can best

algorithms
most
be found by employing a combination of heuristics and _algorithms_. In this case the (most/least) probable solution would be tried first.

Learning Objectives

9. What are the four steps involved in hypothesis testing?

10. What is an algorithm? What is the major deficiency of the algorithmic approach to problem solving?

11. What is the heuristic method of problem solving? What is "subgoal analysis"?

Categorizing the World

16. One of the important aids in problem solving is the ability of human beings to

categories
learn to place things in _categories_. This means that they can group things together on the basis of one or more common characteristics. For example, a cat, a rat, and a dog all share common characteristics that place them in

category
the _category_ of mammals.

17. There are two general explanations as to how human beings learn to categorize. One explanation assumes that they form a hypothetical ideal model, or

prototype
prototype, by averaging all the specific members of a category. The prototype is then used as a basis for deciding whether or not objects

belong (fit)
belong within a particular category.

18. The other general explanation as to how people learn to categorize assumes that instead of forming a prototype, they tend to notice what particular sets of

features   _features_ accompany category membership and then develop the categories around these *features*. Thus a creature that has two wings, two legs, a beak, and is covered with feathers would have the particular

features   _features_ that categorize it as a bird.

19. The importance of categorizing for problem solving is that it allows for using

the same   (the same/a different) solution to many problems that at first glance may appear to be dissimilar. For example, if a winter vacation on a Florida beach results in a painful sunburn, one is likely to take precautions against sunburn the following winter while skiing in Colorado.

Computer Simulation

20. The General Problem Solver (GPS) is a computer program that approaches problems in a manner similar to that used by human beings—that is, by

heuristics   the use of _heuristics_. Computers using this heuristic approach
do not   (do/do not) exactly duplicate human memory and thinking. Moreover, at the
fall below   present time they (exceed/fall below) the ability of human beings at solving similar problems.

Learning Objectives

12. What is meant by categorization? How does the ability to categorize aid in solving problems?

13. What are the two general explanations as to how human beings learn to categorize?

14. What is the General Problem Solver? In what two ways does the GPS differ from human beings with respect to the ability to solve problems?   Computer

Impediments to Problem Solving

21. *Fixation.* When we continue to apply an ineffective strategy to a particular problem simply because the strategy has worked with similar problems in the past,

fixation   we are engaging in _fixation_.

hindered

22. The "water jar" problem used by Luchins provides an example in which adopting a particular strategy or set eventually (aided/hindered) the solution of a problem. In Luchins's study (Figure 10.5 in the text), the first five problems can be solved by employing the same formula. The sixth problem, however, requires a

different (new)

different formula. Solving the first five problems thus produces a

fixation

rigidity, referred to as _fixation_, which interferes with solving the sixth problem. When people are given the sixth problem *before* the other five,

usually

they (infrequently/usually) solve it.

23. Another kind of fixation frequently occurs when a person is asked to solve a problem that requires the use of familiar objects in unfamiliar ways—a matchbox as a candle holder, for example. This kind of fixation is called

functional fixedness
away from

functional Fixedness. In this case people are unable to change their mental sets (away from/toward) the common *function* of an object.

inhibits

24. Regardless of the form in which it occurs, fixation always (inhibits/facilitates) the solving of a problem because of the inappropriate transfer of a *mental*

set

set from one task to another.

25. *Motivational Level.* While the effects of past experience on problem solving may become stable characteristics of the problem solver, motivational level is only a

temporary (short-term)

temporary characteristic.

26. When performance is plotted as a function of motivational level (arousal), an inverted-U relationship has been found to exist. This relationship is known as the

Law

Yerkes-Dodson _Law_.

Yerkes-Dodson
poor

27. The _Yerkes_-_Dodson_ *Law* states that performance in a variety of tasks is (poor/good) at low levels of arousal. However, as arousal

increase (improve)

increases, performance begins to _increase_, but only up to a point

optimal

called the _optimal_ arousal level. Beyond this point performance

decrease (decline)

once again begins to _decrease_ as arousal continues to rise.

28. Thus, under conditions of high arousal, such as in either simulated or real battle

deteriorate (decline)

conditions, it can be expected that performance will _deteriorate_. However, continued exposure to dangerous conditions and the subsequent development of expertise may slow this deterioration.

Learning Objectives

15. Describe what is meant by fixation. How did Luchins demonstrate fixation?
    Applying same technique to solving a problem because it worked before, even
16. What is functional fixedness? *when it doesn't work on new problem filling jars*
    When you see an object functioning in one way it becomes hard to use it in a different situation
17. In what way do all forms of fixation impede problem solving?
    It inhibits problem solving
18. Describe how motivational level affects problem-solving ability, using the Yerkes-Dodson Law to explain your answer. *low motivational level - low solving ability*

19. In what way does motivational level differ as an impediment to problem solving compared to other effects of past experience, such as fixation?

DECISION MAKING

Heuristics in Judgment

past experience

29. When making important decisions, human beings are most likely to turn to heuristics and place the greater emphasis on (past experience/pertinent information) when making a choice.

30. *Representativeness.* One of the two major heuristics employed in decision making is to base the prediction of an event on how closely it *represents* a typical

representativeness

event. This heuristic is called ___representativeness___ Using the heuristic of representativeness and assuming this book is typical of books in general, one

200

would predict that page 199 is followed by page ___200___ .

31. In addition, the representativeness heuristic can also base a prediction on the degree to which a predicted outcome is a typical result of the process that

generated (produced)
duck

___generated___ it. For example, one would predict that a fertile egg layed by a female duck would produce a (duck/turtle).

32. The other major heuristic employed in decision making is to make decisions by comparing the current situation with similar past situations. Since this heuristic requires that similar past situations be *available* in the memory store, it is aptly

availability

named the ___availability___ heuristic.

33. If one predicts that he or she will catch a cold sometime during the current year because this has happened during the previous six years, he or she is using the

availability

heuristic of ___availability___ .

Learning Objectives

20. What are the two assumptions on which the representativeness heuristic bases predictions?

21. What is the assumption made by the availability heuristic? What must an individual have before he or she can apply this heuristic?

22. Below are three statements employing either the representativeness or availability heuristic. Name the heuristic being employed.
    a. I'm always chasing rainbows and probably will continue to do so. *avail*
    b. Like father, like son. *represent*
    c. Isn't that just like a man? *represent*

Biases in Judgment

less

34. Employing a heuristic can produce erroneous results when the information it calls for is ((less)/more) relevant than other information available at the time.

35. *Biases in Representativeness and Biases in Availability.* Below are four examples of biases that can occur because of the inappropriate application of either the representativeness or availability heuristic. Identify which misapplication is at fault.
    a. While at a visiting carnival, you lose ten dollars in a shell game because you felt that the dealer looked like an honest man. He reminded you of a minis-

representativeness

   ter. This illustrates the misapplication of the ___representativeness___ *heuristic*.
    b. You board an airplane headed for Shangri-la even though you notice one of the wings appears to be badly damaged. You assume that airplane crashes are very infrequent. The airplane crashes on takeoff. This illustrates the mis-

representativeness

   application of the ___representativeness___ *heuristic*.
    c. You buy a used Invincible automobile from a sleazy-looking used-car lot because you feel that this particular make of car represents the pinnacle in automotive engineering. The engine explodes fifteen minutes after you have closed the deal. This illustrates the misapplication of the

representativeness

   ___representativeness___ *heuristic*.
    d. After living in the Midwest for twenty years you have experienced many tornado warnings but never a tornado. You decide to ignore the latest warning even though conditions seem unusually threatening and the radio announcements are adamant about the potential danger. You barely escape with your life when the tornado hits. This illustrates the misapplication of

availability

   the ___availability___ *heuristic*.

36. A particularly important influence on the availability heuristic is the fact that

vivid

very _____vivid_____ information has a much stronger impact than *less vivid* information. Thus, the decision by women to begin periodic examinations for possible breast cancer is more likely to be triggered by reports of the

prominence

(number/prominence) of women getting breast cancer.

37. Several reasons have been suggested to account for the effect of vividness, but the important point is that vivid information, as compared to equally relevant but less vivid information, is more likely to be stored in memory and more likely to be retrieved at a later time. It is for this reason that vividness can lead to a

bias

_____bias_____ when employing the availability heuristic.

38. *Biases in Anchoring.* Biases in decisions can also result because of the starting point from which one bases a judgment. In this case the starting point acts as an

anchor

_____anchor_____, which may slow the observation of other relevant information. This tendency of a starting point to gain an undue amount of attention is

anchoring

called _____anchoring_____.

39. *Biases in Hindsight.* When a person informs a friend that her grandparents were stupid for buying tickets on the maiden voyage of the *Titanic*, that person is en-

hindsight

gaging in the bias of _____hindsight_____.

40. Bias in hindsight refers to the fact that people often make judgments after an event that they (would/would not) have made before the event. Their failure to

would not

realize this is the actual bias.

Learning Objectives

23. Under what conditions should the heuristics of representativeness and availability not be employed?
When information is less relevent than other information available

24. In what way does vividness influence the availability heuristic?

25. What is anchoring?

26. What is meant by "biases in hindsight"?

Framing Decisions

41. Most people prefer a glass that is half full to one that is half empty. This illus-

framing

trates the point that the phrasing, or _____framing_____, of a problem can influence the decision that is made.

losses

42. Research shows that people are more willing to take a risk when a problem is framed in such a manner as to involve possible (losses/gains). This is true even though the actual outcome is not changed by how the problem is framed.

43. Thus, when people are given the following two messages by an advertiser—
    a. "Your chance of not catching a cold is 50 percent if you take Zapo"
    b. "Your chance of catching a cold is 50 percent if you do not take Zapo"

b

—message _____b_____ is most likely to result in greater sales of Zapo. This reflects the fact that emphasizing the possible displeasure of loss has

greater

a (greater/lesser) effect on decisions than emphasizing the possible pleasure from gain.

44. An announcement on the evening news that 10 percent of the population is now unemployed may strike terror in much of the population. However, framing this same statistic in a different way by saying that 90 percent of the population is

a very different

now employed has (the same/a very different) effect on the reaction of the population and their subsequent decisions. This illustrates that the starting point, or

anchor

_____anchor_____, plays an important role in the framing bias.

45. Another way of saying the same thing is that one can manipulate the anchor

framed

point by the manner in which a question is ___pFramed___. Thus the

anchoring

bias in framing often occurs because of ___anchoring___.

Learning Objectives

27. How should a problem be framed so as to most influence decision making? If it involves losses people will take a risk

28. In what way do framing and anchoring interact? by the emphasis it puts on a statement

CREATIVITY

46. Combining two previously unconnected events or elements in a new and useful

creative

way requires ___creative___ thought; and the greater the distance be-

creativity

tween the newly combined elements, the greater the ___creativity___ involved.

47. The two key elements in the creative process are that the combination of ele-

new (novel)

ments is ___new___ and the resulting idea is *useful*. For example, while the idea of combining a bug repellent with vinegar and oil to make a new bug-repelling salad dressing for picnics is probably new, it would not be consid-

useful

ered as an instance of creativity because it is not ___useful___.

The Creative Process

48. Wolfgang Kohler's chimpanzees demonstrated an ability to place hollowed-out sticks together to make a long rakelike tool with which they could then secure food located some distance from their cages. The sudden onset of this creative

insight   thought is an example of ___Insight___ (the sudden birth of a creative idea).

49. Birch later tried to replicate Kohler's original study, using chimpanzees who did not have the previous experience of playing with the hollow sticks (as did the

not   Kohler chimps). Birch found that his chimps could (also/not) solve the problem. The missing element here was the previous experience of playing with the

sticks   ___sticks___. Thus, while insight may appear suddenly, it does not

experience   occur without the relevant past ___experience___.

50. Actually, the insightful solution to a problem occurs near the end of the creative process, which can be divided into four successive stages. The first stage in

preparation   which a solution is sought without success is called the ___preparation___ stage. The second stage in which the problem is set aside and not given con-

incubation   scious attention is called the ___incubation___ stage. The third stage in

illumination   which the sudden insightful solution arrives is called the ___illumination___ stage. The final stage occurs with the testing and *verification* of the solution and

verification   is called the ___verification___ stage.

Learning Objectives

29. What are the two key elements that make up the creative process? ___Novel and useful things___

30. Use the example of Kohler's chimps to illustrate the phenomenon of insight. What new light did Birch's later replication of this experiment cast on the nature of insight?

31. List the four stages in the creative process. ___preparation, incubation illumination and verification___

The Creative Person

51. Daydreaming, remembering night dreams, risk taking, and self fault finding are

creative   all characteristics commonly found among ___creative___ persons. It has also been found that in comparison to uncreative persons, the attention of

less   creative people is (more/less) focused. They are more likely to pay attention to a broad variety of details that might escape the average person's attention.

arousal

52. Martindale has proposed that the major difference between creative and uncreative people can be traced to differences in their _____arousal_____ systems. Arousal level increases with an increase in stimulus intensity among all persons. However, when the stimulus intensities become strong, creative people show a

dip

_____dip_____ in their arousal level not found with uncreative people. It is this dip in arousal and lack of focused attention that coincide with the illumination phase of the creative process.

more

53. In any case, in comparison to uncreative people, creative individuals appear to be (less/more) enthusiastic about unconventional ideas and moderately intense stimuli that uncreative people find uncomfortable.

Learning Objectives

32. List five characteristics that appear to be found among creative persons.   Dreaming,

33. What did Martindale propose as the major difference between creative and uncreative persons?   arousal level,

PRACTICAL APPROACHES TO PROBLEM SOLVING

more

54. Creative thinking is (less/more) difficult than reductive thinking because the latter only requires the retrieval of stored solutions from among the mass of information stored in the memory.

55. Thus, when faced with the need to solve many problems in a particular area, the

expertise (experience)
reductive

best problem-solving technique is to gain a good deal of _____expertise_____ in that area. For example, chess masters depend on (reductive/creative) thinking. Because of their many years of experience they need only select the proper move from among the many thousands stored.

56. Since one cannot possibly gain expertise in the numerous areas that might require

creative

problem-solving abilities, _____creative_____ thinking will be required from time to time. Applying the information gained from this chapter may prove useful here.

Learning Objectives

34. What is the best approach to use when faced with the need to solve many problems in a particular area? Explain the reason for your answer.   heuristics, become an expert in that area

Chapter Eleven
Early Development

General Objectives

1. Describe the relationship between DNA, chromosomes, and genetic inheritance.

2. Explain how twin studies reflect on the heredity-versus-environment issue in human development.

3. Describe the phases of prenatal development, and discuss the impact of various environmental stresses on the course of prenatal development.

4. Describe the early reflexes (stepping, swimming, and so on), and suggest an explanation for their pattern of appearance, loss, and reappearance.

5. Describe the sensory and perceptual capacities of the young infant.

6. Describe the imitative behavior of the infant.

7. Explain how the early capacity to perceive depth, locate sounds, and imitate resembles the early reflexes in the pattern of appearance, loss, and reappearance.

8. Discuss the evidence relating self-awareness to early social interaction.

Early Development

Learning Objectives appear at
the end of each major section.

THE PROCESS OF DEVELOPMENT

Developmental Sequences: The Question of How

sequential (orderly, predictable)

1. One of the main points the text makes concerning development is that developmental changes occur in a(n) ___sequential___ pattern; that is, one stage follows another in a particular sequence. For example, most babies crawl before they walk.

averages (norms)

2. A second point is that the sequences do not represent "normal" or ideal develop-
ment but are simply mathematically calculated _averages_ of what babies do at a particular age. Thus, while the "average" baby may walk at fifteen months, some perfectly normal children may walk as early as eight months or as late as twenty months.

is not

3. While the stages occur in sequence, some stages may be skipped entirely. Thus, the notion that we must crawl before we walk (is/is not) necessarily true. Some infants pass directly from sitting and standing to walking.

Learning Objectives

1. What is meant by *sequential development?* We learn new things in a certain way/pattern

2. Child *A* skips a developmental sequence (e.g., crawling). Child *B* first walks when she is twenty months old, much later than average. Are these children abnormal? Explain. No they just developed differently

Developmental Sequences: The Question of Why

germen

4. *Hereditary Factors.* Life begins as a single cell formed by the union of a sperm and an egg, the male and female _germ_ cells.

twenty-three

5. With the exception of germ cells, all cells in the human body contain _twenty-three_ *pairs* of chromosomes. The germ cells contain twenty-three *single* chromosomes.

two
single

6. Germ cells are formed through a process called *meiosis,* in which one cell with twenty-three pairs of chromosomes splits apart to form _two_ germ cells with twenty-three (pairs of/single) chromosomes.

pairs of

7. When the egg and sperm are joined, the resulting cell has twenty-three (pairs of/single) chromosomes. These chromosomes determine the genetic structure of the new human being.

DNA

8. Chromosomes are coiled structures composed of long strands of a complex substance called _DNA_ (deoxyribonucleic acid). Certain small por-

genes

tions of the DNA molecule called _genes_ contain codes for producing or combining the various body proteins.

maturation
(development, aging)

9. The genes are the chemical "instructions" for building and maintaining the body. Genes influence not only the structure and behavioral capacities of the organism but also the rate of physical _maturation_

identical

10. While genes influence development, it is clear that environmental factors also play an important role. For example, although identical twins have *genetic* make-ups that are (identical/similar), they do not, of course, develop in exactly the same way or at exactly the same rate.

environmental

11. Since identical twins are genetically identical, any *differences* between them that emerge during development are evidence for the influence of (genetic/environmental) factors. On the other hand, if identical twins are exposed to very different environments but develop at the same rate, this would be evidence for the importance

genetic (hereditary)

of ___genetic___ factors.

the same age as

12. Early research with twins and studies of children in different cultures supported the view that the age at which basic motor skills emerge is determined almost entirely by genetic factors. For example, an early (1940) study of Hopi Indian children, who spent their first year of life restricted in cradleboards, found that these children walked at (the same age as/a later age than) infants in other cultures.

Learning Objectives

3. How many chromosomes are contained in the germ cells of human beings? How many are in all other normal cells?   *23 single chr*   *23 pairs of chr*

4. What is the name of the substance of which chromosomes are composed? What are genes in relation to this substance? What are the functions of genes?   *DNA*   *control development*
   little parts that make up the DNA

5. If *identical twins* differ in development, these differences are attributed to environmental factors. Why is such a conclusion justified? Suppose identical twins separated at birth and brought up in different environments turn out to be remarkably similar in a particular trait. What would this suggest about the relative importance of environment versus heredity for this trait?   *heredity is an important factor in development*

6. One early study with Hopi children found that children restricted in cradleboards walked at the same age as infants who were not so restricted. What did the researchers conclude on the basis of this finding?   *hereditary factors*

is not

13. *Environmental Factors.* While more recent twin studies have found that genes clearly influence development, scientists now know that heredity (is/is not) the sole influence. Evidently the range of environmental differences in the early studies of motor development had been too limited to reveal this fact.

strongly retarded

14. A study of a foundling home in Lebanon demonstrated that a severely impoverished environment (strongly retarded/had no effect on) the motor development of infants. Infants in the foundling home had spent the first year on their backs, ignored by adults.

improved enormously

15. When the environment of the foundling-home infants was changed by propping them up in a sitting position and allowing them to play with simple objects, their motor development (was unaffected/improved enormously).

environmental

16. Thus, ~~Environmental~~ factors had strongly contributed to the infants' def-

environment

icit in motor development, and a change in the ___environment___ helped to remedy the deficit.

17. Furthermore, a recent study has found that foundlings who receive sight and sound enrichment, along with human attention, develop

as rapidly as

(less rapidly than/as rapidly as) infants from middle-class homes.

18. The walking reflex refers to the tendency of newborn infants to place their feet as if walking when they are held upright. One study has found that if practiced,

will

the reflex will persist and (will/will not) result in earlier walking. The difference in age of walking was slight, but the main point is that developmental sequences,

environment

within limits, respond to changes in the ___environment___.

19. It may well be that environmental enrichment enhances mental functioning as well as motor skills. For example, premature infants who were massaged,

memory

rocked, and talked to showed better recognition ___memory___ at six months than did a group not given the extra stimulation.

20. More convincing of the potential importance of environment for mental function-ing is the finding that, relative to rats raised in an enriched environment (with many objects to explore), rats raised in an impoverished environment had smaller

cortexes

cerebral ___cortexes___ and other marked changes in brain structure.

21. Your text concludes the section on environmental factors by suggesting that, for most infants, extra enrichment beyond the environments found in most homes

only slight

would produce (only slight/powerful) gains in development.

22. *Sensitive Periods of Development*. A sensitive period is a time during develop-ment when an organism is particularly susceptible to certain kinds of environ-mental influences. For example, dogs are likely to become attached to a human

sensitive

master only if exposed to people during a ___sensitive___ period from three to twelve weeks after birth.

23. While the optimal period for language acquisition seems to be between two and thirteen years, psychologists disagree concerning whether or not there are true

sensitive periods

___sensitive   periods___ in human development. Psychol-ogists point out, for example, that human beings are extremely resilient and can generally overcome harmful early experiences.

24. Given the ethical constraints on research with human beings, it will probably be impossible to establish the relative contribution of environment and heredity to human development. One thing which is clear, however, is that the typical course of human development involves (heredity/environment/

a combination of both

a combination of both).

Learning Objectives

7. Describe how each of the following studies demonstrates the importance of *environmental* factors in human development:
   a. The "foundling home" study.
   b. Practice of the walking or stepping reflex.
   c. Study of enriched versus impoverished environments of rats.
   d. Environmental enrichment for premature infants.

8. What conclusion was reached regarding the importance of "extra enrichment" for infants in most home environments? It helps put them ahead

9. What is a sensitive period of development? What conclusion was reached concerning whether or not there are sensitive periods in human development? Period when animals are greatly influenced by surroundings
   No.

PRENATAL DEVELOPMENT

Prenatal Growth and Behavior

25. Development in the womb, from a single fertilized egg to a mature fetus, may be divided into three basic periods. During the first period, the

germinal
identical

_____germinal_____ period, the egg initially divides into cells that are (identical/highly differentiated) in nature.

26. After about the first two weeks, the cells differentiate into

three

_____3 Three_____ primary layers from which the various tissues and organs are produced.

embryonic

27. The second prenatal period, the __Embryonic__ period, begins within

four

_____four_____ weeks after conception. During this phase, the develop-

embryo

ing organism, now referred to as an __embryo__, is nearly all head but has the beginnings of several internal organ systems.

eighth

28. The embryonic period ends at about the __eighth__ week, at which

one inch

time the embryo is almost __one____inch__ in length.

fetal

29. The third period, the __fetal__ period, begins at about the

eighth

_____eighth_____ week and ends at about the thirty-eighth week, when the child is born. During this period, the developing organism is known as a

fetus

_____fetus_____.

30. By eight weeks after the beginning of the fetal period, which is the

sixteenth   _sixteenth_ week of development, the fetus has taken on a distinctly human appearance. The internal organs also have the general shape they will

do not   eventually attain, but they (do/do not) have the capacity to maintain the fetus outside the uterus.

31. During the fetal period the fetus grows from one inch to the average birth length

thirty   of about twenty inches. The fetal period lasts about _thirty_ weeks and ends with the birth of the baby, about thirty-eight weeks after conception.

Learning Objectives

10. List the names of the three periods of prenatal development. Next to these names, list the approximate time span these periods cover. _Germinal conception to 4weeks._ _Fetal 8to38weeks_ _Embryonic 4to8weeks_

11. What occurs during approximately the first two weeks of the germinal period? What occurs during the remaining two weeks of the germinal period? _cell division_ _three tissue layers form_

12. What is the developing organism called during the second period of prenatal development? What is it called during the third period? _Embryo, Fetus_

13. What portion of the embryo is largest? Approximately how long is the embryo at the end of the embryonic period? Approximately how long is the average baby at birth? _1head_ _1inch_ _.28inches_

14. By approximately what age, and during what period, does the developing organism take on a distinctly human appearance? _Sixteenth week Fetal period_

Environmental Influences

32. Development of the embryo and fetus involves not only genetic but environmental factors, especially the environment inside the womb. If the environment is deficient, prenatal growth will be affected. For example, studies with lower ani-

protein   mals have established that a deficiency of _protein_ in the diet of

brain   the mother causes an irreversible reduction in _brain_ weight and later learning capacity in the offspring.

33. Furthermore, the learning-disabled offspring of protein-deprived female rats

are also   themselves produce offspring that (are also/are not) learning-disabled. This oc-

adequate   curs even though the diet of these mothers is (adequate/inadequate), probably be-

placenta   cause they are unable to form a normal _placenta_.

34. Thus, learning disabilities caused by protein deficiency may be transmitted to a

grandmother   second generation, an effect referred to as "the _grandmother_ effect."

35. Drug consumption by mothers may also affect fetal development. For example, alcoholic mothers may produce babies with a variety of disorders including men-

retardation   tal _retardation_ ; and during the early 1960s, mothers who took the

thalidomide   sedative _thalidomide_ during the early weeks of pregnancy produced babies with severely deformed arms and legs.

36. In addition, mothers who smoke during pregnancy produce infants that are, on

smaller (lighter)   the average, _smaller_ than normal.

37. The most damaging effects of disease, drugs, or malnutrition occur during the

trimester   first _Trimester_ , the first third of pregnancy, especially during the second and third months.

Learning Objectives

15. What are the probable effects of maternal protein deficiency on the newborn child? _small brain_ If the female offspring of a _Yes_ protein-deprived mother is not protein-deprived, is it likely that her offspring will be learning-disabled? In this case, how is the disability transmitted to the grandchildren? _genes_ Were the studies of these problems done with rats or human beings? _rats_

16. What are the effects on the newborn child of a mother who smokes cigarettes or is an alcoholic? _small infant_ _– retardation_

17. During which phase of pregnancy are disease, malnutrition, or consumption of drugs by the mother likely to have the most damaging effect on the prenatal organism? _First Trimester_ Which two months of this period are most critical? _2nd & 3rd_

The Competency of the Newborn

38. Most animal species are born with either very well-developed or very poorly developed sets of sensory and motor capacities. The former species are classified as

precocial   _precocial_ and the latter as _altricial_.

both   39. Like other primates, human babies are (precocial/altricial/both). Thus, while babies are relatively weak and dependent on their caretakers, they have remarkably mature sensory systems.

motor   40. While human babies have limited (motor/sensory) capacities, they do come equipped with some important reflexes. When a baby's cheek is touched, it usually turns its head in the direction of the object touching it. This is the

rooting   _rooting_ reflex. Babies also tend to grip firmly a finger or other

grasping   object placed in their hands. This is the _grasping_ reflex.

41. Unusual among infants' reflexes are the walking or stepping reflex, discussed

swimming

earlier, and the ___swimming___ reflex, which occurs when infants are placed face down in water. The swimming reflex appears first when the baby is

weeks

only a few ___weeks___ old and reappears, in a different form, when

one

the baby is about ___one___ year old.

42. In addition to swimming, other reflexes, such as walking and reaching, also show the pattern of appearance, loss, and reappearance. Researchers have suggested that these changes may reflect changes in the developing brain, with shifts

cortical (cortex)

in control from subcortical to ___cortical___ structures. With a shift to more "voluntary" areas, the behavior must be learned.

Learning Objectives

18. Define the following, and indicate how human and other primate babies are unique in terms of these classifications:
    precocial – *motor sense*
    altricial   *sensory sense humans have both*

19. Describe the following reflexes:
    rooting – *touch cheek baby looks where it was touched*
    grasping – *hold on tight to a finger etc*
    swimming – *two weeks old babies can swim to some degree*

20. At what age does the swimming reflex first appear? When does it reappear?
    two weeks   *1 year old*

21. What do the appearance, loss, and reappearance of swimming, stepping, and reaching suggest about cortical development?   *It switches as the baby develops*

Sensory and Perceptual Abilities

43. Do newborn infants perceive a world made up of stable objects and distinct sounds, or is the baby's world essentially disorganized and chaotic? Recent investigations have indicated that the (former/latter) view is probably more accurate.

former

44. *Vision.* The visual capacity of newborns is limited by the fact that they have poor peripheral vision and can only see objects about (nine inches/three feet) from the eyes, and those objects probably appear blurred.

nine inches

45. Such visual limitations reduce the stimulation and probably (increase/lessen) the confusion of the newborn's early weeks. Vision improves rapidly, however, and

lessen

by the age of ___six___ months babies can see as clearly as the average adult.

six

46. When an object is moved toward a newborn's face, the baby will pull his or her head back. This and other evidence has established that infants have some sense

depth

of ___depth___ perception.

47. Newborns also appear to distinguish between an approaching object that is likely to hit them and one that will sail harmlessly past. Babies who are slightly older, however, seem to (lose/improve) this depth-perception response.

lose

48. By the time babies are five months old they appear to have regained their depth-perception capacities. It may be that early depth perception is like the stepping, reaching, and swimming ___reflexes___ , which disappear and reappear

reflexes

subcortical

as behavior shifts from ___subcortical___ to cortical control.

potentials

49. Research using visually evoked ___potentials___ has found evidence of three-dimensional vision in babies older than four or five months but not among babies less than ten weeks of age. This physiological evidence reflects the behavioral shifts discussed above.

50. Development of motor and perceptual capacities are related, as is evident in the visual-cliff studies. In those studies it was found that a fear of the "deep" side of the cliff was present in babies who (could/could not) crawl. Such a fear, which occurs in a number of animals as soon as they can move about, has clear survival value.

could

51. By examining the length of time babies look at different colors presented to them it has been determined that babies can classify colors into basic categories of red, green, yellow, and blue, color categories that seem to be universal. This capacity occurs long (before/after) they acquire the language capacity to name these colors.

before

Learning Objectives

22. Describe the visual capacities of newborn infants in terms of peripheral vision and distance at which they can see objects. What function does such limited vision serve? At what age can infants see as clearly as adults? *– six month* *nine inches no peripheral vision very limited*

23. What evidence suggests that newborn infants have a type of depth perception with regard to objects moving toward them? *They put their hands up to block it*

24. The early "depth perception" response of newborns (to objects moving toward them) disappears shortly after birth. By what age does it reappear? How might the appearance, disappearance, and reappearance of depth perception be related to swimming and stepping, subcortical and cortical development, and reflexive and learned behavior? *six months it is reflexive?*

25. At about what point does fear of the visual cliff seem to develop? What is the survival value of this fear? *Protect you when babies start to crawl from falling or killing yourself*

26. What do babies learn first, the names of colors or an ability to classify colors in four basic categories? Are these color categories used only by American and European infants, or do they seem to be universal?

52. *Hearing*. Babies are able to locate sounds at a very young age. One study found

minutes
reflexive

that an infant only a few _minutes_ old turned toward the source of various sounds. This coordination is probably (reflexive/learned), since another study found that the behavior drops out and reappears around the age of three months.

53. Babies are also capable of discriminating between similar speech sounds—such as their mother's voice and that of another woman, or the sounds "pa" and "ba." Since young infants cannot talk, these studies have been done by examining the

pacifier

frequency and vigor with which babies suck on a _pacifier_ wired

month

to produce sounds. Before babies are one _month_ old they can tell a familiar from an unfamiliar voice.

54. *Taste, Smell, and Touch*. Newborns can also discriminate basic sensory information concerning taste, smell, and touch. In a recent study involving taste, for

day

example, babies less than one _day_ old differentiated between

expressions

sweet, sour, and bitter by making the same _expressions_ that adults associated with these tastes.

Learning Objectives

27. Newborn infants are able to locate sounds by turning toward them. In what way does this behavior seem related to such behaviors as early depth perception, swimming, stepping, etc.? What other sound-discrimination capacities do young infants have? _Reflexive Appears disappears and reappears_

28. What evidence is there that very young (one day old) infants can discriminate among tastes?
Make faces

The Roots of Cognitive and Social Development

55. Why do babies smile when looking at the face of a smiling adult? Do they have an innate preference for faces, or is this behavior largely acquired? Fantz demonstrated that infants will spend more time gazing at disks with faces represented on them than at disks with other patterns, and he suggested that infants have an

innate

(innate/acquired) preference for human faces.

was not

56. This conclusion (was/was not) supported by later research. Later research revealed that it wasn't simply faces that infants prefer but a variety of simple, high-contrast patterns. By the age of two months, however, infants do seem to

faces

have acquired a distinct preference for (faces/high-contrast patterns).

57. When very young infants gaze at a face, they tend to look most at high-contrast areas—the edges of the face, including the hairline. By the time they are two months old, however, they increase the amount of time they spend looking at the

eyes   ___*eyes*___ of a human face. This may occur because eye contact is

reinforced   ___*reinforced*___ by the parents.

58. *Imitation.* One recent study found that babies begin to imitate the gestures and

weeks   expressions of adults within two ___*weeks*___ after they are born. The

tongue   behaviors imitated included movements of the mouth, ___*tongue*___, and fingers.

59. The reason for this imitation, according to the researchers who conducted the study, is that imitation:
    a. is the result of an innate releasing mechanism.
    b. has been specifically reinforced.
    c. is an innate ability which involves mental representation.
    d. is reflexive.

c

60. The above interpretation has been challenged, and based on further research your text suggests that early imitation—like early reaching, swimming, and stepping—

automatic (reflexive)   is largely a(n) ___*reflexive*___ response which drops out as control passes to the cortex.

61. Your text also interprets early smiling, triggered by the sight of the human face, as:
    a. important for strengthening bonds to a caregiver.
    b. a reflexive response.
    c. an automatic response.
    d. all of the above.

d

Learning Objectives

29. Infants smile when looking at the face of a smiling adult. Is this an innate preference for *faces,* or is there something else about the pattern presented by faces that newborns seem to like? *Something else about the Pattern of faces*

30. When and why do infants change from gazing at the edges of the face to looking at the eyes? *two months old reinforced → two weeks*

31. One study found that babies imitate adults at a remarkably young age. Approximately how young? What types of gestures do they imitate? Did the researchers assume this behavior to be acquired or innate? What interpretation of these data does your text seem to favor? *Imitate movements of mouth, Tongue and fingers Innate Innate*

32. According to your text, is smiling by the very young infant in response to a human face a reflexive or acquired response? What is its function in terms of the child-parent relationship? *Reflexive strengthens bond between caregiver and baby*

62. *Self-Awareness*. One point of view assumes that self-awareness emerges only after people have had the opportunity to observe others through *social interac-*

isolation

tion. According to this view, a person raised in ___isolation___ would not develop a true sense of self.

63. Such a point of view has been supported by research with both chimpanzees and human beings. In one study, some chimps were raised in isolation, and others in the company of other chimps. When later placed in a cage with a mirror, the chimps raised with others eventually acted as if they

recognized

(recognized/did not recognize) their own reflection.

64. In contrast, the chimps raised with others continued to act as if the reflection

another animal

were (themselves/another animal).

65. Further, when red spots were painted on the chimpanzees and the chimps were

ignored
touched

returned to the mirror, those raised in isolation (touched/ignored) the spots, while those raised with others continually (touched/ignored) the spots.

66. Similar tests with human infants suggest something about the developmental aspects of self-awareness. When spots were secretly painted on children's noses (by their mothers), most children older than two years

responded

(responded/did not respond) with recognition by grabbing their noses when they

nine

looked in a mirror. Babies less than ___NINE___ months of age did not show such recognition.

67. Newborn infants seem to show a type of self-awareness in another way. In re-

cry
stop crying

sponse to crying by other infants, newborns will (cry/stop crying). In response to a recording of their own crying, newborns will (cry/stop crying).

68. Newborn infants will cry in response to:
    a.   the crying of an infant chimp.
    b.   the crying of an eleven-month-old baby.

c (Note: They *don't* respond to chimps and older babies!)

    c.   the crying of another newborn.
    d.   all of the above.

69. As further evidence of early self-recognition, studies have found that infants as young as nine months respond more to videotapes of

themselves

(themselves/other babies).

Learning Objectives

33. What evidence is there that self-awareness (or self-recognition) depends on social interaction? Explain, using the studies with chimps and human infants.

34. What is the response of a newborn to crying by other newborns? How does the newborn respond when he or she hears a recording of his or her own crying? Starts to cry — starts to cry

Chapter Twelve
Cognitive Development

General Objectives

1. Describe Piaget's concepts of scheme, assimilation, accommodation, and equilibration.

2. List the five divisions of cognitive growth used by your text and the approximate equivalents in Piaget's four stages of development.

3. Describe the major changes in cognitive capacity which occur across the phases of development, especially with regard to:

    a. the concept of object permanence.
    b. representational thought.
    c. the concept of conservation.
    d. memory strategies and metacognition.
    e. systematic experimentation and abstract thinking.

4. Discuss differences in cognitive abilities between the sexes and changes in the memory systems across age.

Cognitive Development

Learning Objectives appear at
the end of each major section.

1. Psychologists are not in agreement concerning how mental activity changes during development, and your text describes three major views. One view stresses *gradual, cumulative learning* in which changes in thinking are considered to be largely (quantitative/qualitative).

quantitative

2. A second view asserts that there are radical shifts in thinking capacities which

stages
qualitatively

may be described in terms of cognitive ___stages___ of development. Under this view, thinking at one stage is (quantitatively/qualitatively) different from that at another stage. The thinking processes of an adult, for example, would not simply be "more" of the thinking processes of a child but would be of a very different type.

3. The third view stresses the importance of learning or experience but indicates

biological
more
that what can be learned at any age is limited by _biological_ constraints. This view would see (more/fewer) commonalities in the thinking of
young and old than would the second point of view.

THE PROCESS OF COGNITIVE DEVELOPMENT: PIAGET'S FRAMEWORK

4. One of the major figures in developmental psychology is the Swiss psychologist

Piaget
qualitatively
Jean _Piaget_. Since he proposed that cognitive development
occurs in (qualitatively/quantitatively) different stages, he would fall under the
second viewpoint described above.

Some Basic Concepts

5. Piaget identified three processes as central to intellectual development: scheme,
assimilation, and accommodation. The recurrent *action patterns* which children

schemes
use to find out about their environments are termed _schemes_. For

grasping (sucking, throwing)
example, one of the schemes used by young infants is _grasping_
(name one of three mentioned).

6. While the schemes of very young infants involve overt physical

action
action patterns, the schemes of older children become

internalized
internalized. For example, while a young infant may explore gravity
by dropping marbles, an older child already knows that marbles fall without performing this action.

7. An individual's attempts to incorporate new information through the use of *exist-*

assimilation
ing schemes is referred to as _assimilation_. When the new knowledge
does not fit the existing schemes, the individual must change the schemes

accommodation
through the process of _accomodation_

8. For example, a child may apply a grasping and pulling scheme to a new toy,

assimilation
such as a wagon, through the process of _assimilation_. The scheme
may work for a while, but if the environment imposes new demands, as when a
wheel gets caught in a doorway, the child will have to modify the scheme

accommodation
through the process of _accomodation_.

9. In Piaget's view, cognitive development consists of a continual search for balance between assimilation and accommodation, a process he termed

equilibration _equilibration_

10. For example, meeting a new situation that cannot be assimilated with old schemes or developing a new but untried capacity to accommodate creates imbal-

equilibrium ance. Balance or _equilibrium_ is restored through accommodation, with the resulting advance to a higher level of cognitive organization.

Learning Objectives _qualitative   scheme - action patterns_
quantitative   assimilation incorporate new ideas through use of
constraints   existing schemes

1. Briefly describe the three general viewpoints of cognitive development presented. _existing schemes_
accomodation - changing existing schemes to allow for new knowledge

2. Name the psychologist primarily responsible for the theories of development discussed in this section. Under what viewpoint does he fit? _Piaget   Qualitative_

3. Define or give an example of the following:
scheme - _action patterns ideas we have about the world_
assimilation _new ideas by existing schemes_
accommodation _changing existing schemes to allow for new knowledge_
internalized action or scheme
equilibration

Stages of Intellectual Development

four 11. Piaget listed _four_ main periods, or stages, of intellectual development. He asserted that the order or sequence in which these stages occur

is invariable (is invariable/may vary).

12. While a more detailed description of each of Piaget's stages follows, it is important at this point to have an overview of this sequence. In the blanks below, write the name of the developmental period that corresponds to the approximate age range given. (Some patterns that characterize these stages are presented in parentheses.)

sensorimotor a. _sensorimotor_ period. Birth to two years (action schemes).

preoperational b. _preoperational_ period. Preschool years (internalized schemes, symbolic play, illogical thinking).

concrete-operational c. _concrete_ - _operational_ period. Early school years (logical, but concrete, thinking).

formal-operational d. _formal_ - _operational_ period. Adolescence through adulthood (abstract reasoning).

Learning Objectives

4. List the four main stages of intellectual development proposed by Piaget. Next to the name of each stage indicate the approximate age range.

5. According to Piaget, can the order in which these stages occur vary? *No*

INFANCY

13. In this and following sections more general labels for the developmental periods are used along with the ones developed by Piaget. For example, infancy, described as roughly the first two years of life, would be the stage that Piaget

sensorimotor   would have referred to as the _sensorimotor_ period.

The Infant's Capacity for Learning

14. *Conditioning and the Newborn*. Not surprisingly, infants are capable of learning by operant conditioning. For example, babies have been taught to pace their

sucking   _sucking_ responses for the reward of hearing music.

15. *Learning for the Fun of It*. The point being made in this section is that discovery of a contingency—that is, discovery of the connection between a behavior and

reinforcer (consequence)   the _reinforcer_ that follows it—is pleasurable. Thus, according to your text, it is not simply that behavior increases in frequency when reinforced

pleasure   but that human beings derive subjective _pleasure_ from discovering their power over the environment.

Infant Memory

16. Since infants cannot *tell* researchers what they remember, studies of infant mem-

habituation   ory use the _habituation_ technique, in which babies are exposed to a stimulus until the point at which they stop looking at it (that is, are habituated to it). If the same stimulus is then presented along with a new stimulus, and if babies pay attention to the new one, it is assumed that they

recognize (remember)   _recognize_ the old one.

17. *Recognition and Recall*. Using the habituation technique, researchers have been able to demonstrate that newborn infants can retain a memory of a stimulus for five to ten seconds. The form of memory demonstrated here is termed

recognition   (recognition/recall).

18. Older infants, between the ages of four and six months, have shown

recognition   ~~recognition~~ memory of a human face for as long as two weeks.

recall   While there has been little experimental evidence of ___recall___ memory in infants, there have been many reports of instances in which infants seem clearly capable of recall.

19. *Infant Amnesia.* We seem to remember little, if anything, from our infancy, and some research suggests that such forgetting, or lack of memory, is due to the

immaturity   ~~immaturity~~ of infants' neurons or brain structures.

20. In an experiment with baby rats, some of the rats were classically conditioned with a sound and shock when they were very young (eleven to sixteen days old) and others when they were slightly older (seventeen days old). Six weeks later,
slightly older   only the rats conditioned when they were (very young/slightly older) showed any evidence of conditioned fear. These results were interpreted as support for the notion that absence of memory in infants, termed "infantile amnesia," may be

neurons (brain structures)   due to the immaturity of the ___neurons___ involved.

21. Another study with human infants, trained to operate a mobile by kicking their feet, indicated that certain experiences may become
temporarily inaccessible   (wiped from memory/temporarily inaccessible). In this study, memory of the connection between the motion of the mobile and kicking seemed to recur for those infants who saw the mobile the day before the test day.

Learning Objectives

6. By what term did Piaget refer to the infancy phase, roughly the first two years of life? *Sensorimotor*

7. What evidence is there that infants may be operantly conditioned?

8. Aside from increasing the frequency of behavior, what function does discovery of a contingency have for human beings?

9. Describe the use of habituation as a technique for investigating infants' memories.

10. According to research using the habituation technique, how long can newborn infants retain memory of a stimulus? What type of memory is involved? Do infants seem capable of recall?

11. According to your text, what factor is probably important in explaining "infantile amnesia"? Briefly state the results of the study involving rats and classical conditioning.

12. Explain how the study with infants and the mobile relates to the notion that memories may simply be inaccessible rather than totally removed.

Sensorimotor Intelligence and the Object Concept

two

22. As previously indicated, the infancy or sensorimotor period occurs between birth and approximately ___2 two___ years of age.

object

23. During this stage children develop the object concept, which involves the concept of ___object___ permanence or the awareness that objects continue to exist when out of sight.

will not

24. For the very young infant, an object that cannot be seen or touched does not exist. For example, if an object that the infant has been watching is covered, the infant (will/(will not)) look at the area where the object was previously visible.

fourth
partially visible

25. The first signs of object permanence seem to appear around the ___fourth___ month of life, or even earlier. At this point the child will reach for a toy if it is ((partially visible)/totally obscured) behind a blanket or pillow.

first

26. Between the eighth and twelfth months the child will reach for completely hidden objects, but there are still limitations on his or her understanding of objects. For example, if an object is first hidden under one pillow and then, as the child watches, moved to a second one, he or she will look for it under the ((first)/second) pillow.

fourth

27. During the twelfth to the eighteenth month, the child becomes capable of following all *visible* movements of an object. For example, if a toy is moved to a second, then to a third, then to a fourth pillow, the child will look for it under the ___fourth___ pillow.

in the box

28. At this point the child is still unable to understand actions not seen, however. For example, in one demonstration described in the text, a toy is first placed in a box, the box placed under a pillow, and the toy then secretly removed from the box and left under the pillow. When the empty box is then presented to the child, he or she looks for the toy only ((in the box)/under the pillow).

two

see

29. It is only during the last part of the sensorimotor period, between eighteen months and ___two___ years of age, that children understand that an object can be moved even when they do not ___see___ it being moved.

deferred

30. At the same time children also begin to develop ___deferred___ imitation, the ability to mimic in play something observed at an earlier time.

Learning Objectives

13. Describe the gradual changes in the concept of object permanence that occur between approximately the following ages:
    birth to the fourth month
    the fourth to the eighth month
    the eighth to the twelfth month
    the twelfth to the eighteenth month
    the eighteenth month to two years

14. Aside from the ability to follow unobserved movements of an object, what other capacity begins to develop after the eighteenth month? *object can be moved even though they don't see it being moved*

EARLY CHILDHOOD

31. The second major period of development described by Piaget begins at about the

    two

    age of ___*two*___ and ends about the time the child enters school, between the ages of five and seven. Piaget termed this early childhood period the

    preoperational

    ___*preoperational*___ stage.

Advances in the Young Child's Thinking

32. The ability to follow unobserved movements marks the end of infancy and the

    representational

    beginning of ___*representational*___ thought, the capacity to mentally represent objects not directly seen.

33. In the preoperational phase the ability to mentally represent engenders a number of other accomplishments, including language development and an expanded use

    imitation

    of deferred ___*imitation*___, an ability that began to develop at the end of the sensorimotor period.

    insight

34. In addition, the preschool child shows ___*insight*___ learning, in which the solution to a problem seems to occur all at once. The child at this stage also shows some ability to understand counting and the concept of

    number

    ___*Number*___.

35. Despite the advances that accompany representation, there remain immature aspects of preoperational thinking. The child at this stage is characterized by (a) egocentric thinking, (b) complexive thinking, and (c) an inability to conduct tasks that require self-direction, in which external cues are absent. In the blanks below write the letter (a, b, or c) that best illustrates the type of limitation described.

b   _____b_____ The child's sentences do not express coordinated thought, and they jump from one idea to another.

a   _____a_____ The child is unable to visualize or understand something from another's point of view.

c   _____c_____ The child cannot stack building blocks unless indentations show how they fit together.

Learning Objectives

15. What name did Piaget give the second major period of development, the period that your text terms early childhood? Approximately what ages does this period span? *Preoperational Stage*

16. What is representational thought? What new abilities accompany the capacity for representational thought?

17. Name and describe three immature aspects of the thinking of the preoperational child. *egocentric complexive self direction*

MIDDLE CHILDHOOD

concrete-   36. Piaget referred to this stage as the ___Concrete -___

operational   ___operational___ period. It begins when the child is between five and

school   seven years old, at about the time he or she begins ___school___, and ends at about adolescence.

The Concept of Conservation

37. Gradually across the course of development in middle childhood the child learns

conservation   ___conservation___, the principle that irrelevant changes in an object's appearance have no effect on the object's quantity.

38. For example, if there are equal amounts of water in two squat containers, and if water from one of them is poured into a tall, narrow container, a *preoperational* child will say that:

a   a. there is more water in the tall container.
           b. there are equal amounts of water in the two containers.
           c. there is more water in the squat container.

39. On the other hand, a child well into the *concrete-operational* period (an eight-

b   year-old, for example) will probably report that ___b___. (Pick a, b, or c, above.)

40. There are other principles of conservation learned as well during this period, including conservation of length, weight, and number. For example, if two equal rows of marbles are lined up and one row is then spread out, a child in the

concrete-operational

concrete-_operational_ period will report that there are equal numbers in the two rows.

41. It should be noted that simple changes in a conservation task, such as allowing the children to pour the water or failing to indicate that the experimenter's actions are important, (increase/decrease/don't affect) the proportion of five- and six-year-olds who answer the critical question correctly.

increase

42. Thus, while there are differences between preschoolers and schoolchildren in responses to these tests, it (is/is not) possible to state with certainty that the tests indicate _qualitative_ differences in thinking between the two groups.

is not

Learning Objectives

18. What is Piaget's name for "middle childhood"? Approximately what ages does this period span?
concrete operational 7-12

19. What is the principle of conservation (of quantity)? Explain by describing the preoperational and concrete-operational child's response to the following problems:
    a. the containers of water.
    b. two rows of marbles.

20. Do preoperational children invariably respond to the conservation problems with the "wrong" answers, or does it depend on how the problems are presented? Explain.

21. What does your text conclude with regard to whether or not children's thought varies qualitatively across stages?
They do not vary across stages

Memory Strategies in Children

43. Older children do much better than preoperational children on tests of

memory

memory. This improved performance is due largely to the older

strategies

child's capacity to use memory _strategies_, techniques for storing and retrieving information.

44. For example, the study with six-, eight-, and eleven-year-old children found that the older the children, the more likely they were to use the

cue

retrieval cue cards which helped them categorize and remember the objects.

Organizing Concepts

one category

45. Preschoolers develop a wide range of concepts by which they are able to classify objects or events. A two-year-old can probably sort objects into two categories but will probably do so by creating (one category/two categories) at a time.

does not have

46. A late preschool child can sort into several categories and answer questions about the classification. Such a child (also has/does not have) a *complete* understanding of the *hierarchical* use of classes—that is, the adult's use of subclasses.

and also

47. While children in the late preoperational stage have some understanding of a hierarchy of classes, their understanding is not complete. A late preoperational child will probably be able to correctly label oranges, apples, and bananas (and also/and not) be aware that these are all called fruit. However, further questioning will make it clear that the child does not really understand the hierarchy.

48. If the child is shown seven oranges, three apples, and two bananas and asked whether there is more fruit or more oranges (!), the child is likely to answer that

oranges

there are more ___oranges___. This suggests that the child cannot think of classes and subclasses at the same time.

49. According to Piaget, the child in the preoperational period cannot think in terms of classes and subclasses *at the same time*, while the child in the

concrete-operational

___concrete___-___operational___ period is able to do so. Despite this assertion, it has been found that many eight- and nine-year-old children respond in the same manner as do preschoolers.

50. Another difference between the two groups is the development of

metacognition
did not notice

___metacognition___ an understanding of the cognitive processes, the ability to think about thinking. For example, six-year-olds (noticed/did not notice) the absence of crucial elements in instructions for performing a task. Eight-year-olds noticed the absence immediately.

Learning Objectives

22. Discuss differences between the preoperational and concrete-operational child with regard to:
    a. use of memory strategies.
    b. use of categories and subcategories (a hierarchical classification system).

23. Using an example, explain what is meant by the statement that even late preoperational children cannot think in terms of categories and subcategories at the same time. What appears to be in conflict with this statement?

24. Provide a rough definition of the term *metacognition*. to think about how you think

GENDER DIFFERENCES IN COGNITIVE DEVELOPMENT

language/visualization

51. As children go through school, differences in cognitive ability between the sexes become increasingly apparent. Females, on the average, show superior (language/visualization) skills, and males show superior (language/visualization) skills.

boys

52. Among junior-high-school students tested in one recent study, both sexes did equally well on the verbal section of the test, but the (girls/boys) did better on the mathematical section.

53. The superiority of males over females in mathematical ability is due to:
    a. genetic differences.
    b. differences in experiences outside the classroom.
    c. conformity to prescribed sex roles.

d

    d. unknown factors. Any or all of the above are possible explanations.

54. One study with three-month-old infants found that boys learned fastest when

visual

given a _____(color) visual_____ reward and girls learned fastest when rewarded

sound

with a _____sound_____. If found to be reliable, such a result would suggest a reason for girls' superiority in language and boys' superiority in processing of visual-spatial information.

Learning Objectives

25. In what general cognitive capacity are males, on the average, superior to females? Females superior to males?
    math visual   *language*

26. Are the differences between males and females in mathematical ability due to genetic (or biological) factors? List two additional alternative explanations for the sex differences found. *No, Environment outside classroom prescribed sex roles*

27. What does the study with three-month-old infants suggest about gender differences in cognitive development? *Nothing genetic*

ADOLESCENCE

formal

55. Piaget termed the last major stage of development the *Formal*-operational stage. It begins at about the age children move into

adolescence

_____adolescence_____ and continues throughout adulthood. (Note that your text divides this stage, treating adolescence and adulthood separately.)

formal-

56. Not all people develop the capacity for *formal*-

operational

_____operational_____ thinking, however. Most studies find that only approxi-

40 to 60

mately _____40 to 60_____ percent of college students and adults have attained this level.

Systematic Experimentation

57. One of the capacities that develop during adolescence is the ability to reason scientifically, the capacity to consider all possible combinations of factors that may

systematic (scientific)   cause an event and to test them in a _systematic_ manner.

58. For example, in the demonstration involving combinations of liquids discussed in the text, a child in the formal-operational period is able to consider

all possible   _all   possible_ combinations of liquids to arrive at a solution. The preadolescent child is generally unable to use such a systematic approach.

Hypothetical Ideas and Abstract Thinking

59. Formal-operational thinking also involves two other capacities: the capacity to

hypothetical   consider _hypothetical_ ideas and the capacity to engage in *abstract thinking*.

60. For example, I just called my daughter Samantha and asked her the following: "Suppose you had a twenty-foot-long carrot which you could eat at the rate of two feet per minute. How long would it take you to eat the carrot?" If Samantha is preadolescent, which of the following is likely to have been her response?

a   a.) There's no such thing as a twenty-foot carrot.
    b.   Ten minutes.

61. Actually, Samantha, who is not quite ten, did say that there was no such thing as a twenty-foot carrot. But then she set about trying to solve the problem. She is

hypothetical   beginning to develop the capacity to consider _hypothetical_ ideas, ideas not bound by physical reality.

62. In addition to hypothetical ideas, the adolescent is able to understand general

abstract   or _abstract_ principles important for understanding such fields as mathematics, science, economics, and law. Adolescents may also become preoccupied with abstract and idealistic principles, including notions related to ethics and conformity.

Learning Objectives

28. What name did Piaget give to the fourth stage of development? When does it begin?   Formal-operational   adolescence

29. Approximately what proportion of individuals are thought to be able to engage in formal-operational thinking?   40 to 60

    of college students

30. List three new capacities that emerge during this period. Briefly describe each of these capacities.

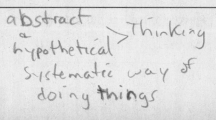

abstract
a hypothetical } Thinking
Systematic way of
doing things

ADULTHOOD

Cognitive Skills in Early and Middle Adulthood

twenty/forty

forty

sixty

63. The text defines early adulthood as the years between ages

_____20_____ and ____40_____ . It considers middle adult-

hood to be the years between ages ____40_____ and

_____60_____ .

middle

early

64. A study of intellectual performance has shown that IQ generally increases into

the ___middle____-adulthood years. While flexibility in thinking is

likely to peak in ___early_____ adulthood, it will probably remain at
this high level through the middle-adulthood years.

Cognitive Skills in Later Adulthood

sensory (perceptual)

65. *Changes Associated with Aging.* Aging is accompanied by a general tendency to
"slow down," with initial changes in vision and hearing producing a decrease in

___sensory_____ input.

two
sensory

66. Memory also changes during the aging process. For example, when shown a
brief presentation of seven letters, of which younger people will recall three,

older people will recall, on the average, ___2_____ letters. Thus,
the (sensory/long-term) memory of older people is worse than that of younger
people.

reorganize

backward

67. Older people can hold about as much information in short-term memory as can

younger people except when they must ___reorganize__ information in
short-term memory or when the task requires a division of attention. For example, older people do worse than younger people when they must repeat a list
(forward/backward/both).

attention

extinguished

68. Older people's performance on the light bulb and key task is inferior to that of

younger people if the task requires a division of ___attention_____ . Thus,
older people did worse when the key that extinguished the light bulb was located
below the bulb which had just been (lit/extinguished).

are not

69. Outside the laboratory, most of the differences between short-term memories of
older and younger adults (are/are not) readily noticed.

incorrect

70. A popular stereotype about the elderly is that their memory for distant events is much better than that for recent events. Research has shown this assumption to be (correct/incorrect). When memory retention for news stories was tested across several months, it was found that the amount of information recalled declined

all ages

with the passage of time for (the young/the aged/all ages).

sensory

71. To review, older people do show some decrement in ___sensory___

short-term

memory and also in ___short___-___term___ memory if reorganization or a division of attention is required. With regard to long-term

do not

memory, older adults (also/do not) show decrement in recall. The major decrement in cognitive skills experienced by the elderly involves not so much memory

reorganize

capacity as the ability to ___reorganize___ information stored so that inferences from it can be drawn.

72. *Minimizing Cognitive Decline.* While certain cognitive changes tend to be associated with aging, such changes are not inevitable. There is considerable evidence

a small percentage

that (most/a small percentage) of the elderly suffer no decline in cognitive functioning.

73. There is, then, considerable variability in response to aging. In part, genetic factors are involved, as is evidenced by the fact that, forty or more years after fin-

identical twins

ishing school, ___identical twins___ are more similar in cognitive functioning than are unrelated individuals or fraternal twins.

74. Environmental factors are also important, especially the extent to which an older

physically

person has the opportunity to remain ___physically___ and

intellectually

___intellectually___ active. Depression, lack of hope, and other

emotional

___emotional___ problems may add enormously to the decline that may occur with aging.

75. Finally, recent research has demonstrated that older people may be taught strategies that help them encode, retrieve information, and use systematic testing in problem solving. Thus, although genetic factors are important determinants of

environment

cognitive decline, changes in the ___environment___ may help the elderly compensate for such declines.

Learning Objectives

31. What age range does the text consider to be early adulthood? Middle adulthood?
    20 to 40   40 to 60

32. During what stage of adulthood is IQ likely to peak? During what stage is flexibility in thinking likely to peak? Will flexibility decline or stay the same during the following stage?
    middle   20 to 40
                    Stay the same

33. Describe changes in the following capacities that generally accompany aging, giving examples of research where appropriate:
    sensory input
    sensory memory
    short-term memory storage
    short-term memory involving reorganization or division of attention
    long-term memory

34. Are the memories of the aged for distant events better than their memories for more recent events? Describe the results of a study that examined this question.

    No

35. What factors contribute to the decline that may occur with aging, and what can be done to reduce the impact of these factors?   *learn new strategies*

Chapter Thirteen
Acquiring and Using Language

General Objectives

1. Describe some of the major aspects of the nature and structure of language.

2. Discuss some of the important features that aid in the production and comprehension of language.

3. List the characteristics that define human language and that make it unique.

4. Describe the ways in which human beings are biologically adapted for human language.

5. Discuss the various phases in the acquisition of language by children.

6. Explain the three theories as to how children acquire language.

7. Describe the ways in which language influences thought and the ways in which thought influences language.

Acquiring and Using Language

Learning Objectives appear at
the end of each major section.

1. The text gives several examples and anecdotes of how meaning can be confused by the users of language and points out that these kinds of confusions (can/cannot) arise even when the users have a thorough knowledge of the language's structure.

can

THE NATURE OF LANGUAGE

2. Two important and separate aspects of language are *performance* and *competence*. The way language is used in either speaking or listening is referred

performance

to as linguistic _performance_, while the abstract knowledge of the rules and principles of a language is referred to as linguistic

competence

competence.

174

3. Improper linguistic performance does not necessarily indicate a lack of linguistic competence. For instance, the passenger who answers the flight attendant's offer of coffee, tea, or milk by saying "yes" is obviously showing an error in linguis-

performance

tic _performance_. This does not necessarily mean, however, that the

competence

passenger has a deficit in linguistic _competence_. The passenger may have merely been trying to be funny, for example.

4. As was illustrated by the child who could not speak, it is entirely possible to

performance

show a severe deficit in language _performance_ while still having linguistic competence.

communication

5. The basic function of all language is _communication_. The study of how language functions to carry out communication is called

pragmatics

pragmatics —how one uses language to accomplish a goal that requires a listener's comprehension.

6. Intimately related to the function of language are the rules that specify how the language is to be used. These rules make up the structure, or

grammar

grammar, of language, and they can be subdivided into three major divisions: *phonology, syntax,* and *semantics.* Identify each of these divisions from the descriptions given below.

a. The rules that govern how words should be combined to form sentences.

syntax

Syntax

b. The rules that prescribe the meaning of words and sentences.

semantics

semantics

c. The rules that identify the particular sounds that are linguistically meaningful and prescribe how they should be ordered to form words.

phonology

phonology

Learning Objectives

1. Distinguish between linguistic performance and linguistic competence.

2. What is the basic function of all language?   communication

3. What is pragmatics? how we use language to acquire a goal that require a listeners comprehension

4. What is the structure of language called, and what are its three major divisions?   grammar

1 syntax
2. Phonology
3 semantics

Producing Language

7. *Context and Intention*. The ease with which we produce meaningful speech in going about our daily lives obscures the complex process that underlies its production. Two aids that help to simplify this complex process are *context* and *intention*. For example, the words "Do you want fries with these?" are easily understood when ordering a meal at a drive-in because of the

context   _____context_____ in which the verbal exchange is carried out. Moreover, the exchange between a carhop and a customer is also made easier because each

intention   knows the _____intentions_____ of the other; the carhop wants to take an order and the customer wants to give one.

8. *Choice of Form*. The structure of language generally allows for

several   (several/only one) way(s) to express an intention. Since the speaker has to decide which of the possible options to use, expressing an intention may be thought of

problem   as solving a _____problem_____ .

9. *Production*. By studying slips of the tongue it has been revealed that speech is

six or seven   planned no further than (six or seven/twenty or thirty) words in advance as a speaker begins to produce an utterance.

Learning Objectives

5. What are two aids that help to simplify the complex process of speaking and understanding language?
   context and intention

6. In what way might the decision to express an intention be thought of as solving a problem?
   We can express things different ways. So you choose how to put your intention

7. How do we know that a speaker plans no further ahead than six or seven words when beginning to speak?
   We know this because people make slips of the tongue

Comprehending Language

10. The comprehension of speech is an extremely complex process. The most ad-
cannot   vanced computers (can/cannot) perform this task as well as a human being.
syllables   Human beings process speech patterns at the level of (phonemes/syllables), using both the sound and the context to aid in the decoding process.

11. When words have more than one meaning (*bright,* for example), the listener retrieves all meanings from semantic memory and holds them until the

context   _____context_____ makes the speaker's meaning clear. Thus when somebody is telling us "The bright and the beautiful people have it made," we learn
intelligent   from the context that the intended meaning here of *bright* is (shiny/intelligent).

12. Another aid in the decoding process is the ability to predict the words and phrases that are likely to follow previous words. This is accomplished with the

syntax   aid of _____syntax_____ , the rules that govern how words should be combined to form sentences.

13. A third important aid in the decoding of speech is the *given-new strategy,* in which the listener may comprehend *new* information by integrating it with old,

given

_____*given*_____ information already in the memory store. In the English language, for example, the definite article *the* is used to tag

given (old)

_____*given*_____ information, while the indefinite article *a* is used to indi-

new

cate _____*new*_____ information.

14. When old and new information are both introduced by a speaker but not clearly

assumptions

specified, the listener then makes _*assumptions*_ that connect the old and the new information in a sensible manner. In the example used by the text, "Mary got some picnic supplies out of the car. The beer was warm," the listener

assuming

makes sense out of this statement by _*assuming*_ that the beer had previously been referred to as part of the picnic supplies.

Learning Objectives

8. How do human beings and computers compare with respect to comprehending spoken language?
   Computers can't comprehend things as well as People

9. At what level do human beings process speech patterns?
   syllable

10. In what way does context help in the decoding of speech? *How a sentence is put into context allows you to figure out the meaning*

11. In what way does syntax help in the decoding of speech?
    How words are going to be arranged in a sentence

12. What is the given-new strategy? How does it aid in the decoding of speech?
    Integrating of new and old information

13. What procedure does a listener follow when a speaker introduces both old and new information without clearly speci-fying their interconnection? *Make assumptions*

HUMAN LANGUAGE AND ANIMAL COMMUNICATION

15. While virtually all species of animals can communicate with one another in some fashion, the pattern or form of communication used by each of these species is

species-specific

*species - specific*, which means that all members of the species will demonstrate this ability to communicate and the ability will be

biological (anatomical)

based on _*biological*_ structures unique to the species.

species-

specific

does

16. Some psychologists regard human language as a ___species -___ ___specific___ behavior that is radically different in kind from the communication of all other animals. It is clear that human communication (does/does not) meet both of the specifications listed above for species-specific behavior. But if human language is truly different in kind from animal communication, then no other animal will be able to acquire human language.

The Uniqueness of Human Language

17. Your text lists six characteristics that define human language. They are (1) semanticity, (2) discreteness, (3) displacement, (4) productivity, (5) iteration, and (6) recursion. Match these terms with their descriptions given below:

iteration

a. Adding new constituents to old statements is called ___iteration___.

b. Achieving meaningfulness by attaching arbitrary meaning to each separate

semanticity

word is called ___semanticity___.

displacement

c. Referring to distant objects and events is called ___displacement___.

d. The capacity to combine units into an infinite number of statements is called

productivity

___productivity___

discreteness

e. The possession of distinct units is called ___discreteness___

f. The ability to embed one meaning structure within another is called

recursion

___recursion___.

18. Among all the forms of animal communication, only the language of

human beings

___human beings___ has all of these characteristics. Therefore, the use of human language can be said to be a

unique

___unique___ form of communication.

does not

19. Language (does/does not) require sound. For example, the American Sign Language used by the deaf has all of the six essential features of human language.

ten-month-old
cannot

20. Although chimpanzees have learned to communicate using signing, plastic tokens, and computer terminals, none has yet demonstrated a grasp of language more advanced than that shown by a (ten-month-old/ten-year-old) child. At this time it (can/cannot) be said that chimpanzees have the capacity to use language in the same manner as human beings. The question remains unresolved.

Learning Objectives

14. What is meant when it is said that the communication system used by each species of animal is species-specific?
    It is only unique to their species

15. Why do some psychologists regard human language as a species-specific behavior? *– Because it satisfies the definition?*

16. List and describe the six characteristics that define human language. *recursion, iteration, displacement, discreteness, semanticity, productivity*

17. Why can it be said that human language is unique? *– We are the only animals on earth that have all six characteristics*

18. Illustrate by an example that a language does not have to have sound.
    Sign language people who can't talk use this

19. Can chimpanzees use human language the same way as human beings do? *No*

Biological Adaptation for Human Language

a far greater

21. *Vocal and Auditory Specialization.* In terms of our anatomical structure, human beings are equipped to make (about the same/a far greater) number of sounds than any other animal. Even our closest relatives, the chimps, lack the necessary vocal apparatus for complex speech.

22. In addition, human beings are well equipped to hear a wide variety of sounds.

weeks

Infants only a few __weeks__ old can discriminate between such similar speech sounds as *ba* and *pa*. The vocal and auditory specialization found

biologically

in human beings suggests that they are __biologically__ prepared to acquire language.

left

23. *Brain Specialization.* In most human beings, the __left__ cerebral hemisphere dominates for language abilities. This feature of the human brain in which each of the cerebral hemispheres has specialized roles is called hemi-

lateralization

spheric __lateralization__

does

24. The dominance of the left cerebral hemisphere with respect to language (does/does not) suggest a possible distinct neural basis for language, but many psychologists believe that human language ability also depends on general human

cognitive
rejects

__cognitive__ abilities and that language is simply one aspect of these abilities. This view (accepts/rejects) a distinct neural basis for language.

25. The fact that chimpanzees have not been able to go beyond a ten-month-old child

unique (distinct)

in language ability argues for a __unique__ neural basis for human language. However, the fact that retarded children show deficits similar to those of chimpanzees in acquiring language while highly intelligent children acquire language very rapidly argues for the notion that language is dependent on general

cognitive

__cognitive__ abilities. Thus whether or not a unique brain organization is responsible for human language remains to be established.

Learning Objectives

20. How is the vocal and auditory specialization found in human beings related to their ability to acquire language?
we can make a lot of different sounds

21. Which of the two cerebral hemispheres dominates with respect to language ability? What does this particular example of hemispheric lateralization suggest? *left*
Neural basis for language

22. What is the alternative explanation that rejects a unique neural organization as the basis for human language? What evidence supports this view? What evidence supports the alternative view?
Cognitive Tests done on monkeys

Sensitive Periods

sensitive

26. It has been suggested that there is a ___*sensitive*___ period in which human beings find it especially easy to acquire a language. This period is said to

puberty

   occur between the ages of two and ___*puberty*___.

more

against

27. If, in fact, a true sensitive period does exist for human language, then persons learning a second language after puberty should find it (more/less) difficult than learning it before puberty. Research evidence argues (for/against) this supposition; postpuberty children were found to learn a second language more easily than prepuberty children.

accent

28. It was found, however, that the prepuberty children were less likely to have an ___*accent*___ in the new language than older children. Nonetheless,

sensitive

   there does not appear to be a true ___*sensitive*___ period for human language.

Learning Objectives

23. Between what ages is the sensitive period for acquiring human language said to occur?
between two and puberty.

24. What differences should be found between prepuberty and postpuberty children if there is a true sensitive period for human language acquisition? What differences were found?
Prepuberty wont have an accent. Prepuberty will *less difficult to learn for prepuberty than*

25. Is there a true sensitive period for human language acquisition? *postpuberty children*
No

HOW CHILDREN ACQUIRE LANGUAGE

The Stages of Language Acquisition

29. *Prespeech Communication.* The earliest form of communication of an infant is crying, which seems to have three different patterns: a basic

rhythmic/anger

____rhythmic____ pattern, a cry expressing ____anger____, and a

pain

cry expressing ____pain____.

are not
all

30. During the first six months or so the sounds a baby makes (are/are not) limited to the sounds it hears in its environment. Babies seem to produce sounds from (one/all)

deaf

languages. Furthermore, the fact that babies who are ____deaf____ cry

independent of

and babble like hearing babies indicates that early vocalizations are (dependent on/independent of) what the child hears.

gestures

31. In addition to sounds, infants also use ____gestures____ to communicate, and at about ten months they begin seeking help from adults—to reach a toy, for example—through gestures. This probably represents the beginning of children's

communication

realization of the importance of ____communication____.

32. Between the ages of seven months and a year or so infants'

intonations

____intonations____ begin to closely follow those of the adults in their culture. For example, they express intonations that signify commands or questions. This early acquisition of intonation patterns is important in the further develop-

meanings

ment of language, since the ____meanings____ of words can be changed by changes in intonations.

33. *First Words.* Children usually begin to produce their first words by the time they

one

are ____one____ year old. During this stage children employ gesture,

intonation

context, and ____intonation____ to give meaning to their one-word sentences.

34. Also during this stage children often extend the meaning of words to cover objects or actions for which they have no words, a process called

overextension

____overextension____. For example, a child who learns the word *doggie* may

"doggie"

also call the family cat ____doggie____.

does not

35. Overextension (does/does not) always indicate a confusion of meaning on the part of the child. For example, the child who calls the family cat "doggie" will

only a dog

often point out (only a dog/a dog and a cat) when asked to identify a "doggie" from among many pictures of animals.

36. *First Sentences.* At around two years of age, children begin constructing sen-

two

tences composed of only _____two_____ words. These two-word sentences omit nonessential words, such as articles and prepositions, much like the
wording in a telegram. Thus these utterances are referred to as

telegraphic

_____telegraphic_____ speech.

37. Even a child's two-word utterances show a distinct structure. By saying "Drink
juice," thus indicating that juice is the object rather than the subject, a child

rules (structure)
the same

demonstrates conformity to certain grammatical ___rules___ . Children from different cultures show (the same/a different) range of concepts in
constructing their two-word sentences.

38. *Acquiring Complex Rules.* Children continue to construct new grammatical rules
and discard old ones as they progress toward adult language. In this progress
they quite frequently extend rules to cases where they do not apply, an error

overregularization

called _overregularization_ . For instance, use of regular past tense for verbs

irregular

that have an ___irregular___ form or use of incorrect plurals is common
in young children.

Learning Objectives

26. Name and describe the three different patterns of crying, the child's earliest attempts at communication.
rhythmic, anger, pain

27. What evidence indicates that the sounds a baby makes during its first six months are not determined by what he or
she hears? Because Deaf Babies also make these sounds.

28. In addition to vocalizations, in what other way does a ten-month-old infant communicate?
By using gestures

29. At about what age range do infants' intonations begin to follow the intonations of adults? What is the significance of
this development? Seven months to a year. Helps them with communication

30. At about what age do children begin to say their first words? How do they clarify the meaning of these one-word
utterances? What common mistake do children make in using these words? One year old
gestures context and intonation   overextension

31. At about what age do children begin to use two-word sentences? Describe the composition of these sentences.
Two Years of Age   omit nonessential words articles, prepositions

32. What evidence suggests that even for two-word utterances a child is following a set of grammatical rules?
The way they say these sentences using obj instead of a subj

33. Between the ages of two and five, children are said to acquire temporary sets of grammatical rules. What common
error do they make in applying these rules? Overregularization

Explaining Language Acquisition

39. The text describes three different explanations as to how children acquire language. Noam **Chomsky** subscribes to a biological view in which the acquisition of language is primarily a matter of **maturation**. This maturational pattern is based on special cognitive abilities built into the human brain.

40. Some behaviorists, especially B. F. **Skinner**, disagree with Chomsky and see language acquisition as simply the result of **operant** conditioning. According to this view, the child acquires language skills because he or she is **reinforced** by parents or significant others for doing so.

41. The social-learning theorists have still another explanation for the acquisition of language. According to this view, **imitation** is the major factor in the acquisition of language by children. In other words, they acquire language through imitating their parents and significant others.

42. It appears, however, that reinforcement is evidently not adequate to account for children's language acquisition. In studies of parent-child interactions, for example, it has been found that while parents pay attention to the intelligibility or accuracy of children's statements, they rarely pay attention to incorrect grammar, nor do they reinforce correct grammatical usage. Thus, direct **reinforcement** alone cannot account for the acquisition of grammatical rules.

43. Nor is imitation an adequate explanation for the acquisition of grammar. When children overregularize, for example, they are not imitating adults; adults generally do not overregularize. In addition, in many cases children do not exactly imitate the speech of adults; they tend to filter what is heard through their own system of grammatical **rules**.

44. A more recent view of language acquisition is based on **pragmatics** and sees language as emerging out of the social interaction between infant and caregiver. In this case the acquisition of language is made easier by the **special** language all adults adopt when talking to children.

Chomsky

maturation

Skinner

operant

reinforced

imitation

reinforcement

rules

pragmatics

special (simplified)

Learning Objectives

34. What is Noam Chomsky's explanation as to how children acquire language? *Biological View*
Acquire language through maturation

35. What is B. F. Skinner's explanation as to how children acquire language? What evidence argues against this explanation? *Children acquire language through reinforcement by adults*
operant conditioning   social-learning theory

36. What is the social-learning theorists' explanation as to how children acquire language? What evidence argues against this explanation? *Through imitation of other adults*
children use there own grammatical rules through pragmatics

37. How does the view based on pragmatics explain how children acquire language? *They filter out what*
they hear and apply their own grammatical rules to it

LANGUAGE AND THOUGHT

45. While it is obvious that language and thought interact, it is less obvious whether it is thought that influences language or whether it is language that influences

thought   _thought_ .

How Language Affects Thought

46. A society that did not have a word for war might think (and behave) differently

linguistic   from one that did, according to Benjamin Whorf's _linguistic_

relativity   _relativity_ *hypothesis.* The basic notion of the linguistic relativity

thought   hypothesis is that language determines _thought_ .

47. If this is true, then Americans, who have only a single word for snow, will be unable to perceive or think about snow in the same manner as Eskimos, who

twenty   have more than _twenty_ names for various types of snow. It has been found, however, that when distinguishing between various types of snow becomes important, such as is the case with English-speaking skiers, they

do   (do/do not) discriminate between various kinds of snow and develop a specialized vocabulary to label the distinctions.

48. Although vocabulary may make it easier or harder to perceive certain distinctions, it does not make the perception of these differences impossible. Thus

incorrect   Whorf was (correct/incorrect).

49. If vocabulary affects thought, it does so by affecting the way information is en-

memory   coded into _memory_ , such as when an ambiguous figure is remembered differently when it is labeled as "eyeglasses" than when it is labeled as a "dumbbell."

50. Vocabulary can also affect thought by encouraging people to notice similarities between different stimuli by attaching a common category

label

label to them. For example, the common category label

similarities

"mammal" causes us to notice the _similarities_ between a dog and an elephant while downplaying the differences.

51. Finally, language (labels) can affect thought by changing a person's

self-concept
more

self-_concept_. People who were arbitrarily labeled as being "charitable" were later found to be (more/less) likely to give to charitable appeals than people who had been arbitrarily labeled as "uncharitable."

52. Another facet of the linguistic relativity hypothesis was that

grammar
rejected

grammar affects the way people think about time, space, and matter. Research in this area has (confirmed/rejected) this hypothesis.

Learning Objectives

38. What is the basic notion behind Benjamin Whorf's linguistic relativity hypothesis?   _language determines_ _thought_

39. Are Americans capable of perceiving or thinking about snow in the same manner as Eskimos? How does this reflect on the linguistic relativity hypothesis?   _Yes. That we shouldn't be able to do it according to the hypothesis_

40. List three ways in which vocabulary (labels) can affect thought. Give an example of each.   _memory_ _self concept_   _similarities_

41. What is the significance of grammar according to the linguistic relativity hypothesis? What does research say about this?   _Affects the way people think about space time and matter_ _It is rejected_

How Thought Affects Language

53. The influence of language on thought is now felt to be much less than was proposed by Whorf, and interest has shifted toward how thought affects

language

language. It may be, for example, that the universal characteristics of human thought processes create universal _linguistic_

linguistic (language)

structures.

54. The search for linguistic universals that depend upon human perceptual and cognitive capacities has focused on color terms. Studies have found that the lack of

does not

color terms in a culture's language (does/does not) limit the capacity of its members to make universal distinctions in color.

almost identical

55. In one study, for example, people from a wide variety of cultures were asked to select from a color chart the best examples of color terms in their language. Although the color chart contained 320 different hues, their choices were (almost identical/very different). In other words, while there are many different names for the color we call "red" and some cultures have no name for this color,

red (color)

all human beings see the same ___red___ we see.

56. It appears, then, that color categories are a reflection of the physiological, per-

cognitive

ceptual, and ___cognitive___ capacities of human beings. These capacities allow human beings to discriminate subtle variations in all kinds of environ-

names (labels)

mental events and then give ___names___ to these variations that they perceive and think about. Thus it can be said that human thought does, in fact,

language

affect human ___language___ .

Learning Objectives

42. Explain why the lack of words for different colors in a culture does not indicate the inability of its members to make universal color discriminations. ___Because we all see the same colors___

43. In what way are the perceptual and cognitive abilities of human beings reflected in their words for colors? What does this say about the relationship between thought and language?

Chapter Fourteen
Personality and Social Development

General Objectives

1. Describe the development of personality and social behavior from the psychoanalytic, cognitive-developmental, and social-learning perspectives.

2. Describe the phases of attachment formation in infancy and the effects of attachment deprivation.

3. Discuss the evidence that suggests that biological as well as cultural factors may contribute to gender role behavior.

4. Describe the importance of peer relationships and play for socialization, and discuss the changes in prosocial behavior that occur as the child matures.

5. List and give examples of the three levels of moral development proposed by Kohlberg.

6. Explain how reinforcement and modeling affect aggressive behavior.

7. Explain the distinction between puberty and adolescence, and discuss the importance of adolescence in Western societies.

8. Describe the stresses and changes in perspective that accompany aging.

Personality and Social Development

Learning Objectives appear at
the end of each major section.

PERSPECTIVE ON PERSONALITY AND SOCIAL DEVELOPMENT

The Biological Perspective

identical

fraternal

genetic

1. One recent study found that ___identical___ twins are much more similar in temperament than are ___fraternal___ twins. These findings suggest that temperament and personality are at least in part determined by (genetic/environmental) factors.

2. It has also been found that vocational interests and the extent of authoritarian attitudes are more similar in biological than adoptive families. Again, these data

genetic

suggest that personality is in part determined by ___genetic___ factors.

3. The emphasis throughout the text, however, is that neither environment nor heredity is solely responsible for personality development. There is always as-

interaction

sumed to be an ___interaction___ between these two factors.

Freud's Theory of Psychosexual Development

4. According to Freud, human beings are motivated by powerful biological instincts to seek pleasure. As the child grows, different parts of the body, termed

erogenous zones

___erogenous zones___, become the focus of this pleasure.

5. The shifts in erogenous zone coincide with five stages of psychosexual develop-ment. Unresolved conflicts at a particular stage will produce

fixation

___fixation___ at that stage, which will in large part determine the adult personality.

6. The Freudian stages are covered in more detail in Chapter 18. As a review, list the names of the five developmental stages in the blanks next to the *approximate* age ranges.

oral

anal

phallic

latency

genital

___oral___ birth to one year

___anal___ two to three years

___phallic___ three to five years

___latency___ six years to puberty

___genital___ puberty to adulthood

phallic

7. The most important conflict in the child's development, according to Freud, occurs during the ___phallic___ stage and is known as the

Oedipal
same-sex

___Oedipal___ conflict. It involves the child's desire for the affection of the opposite-sex parent and rivalry with the (same-sex/opposite-sex) parent.

8. Which of the following aspects of Freudian theory are widely accepted by psychologists today?
   a. Freud's notion that events in the oral phase cause the traits associated with the oral personality.

b

   b. Freud's belief that early childhood experiences have a crucial impact on adult personality.

Learning Objectives

1. What evidence supports the idea that temperament or personality is in part influenced by genetic factors? Similarity between Identical twins

2. What produces fixation, according to Freud? unsolved conflicts at a particular stage of Development

3. Name and describe the five developmental stages in psychoanalytic theory and the approximate ages at which they occur. oral - birth to 1 year   phallic 3 to 5   genital puberty to Adulthood   anal - two to 3   latency 6 to puberty

4. What is the name of the most important conflict occurring in a child's development, according to Freud? Briefly describe the conflict, and indicate in which stage it occurs. Oedipal conflict   It occurs in the phallic stage, when child lusts after parent of opposite sex

The Cognitive-Developmental Perspective

stages

9. Both the Freudian and cognitive-developmental perspectives use the concept of ___stages___ of development. The Freudian system, however, emphasizes conflict between the instincts and the demands of society, while the cogni-

thinking

tive-developmental viewpoint emphasizes ___thinking___, reasoning, and role taking.

Piaget

10. The cognitive-developmental perspective was heavily influenced by Jean ___Piaget___, whose theories are also discussed in Chapter 12.

sensorimotor

11. Under this view, social development in the first stage, the ___sensorimotor___ stage, begins with recognizing people and forming attachments to them. During the preoperational stage, as the child grows and develops a sense of independence, the child develops the capacity for planning and

representational

___representational___ thinking. These skills permit the child to

imitate

___imitate___ the behavior of others.

12. During the concrete-operational period the child becomes capable of

role
_____role_____ *taking*, assuming the perspective of another person.

adolescence
13. Later, during _adolescence_ (at the beginning of the formal-operational

abstract
phase), the child becomes capable of _abstract_ reasoning and begins to question the beliefs and teaching of her or his parents. It is during this

identity
period that an _identity_ crisis may occur.

Learning Objectives

5. List the four major stages in Piaget's developmental system. Next to the name of each stage describe a capacity that
develops during that stage. sensorimotor   concrete-operational
preoperational   formal-operational

6. At about what age or period does an identity crisis tend to occur?
Adolescence

The Behavioral Perspective

14. The development of personality and social behavior may also be explained on the
basis of the principles of learning presented in Chapter 8. Under this view, be-

reinforcement
havior is affected by its consequences—namely, _reinforcement_ and

punishment
punishment.

15. For example, if a child's whining behavior is followed by reinforcement (for ex-

increase
ample, attention from an adult), the behavior will _increase_ in frequency and perhaps become a personality trait.

16. While many social behaviors are acquired through operant conditioning, emotional responses, such as an infant's attachment to his or her caregiver, are

classical
thought to be acquired through _classical_ conditioning based on the
warmth, comfort, and reduction of hunger associated with the caregiver.

17. In addition to acquiring characteristics directly, by experiencing reinforcement
and punishment, children may acquire social behaviors vicariously, through ob-

imitating
serving and _imitating_ a model's behavior. People are particularly

reinforcement
likely to imitate behavior that leads to _reinforcement_ for the model.
Gender role identity is assumed to be acquired, at least in part, through

imitation (modeling)
imitation of the same-sex parent.

Learning Objectives

7. Name the major principles of learning assumed to influence behavior under the behavioral perspective. Give examples of each. *reinforcement punishment, imitation conditioning*

INFANCY

two

18. The term *infancy* is used here to refer to approximately the first _____*two*_____ years of life. The important social and personality

attachment

developments discussed involve the phenomenon of _____*attachment*_____, the emotional bond between infant and caregiver.

Attachment

19. Attachment to the mother derives in part from the fact that she is the source of food, warmth, and comfort. Bowlby also viewed attachment as having

adaptive (survival)

_____*adaptive*_____ significance. It seems reasonable to suppose that during the process of evolution, an infant who formed a strong attachment to an adult

survival

would have a better chance for _____*survival*_____.

20. The parent also forms an attachment to the infant. According to the ethologists, such an attachment may well be a natural response evoked by the baby's

cute

" _____*cute*_____ " appearance.

21. The development of attachment in human infants seems to go through four phases. In the first two or three months of life the child responds to

anyone

(*anyone*/only the mother). In fact, during this phase the child seems to have no special attachment to the mother.

22. During the second phase the baby begins to respond to its

mother

_____*mother*_____ in special ways but does not protest being left with a sitter.

six or seven

23. During the third phase, which begins at about the age of _____*six or seven*_____ months, genuine attachment develops, and the baby attempts to remain close to the mother. During this phase babies also show *separation*

distress

_____*distress*_____, protesting with great intensity when they are parted from their mothers.

24. A month or two later, at seven to nine months, babies also develop *wariness of*

strangers

_____*strangers*_____.

25. Anyone who has witnessed this third phase, occurring sometime between six months and two or three years of age, can attest to its intensity. My daughters (Vanessa and Samantha) certainly showed the behavior, evincing great distrust or

wariness _wariness_ of strangers, which was especially intense when their
absent caregiver was (absent/present).

26. In the fourth stage of attachment, beginning when the child is about two or

three _three_ years of age, attachment becomes more flexible and

separation _separation_ distress vanishes.

27. Only recently have studies examined the attachment between fathers and infants, and the conclusion from these studies is that attachment to fathers is of
about the same (about the same/somewhat less) intensity as it is to mothers.

28. According to studies both in Israeli kibbutzim and American day-care centers, it
nature is the (nature/amount) of the interaction between child and caregiver that is important. Apparently children who spend most of their day away from their parents, in a high-quality care environment, develop normally if they have a supportive relationship at home.

29. To examine the attachment relationship Harlow raised rhesus monkeys in a cage that contained two surrogate mothers, one covered with soft terrycloth and the
cloth other made of wire mesh. Attachment was stronger to the (cloth/wire) mother,
wire even though the (cloth/wire) mother supplied milk for the infant. Evidently com-
more important fortable contact (or softness) is (more important/less important) than is feeding for establishing an attachment relationship.

Learning Objectives

8. Approximately what age range is covered by the period referred to as infancy? _birth to two yrs old_

9. What does it mean to say that an infant's attachment may have "adaptive significance"? _It will help the baby survive in life_

10. Describe the four phases that infants seem to go through in developing attachment. Make special note of the stage and age range in which separation distress and wariness of strangers occur.

11. How does the intensity of attachment of infants for their mothers seem to compare with that for their fathers? _About the same_

12. What effect does separation of a child from its parents in a high-quality day-care environment seem to have on development? _No effect at all_

13. What is the conclusion of the Harlow "surrogate mother" studies with regard to attachment?

Comfortable contact is more important than feeding for establishing an attachment relationship.

Attachment Deprivation

temporary

30. Brief separations of young children from their parents, as when children are admitted to a hospital, will generally have (no/temporary/lasting) effects on the parent-child relationship and the child's later personality.

are not

31. Longer periods of attachment deprivation may produce more profound effects: rhesus monkeys raised in total isolation have exhibited abnormal behaviors similar to those of human schizophrenics. Caution must be used in generalizing these results to human beings, however, since the same behaviors (are also/are not) exhibited in two closely related species of monkey, the crab-eating and pigtailed macaques.

younger

32. In addition, rhesus monkeys do recover from most of the effects of isolation if they are placed in contact with monkeys that are (younger/the same age). The younger monkeys gradually draw the isolates into social interaction and play.

can be

33. With regard to human behavior, infants who have not had the opportunity to form secure attachments are at a clear disadvantage, but evidence from adoption of homeless children from war-torn countries has shown that the experiences of infancy (can be/cannot be) reversed. If a child passes through a series of foster homes, however, never having had the opportunity to form a secure attachment, the child may have difficulty forming deep relationships.

The Beginnings of Social Interaction

34. Although babies show attachment and have dependency needs, they also show the beginnings of autonomy. They are attracted to novel situations and people, and they enjoy playing with other children. However, peer relationships probably do not become a major influence until the children acquire

language

language and can begin to understand their peers' intentions.

Learning Objectives

14. What are the effects of total attachment deprivation in rhesus monkeys? What evidence suggests caution in generalizing this result to other primates, including human beings? _Isolated monkey have developmental problems Similar experiments with other monkeys did not have the same results_

15. What procedure seemed to remedy the behavioral problems of the isolated rhesus monkeys? _Putting them with younger monkeys_

16. What factor seems important in determining whether or not damage results from attachment deprivation in human children? _War-torn children who are adopted_

CHILDHOOD

35. As children grow, the parents' primary role changes from providing nurturance

socialization

to being an agent for _Socialization_, the process by which children begin to absorb society's values and customs.

Acquiring Gender Roles

36. *The Impact of Biology.* While there is no way to assess exactly how biology affects the behavior of boys and girls, some gender role differences may be attributable to biological factors. For example, one study has found that newborn

awake (active)   boys were _awake_ more than newborn girls and showed more general activity. Such differences could underlie some of the observed gender differences in aggressive play behavior.

37. In addition, prenatal exposure of children to male hormones increased the level

aggressive   of _aggressive_ play in both boys and girls.

38. *The Power of Socialization.* Despite possible biological influences, gender roles are clearly influenced by *socialization* in the particular society in which people grow up. For example, your text notes that in Iran women are viewed as the

logical   (emotional/logical) sex.

39. It is easy to understand how environment influences gender role development.

were not   For example, one study observed that toddler girls (were/were not) rewarded for playing with blocks; toddler boys were rewarded for this behavior and, indirectly, for manipulating their environment and behaving independently.

40. While social-learning theory emphasizes rewards, punishments, and modeling, psychoanalytic theory views gender role development as the outcome of the

Oedipal   _Oedipal_ conflict. In successfully resolving the conflict the chil-

identify   dren _identify_ with the same-sex parent.

41. In contrast, the cognitive-developmental perspective asserts that children behave in sex-typed ways not because the behavior resolves the Oedipus complex nor because they are rewarded for it but because they become aware of *gender*

identity   _identity_, the understanding that they are of a particular sex and will remain so.

42. It is very clear, however, that reinforcement, punishment, and observational

gender (sex)   learning are major factors in determining traditional _gender_ roles. Boys who play with dolls are loudly criticized by their peers, for example.

43. With regard to modeling, one recent study found that children who watched tele-

more   vision more than twenty-five hours per week had (more/less) stereotyped views of gender roles than did those who watched fewer than ten hours, an outcome that may be attributable to the more traditional gender roles occurring on television.

Learning Objectives

17. What evidence suggests that there may be genetic differences between males and females that affect gender role behavior? *Boys are more active than girls when they are born*

18. What evidence clearly points to the influence of socialization on gender role behavior? In answering this question provide (a) cross-cultural evidence and (b) evidence from a study with toddlers. *Iranian woman are seen as logical compared with emotional American women. Toddler Girls were not rewarded for playing with blocks*

19. Briefly describe the explanations provided by each of the following theories for gender role behavior:
    a. psychoanalytic theory *- gender role outcome result of Oedipal conflict*
    b. social-learning theory *emphasize rewards punishment and modeling*
    c. cognitive-developmental theory *children behave in sex typed ways because they became aware of gender*

20. Give examples of the way in which punishment and modeling affect gender role behavior. *Children who watch a lot of television had a stereotype of gender roles*

Peer Relationships

peers

44. Peer relationships are important for development because they are between equals; in relationships with adults the power runs one way. It is through interactions with (peers/adults) that children develop independence, social skills, cooperation, and ways to handle aggression.

minimize

45. *Play.* According to Bruner, one of the functions of play is to (minimize/maximize) the consequences of a child's actions. Children can try out adult roles or experiment with new solutions to problems without the risk that may characterize the real world.

preschool

46. Play involving make-believe is particularly evident in (preschool/elementary school) children. Thereafter make-believe becomes internalized in the form of fantasy and dreams.

rules

binding

47. During the school years games involving shared ___rules___ take the place of make-believe. While younger elementary school children view the rules as (flexible/binding), older children understand that rules are arbitrary and can be modified if all agree.

adolescence

48. *Friendship.* In the early school years friends are valued only because they do what the child likes to do. As children mature, friendship becomes more reciprocal until in *adolescence* there exists a sense of shared identity.

e

49. Friends generally resemble one another. For which of the following characteristics is this statement true?
    a. age
    b. sex
    c. race
    d. interests or enjoyments
    e. all of the above

50. *Groups*. Children also socialize one another, valuing such characteristics as physical attractiveness, sociableness, intelligence, and generosity—attributes that

popular

make children ___popular___ with their peers. Children socialize peers in another way by keeping out of the group individuals whose aggressive behavior or verbal abuse tends to disrupt the group.

51. Susceptibility to peer influence increases with age, reaching a peak in perhaps the ninth grade and declining thereafter. While peer pressure can erode the power of parental and social value systems, research indicates that serious conflict be-

mostly illusory

tween the child and adult values is (mostly illusory/general and intense).

Learning Objectives

21. What is the importance of peer relationships and play for child development? play lets children act like
Important because children are then between equals adults but minimizes the real outcome

22. How do the following change across the school years?
   a. Play (the use of make-believe and shared rules) make believe internalized into daydreams in older
   kids. when kids get older they find all rules are not binding if
   b. Friendship (reciprocity) everyone agrees to change them
   grow closer as children get older

23. In what way do children use popularity and the formation of groups to socialize each other?

24. How does susceptibility to peer influence change across the school years? Kids are increasingly susceptible
up to the 9th grade and then it seems to peak.

Prosocial Development

52. Action intended to benefit another person, taken without expectation of external reward and generally involving some cost, is referred to as

prosocial

___prosocial___ behavior, which is roughly synonymous with *altruism*.

very little

53. *Moral Behavior*. Preschool children engage in (very little/a lot of) altruistic behavior and are generally reluctant to share. During the school years children become increasingly more generous, with prosocial behavior leveling off at about

ten

the age of ___ten___ years.

54. If children are reinforced for being generous, their generosity will generally increase. Among eight-year-olds, praise for generous behavior was more apt to

children

generalize to a later situation if the (children/act) had been praised—that is, if the children were told that they had been helpful rather than that the thing they had done was helpful.

ten

55. Among ___ten___-year-olds generosity generalized regardless of the wording of praise, perhaps reflecting more flexibility in interpreting rules of language.

56. *Moral Judgment.* According to psychoanalytic theory, children internalize a parent's moral code at the end of the Oedipal conflict, when they

identify

_____identify_____ with the same-sex parent.

57. Social-learning theorists, on the other hand, stress the effects of reinforcement,

imitation (modeling)

punishment, and _____imitation_____ on the formation of moral behavior.

58. Referring neither to identification nor to consequences of behavior, the

cognitive

_____cognitive_____-developmental theorists stress the thinking or reasoning processes that the child uses. Kohlberg has proposed that the child passes

stages
invariable

through six distinct developmental _____stages_____ of moral judgment. The sequence in which these stages are assumed to occur is (invariable/flexible); each stage is more complex than, and develops out of, its predecessor.

universal

59. In addition, Kohlberg assumes that the stages are _____universal_____, that they characterize moral development in all societies.

three

60. The six stages occur in _____three_____ levels of moral judgment. Hence, each level is composed of two stages. The first level is the

preconventional

_____preconventional_____ level and involves a view of morality in terms of its immediate consequences, the pain or pleasure resulting from the behavior.

conventional

61. The second level, the _____conventional_____ level, emphasizes meeting the standards of others and maintaining the social order.

principled/is not

62. The highest level of moral reasoning, the _____principled_____ stage, (is/is not) reached by most adults. At this stage the individual adheres to

universal

_____universal_____ ethical principles based on the ideas of reciprocity and human equality.

63. Kohlberg's theory has been criticized on several counts, but some interesting research has emerged. For example, among boys, more principled reasoning has been found to occur under child-rearing conditions that (were punitive/

encouraged autonomy

encouraged autonomy). Among girls, on the other hand, both encouragement of autonomy and a high degree of control by the father seemed linked to

principled

_____principled_____ reasoning.

64. For both sexes in the study just described, a nurturing child-rearing environment involving encouragement and warmth was linked to the development of

principled

_____principled_____ reasoning.

65. In support of the notion that reasoning is involved in Kohlberg's stages, it has

cognitive

been found that _cognitive_ development, judged by the child's ability to perform Piagetian logical tasks, is related to the level of moral reasoning.

Learning Objectives

25. What is prosocial and altruistic behavior? How does altruism change across the school years?
Action taken that will suppasedly benefit another person. It increases over the school years.

26. How does reinforcement in the form of praise affect generosity in children? How does the wording of praise affect generalization among eight-year-olds? Among ten-year-olds? — *They'll be generous no matter how you word It increases their generosity* ← *If you praise child he'll it don't again. If you praise the thing he did he won't be generous again*

27. How do children acquire a moral code, according to psychoanalytic theory? According to social-learning theorists?
By the oedipal conflict who they identify with a parent. Social-Learning say we acquire it through punishment, imitation, reinforcement.

28. Name and describe the three levels of moral development proposed by Kohlberg. Discuss research that seems to support Kohlberg's position that the stages form a hierarchy which depends on cognitive development.
Child-Rearing between boys & girls
preconventional, conventional & principled

Control of Aggression

hostile

66. Children and adults show two major forms of aggression: _hostile_

instrumental

aggression, aimed at hurting another person, and _instrumental_ aggression, aimed at acquiring objects, territory, or privileges.

67. For example, a child who knocks another child down to obtain a toy truck would

instrumental

be using primarily _instrumental_ aggression. Very young children use

instrumental

predominantly _instrumental_ aggression.

68. Vanessa has found that a quick kick in the shins will tend to stop Samantha's teasing, at least temporarily. This example illustrates learning through

negative

negative reinforcement, a method according to Patterson that is particularly important in increasing aggressive behavior.

modeling

69. Aggression is also learned through _modeling_ the behavior of siblings, peers, television and film characters, and parents. When a parent spanks a child, the major effect may be that the parent serves as a model of aggressive behavior.

uncertain

70. While the long-term effects of watching televised violence are (uncertain/ very clear), most research to date has found that watching televised violence has tended to increase aggressive behavior at least in the short run.

Learning Objectives

29. Name and illustrate the two types of aggression discussed. Which predominates among very young children? *Instrumental*

hostile a Instrumental

30. Give an example of the ways in which negative reinforcement and modeling increase aggressive behavior.

By hitting someone it stops their behavior you seeing older brothers or sisters fighting are negatively reinforced - learning

31. What does most research on the effects of televised violence seem to indicate, and what is the conclusion about the long-term effects? *— uncertain about longterm effects*

Increase in aggressive behavior in the short run

Adolescence

71. The text distinguishes between adolescence and puberty as follows:

puberty

_____puberty_____ is viewed as the period of *physical* sexual maturation

adolescence

during which the child is transformed into an adult; _adolescence_ involves the *social* development necessary for an individual to be considered a
functioning member of the adult community.

Physical Maturation

72. Puberty involves the development of secondary sex characteristics, such as facial
hair in males and breasts in females. It usually begins between the ages of

ten/twelve

_____ten_____ and twelve for girls and ___twelve___ and
fourteen for boys.

Social Maturity

73. While the child who has passed through puberty has the physical characteristics
of an adult, he or she may not have the social behaviors that characterize adulthood in a particular society. In Western societies, puberty is followed by an ex-

transitional

tended adolescence, a _transitional_ period during which individuals
are not yet considered to be adults.

Establishing an Identity

74. The major developmental task of adolescence is the establishment of independence from one's parents and the development of a separate

identity

_____identity_____.

75. Adolescence is a period of change, an awareness that one is not the same person
he or she has been in the past or will be in the future. This realization may

crisis

produce an identity ___crisis___, which may be resolved by the development of a sense of continuity or sameness between the past and future
person.

greater

76. In attempting to resolve the identity crisis, the adolescent may try out and discard a variety of roles. It is this process that permits (greater/less) flexibility in choice of adult roles than occurs in societies with a short period of adolescence or none at all.

does not

agree

77. It is commonly assumed that adolescence is a stormy period of great conflict. Such turmoil (does/does not) commonly accompany adolescence, however. In addition, the generation gap is probably not as great as has been thought, since research has indicated that parents and adolescents (differ/agree) on most matters.

Learning Objectives

puberty - physical development
Adolescence - social development

32. What distinction does the text draw between adolescence and puberty?

33. At approximately what age does puberty begin for males? For females?
twelve - males   Ten - Females

34. What does the text mean when it points out that in some societies there is no period of adolescence?
Kid go from being a child right into Adulthood ready to take on the world

35. What is the main developmental task that occurs in adolescence? What does the term *identity crisis* mean, and how is this crisis resolved? *Getting Your Identity - when you are not at ease with your present situation. By getting sameness and continuity*

36. In terms of flexibility of choice in selecting adult roles, what is the advantage of societies that have a relatively prolonged period of adolescence? *greater Flexibility in choosing roles*

37. Discuss the text's viewpoint with regard to:
    a. the assumption that adolescence is a period of great turmoil. *- normally it doesn't accompany*
    b. the existence of a generation gap. *adolescence*
    most parents and Kids agree on most matters

ADULT DEVELOPMENT

Changes in Personal Concerns

more

78. People's personal concerns change across the life span. Married men are (more/less) compassionate, for example, than single men, and having children

traditional

seems to make people more *traditional* .

79. When they become parents, women increase in feelings of tenderness and men in feelings of leadership and autonomy. When they become grandparents, women

leadership/autonomy

increase in feelings of *Autonomy* and *leadership* and

tenderness (compassion)

men in feelings of *tenderness* .

80. Neugarten found that the middle-aged show a greater concern with

inner
left to live

inner life, that they become more introspective. They also begin to measure their lives in terms of time (left to live/since birth). As people age they also become aware that death is a real possibility for the self, that life is in fact finite.

Ways of Aging

81. Most people cope with major life transitions, such as retirement or the death of a spouse, without undue stress. These events become traumatic only if they are

unexpected

unexpected. Thus, the death of a child is more stressful than the death of a parent; divorce is more stressful for a younger woman than widowhood at a later age.

unexpected

82. Similarly, an _unexpected_ retirement is more stressful than one that is part of a life's plan. Even the prospect of dying is more stressful for people in unfamiliar surroundings than for those in a familiar, stable environment.

Learning Objectives

38. Describe the changes in people's personal concerns that seem to coincide with marriage, becoming parents, and becoming grandparents. _People become more traditional, caring, leadership & autonomy_

39. Give examples of changes in perspective that accompany middle age. _People have a greater concern with inner life_

40. What factor seems to increase the stress associated with major life transitions? Give some examples.

unexpected happenings like death of a child, early retirement, divorce and death in unfamiliar surroundings.

Chapter Fifteen
Emotions

General Objectives

1. Define the term *emotion,* and list and describe its major sources and major components.

2. Describe the role of some of the more important physiological correlates of emotion, and tell how they are measured.

3. Describe the role of behavioral and cognitive correlates of emotion.

4. Discuss how biology and learning interact in the expression of emotions.

5. Describe the James-Lange theory of emotion, including the evidence both for and against it.

6. Explain the Schachter-Singer theory of emotion and the role of initial cognitive appraisal in emotion.

7. Explain and illustrate how emotions, cognitions, and behavior can interact to influence one another.

8. List the sequence of events that appears to be similar for all emotions, and explain the significance of this sequence.

Emotions

Learning Objectives appear at
the end of each major section.

THE NATURE OF EMOTIONS

1. While it is difficult to formulate a general definition of emotion, all emotions arise from three general sources—biological, sensory, and cognitive. The embarrassment felt when remembering being caught in a foolish act illustrates

    cognitive   the <u>cognitive</u> source; the elation felt following a <u>glass</u> of

    biological   <u>champagne</u> illustrates the <u>biological</u> source; and fear experienced

    sensory   when approached by a large, snarling dog illustrates the <u>sensory</u> source.

2. Some sensory sources of emotion, such as the fear one feels at the sudden loss of support or the chilling effect of very cold water, (do/do not) require previous learning experience. Other sensory sources of emotion, such as a funny joke or an A on a term paper, do require prior knowledge that must develop out of pre-

do not

experience

vious _experience_. Thus some emotions are *unlearned,* while others

learned

are _learned_.

3. All emotions, whether learned or unlearned, have three major components. The first consists of the physiological changes that accompany emotions and is the

arousal

arousal component. The second consists of the behavioral acts

expression

elicited by emotions and is the _expression_ component. The third consists of the subjective feelings that accompany emotions and is the

experience

experience component.

Learning Objectives

1. Name the three general sources of emotions, and give an example of each source. *cognitive / biological / sensory*

2. Give an example of a sensory source of emotion that requires previous learning. Give an example that does not require previous learning.

3. List the three major components of emotions. *arousal / expression / experience*

Physiological Correlates of Emotion: Arousal

4. Strong emotions are usually accompanied by internal physiological changes re-

autonomic

sulting from activation of the _autonomic_ nervous system. This system has some control over most visceral muscles and glands.

5. The autonomic nervous system is composed of two general divisions that usually

opposition (antagonism)

act in _opposition_ to each other. The *sympathetic* division is most

sympathetic

active during emergency or stress situations. Thus, the _sympathetic_ nervous system promotes energy expenditure. The *parasympathetic* division tends to dominate during conditions of relaxation. Thus, this system tends to

conserve

conserve energy.

6. The text cites several examples of the physiological changes that occur when the sympathetic nervous system is activated. Place a check mark in the appropriate column below to indicate whether activation of the sympathetic nervous system results in an increase or decrease of the physiological processes listed.

	INCREASE	DECREASE
increase — heart rate	✓	
decrease — movement of gastrointestinal tract		✓
increase — release of blood sugar by liver	✓	
increase — breathing	✓	
decrease — salivation		✓
increase — visual sensitivity	✓	

7. Once an emergency situation has ended, all of the above physiological changes begin to reverse their direction as the opposing effects of the

parasympathetic   ~~parasympathetic~~ system begin to dominate.

8. *Measuring Physiological Correlations of Emotion: The Polygraph.* A polygraph is simply an instrument that measures the visceral and glandular changes that oc-

emotional   cur during _emotional_ arousal. Thus, while it is frequently referred

emotion   to as a *lie detector,* it is more properly called an _emotion_ detector.

9. When a polygraph is used to detect lies, the examiner is actually measuring the difference in physiological responses to routine questions as compared to *critical* questions. The level of physiological response during the routine questions is

slight   called the *base line*. An innocent subject should show (slight/large) variations in his or her physiological responses to base-line and critical questions.

is not
difficult

10. When used as a "lie detector," the polygraph (is/is not) always dependable. For example, a person who is a habitual liar would be (difficult/easy) to detect, or a guilty person may practice lying in order to better control his or her emotional responses to critical questions. Another problem is that a person can lie during

base line   the routine questions and thus raise the _base line_ so that it is difficult to detect actual lying during the critical questions.

11. Not only is it possible for guilty persons to appear innocent on a lie detector test,

guilty   but it is also possible for innocent persons to appear _guilty_. For example, simply being questioned about certain topics such as rape may cause an

increase   _increase_ in arousal level among innocent male subjects.

12. *Emotion and the Brain*. The autonomic nervous system is actually coordinated by

brain

the ___brain___. In fact, direct electrical stimulation of particular areas of the *hypothalamus* in cats will elicit an emotional response that can be

rage
different

interpreted as ___rage___. Stimulation of other brain areas will elicit (different/the same) emotional responses, even emotions that the animal has never exhibited before.

13. In human beings, stimulation or damage to the *limbic system* has also been ob-

emotional

served to affect ___emotional___ behavior. The limbic system is closely

hypothalamus

connected in function with the ___hypothalamus___, which was shown to be of importance in arousing emotion in cats.

right

14. The cerebral cortex, especially the (right/left) cerebral hemisphere, plays an important role in emotion. The dominance of the right hemisphere is also evident in the facial expressions that accompany emotions. For example, research has shown that the facial expressions of the *left* side of the face are more expressive

right

of emotions than those of the ___right___ side of the face. The left

right

side of the face is controlled by the ___right___ cerebral hemisphere.

Learning Objectives

4. What are the two divisions of the autonomic nervous system? Briefly describe the role of these two divisions.
   *Parasympathetic > They work in opposition of each other increasing
   Sympathetic   or decreasing*
5. List at least five physiological changes that occur when the sympathetic nervous system is activated.
   *Heart beat faster, Blood Sugar rises, breath faster, visual sensitivity greater,
                                                    salivation decreases*
6. Briefly describe how the polygraph is used to detect lies. Be sure to use the term *base line* in this description.
   *During routine questioning a base line is established. When asked critical question their
                        is a change in base line implying your are lying*
7. List two ways by which a guilty person might fool a "lie detector" test. How might an innocent person appear guilty on this test?

8. How were psychologists able to produce rage in cats? What brain structure in human beings has been found to be involved in similar behavior? *Stimulation of hypothalamus
   limbic system connected to hypothalamus.*
9. What evidence supports the idea that the right cerebral hemisphere is more dominant in emotion than the left cerebral hemisphere? *When a person uses facial expression left side of face
   is more impressive*

Behavioral Correlates of Emotion: Expression

angry

15. When people watch a scene from a silent movie in which the villain bares his teeth and clenches his fists, they usually agree that he is (angry/bored). This il-

good

lustrates the point that the behavior that accompanies strong emotions can often be observed, and there is (good/little) agreement among observers as to which emotion is being displayed.

Cognitive Correlates of Emotions: Subjective Experiences

awareness

16. When we speak of the subjective feelings that accompany emotions, we have in

    mind the personal ___awareness___ of the feelings that accompany the
    emotion. Every emotion has this subjective component, although it is not always

observed

    easy to describe, nor can it be ___observed___ by others.

17. Rating scales have been developed to record and measure the subjective feelings
    that accompany emotions, and the results have shown that human beings gener-

similar

    ally have (similar/dissimilar) subjective feelings to a given emotional event.

Learning Objectives

10. What makes it possible for an actress to display an emotion by facial expression alone? ?Strong emotions
    can be observed

11. In what way does the subjective experience of an emotion differ from the overt expression (such as facial expression)
    of an emotion? Can these subjective events be measured? Yes rating scales
    Subjective hard to describe + observe

PERCEIVING AND UNDERSTANDING THE EMOTIONS OF OTHERS

Interpreting Nonverbal Communication of Emotion

18. One aspect of nonverbal emotional communication is the way in which people
    express their emotions by means of facial expressions, gestures, tone of voice,

words

    and so forth, without actually using ___words___. The other aspect
    needed to complete the communication is the correct interpretation of the emo-

person

    tion being expressed by another ___person___. The evidence is clear
    that emotions can be communicated reliably without the use of

words

    ___c words___.

are not

19. Research in laboratories and observation of animals in the wild have shown that
    human beings (are/are not) unique in their ability to express emotions
    nonverbally.

20. For example, one monkey was able to prevent shock to another monkey by
    pushing an "avoidance bar" at the appropriate time. The only cue the monkey
    had to signal the appropriate time was the other monkey's

facial expression

    ___facial expression___ seen on a television screen.

Learning Objectives

12. What is meant by nonverbal communication of emotions? What two essential aspects are necessary for nonverbal communication to occur? *not using words to express emotions. Not using words and another person interpreting your emotion correctly*

13. How was it demonstrated in the laboratory that monkeys could correctly interpret the facial expressions of other monkeys? *Showed a monkey ready to be shocked another monkey aware of his facial expression stoped him from being shocked*

The Role of Biology and Learning

21. Both the expression of emotions and their interpretation by others are apparently

    biological

    based on a combination of learning and ___*biological*___ factors.

22. It has been observed, for example, that people from a wide diversity of cultures exhibit a great deal of similarity in the manner in which they express common

    biological

    emotions. This would suggest the importance of ___*biological*___ factors in the expression of emotions.

23. However, there are also some obvious cultural differences in the way people express their emotions. For example, Chinese people often scratch their ears and cheeks to let others know that they are happy, an expression that would probably be misinterpreted in our culture. This would suggest the importance of

    learning

    ___*learning*___ in the expression and interpretation of emotions.

24. *Biological Universals.* Charles Darwin believed that many of the features of hu-

    inherited

    man emotional expression are ___*inherited*___ and at one time probably had survival value. He suggested as an example of this the fact that human

    teeth

    beings, like other animals, bare their ___*teeth*___ when they become angry. Human beings, like other animals, also usually prefer to take action other than fighting when given a clear signal that a fight is likely to occur, and they are likely to live longer if they do. Thus, baring the teeth perhaps had

    survival

    ___*survival*___ value in that it provided a warning to possible adversaries that a fight was likely to occur unless other actions were taken.

25. Several lines of evidence suggest that Darwin was at least partly correct in his contention that emotional expressions are inherited. Studies of identical and fra-

    identical

    ternal twins have shown that ___*identical*___ twins are more alike in their general emotional dispositions.

26. Goodenough's observation of a ten-year-old blind girl reacting to a variety of situations with recognizable emotional expressions also supports Darwin's con-

inherited (innate)   tention. These expressions must have been primarily _inherited_, since the girl could not have learned them by watching others.

27. Finally, Darwin is supported by comparisons of cross-cultural expressions of emotion, which indicate that many basic emotional expressions (are/are not) recognizable across cultures.

are

28. *Cultural Differences*. When we find cross-cultural differences in the manner in which people express a given emotion, we have evidence for the role of

learning   _learning_ in emotional expression. The earlier example of Chinese people indicating happiness by scratching their ears and cheeks illustrates this point nicely.

29. The situations that elicit emotions, as well as the expressive form they take, also show cross-cultural variations, implying a learning factor. For example, Ugandan adolescents are likely to equate happiness with success in

school (academic subjects)   _school_, whereas American adolescents are likely to equate hap-

social   piness with success in their _social_ lives.

30. Studies of monkeys reared in isolation from other monkeys found that those isolated were significantly retarded in both their ability to display appropriate *facial*

facial   expressions and their ability to respond properly to the _Facial_ expressions of other monkeys.

31. This study indicated that there might be a period in early life that is

critical   _critical_ for the proper development of emotional expressions in
during   monkeys. This critical period is evidently (during/after) the first year of life.

Learning Objectives

14. What are the two major factors in the expression of emotions and their interpretation by others?
Biology and Learning

15. List three lines of evidence that support Darwin's view that many of the features of human emotional expressions are inherited. identical twins   survival value
Blind people

16. Explain why the Chinese expression of happiness supports the role of learning in expressing and interpreting emotions. It is different from how we express hapiness

17. What differences were found between Ugandan and American adolescents in the kinds of situations that elicit certain emotional expressions? To what are these differences attributed?
doing school elicits happiness goodin
success social lives elicits happiness in American kids

To what you have learned cultural or whow you were brought differenceyup

18. What effects have been observed with monkeys who have been reared in isolation from other monkeys? *They can not interact with other monkey – making facial expression*

19. What did the above study on monkeys indicate regarding a critical period for the development of their emotional expressions? *First year of life is a critical period for emotional development*

PERCEIVING AND UNDERSTANDING OUR OWN EMOTIONS

The James-Lange Theory

results from

32. The James-Lange theory of emotion proposed that the experience of an emotion (causes/results from) the bodily changes we experience when confronted with an emotionally arousing situation. According to James, it is our perception of these

emotion

bodily changes that is the ___emotion___; thus each emotion must have its own *unique* pattern of bodily changes.

33. Suppose a friend returns one of your valued books he has borrowed. You observe that the book is now badly mangled and the cover is missing. Your friend explains that his dog played with the book. According to the James-Lange theory (circle the correct answer):

   a. heart rate and blood pressure would increase because you are angry.

b

   b. you become angry because your heart rate and blood pressure increase.

34. Walter Cannon pointed out three major criticisms of the James-Lange theory. First, persons injected with a drug such as adrenaline, which produces visceral

do not

arousal, report that they (do/do not) consciously experience the visceral arousal as an emotional experience. Second, the experience of an emotion usually occurs

before

(before/after) the visceral changes that accompany the emotion. One's elation with the last-second shot that wins the game for Farquhar University is instanta-

after

neous; the visceral responses occur (before/after) the immediate elation.

35. Finally, physiological responses to emotions, especially the more subtle ones, are

similar

too (similar/different) to account for the distinctiveness we can attach to our emotional experiences. Moreover, the general pattern of physiological responses that has been identified for such emotions as anger and fear can vary among individuals and even from situation to situation in the same

individual (person)

___individual___

36. Although bodily changes may not cause emotions as proposed by the James-

does

Lange theory, the absence of these bodily changes (does/does not) affect the manner in which one experiences an emotion. Thus men who had experienced damage to the spinal cord and no longer had a fully operative autonomic nervous system found their experience of anger

changed in quality

(changed in quality/increased in intensity).

37. A hypothesis similar to the James-Lange theory holds that the subjective experience of emotion arises from the feedback from the facial expressions that accompany emotions. This is called the *facial* _feedback_ hypothesis.

feedback

38. According to the facial feedback hypothesis, if one feels angry, it is because one _looks_ angry. While some research evidence supports this hypothesis, other research evidence does not.

looks

Learning Objectives

20. What accounts for the subjective feelings that accompany emotions according to the James-Lange theory?
bodily changes we experience when confronted with emotional situation

21. How did James account for the diversity of human emotions?
each emotion has its own unique pattern of bodily changes

22. List three criticisms of the James-Lange theory of emotion.
People injected with adrenaline did/not experience visceral arousal

23. How does the study of men with damaged spinal cords support the James-Lange theory?
Absence of bodily changes does change emotions you feel →

24. What is the facial feedback hypothesis?
How you look is how you feel

The Schachter-Singer Theory

39. Marañon injected subjects with adrenaline and then asked them to report on the effects. A majority of the subjects reported physical symptoms, but no _emotional_ reaction. Those who did report emotional reactions found them somehow lacking in quality; the emotions were without meaning to the

emotional

subjects. They were what Marañon called "_as_

as

_if_" emotions.

if

40. The few subjects who did report a genuine emotional experience did so by combining the physiological reactions they were experiencing with an emotion-arousing _experience_ they recalled from their own past lives.

experience (situation)

41. Schachter and Singer's experiment on emotion consisted of injecting _adrenaline_, a drug producing visceral arousal, into three groups of subjects. All three groups of subjects were *incorrectly* informed that the injected

adrenaline

drug was a _adrenaline_.

vitamin

42. However, the first group was correctly informed of the actual side effects to be expected. The second group was incorrectly led to expect side effects not usually associated with adrenaline, and the third group was incorrectly informed that there would be no side effects. When confronted with emotion-producing situations designed to elicit euphoria or anger, the

misinformed groups (correctly informed group/misinformed groups) reacted more emotionally.

43. Schachter and Singer assumed that the reason for this difference in emotional arousal was that the group correctly informed of the actual side effects interpreted the visceral arousal they felt in the presence of the emotion-producing sit-

drug uation to be the result of the effects of the (adrenaline) drug.

44. On the other hand, the two groups that were misinformed interpreted the visceral arousal they felt in the presence of the emotion-producing situation to be the re-

situation sult of the _situation_. In other words, they *attributed* their emotional arousal to the situation they were in at the time, while the correctly in-

attributed formed group _attributed_ their arousal to the drug.

45. Thus the Schachter-Singer theory postulates that emotions are composed of

two _two_ factors. One factor is the change in level of arousal or

interpretation activation, and the other factor is the cognitive _interpretation_ given to

have an emotional situation. Other experiments (have/have not) found additional evidence supporting a two-factor theory of emotion.

46. The Schachter-Singer two-factor theory also predicts the large number of different human emotions that William James felt needed to be explained by an adequate theory of emotion. According to the two-factor theory, there could be as many different emotions as there are different emotion-arousing

situations _situation_.

is not 47. The Schachter-Singer theory (is/is not) entirely correct. For example, research on the effects of several of the depressant drugs has shown that these drugs can produce the physiological and behavioral effects of depression, and a person who takes them will actually feel depressed. Thus depression, at least, can be pro-

interpretation duced without the *cognitive* _interpretation_ claimed to be necessary by the Schachter-Singer theory.

The Effect of Cognitive Factors on Arousal and Experience of Emotion

appraisal 48. It has been suggested that both factors in Schachter and Singer's theory may be effects that follow the initial cognitive _appraisal_ of an event.

49. This view is supported by research in which experimental subjects who listened to a "denial" sound track before watching an emotionally arousing film showed (more/less) physiological arousal than subjects not previously exposed to the "denial" sound track. This indicates that cognitive processes not only determine

less

the __interpretation__ we give to an event (pleasant, frightening,

interpretation (label)

and so on) but also determine to a large extent the __level__ of our emotional arousal to that event.

level (intensity)

Learning Objectives

~lacking quality

25. What did Marañon mean by "as if" emotions? How were these "as if" emotions produced in his subjects?
emotions without meanings   'used Adrenaline injections to produce "as if emotion"

26. What are the two components of emotions according to the Schachter-Singer theory?
arousal/activation and interpretation

27. Briefly describe the Schachter and Singer study, and explain the role of "attribution" in the study's conclusion.

28. What evidence involving depressant drugs shows that the Schachter-Singer theory is not entirely correct?

29. In what way might the initial cognitive appraisal given to events be involved in the subjective experience of emotions? What two facets of emotions appear to be influenced by initial cognitive appraisal?

The Effect of Expression on Arousal and Experience

50. It is quite easy for human beings to change a heightened state of tension to a state of calmness and tranquility by intentionally relaxing their muscles. This illustrates the point that overt behavior can (cause/result from) emotional feelings.

cause

51. This same point was also illustrated by the study in which subjects were requested to either move their heads up and down or from side to side as they listened to taped messages on earphones. Although both groups listened to the same messages, it was found that the subjects who (nodded/shook) their heads were more likely to agree with the taped messages when questioned later.

nodded

52. Many aspects of behavior, and especially preferences, are under the control of (rational thinking/emotions). For example, one theory of music appreciation suggests that one's preferences for music are based on *familiarity* with the music. Thus people are most likely to prefer (unfamiliar/familiar) music.

emotions

familiar

53. Research studies have shown that people still prefer familiar things even when they cannot identify them. For instance it was found that smokers preferred their own brand of cigarettes over other brands even though their own brand could not

identified/emotional

be __Identified__. It is obvious that (cognitive/emotional) factors must be responsible for this preference.

54. Thus while some behavior appears to be primarily controlled by emotions, other behavior is primarily controlled by cognition or reasoning. However, the question as to whether emotion or cognition controls behavior is

meaningless   <u>meaningless</u>. The answer is that to a greater or lesser extent, depending on the situation, they both do.

Learning Objectives

30. List two examples to support the point that overt behavior can influence or cause emotions. *People who nodded while listening to recording tended to agree with what was said, later on. By relaxing your muscles you can become tranquil*

31. What point is illustrated by the study in which smokers preferred their own brand of cigarettes even though they could not pick out their brand from among other brands? *emotions, people like familiar things. People prefer familiar things even when they can't be identified*

32. What is apparently a major factor in determining preferences? Is this an emotional or a cognitive factor? *familiarity   emotional*

RELATIONSHIP AMONG THE CORRELATES OF EMOTION

55. All emotions seem to progress through the same sequence of events. These events are listed below. Arrange them in the correct sequential order:

d   Event 1 ___*d*___   a. behavior

b   Event 2 ___*b*___   b. interpretation of stimulus

e   Event 3 ___*e*___   c. goal

a   Event 4 ___*a*___   d. eliciting stimulus

c   Event 5 ___*c*___   e. feeling

E.I.FBG

BIGEF

56. The importance of this sequence of events for human beings, and other animals as well, is that it allows for adaptation to the environment and so for

survival   <u>Survival</u> of both the individual and the species.

Learning Objectives

33. List the sequence of the five events that appears to be similar for all emotions. *eliciting stimulus, Interpretation Feeling Behavior Goal*

34. What is the significance of these five sequential events? *For Adaptation to Environment and Survival*

Chapter Sixteen
Motivation

General Objectives

1. Define the term *motive,* and name and explain the two major components of motivation.

2. Describe how motivation operates to control thirst and water balance, hunger and weight regulation.

3. Describe how needs can exist without specific drives and how these needs can be satisfied.

4. Identify some of the motives without specific primary needs, and describe some of the theories that attempt to explain these motives.

5. Describe achievement motivation, how it is measured, and some of the findings with respect to this motive.

6. Describe some of the research and theories that attempt to account for sex differences in achievement motivation.

7. Explain the theories of cognitive balance, cognitive dissonance, and impression management.

8. Distinguish between intrinsic and extrinsic motivation, including their differential effects on behavior.

9. Explain Maslow's hierarchical conception of human motivation.

Motivation

Learning Objectives appear at
the end of each major section.

little

1. Catching a glimpse of Cragmont as he hurries across campus carrying his prized collection of pressed flowers tells us (little/much) about his reason, or motive, for doing so. We follow him, however, and observe that he sells his prized collection and then hurries to stand in a line of people waiting to buy tickets for an upcoming rock concert. From this *organized* pattern of behavior we can now in-

state

fer the *end* ___State___, or goal, Cragmont wishes to achieve.

2. Thus Cragmont's behavior was organized around the end state of attending a rock concert. The property that organizes behavior and defines its end state is

motive
cannot

called a ___motive___. Motives, and their corresponding process, motivation, (can/~~cannot~~) be directly observed. Motivation can only be inferred after viewing an organized pattern of goal-directed behavior.

3. Theories of motivation attempt to account for the *initiation, direction,* and

persistence

___persistence___ of goal-directed behavior at any given moment. For instance, why are Cragmont's efforts directed toward attending a rock concert rather than a flower show, and what maintains these efforts? It is obvious from

are not

this example that many human motives (are/~~are not~~) directly related to physiological needs, even though many are.

Learning Objectives

1. What is a motive? How do we infer motives or motivation?

2. Theories of motivation generally try to account for what three aspects of behavior?

MOTIVATIONAL BASIS OF BEHAVIOR

4. The psychological concept of motivation holds that motives have

two

___two___ major components. One component consists of internal

drives

motivational factors called ___drives___. The other component

incentives

consists of external motivational stimuli called ___incentives___.

5. Thus if we view a student devouring an inedible meal at the college cafeteria, we

hunger

might infer that the student's inner-drive state is one of ___hunger___ that is being satisfied by a goal or incentive—in this case

food

___food___.

6. However, saying that this student is devouring food because he or she is *hungry* has three serious shortcomings. One is that we are inferring a motive on the basis of observed behavior and then using this inferred motive to explain the be-

circular

havior. This is an example of ___circular___ *reasoning.*

7. A second shortcoming is that explaining behaviors by merely labeling them with

does not

a motive (does/~~does not~~) make clear why the same motive may result in different patterns of behavior. For example, in the illustration of the hungry student, many other students may be equally deprived of food but may choose to go elsewhere after viewing the menu.

8. A final shortcoming is that a simple motivational label does not explain how in-

different (various)

dividuals are able to identify ___different___ drive states within themselves. In other words, how does an individual know he or she is hungry rather
than thirsty?

Learning Objectives

3. What are the two components that are said to comprise motives? *no drive a incentives*

4. What are the three shortcomings in the statement "The woman is eating because she is hungry"? In other words,
   what is wrong with explaining behavior on the basis of inferred motives?

MOTIVATION AS A REGULATORY PROCESS: PRIMARY DRIVES

9. All healthy animals seek to maintain a relatively constant state of internal

homeostasis

physiological equilibrium called ___homeostasic___. A good deal of

motivated

behavior is ___motivated___ by the necessity to restore homeostatic
conditions. For example, when an animal is thirsty, it seeks water.

Thirst and Water Balance

10. Two questions arise when attempting to determine how deviation from homeosta-
    sis produces behavior motivated to restore the homeostatic condition. The first

when

question is: How does an animal know ___when___ an adjustment is
necessary? The second question is: What is the physiological

mechanism

___mechanism___ that regulates this adjustment? The text uses the research
on thirst and water balance to illustrate how researchers pursue answers to these
questions.

11. It has been found that there are three types of stimuli that induce thirst and

salt

drinking in mammals. The first is an increase in the ___salt___ concentration of various bodily fluids. Cells located in the *hypothalamus* monitor the
salt content of the body fluids and signal a thirst condition whenever the salt

high

concentration becomes too (high/low).

12. A second stimulus that has been found to induce thirst is a

decrease

not

decrease in the volume of fluid in the circulatory system. A change in chemical concentration is (also/not) involved here. The detection of a

kidneys

decrease in volume is first sensed by the _Kidneys_, which in turn release a chemical that alters the structure of a substance in the blood. This al-

hypothalamus

tered substance then acts directly on several areas in the _hypothalamus_ to elicit thirst and drinking.

13. The third major stimulus for thirst is produced by an increase in body tempera-

exercise (exertion)

ture or by _exercise_. The mechanism involved here is once again

hypothalamus

the cells in the _hypothalamus_ that detect salt concentration in bodily fluids. Both exercise and increased body temperature result in sweating and thus

increase

an _increase_ in the salt concentration of the fluids remaining in the body.

14. There are several stimuli that serve to stop drinking once bodily needs have been

stomach

satisfied. One of these is distension of the _stomach_. Another is fluid passing through the mouth, which is monitored by a

mouth

"_mouth_-metering" mechanism.

15. If the "mouth-metering" mechanism is circumvented by injecting water directly

will

into the stomach, thus bypassing the mouth, an animal (will/will not) maintain an adequate water balance.

Learning Objectives

5. What is homeostasis? What does homeostasis have to do with motivated behavior? _Internal regulation_

6. List and briefly explain the three types of stimuli that induce thirst and drinking in mammals.
High salt content - decrease in volume of fluid in blood, exercise

7. List and briefly explain the types of stimuli that stop drinking in mammals once bodily needs have been met.
Stomach distension   mouth metering

Hunger and Weight Regulation

16. As with thirst, the brain control centers that regulate hunger and eating are lo-

hypothalamus

cated in the _hypothalamus_. These centers react to substances in the blood that change with food intake and food deprivation.

17. To a large extent, eating behavior is also governed by *external* as well as internal physiological factors. How the food looks, tastes, and smells, the social customs, and the amount of effort required to obtain the food are all examples of these

external

_____external_____ factors.

18. Some research has demonstrated that these external factors appear to play a larger role in the eating behavior of (normal-weight/obese) persons. Persons of normal weight, on the other hand, appear to rely more heavily on

obese

internal

_____internal_____ cues to regulate their food intake.

19. It is important to remember, however, that this difference between obese persons and persons of normal weight (is/is not) a consistent finding. Some people who

is not

obese

are highly sensitive to external cues never become _____obese_____.

20. Moreover, external and internal cues can *interact,* or influence one another. For example, a well-fed chicken was shown to begin eating again after being placed

chicken

near a hungry _____chicken_____ that eats in its presence. A person who once again feels hungry when offered a favorite dessert following a full meal is

interaction

demonstrating a similar _____interaction_____ between internal and external cues.

NOTE: Two general conclusions are becoming widely accepted after years of scientific study in this area. One conclusion is that body weight results primarily from a genetic predisposition; thin people will remain thin and obese people will remain obese unless they are willing to live in continuous discomfort. The second and more cheerful conclusion is that the body weight dictated by current fashion is generally well under the body weight dictated by good health.

Learning Objectives

8. Where are the centers that control thirst and hunger located in the brain? hypothalamus

9. What are some of the external factors (cues) that control eating in human beings?

10. In what way do obese and normal persons differ with respect to internal and external hunger cues? Is this always found to be true?

11. Illustrate how internal and external hunger cues can interact.

Needs without Specific Drives: Learning What to Eat

21. As a general rule, as a biological need becomes greater, the accompanying drive becomes (more/less) intense and the organism becomes (less/more) single-minded in satisfying this need.

more/more

22. This was demonstrated by a study in which volunteer subjects spent six months on a diet restricted to less than half of their normal caloric intake. These subjects soon found that all of their thoughts and conversations revolved around

food (eating)

food .

may not

23. A biological deficit or need (will always/may not) result in a drive to reduce the need. The text cites the example of many early Arctic explorers who died of

C

scurvy because of a severe lack of _vitamin_ _C_ in their diets. Although a rich source of vitamin C was easily available to them in animal fats,

drive

the explorers experienced no _drive_ to obtain this vitamin.

24. The health of the Eskimos who live in Arctic regions without getting scurvy demonstrates that certain healthful eating habits can exist even without an ac-

drive

companying specific _drive_ . The fate of the explorers demon-

learned (previous)

strates that _learned_ eating habits can interfere with the demands of a new feeding situation.

25. A study by Rozin demonstrated how animals—rats in this case—were able to satisfy basic biological needs that are not accompanied by specific drives. When their well-balanced diet was made deficient in some essential vitamins and min-

aversion

erals, the rats quickly developed an _aversion_ to this diet and a corresponding preference for new foods.

26. The rats continued to seek new diets until the deficiency had been corrected and

recovery
would not

then tended to favor the diet associated with their _recovery_ from the deficiency. Moreover, the rats (would/would not) return to the original diet after the deficiency had been corrected.

27. Thus it appears that many animals, including human beings, are able to

learn

learn , often by trial and error, to satisfy biological needs that have no specific drives.

Learning Objectives

12. Use the example of the Arctic explorers and the Eskimos who live in this region to illustrate the following points:
    a. A biological need may not always result in a specific drive to reduce the need.
    b. Healthful eating habits can exist even without specific drives for all the essential ingredients in an adequate diet.
    c. Previously learned eating habits can interfere with the demands of a new feeding situation.

13. How do rats—and presumably other mammals—maintain an adequate diet even though they lack accompanying drives for specific deficiencies? _learn what they need_

Motives without Specific Primary Needs

needs

28. Numerous studies have shown that much animal and human behavior, such as exploring the environment and manipulating objects, appears not to serve any

    specific primary (biological) ___needs___ .

optimal

29. While these "activity" behaviors appear to be intrinsically rewarding, and perhaps have future survival consequences, the internal biological mechanisms that regulate them are not apparent. Some theorists have postulated that these behaviors serve to maintain certain "___optimal___" levels of stimulation and activity.

optimal-

level
moderately

30. Theories stressing this idea, called ___optimal___-
    ___level___ theories, assume that each individual becomes adapted to a specific level of activity and stimulation that is (moderately/extremely) different from the accustomed level. Thus the experienced surfer may look longingly for gigantic waves to ride, while the novice seeks a much gentler variety.

changing

31. As the novice surfer gains experience with the gentler waves, he or she will then try to ride waves of moderately increased magnitude. This illustrates the point that the optimal level is constantly (stable/changing).

positive

positive or negative direction

32. There are some restraints on the limits of optimal-level theories. New and different experiences that are (negative/positive) are most preferred. Moreover, events that are extremely different from expectations are evaluated primarily in terms of their (magnitude/positive or negative direction).

33. An alternative theory to optimal-level theories appears to clarify such phenomena as taste aversion, food cravings, attachment, and addiction. This theory assumes that such behaviors involve two opposing processes and is thus called

opponent-process

    ___opponent___-___process___ theory.

secondary

34. According to opponent-process theory, some acquired motivations arise from the opposition of *primary* and ___secondary___ processes. The initial sudden onset of an emotional reaction elicited by a stimulus is the

primary

    ___primary___ process. An opposite emotional response begins to build

secondary

    slowly after the stimulus onset and is called the ___secondary___ process.

strengthened

35. As contacts with a particular stimulus event continue, say riding on a roller coaster, the primary process remains unaltered, but the secondary process is gradually (weakened/strengthened). Thus while a child is usually frightened out of his or her wits on the first roller-coaster ride, with continuing rides the initial

secondary

    terror is gradually surpassed by exhilaration as the ___secondary___ process continues to increase in strength.

Learning Objectives

14. What do behaviors such as exploring the environment and manipulating objects have in common?

15. How do optimal-level theories explain "activity" behavior?

16. What are some of the limits of optimal-level theories?

17. Explain opponent-process theory, using the example of a child learning to love riding roller coasters.

HUMAN MOTIVATION

Achievement Motivation

36. Using pictures from the Thematic Apperception Test (TAT), McClelland and At-

achievement   kinson devised a technique for assessing ___Achievement___ motivation in people. Essentially, their technique consisted of measuring the frequency and

achievement   quality of ___achievement___-*oriented* themes given in response to selected TAT pictures.

37. *Comparison of People with High and Low Achievement Motivation.* Early studies of achievement motivation revealed that differences between high and low scor-

did   ers on need for achievement as measured by the TAT (did/did not) carry over into other contrived achievement-oriented tasks. Persons who got high scores

harder   tended to work (harder/less) at difficult tasks than persons who got low scores,

expert   for instance. High scorers were also more likely to choose (expert/friendly) work partners than were low scorers.

38. Many laboratory studies have confirmed predictions based on McClelland and Atkinson's model. For example, one study showed that persons with low

extreme   achievement motivation scores tended to stand at (extreme/intermediate) distances when asked to perform in a ring-toss game. This meant that they were either assured of easy success or blameless for failure. Persons with high achievement

intermediate   motivation scores tended to stand at ___intermediate___ distances, where the game was a challenge but not impossible.

have   39. Similar results (have/have not) been found to carry over into real-life situations as well. People who score high in achievement motivation tend to explain their

internal   successes on the basis of (internal/external) factors, such as ability and effort,

effort   and they attribute their failures to a lack of ___effort___.

external

internal
skill

40. Low scorers, on the other hand, have been found to attribute their successes in life to (internal/~~external~~) factors, such as good luck, and attribute their failures to _internal_ factors; but in this case they are likely to blame failures on a lack of (~~skill~~/effort).

achievement

41. *Applications: Managing Achievement Motivation.* McClelland and Winter were able to produce an increase in the entrepreneurial activity of businessmen in India by raising their motivation for _achievement_. This increased entrepreneurial activity led to improved economic conditions, including several thousand new jobs.

motivation

42. Moreover, McClelland and Winter found that their project was much less expensive and time-consuming, and had a longer-lasting effect when compared with a much more grandiose program carried out in the Barpali Village in India. The conclusion to be reached from this comparison is that it takes both knowledge and _motivation_ to change people's behavior.

Learning Objectives

18. How did McClelland and Atkinson measure achievement motivation? With TAT test

19. In what way were people with high achievement motivation scores found to differ from people with low achievement motivation scores in contrived laboratory tasks? In real-life situations?

20. How did McClelland and Winter increase the economic activity of Indian businessmen? What conclusion did they reach when comparing their program with a more grandiose effort to improve life in India?

Sex Differences in Achievement Motivation: The Fear of Success

different

43. Research on achievement motivation has disclosed that men and women are (~~similar~~/different) with respect to achievement motivation. At first the difference between the sexes was attributed to a high level of anxiety that was thought to be constitutionally peculiar to women. However, Eleanor Maccoby suggested that the high anxiety levels constantly found in women in certain situations are not

cultural (social)

the result of biological factors, but are _cultural_ ones. Many cultures consider it unfeminine to be success-oriented.

success

44. This led another researcher, Matina Horner, to suggest that in order to accurately assess the achievement motive in women, it is necessary first to assess their fear of _success_ or their *motive to avoid success.* From Horner's point of view, a woman may not express her motive for achievement because its

conflict (interfere)

expression may _conflict_ with the cultural roles regarding femininity.

women
men

45. In her first experiment, Horner was able to demonstrate that (men/women) are more likely to have a fear of success than are (men/women).

competitive

46. In a second experiment, Horner found that men performed at higher levels under (competitive/noncompetitive) conditions, whereas most women did not.

noncompetitive

competitive

men

47. Moreover, Horner found that a large majority of women who rated *high* on the motive to avoid success performed significantly better under (competitive/noncompetitive) conditions. Most of the women who rated *low* on the motive to avoid success performed significantly better under (competitive/noncompetitive) conditions, and in this respect they behaved more like _men_.

avoid success

48. Although the work of Horner and others suggests that the motive to _avoid success_ is responsible for some of the differences in achievement motivation between men and women, the findings do not apply in all situations. For example, while many women may fear success in intellectual and athletic competition, they do not have this fear when

social

social skills are involved.

females

49. While all psychologists do not agree with Horner's explanation for the gender differences in achievement motivation, a recent study has found that among undergraduate students, (males/females) are more likely to fear success.

Learning Objectives

21. According to Maccoby, why are women more likely to exhibit higher anxiety than men in certain achievement-oriented situations? What was the alternative explanation Maccoby was arguing against?

22. What additional motive did Horner believe had to be assessed in order to accurately measure achievement motivation in women?

23. What do women who score low on the motive to avoid success have in common with men? How do they differ from women who score high on this motive?

24. In what two areas do women most likely fear competition with men? In what area do they not fear competition?

25. Do all psychologists agree with Horner's conclusions? What recent research with college undergraduates supports Horner's conclusions?

Cognitive Consistency

50. By storing information in the form of categories and rules, human beings are able to process new information efficiently. However, a problem may arise when

inconsistent   new information is ___inconsistent___ with any of the previously stored cate-

imbalance   gories. This inconsistency results in a state of *cognitive* ___imbalance___ .

51. Take the case of Ajax, for example. Ajax is fond of Jane, but to his surprise he discovers that Jane is very active in a group favoring environmental protection for crickets, an insect he fears and despises. In this case, Ajax is in a state of

cognitive imbalance   ___cognitive   imbalance___ with respect to his attitude toward Jane.

52. Ajax's state of cognitive imbalance will result in tension and an effort to resolve the imbalance. He has to learn to like Jane a little less or crickets a little more.

motivational (motivating)   In other words, cognitive imbalance has ___motivational___ consequences.

balance   This is the basis of Fritz Heider's theory of *cognitive* ___balance___ : any inconsistent or contradictory information about people or objects creates an imbalance which, in turn, generates motivation to reduce the imbalance and at-

balanced   tain a ___balanced___ view of the world.

Cognitive Dissonance

53. Leon Festinger's theory of *cognitive dissonance* takes an even broader approach to cognitive consistency. It is broader in the sense that it emphasizes the tend-

consistency   ency to maintain cognitive ___consistency___ among all attitudes, thoughts,

dissonance   beliefs, or perceptions. Cognitive inconsistency, or ___dissonance___ , motivates the individual to restore consistency.

54. According to dissonance theory, for example, people seek consistency between their attitudes and their behavior. Thus if a politician publicly says things he does not privately believe, he is likely to increase his belief in his public state-

saying   ments merely because he is ___saying___ them. By increasing his be-

dissonance   lief he is reducing the ___dissonance___ between what he really believes and what he is saying.

55. In addition, if we make a choice between two attractive alternatives, we may tend to *change our attitudes* toward each alternative to make them consistent with our choice (our behavior). Suppose, for example, that in attempting to decide between the purchase of a Rolls Royce or a Mercedes, Mary lists the positive and negative features of each (prestige, cost, comfort, and so on). While the alternatives may appear equally attractive *before* her decision, *after* she decides to buy the Mercedes she will tend to emphasize the (negative/positive) attributes of the Mercedes and the (negative/positive) attributes of the Rolls Royce.

positive
negative

56. Furthermore, in some situations people tend to value more highly (have more favorable attitudes toward) those behaviors that produce less payoff. For example, in the Festinger and Carlsmith experiment described in your text, the group that said they liked the "boring" experiment more was the (twenty-dollar group/one-dollar group).

one-dollar group

57. In this study, subjects were paid either twenty dollars or one dollar for telling other subjects in a waiting room that the boring experiment was interesting. According to the interpretation of the researchers, what the subjects said (their behavior) was inconsistent with what they believed, so all subjects would potentially experience dissonance. However, payment of twenty dollars (reduced/increased) this dissonance, while payment of one dollar did not. Thus, the one-dollar group experienced (more/less) dissonance and underwent (more/less) attitude change toward evaluating the experiment in a positive way.

reduced
more
more

58. An alternative explanation for the above study is that the subjects were not, in fact, bothered by the dissonance. Rather they did not want to *appear*

inconsistent
more

inconsitent. The subjects who were paid only one dollar had a (more/less) difficult task trying to appear consistent than did the subjects who were paid twenty dollars. They had to explain why someone would do such a stupid and boring task for only one dollar.

59. This alternative explanation—that people can tolerate cognitive inconsistency but attempt to impress others that they are not inconsistent—is called

impression

impression *management*.

60. Impression management theory maintains that people can live quite comfortably with cognitive dissonance or inconsistency. However, they cannot live comfortably if they appear to others to be inconsistent and thus will resort to

impression management

impression management.

Learning Objectives

26. According to Fritz Heider's theory of cognitive balance, how does imbalance arise? What are the motivational consequences of imbalance?

27. According to Leon Festinger's theory of cognitive dissonance, why is a politician likely to begin believing his or her own public statements even though initially they were only made for political purposes?

28. According to cognitive dissonance theory, why were the subjects in the one-dollar group more convinced that the experiment was interesting than the subjects in the twenty-dollar group? What alternative explanation is offered by impression management theory?

Intrinsic and Extrinsic Motivation

61. It is possible to divide motivations into two broad classes. Behavior that is undertaken because of some identifiable external reward can be considered to be

extrinsically　_extrinsically_ motivated, while behavior that is undertaken to satisfy personal preferences or long-term goals can be considered to be

intrinsically　_intrinsically_ motivated.

62. As an example of this distinction, a woman who is pulling weeds in a flower garden because she is being paid five dollars can be said to be

extrinsically　_extrinsically_ motivated, while a woman who is pulling weeds because

intrinsically　she enjoys caring for flowers can be said to be _intrinsically_ motivated.

63. Using this same example, one would expect that the most persistent weed-pulling

intrinsically　behavior over time would occur with the _intrinsically_ motivated woman. The woman pulling weeds for extrinsic motivation would cease working when payment stopped.

64. Most daily behavior results from a mixture of both kinds of motivations. Attending college because of a genuine interest in learning would be an example of

intrinsic　_intrinsic_ motivation, while studying late into the night to earn a

extrinsic　good grade on an exam would be an example of _extrinsic_ motivation.

65. There is some evidence that providing additional extrinsic reinforcement for performing a task that is currently intrinsically rewarding may result in weakening

intrinsic　the _intrinsic_ motivation for the task. Thus the person who enjoys
less　weeding a flower garden may find it (less/more) enjoyable after being paid to do it.

mild　66. A more consistent finding is that (mild/severe) punishment can alter the intrinsic motivation inherent in an object or activity. For example, it has been found that when young children are simply requested not to play with a particular toy, they
less　later find the toy (less/more) desirable than children who have been threatened with severe punishment for playing with the toy.

67. The assumed explanation here is that the children who were simply requested not to play with the toy experience some *dissonance*. They have a less valid reason for not playing with the toy than the severely threatened children and thus re-

dissonance

solve their ___dissonance___ by lowering their opinion of the toy.

Learning Objectives

29. Distinguish between intrinsic and extrinsic motivation, giving an example of each. Which form of motivation is more persistent or long-lasting?

30. Describe why mild punishment is more likely to decrease intrinsic attraction to an object or activity than severe punishment.

A Hierarchical Conception of Human Motives

68. Maslow's conceptualization of human motives is an attempt to organize all human needs, both physiologically and cognitively determined, into a three-step

hierarchy/fundamental

___hierarchy___. The hierarchy consists of ___fundamental___ needs

psychological

that are related to physiological deficits; intermediate ___psychological___ needs that are related to security, social acceptance, and self-esteem; and

metaneeds

___metaneeds___ that are related to creativity, justice, and self-actualization.

69. Maslow classifies both the fundamental needs and the intermediate needs as

deficiency

basic, or ___deficiency___, needs. In Maslow's scheme, the fundamental

intermediate

needs must be satisfied before the ___intermediate___ needs can be realized. In turn, both the fundamental needs and the intermediate needs (the deficiency

metaneeds

needs) must be satisfied before the ___metaneeds___ can be met. In other words, the metaneeds, leading to creativity and self-actualization, can only be

deficiency

realized after the ___deficiency___ needs are satisfied.

Learning Objectives

31. List the three groups in Maslow's hierarchy of needs, and briefly describe the kinds of needs found in each of these three major groups.   Fundamental, psychological metaneeds

32. According to Maslow, what are basic, or "deficiency," needs? In what way are they important to metaneeds?

Chapter Seventeen
Human Sexuality

General Objectives

1. Explain what is meant by gender, and describe the sequence of genetic and biological factors that initially influences gender.

2. Distinguish between gender identity and gender roles, and explain the function of biological and environmental factors in their formation.

3. Describe the four methods used to study human sexual behavior, and discuss the problems associated with each of these methods.

4. List and describe the four phases that Masters and Johnson have found to characterize the human sexual response.

5. Describe the similarities and differences in the male and female sexual response.

6. Discuss some of the more important stimuli that produce sexual arousal in human beings.

7. Describe how the sexual response is affected by aging.

8. List and define the most common sexual dysfunctions in men and women.

9. Name and define the various forms that human sexual behavior may take.

10. Describe the changing attitudes toward sexual behavior in the United States.

Human Sexuality

Learning Objectives appear at
the end of each major section.

INFLUENCES ON GENDER

a composite of

1. Gender refers to the maleness or femaleness of an individual. Gender is determined by (biological/a composite of) factors.

Genetic and Hormonal Influences

conception

2. Genetic sex is determined at the moment of _conception_. The eggs

X

produced by women always contain an _X_ chromosome; the

Y

sperm produced by men may contain either an X or a _Y_ chromosome.

3. If fertilization results in the uniting of two X chromosomes, the child will be a

female

female. If an X chromosome and a Y chromosome are united,

male

the child will be a _male_.

4. The sex organs of both males and females arise from the same embryonic struc-

gonad

ture, called the _gonads_, which performs identically in both sexes for the first six weeks following conception.

5. At this point in time if the gonad begins to secrete *androgens,* then the embryo

male

will become a _male_ and the gonad will begin to develop into

testes

testes. The presence of androgens not only leads to the development of testes, but also causes a male pattern to develop in the

hypothalamus

hypothalamus. The male pattern in the hypothalamus brings about a continuous production of androgens.

6. If androgens are not produced by the gonad, then the embryo will develop into a

female/ovaries

female. The gonad will develop into _ovaries_

hypothalamus

and the female pattern will develop in the _hypothalamus_. The female pattern in the hypothalamus leads to the cyclical hormone pattern that maintains the female reproductive system.

can still

7. An embryo (can still/cannot) develop if it receives only a single X chromosome. The fetus will develop into an anatomical female, but without ovaries and sec-

Turner's

ondary sex characteristics. This condition is known as _Turner's_ *syndrome.*

cannot

8. An embryo (can still/cannot) develop if it receives only a single Y chromosome. The X chromosome apparently carries information vital for development.

9. A genetically male fetus (XY chromosomes) may fail to respond to androgens, a

androgen

condition known as _Androgen_ *insensitivity syndrome*. Although ge-

female

netically a male, the child will have _Female_ anatomy at birth and
be reared as a female. Biologically, both the male and female patterns of devel-

female

opment appear to evolve from a _female_ pattern of development.

Learning Objectives

1. What is the meaning of the term *gender?* What determines gender? biological/environmental factors

2. What chromosome is always found in the eggs of a female? What two chromosomes are found in the sperm of a male? X,Y   X

3. What combination of chromosomes produces a female child? What combination produces a male child? X Y
XX

4. Describe the developmental sequence that leads to a male fetus and to a female fetus.

5. What is Turner's syndrome? One X chr,

6. What is the androgen insensitivity syndrome? Genetic male but anatomical female

7. What happens to an embryo with only a single Y chromosome? Doesn't survive

8. What appears to be the basic pattern of development from which both males and females evolve? female pattern

Social Influences: Gender Identity and Gender Roles

10. Gender identity refers to the sex one identifies with, while gender role refers to
the differences in behavior society expects of males and females. In our society,
for example, it is expected that little boys will be more adventurous and aggressive than little girls. Boys and girls are ascribed different gender

roles

roles.

11. While genetic influence on gender identity begins at the moment of conception,
social influences on gender identity begin at the moment of

birth

birth. By the age of three or four years, most children think
of themselves as either boys or girls. In other words, they have developed a

identity

strong *gender* _identity_.

12. Children raised in gender roles that are incompatible with their biological sex

do not

(do/do not) always adjust to their altered gender role. For example, the infant
boy whose anatomical sex was changed to female following the mutilation of his

masculine

genitals began to exhibit (masculine/feminine) behavior patterns around thirteen
years of age.

female

13. However, nine out of ten genetic boys who were raised as girls because they had androgen insensitivity syndrome later developed stable _Female_ gender identities.

masculine

14. Physiological factors, particularly prenatal hormones, may also influence the development of gender role and gender identity. A study of female children who were exposed before birth to unusually high levels of androgens in the uterine environment found that they displayed more (masculine/feminine) behavior than is typical of girls their age. Nonetheless, the girls in the study who had reached adolescence were found to express romantic interests similar to those of

girls

(boys/girls).

transsexuals

15. Persons who at an early age develop a gender identity opposite to their biological sexual identity are called _Transsexuals_. Transsexuals differ from homosexuals in that the latters' gender identity matches their biological sexual identity. For example, a male homosexual thinks of himself as a

male

male, while a male transsexual thinks of himself as a

female

female.

did not

16. Surgical intervention has been used to change the sexual anatomy to the preferred sex. However, transsexuals receiving this form of treatment (did/did not) always adjust well to this change. A major problem here is that the cause or causes of transsexualism remain to be identified.

Learning Objectives

9. What is meant by gender identity and gender role? *sex you identify with* *role you take on after learning*

10. At what point do social factors begin to influence gender identity? *birth*

11. What was observed in the study of the boy who was surgically changed to a girl because of mutilated genitals?

12. What was observed in the study of female children who had been exposed to high levels of androgen in the uterine environment?

13. What was observed in the study of ten genetic boys who were reared as girls because of androgen insensitivity syndrome?

14. What are transsexuals? How do they differ from homosexuals?

METHODS OF STUDYING SEXUAL BEHAVIOR

Cross-Cultural Studies

17. Cross-cultural studies of sexual behavior have shown that what may be considered to be abnormal sexual behavior in one culture may be considered

normal
few

normal sexual behavior in another culture. In other words, there are (few/many) sexual practices that are considered to be abnormal by all cultures.

normal
should

18. For example, one study observed that the Mangaian people believe that masturbation among children is (normal/abnormal) and that unmarried adolescents (should/should not) engage in sexual relationships in order to prepare themselves for later marriage.

different

19. The pattern of sexual behavior observed among the inhabitants of Inis Beag, a small island near Ireland, was dramatically (similar/different) from the sexual behavior found among the Mangaians, however.

20. One end result of the sexually restrictive culture found on Inis Beag was that

orgasm

almost all of the women failed to experience _orgasms_ during sexual activity. Orgasm was almost universal among the Mangaian women.

21. Another point revealed by cross-cultural studies is that every society imposes

restrictions (rules)

some _restrictions_ on sexual behavior. No culture permits complete sexual freedom.

Learning Objectives

15. What general point is illustrated by the difference in sexual practices among the Mangaian people as compared to the people of Inis Beag?

16. What other general point can be drawn from cross-cultural studies of sexual behavior?

Surveys

22. The first major survey of the sexual practices of American men and women was

Kinsey

conducted by Alfred _Kinsey_. Kinsey collected information

interviews

through detailed, confidential _interviews_ with men and women, concentrating primarily on their sources of sexual outlets.

volunteers

23. There are two principal criticisms leveled at Kinsey's studies. First, the subjects were (volunteers/randomly selected). Critics point out that the sexual behavior of persons who volunteer may be different from that of a randomly selected sample of subjects.

segments (portions)

24. The second criticism is that major ___segments___ of the population were not represented, particularly black, rural, and poorly educated Americans.

25. Therefore, the Kinsey studies should be interpreted as a compilation of data on what white, middle-class, educated persons (say they do/actually do) with respect to sexual behavior. Nonetheless, the Kinsey studies represented the most comprehensive attempt, until the mid-1960s, to study the sexual practices of American men and women.

say they do

popular

26. Many of the surveys on sexual behavior that have been conducted following the Kinsey surveys, such as *The Hite Report*, have been for the purpose of (popular/scientific) interest. As such, they have many flaws and do not necessarily reflect the actual sexual behavior of the population.

Learning Objectives

17. Who conducted the first major survey of the sexual practices of American men and women? How did he collect the survey information? *Kinsey* *confidential interviews* *not prop*

18. What are the two principal criticisms leveled at Kinsey's studies? What is perhaps the most appropriate way to interpret these studies? *Improper rep. of population, volunteers: compilation of data on white—middle class American*

19. On what basis are surveys such as *The Hite Report* subject to criticism? *Done for popular interest*

Observational Studies

27. A long-term study employing direct observation (filming, making physiological measurements, and so on) of persons engaged in various sexual practices was

Masters/Johnson

conducted by ___Masters___ and ___Johnson___.

28. Criticisms similar to those leveled at the Kinsey studies have been raised with respect to the work of Masters and Johnson. For example, their subjects were

volunteers

also ___volunteers___, who may not have been representative of the general population. Also, sexual behavior taking place in a laboratory in the pres-

different

ence of observers may be ___different___ from sexual behavior conducted in private.

Controlled Experimentation

more

29. Julia Heiman performed a controlled experimental study to test Kinsey's hypothesis that men are (less/more) aroused by psychosexual stimuli (nude pictures, erotic language, and so forth) than are women.

equally

30. Heiman found that men and women were ((equally)/differentially) aroused by listening to erotic material on a tape recorder. Heiman also found that sexual arousal from listening to romantic material without any reference to sexual con-

both men and women

tact resulted in little sexual arousal among (men/women/(both men and women)).

contradicts

This finding ((contradicts)/supports) the cultural stereotype that women are more aroused by romantic love than by nonemotional sex.

31. Of the four methods used to study human sexual behavior described by the text (cross-cultural studies, surveys, observational studies, and controlled experimen-

controlled-experimentation

tation), only the _Controlled_ _experimentation_ method allows for testing and discarding of hypotheses. The first three methods are primarily

descriptive

descriptive in nature.

Learning Objectives

20. How did Masters and Johnson study human sexual behavior? What are two major criticisms of their work?
    observations of people   *used volunteers* *not done in normal enviornment*

21. Explain what Julia Heiman's controlled experimental study showed with respect to the following:
    a. Kinsey's hypothesis that men are more aroused by psychosexual stimuli than are women. *False*
    b. the cultural stereotype that women are more sexually aroused by romantic love than by nonemotional sex. *False*
    c. the similarity of sexual arousal in men and women to erotic material. *True*

22. List the four methods used to study human sexual behavior that were described in this unit of the text. Which method, or methods, allow(s) for checking and discarding hypotheses?
    -controlled experiment

THE HUMAN SEXUAL RESPONSE

The Physiology of Arousal and Orgasm

32. The sexual response of both men and women can be divided into

four

four phases, according to Masters and Johnson. The first

excitement

phase, called the _excitement_ phase, is characterized by an increase in respiration and heartbeat rates and an increase of blood flow to the genitals,

penis

causing an erection of the _penis_ in men and a swelling of the

clitoris

clitoris in women.

plateau

33. The second phase is called the _plateau_ phase and is primarily characterized by the completion of the physiological readiness of the sex organs for intercourse.

orgasmic (orgasm)

34. The third phase is called the ___Orgasmic___ phase and is primarily characterized by strong, rhythmic muscular contractions, which most people find intensely pleasurable. In men, the orgasmic phase is also characterized by

ejaculation
does

___ejaculation___. It has been recently observed that a similar form of ejaculation ((does)/does not) occur in some women.

resolution

35. The fourth and final phase is called the ___resolution___ phase. It is dur-

normal (preexcitement)

ing this phase that the body gradually returns to its ___normal___ physiological state.

similar

36. Masters and Johnson found that the physiological responses during these four stages are ((similar)/different) for masturbation and intercourse. If anything, the

masturbation

orgasms produced during ___masturbation___ are more intense, perhaps because of the more precise control the person has over this form of sexual stimulation.

37. Although men and women experience the same general subjective emotional experience during orgasm, there are two physiological differences between the

men

sexes. One is that it is primarily only ___men___ who experience ejaculation. The other is that multiple orgasms within a short period of time are

women

found only among ___women___. Men, on the other hand, experience

refractory

a ___refractory___ *period* in which no further orgasms are possible for several minutes or even hours or days.

Learning Objectives

23. List the four phases that Masters and Johnson have found to characterize the human sexual response. Include the general features that are representative of each phase. Excitement, Plateau, orgasmic, & Resolution

24. What did Masters and Johnson find with respect to physiological arousal through masturbation as compared with arousal through intercourse? approx same physiological arousal happens - Not much difference very good feelings

25. How do men and women differ, if at all, in their general emotional response to orgasm? How do they differ in their physiological responses to orgasm? - Men can not have multiple orgasms - women can have one after another

26. What has been a recent finding with respect to ejaculation in women? + some women appear to ejaculate

Stimulation and Arousal

the same as

38. The physiological responses that occur in response to erotic material, books, films, and so on are (different from/(the same as)) those that occur in the initial stages of intercourse. However, it is important to note that the particular stimuli

different

that are most sexually arousing are (similar/(different)) across individuals.

39. While both men and women are sexually aroused by many varieties of tactile, visual, and auditory stimuli, research has not yet found a consistent arousal effect from _olfactory_ stimulation.

olfactory

40. Perhaps the most powerful stimuli of all for inducing sexual arousal are an individual's own _fantasies_. One study of suburban housewives found that a majority of them used fantasies during intercourse to increase their enjoyment.

fantasies

Learning Objectives

27. How does the arousal that occurs in response to erotic material compare to the arousal produced by the initial stages of intercourse? _It appears to be the same: material produces same initial arousal_

28. What is important to note about the particular stimuli that are most sexually arousing to individuals? What about olfactory stimuli? _stimuli affects different people in different ways. Research has not proven olfactory stimuli as valid yet._

29. What is perhaps the most powerful stimulus with respect to sexual arousal? What did a study of suburban housewives find regarding this form of sexual stimulation? _Fantasies - It increased there enjoyment of sex_

Sexual Responsiveness and Aging

41. A study of college students found that they were most likely to (underestimate/overestimate) the frequency of sexual intercourse by their parents. The general cultural stereotype is that sexual behavior is very infrequent among older persons.

underestimate

42. Kinsey's studies revealed that sexual behavior is much (more/less) frequent among persons over sixty-five than commonly believed. The average reported frequency of sexual intercourse for men over sixty-five was about

more

four times a month. More than 25 percent of the men in this age group reported that they regularly practiced masturbation.

four

43. It is clear, then, that sexual interests and behavior do not suddenly cease at any given age. Rather, people continue to maintain relatively active sex lives into old age. The most sexually active people in old age are those who were (least/most) active in their younger lives.

most

44. There (are/are not) physiological changes that occur with aging that may serve to inhibit sexual behavior. For example, vaginal lubrication and erectile vigor diminish. However, older persons who do continue to enjoy sexual intercourse find that it lasts for a (shorter/longer) period of time.

are

longer

Learning Objectives

30. In what way does the cultural stereotype differ from research evidence (the Kinsey studies) with respect to the sexual practices of older persons? *The stereotype is that old people are sexually inactive but kinsey four old people are very sexually active*

31. What physiological changes occur in men and women with advancing age that may serve to inhibit sexual behavior? What advantage accrues to older persons who continue to engage in sexual intercourse? *Physiological problems vaginal lub. & erectile failure*
sexual intercourse lasts longer.

32. Who are the most sexually active older people? *- The ones who were sexually active when they were younger*

Sexual Problems and Therapy

45. The inability to engage in a preferred sexual relation or to achieve orgasm is

dysfunction   called a *sexual* ___dysfunction___ . Sexual dysfunction refers only to prob-

response   lems involving an inadequate sexual ___response___ and not to problems
of sexual preferences or "sexual deviancies."

46. *Sexual Dysfunction in Men and Women.* As used by the general public, the terms
incorrectly   *impotence* and *frigidity* (correctly/incorrectly) suggest that the sexual dysfunctions
being described are permanent. These terms are also grossly imprecise.

47. The text describes several sexual dysfunctions commonly found among men.
Identify them from the descriptions given below.
    a. The complete absence of the ability to achieve and maintain an erection is

primary   called ___primary___ *erectile failure.*
    b. The inability to achieve and maintain an erection in some or all desired situ-

secondary   ations is called ___secondary___ *erectile failure.*
    c. The inability to contain orgasm (ejaculation) for an appropriate period of

premature ejaculation time is called ___premature___ ___ejaculation___.
    d. The inability to achieve orgasm (ejaculation) with a partner is called

inhibited ejaculation ___inhibited___ ___ejaculation___.

primary   48. All of these sexual problems, with the exception of ___primary___ erectile failure, are found among virtually all men at one time or another and represent normal variability in an individual's sex life. Not until they become persistent or greatly upsetting to the individual are they considered to be truly

dysfunctional   ___dysfunctional___

49. The text describes several sexual dysfunctions commonly found among women.
Identify them from the descriptions given below.
    a. Involuntary muscle contractions making vaginal penetration difficult is called

vaginismus   ___vaginismus___.

b. The inability to experience an orgasm by any means is called

primary orgasmic dysfunction   primary orgasmic dysfunction.

c. The inability to experience an orgasm with a desired partner is called

secondary orgasmic dysfunction   secondary orgasmic dysfunction.

secondary   50. The most common of these problems among women is secondary orgasmic dysfunction. It is not considered to be a true dysfunction until it becomes persistent or particularly upsetting to the woman. Most women

will   (will/will not) encounter situations in which they occasionally experience secondary orgasmic dysfunction during their sexual lives.

51. While it is not entirely clear why some people respond more freely to sexual stimulation than others, the work of Masters and Johnson shows that this differ-

physiological   ence in responsiveness is rarely related to physiological factors.

52. The inability to freely enjoy sexual behavior, including adequate sexual function-

psychological   ing, seems to revolve primarily around psychological factors. Rigid religious upbringing, fears about performance, and an early experience of sexual abuse are among the many psychological factors that are related to sexual dysfunctions.

53. However, in some cases physiological factors are responsible for certain forms of sexual dysfunctions. Erectile failure in males, for example, may be a result of hormonal deficiencies, medications, or diabetes. One finding in this area is that

do not   men whose erectile failure results from physiological factors (do/do not) experience erections during REM sleep. Men whose erectile failure results from non-

do   physiological factors (do/do not) experience erections during REM sleep.

54. *Sex Therapy*. While there are many distinct approaches to sex therapy, all of the approaches are based on seven basic principles. They are as follows:

a. Sexual dysfunction is a mutual problem between two partners, and therapy

both   focuses on (one/both) partners rather than on the dysfunctional individual.

b. Sexual dysfunction is usually accompanied by misinformation about sex.

education   Therefore, education about sexual anatomy and techniques is an important part of therapy.

changed   c. Negative attitudes regarding sex must be changed.

anxiety (fear)   d. It is necessary to reduce anxiety about sexual performance.

communication   e. Pleasurable sex requires communication and *feedback* between the participating partners.

relationship   f. Sex takes place in the context of the couple's entire relationship.

behavior   g. Changes in actual sexual behavior must be prescribed and practiced.

55. Sex therapy has frequently proven successful. It is intensive, but it is also

brief   _brief_____, usually lasting from ten to fifteen sessions.

Learning Objectives

33. Explain what is meant by each of the following sexual problems found in men:
    primary erectile failure – *can never become erect - penis*
    secondary erectile failure – *inability to have an erection in some or all desired situations*
    premature ejaculation – *ejaculation before appropriate time or before you want to*
    inhibited ejaculation – *inability to ejaculate*

34. Of the four sexual problems listed above, which one *is not* commonly found among men? When does the presence of the other three problems indicate that a serious dysfunction might exist? *Primary when they happen often*

35. Explain what is meant by each of the following sexual problems in women:
    primary orgasmic dysfunction – *inability to have orgasm*
    secondary orgasmic dysfunction *inability to have orgasm at certain time or with partner*
    vaginismus *involuntary muscle contractions making penetration into vagina very difficult*

36. What is the most common sexual problem in women? At what point does the presence of this problem represent a serious dysfunction? *secondary orgasmic dys. when it starts happening often enough that it affects the person*

37. Psychological, rather than physiological, factors are generally responsible for sexual dysfunctions. List three of these psychological factors. *Religious upbringing, sexual abuse early, fears about performance*

38. In what way do men whose erectile failure results from physiological factors differ from men whose erectile failure results from psychological factors? *In REM sleep men with physio problems don't achieve erections, I REM sleep men with psycho. problems do.*

39. List the seven principles upon which all sex therapy is based. *education, behavior, both partner, changed, anxiety communication relationship involved*

SEXUAL BEHAVIOR

56. Human beings engage in such a wide variety of different sexual practices that it is very difficult to draw a sharp distinction between "variations" and

deviations   " _deviations_ ."

Celibacy

57. Refraining from sexual activity with other persons is referred to as

celibacy
few   _Celibacy_____. While many persons experience temporary celibacy, (few/many) choose it as a permanent life style. Little is known about the effects of celibacy after having been accustomed to a regular sex life.

Masturbation

acceptable/young

58. Surveys have found that a majority of both young and old adults consider masturbation to be (wrong/(acceptable)). However, ((young)/older) adults report the highest percentage of acceptance of this practice.

increase

59. When compared with the data from the Kinsey studies conducted in 1948 and 1953, the Hunt survey conducted in 1974 showed an ((increase)/decrease) in frequency of masturbation among both young men and young women. This increase

women

in frequency was especially marked in young ___women___. In comparing these two studies, it was also found that boys and girls are beginning this

earlier

practice ((earlier)/later).

encourage

60. Some sex therapists ((encourage)/discourage) the practice of masturbation. These therapists have proposed that this is an important part of self-discovery.

Learning Objectives

40. Why is it difficult to draw a sharp distinction between sexual "variations" and sexual "deviations"? *Because people engage in such a wide variety of sexual practices*

41. What is celibacy? What are the long-term effects of celibacy? *Abistenance from sexual intercourse — No one knows the long term effects*

42. How do we know that masturbation is an accepted practice among the American people? What age group is most accepting of this practice? *Because of Kinsey and Hunts research — Young adults*

43. What differences can be noted in masturbation practices when comparing the Kinsey studies with the later Hunt study? *Increase in no. of women who practice mastur. from time of Kinsey report*

44. How do some sex therapists regard the practice of masturbation? *They say it is important in self-discovery*

Heterosexuality

heterosexual

61. The most common sexual activity revolves around ___heterosexual___ practices. Sexual relations between a man and a woman involve many different methods of stimulation and many different positions for sexual intercourse. What

individual (personal)

is proper depends entirely on ___individual___ taste; there are no "proper" and "correct" heterosexual practices.

had

62. *Premarital Sex.* Kinsey's studies found that a clear majority of men ((had)/had not) experienced premarital sexual intercourse. This was true for all educational levels. The incidence of premarital intercourse among women was

lower

found to be (higher/(lower)) than that among men.

slightly/dramatically

63. The more recent survey by Hunt found that premarital sex has increased ((slightly)/dramatically) for men and (slightly/(dramatically)) for women. This does not necessarily reflect a more casual attitude about sex among

women

___women___, since a majority of them tend to restrict their premarital sex to a single partner.

64. The Hunt survey also found that the "double standard" still appears to exist for the two sexes. The majority of both men and women agree that

men

_____men_____ should be permitted more sexual freedom. It was also

men

found that _____men_____ were more likely to grant this same sexual freedom to women.

65. Survey data show that attitudes toward premarital sex among college students

vary

(vary/are the same) across regions and national boundaries. One consistent find-

single

ing, however, is that a trend toward a _____single_____ sexual standard appears to be developing.

66. *Extramarital Sex.* A comparison of the Hunt study with the earlier Kinsey studies

women

shows that extramarital sex has increased sharply among young (men/women). However, more men than women engage in extramarital sex. Moreover, men are much more likely than women to have extramarital sex with

several (six or more)

_____several_____ partners.

67. Attitudes regarding extramarital sex have changed slightly, but most couples still

unacceptable
without

regard this practice as (acceptable/unacceptable) behavior. Thus, most extramarital relationships are carried out (with/without) the consent or knowledge of the other partner. Extramarital sexual practices such as "swinging" and "open mar-

have not

riage" (have/have not) received widespread support among married couples.

Learning Objectives

45. What does a comparison of the Hunt study with the earlier Kinsey studies show regarding:
    a. premarital sex among men? Increased slightly.
    b. premarital sex among women? increased dramatically
    c. the status of the "double standard"? still have a dbl. standard

46. What do surveys show regarding the attitudes of college students toward premarital sex? What is a consistent finding here? They vary across regions.
    Trend toward a single sexual standard

47. What does a comparison of the Hunt study with the earlier Kinsey studies show regarding:
    a. extramarital sex among men? same
    b. extramarital sex among women? increased sharply
    c. married couples' attitudes regarding extramarital sex? still unacceptable

48. In what two ways do men and women differ regarding extramarital sexual practices?
    more men engage in it   men have it with more than one partner

49. What is the current status of "swinging" and "open marriage" among most married couples?
    not widely accepted

Homosexuality

primarily

68. As a rule, psychologists consider a homosexual to be a person who seeks sexual gratification (primarily/exclusively) from members of the same sex. However, there is no universally agreed-upon definition for homosexuality. Moreover, Kinsey found that some form of homosexual practice was much (more/less) frequent than had been suspected.

more

neither

69. Both biological and environmental hypotheses have been suggested to explain why some people develop homosexual preference; (both/neither) of these hypotheses have (has) been adequately documented. The American Psychiatric Association (still/no longer) considers homosexuality to be a "mental disorder." Not all psychiatrists agree with this position, however.

no longer

70. Therapy with homosexual persons has been changing. Many therapists no longer

orientation (preference)

attempt to change the person's sexual _orientation_, unless this is the desire of the client. Instead, therapists concentrate on helping the clients to achieve greater self-acceptance and become more at ease with their sexual preference.

were not

71. While Masters and Johnson have recently reported some spectacular success in treating homosexuals, their results have to be treated with caution. For example, their clients (were/were not) representative of the general homosexual population. Moreover, sufficient time for an adequate follow-up evaluation has not yet elapsed.

Learning Objectives

50. What is the definition most psychologists use to describe a homosexual person? someone who seeks sexual gratification primarily from member of same sex

51. What did Kinsey find regarding homosexual practices among the American population? More people practicing it than expected

52. What two general hypotheses have been suggested to explain homosexual behavior? Which of these hypotheses is correct? Bio / Environ. hypotheses - neither is correct

53. What is the current view of the American Psychiatric Association regarding homosexuality? They no longer consider it to be a mental disorder

54. In what ways has therapy with homosexuals been changing? Therapist no longer try to change homoses preferences they try and help them in their relationships

55. Although Masters and Johnson have reported some impressive results in changing the sexual orientation of homosexuals, why cannot their results be accepted at this time? Clients were not representative of general population
sufficient time has not elapsed for an adequate follow-up evaluation

DEVIANT SEXUAL BEHAVIOR

Rape

rape

72. Sexual intercourse with another person that results from physical force, threat, or intimidation is called _rape_.

is not   73. Most psychologists feel that the motivation for rape (is/is not) sexual in nature. Rather, most rapists are motivated by either *anger* or the assertion of

power   ___power___ over another individual.

are not   74. Most rapes (are/are not) reported, although the percentage of rapes being reported is increasing. Victims of rape initially exhibit acute

disorganization   ___disorganization___ characterized by shock, disbelief, and anxiety. The initial disorganization may be followed by frightening dreams and a temporary decrease in sexual satisfaction from petting or sexual intercourse.

Learning Objectives

56. Define what is meant by rape. *sexual intercourse brought on by physical force, intimidation or threats*

57. What are the two motives that lead most rapists to commit an act of rape? *—anger and power over another individual*

58. What general statement can be made about the number of rapes that are reported? *# Reported is increasing however, a lot are still unreported*

59. What are some of the symptoms frequently found among rape victims? *- disorganization, shock, disbelief anxiety frightening dreams*

Incest

75. Sexual activity that takes place between closely related persons is called

incest/does not   ___incest___. As generally reported, incest (does/does not) only apply to genital intercourse. In addition to genital intercourse, other sexual behaviors such as oral-genital sex, fondling of the genitals, and mutual masturbation may also be considered as incestuous behaviors—if they take place between closely

related   ___related___ persons.

low   76. The reported incidence of incest is extremely (low/high), but the estimated incidence is much higher. The lack of cases for study and the wide variety of possible incestuous relationships make any generalizations about the motives behind

impossible (difficult)   incest ___impossible___.

Learning Objectives

60. Define what is meant by incest. *sexual activity between two closely related people*

61. Why is it difficult to draw any conclusions regarding the motives for incestuous behavior? *Because of the lack of cases to study and a low report of incidences*

PROSTITUTION

prostitution

hustlers
male homosexuals

over

without

77. The emotionally indifferent sale of sex on a promiscuous basis is the definition

of _prostitution_ . While most prostitutes are women, there are some

male prostitutes, called _hustlers_ , who primarily service
(women/~~male homosexuals~~).

78. The male patrons of female prostitutes are generally (under/~~over~~) thirty years of
age and away from home. They are generally seeking sexual variety
(with/~~without~~) emotional involvement, or else are unable to establish intimate
sexual relationships.

early

lower

79. A common feature in the background of many women who become prostitutes is

that they had _early_ sexual experience, often of a coercive nature. Another common feature is that most prostitutes come from the

lower economic sector of the society.

are not

seven

80. Most female prostitutes (~~are~~/~~are not~~) heavily into drug use. The average prosti-

tute leaves the profession after about _seven_ years.

Learning Objectives

62. Define what is meant by prostitution. _emotionally indifferent sale of sex on a promiscuous basis_

63. What are male prostitutes called, and whom do they primarily service? _hustlers, male homosexuals_

64. List three features that characterize the men who visit female prostitutes. _over thirty, away from home, no emotional involvement wanted_

65. List two features that are commonly found in the background of women who become prostitutes. _lower economic sector, subjects of early sexual experience_

66. What is known about drug use by female prostitutes? How long do these women usually remain in this profession? _not heavily into drug use   seven years_

CHANGING ATTITUDES TOWARD SEXUALITY

attitudes

increased

therapy

81. Perhaps the biggest change that has occurred in American society since the onset
of the sexual revolution is the change in (~~attitudes~~/behavior). Sex has become
much more openly discussed, both for factual information and entertainment
purposes. This has led to an (~~increased~~/decreased) acceptance of persons whose
sexual behavior deviates from traditional patterns. It has also led to an increase

in the provision of _therapy_ for sexual dysfunction.

82. Another change that appears to be gaining momentum is the trend toward a

single

_____single_____ sexual standard. While men have traditionally been

body/person

"_____body_____-centered" and women "_____person_____-centered," the two sexes appear to be moving toward a single gender role that combines both orientations.

Learning Objectives

67. What is perhaps the biggest change to come out of the sexual revolution? What are two by-products of this change?

change in attitudes about sex   Increased acceptance of people who have deviated from normal sexual practices and an increase in sex therapy

68. What other change appears to be gaining momentum?

trend toward a single sexual standard

Chapter Eighteen
Psychoanalytic Theories of Personality

General Objectives

1. Explain Freud's view of the way in which mistakes, dreams, symptoms, and free association provide information about the unconscious.

2. Name and describe the two Freudian instincts and the three psychic structures.

3. Define the concepts of displacement and sublimation.

4. Name and give examples of the defense mechanisms.

5. List and briefly describe the five Freudian stages of development.

6. Describe the major concepts and innovations from the theories of Jung, Adler, Horney, Fromm, and Erikson.

7. Discuss the major criticisms and contributions of psychoanalytic theory.

Psychoanalytic Theories of Personality

Learning Objectives appear at
the end of each major section.

FREUD'S PSYCHOANALYTIC THEORY

stability

1. Personality theories are concerned with two major aspects of human behavior: individual differences and the apparent (stability/inconsistency) of each individual's behavior over time. The present chapter is concerned with

psychoanalytic

approaches that have emerged from _psychoanalytic_ theory, a viewpoint that emphasizes childhood and the power of mental events to influence behavior.

246

the most

2. While he has had many critics, Sigmund Freud is described in the text as (the most/one of the most) influential personality theorist(s). His theory was also

first

the _first_ formal theory of personality and remains the most detailed and original of the theories.

3. Freud's interest in personality began when he attempted to account for certain strange physical symptoms of his patients, symptoms that did not parallel known

hysterical

patterns of nerves. He referred to these symptoms as _hysterical_ disorders.

4. In collaboration with Josef Breuer, Freud found that hysterical disorders might be cured if patients could recall early childhood events. Originally, Freud used

hypnosis

hypnosis to encourage these recollections, but he abandoned this method because many patients could not be hypnotized and because the hysteri-

return

cal symptoms frequently tended to _return_ .

5. After abandoning hypnosis, Freud used a method he called

free association

free _association_ : patients were asked to lie down on a couch and say whatever came into their minds.

6. The content of patients' free associations tended to center on important emotional

conflicts

conflicts . When these conflicts were talked out and better understood, the patient experienced relief from symptoms.

7. Since most patients could not initially remember, or were unconscious of, early childhood experiences or conflicts, Freud was led to develop the notion of the

unconscious

unconscious

8. The unconscious is the reservoir of instinctual and infantile needs that have been

repressed

repressed , or hidden from conscious awareness, because they cause emotional conflict.

9. The content of the unconscious is revealed, according to Freud, not only through

free association

the method of _free_ _association_ , but also in dreams, jokes, accidents, and physical symptoms.

10. For example, Freud thought that the physical symptoms of hysterical disorders represented or symbolized the underlying unconscious emotional

conflict

conflict that caused the symptoms.

11. Dreams were also thought to express unconscious conflict. The surface content of the dream, the story or description given by the dreamer, is known as the

manifest

~~manifest~~ content. The underlying meaning of the dream, arrived at by interpretation of the symbols in the dream, is known as the

latent

latent content.

12. Hysterical paralysis of the legs might symbolize a soldier's fear of going into battle. Since he is unaware of the fear, the fear is said to be

repressed/unconscious

repressed and is contained in his _unconscious_.

13. Like jokes and dreams, accidents involving words, called "Freudian slips," re-

unconscious

veal underlying sources of repressed or _unconscious_ emotional conflict.

14. The name that Freud gave to his theory and treatment procedures is

psychoanalysis

psychoanalysis

Learning Objectives

, Freud

1. Who does your text consider to be the most influential of the personality theorists? What was the name of his theory and method of treatment? _Psychoanalytic theory_   _+free association_

2. For what disorder did Freud use hypnosis, and why did he abandon this technique? _hysterical people   Because hysterical things would return_

3. Define or give an example of the following:
   hysterical disorders ~
   free association — _saying whatever comes to mind_
   the unconscious — _needs that have been repressed_

4. List five ways by which the content of the unconscious may be revealed. _dreams, jokes, accidents_   _free assoc. + Physical symptoms_

5. Gregory reports to his analyst a dream about mixing up his office key and his house key. His analyst interprets the dream in terms of Gregory's unconscious wish to be at his office and his sexual attraction to his secretary. What is the manifest content? The latent content?   _latent content ↗_

Freud's Conceptualization of Personality Structure

15. While Freud's theory was developed from his work with troubled patients, he asserted that his theory of personality explained the behavior of

all people

(the mentally ill / all people).

16. _The Id_. Freud divided the personality into three structures: the

id

_id_, the ego, and the superego.

17. Freud conceptualized the id as the reservoir of all psychic energy, energy that powers or provides "fuel" for the entire personality. Two types of instinctual energy are contained in the id: Eros, the _life (sex)_ instinct, and

life (sex)

death (aggression)

Thanatos, the _death_ instinct.

18. The instincts contained in the id produce tension—tension from the

life (Eros)

life instinct's needs for sex, food, warmth, and touch; and

death (Thanatos)

tension from the _death_ instinct's unreleased aggression.

19. The sole objective of the id is to reduce instinctive tension. This push to reduce

pleasure

tension, to obtain pleasure and avoid pain, is termed the _pleasure_ principle.

20. *The Ego*. While the id is the repository of desires, it has no way to fulfill these

ego

desires. This is the task of the _ego_, the structure that mediates between the id and external reality.

conscious

21. The ego is largely (⟨conscious⟩/unconscious). It is frequently referred to as the executive of the personality because it devises plans and executes actions directed

id

toward satisfying the instinctual desires of the _id_.

22. Since the ego must devise realistic plans based on interaction with the real

reality

world, it operates according to the _reality_ principle.

23. *The Superego*. The concern of the superego is morality, the set of values conveyed to children through their parents. This structure is roughly equivalent to

conscience

what is commonly termed the _conscience_.

24. The major function of the superego is to indicate when the individual is "wrong" according to the particular set of moral beliefs incorporated from his or her par-

prohibit

ents and society. Thus, the superego attempts to (⟨prohibit⟩/encourage) the sexual and aggressive drives of the id.

25. If the ego authorizes an activity disapproved by the superego, the superego retaliates by providing guilt, physical distress, or self-punishing behavior. The super-

punishments

ego, then, is largely a provider of (rewards/⟨punishments⟩) for disapproved behavior.

reality

26. Like the id, the superego is *not* based on the _reality_ principle. It is based on an absolute, and sometimes unrealistic, moral ideal.

Learning Objectives

6. Name the two types of instinctive energy. In which "structure" are these instincts contained? *life + death*
   They are in the id

7. List the three Freudian psychic structures, and briefly describe the function of each. *id - produces tension to*
   ego - is the mediator - based on reality   superego - morality   get things   does what is
   right

8. Which structure is controlled by the pleasure principle? The reality principle?
   id   *Ego*

Freud's Theory of Personality Dynamics

27. Freud viewed the source of personality development as conflict or tension—tension between the psychic structures, between the life and death instincts, and between the instincts and rules of society. According to Freud, nearly all human

tension   behavior is directed toward reducing _____*tension*_____, toward restoring a

homeostasis (balance) state of equilibrium or _____*homeostasis*_____.

28. *Displacement of Instinctual Energy.* According to Freud, all instincts have a *source* and *aim* that remain constant throughout a person's life. For example, the

source   need for sexual release might be termed the _____*source*_____ of the sex

aim   instinct and satisfaction of the need as its _____*aim*_____.

29. Instincts also have *impetus,* which is the force or strength of the need, and *objects*. While the source and aim of instincts remain constant throughout one's

objects   life, the _____*objects*_____ that satisfy these needs may change.

30. A shift from the original object of an instinct to a new object is termed displace-

displacement   ment. For example, smoking is a _____*displacement*_____ of instinctual energy from its original aim, sucking the mother's breast, to a substitute.

31. The particular type of displacement that produces higher cultural achievement,

sublimation   such as artistic creation, was termed by Freud _____*sublimation*_____.

does not   32. Sublimation, like other forms of displacement, generally (does/does not) bring as much satisfaction as does energy attached to the original object.

33. *Anxiety.* Anxiety caused by realistic threats in the environment is referred to as

reality   _____*reality*_____ anxiety. Anxiety resulting from threats from the id, or the fear that the instincts will get out of control, is termed

neurotic   _____*neurotic*_____ anxiety.

moral

34. Anxiety associated with guilt is called ____*moral*____ anxiety. This type of anxiety arises when one behaves, or even thinks of behaving, contrary to his

superego

or her conscience or ____*superego*____.

Learning Objectives

9. According to Freud, the major goal of human behavior is tension reduction. What are the sources of tension?
   psychic structures a life and death instincts   source & aim

10. Name the four characteristics of an instinct. Which of the four remains the same throughout a person's life? What terms did Freud apply to the process by which one changes the *object* of an instinct? Explain or give an example of this process. *Source Aim Impetus & Object   displacement   someone who smokes likes to suck the mothers nipple so they smoke instead.*

11. What is sublimation? _ *displacement that produces higher cultural achievement*

12. Define or describe the following:
    reality anxiety - *caused by realistic threats by the enviornment*
    neurotic anxiety - *Fear that instincts from id will get out of control*
    moral anxiety - *associated with guilt - when you think or behave contrary to your conscience or superego*

35. *Defense Mechanisms.* If anxiety is acute and there appears to be no reasonable way of dealing with it, the ego resorts to a series of tactics referred to as

defense mechanisms

____*defense*____ ____*mechanisms*____.

36. All defense mechanisms have two aspects in common: they deny or distort real-

unconsciously

ity, and they operate ____*unconsciously*____.

37. Carefully reread the section in the text on defense mechanisms before answering this item. Then match the five defense mechanisms listed here with the descriptions below by placing the appropriate letters in the blanks.
    a. repression
    b. fixation
    c. regression
    d. reaction formation
    e. projection

c

____*c*____ The return to an earlier state of development.

e

____*e*____ Attributing one's own feelings or impulses to some other person or object.

a

____*a*____ Extreme forgetting—pushing into the unconscious memories of certain events.

d

____*d*____ The replacement of one feeling with its opposite.

b

____*b*____ A halt in development produced by anxiety concerning the next state of development.

38. The following story of unrequited love, and the examples that follow it, illustrate the functions of the various defense mechanisms. First read the story, and then fill in the blanks with the defense mechanisms that best describe the statements and behaviors of this unfortunate person. Bert loves Alice, but Alice is no longer in love with Bert. In the face of this frustrating situation, Bert experiences anxiety. To reduce anxiety, he engages (unconsciously) in several defense mechanisms.

reaction formation   _Reaction   Formation_   "I don't love her—I hate her."

projection   _Projection_   "But she is still in love with me."

repression   _repression_   He is unable to recall certain aspects of their previous relationship.

regression   _regression_   He throws a temper tantrum.

Learning Objectives

distort a deny reality and operate unconsciously

13. What two characteristics do all of the defense mechanisms have in common?

14. Name and describe, or give an example of, the five defense mechanisms listed in the text.

repression - put bad feeling out of your mind
projection -
regression - go back to early life
fixation - stuck at one stage of development
Reaction-formation - do opp of what you really think

Freud's Psychosexual Stages of Development

39. Freud's theory was unique for its time in that it stressed the importance of

developmental   _developmental_ stages in the formation of personality. (The Freudian stages are also discussed in Chapter 14.)

childhood
prior to

40. Freud placed particular emphasis on infancy and early _childhood_. He believed that basic personality patterns were formed (prior to/after) the time a child enters school.

41. According to Freud, during the first few years of life the child passes through

oral/anal   three *pregenital* stages: the _oral_, _anal_,

phallic   and _phallic_ stages.

42. Following the three pregenital stages, the child passes through a stabilizing, or

latency   _latency_, period. At the end of this period, the development of

genital   adolescent and adult sexuality begins, referred to as the _genital_ phase.

43. Freud assumed that the stages were distinct but that there were no sharp transitions between stages. The final personality structure was assumed to take on

all stages   characteristics from (all stages/the genital stage).

Learning Objectives

15. List the names of the five developmental stages in the blanks next to the approximate age ranges of these stages.

_____oral_____ birth to one year

_____anal_____ one to two years

_____phallic_____ three to five years

_____latency_____ six years to adolescence

_____genital_____ adolescence and adulthood

16. Which of the stages did Freud consider to have the most important influence on the development of personality? *all of the stages influenced personality*

Do not need to know them

DEVELOPMENT OF NEO-FREUDIAN THEORIES

44. Because Freud's theories derived from his own particular experiences and biases, it is not surprising to find that other theorists, with different backgrounds and biases, developed very different theories. Two such theorists were early students

Jung/Adler

of Freud's: Carl _____ and Alfred _____ .

Jung's Analytic Psychology

45. Freud called his theory psychoanalysis. When Jung broke from Freud, he re-

analytic psychology

ferred to his own theory as _____ _____ .

46. Freud believed that behavior was completely determined by past events. Jung

future

stressed not only the past but also an individual's _____ , especially the guiding function of an individual's aims or goals.

47. Jung also proposed that there are two major personality orientations:

introverts

_____ , who are quiet, reserved individuals, and

extroverts

_____ , who are outgoing and excitement-seeking.

48. Like Freud, Jung emphasized the importance of unconscious processes. However, Jung theorized that there are two unconscious structures: the

personal/collective

_____ unconscious and the _____ unconscious.

49. According to Jung, the structure that contains repressed experiences, and that is quite similar to Freud's concept of the unconscious, is the

personal   _____ unconscious.

50. The structure containing memories inherited from humanity's ancestral past is the

collective   _____ unconscious. Within the collective unconscious are the

archetypes   _____, ancient images and predispositions inherited from our animal and human forebears.

Learning Objectives

17. Freud termed his theory psychoanalysis. What name did Jung give to his theory?

18. What differences existed between Jung and Freud in terms of their views of determinants of behavior?

19. What are the two major personality orientations proposed by Jung?

20. Name and describe the two unconscious structures in Jungian psychology. What are archetypes?

Social Determinants of Personality

biological   51. Freud and Jung emphasized the _____ factors in the development of personality. In contrast, Adler, Horney, and Fromm began to emphasize

social   the importance of environmental or _____ factors.

52. *Adler's Individual Psychology.* Alfred Adler, like Jung an early associate of

individual   Freud who broke from him, called his theory _____ psychology.

53. For Freud, the great human motivations were sex and aggression. For Adler, the most important motivation was what he first called the "will to power" but later

superiority   termed "the striving for _____."

54. According to Adler's theory, people strive for superiority to overcome the feel-

inferiority   ings of _____ originating in children's realization that adults can do things which they cannot.

inferiority complex   55. Adler coined the term _____ _____ to describe people who have achieved an outward appearance of strength while maintaining inner feelings of inferiority.

societal goals

56. In addition to striving for individual perfection or superiority, people also have an innate need to achieve (selfish goals/societal goals) that emerges as the individual matures. Adler felt that people have an innate *social interest,* and that by working toward the common good people can compensate for feelings of inferiority.

Learning Objectives

21. In terms of the factors that they emphasized, in what ways are the theories of Adler, Horney, and Fromm more similar to each other than they are to the theories of Freud and Jung?

22. Next to the names of the theorists listed below are the names they gave their theories. Complete the list by indicating the name that Adler gave his theory.
    Freud: psychoanalysis
    Jung: analytic psychology
    Adler: _____ _____

23. In Adler's theory, what is the major motivating force behind human behavior? What accounts for these feelings?

24. Who coined the term *inferiority complex,* and what does it mean?

25. According to Adler, why do human beings work toward societal goals?

---

57. *Horney's Theory of Basic Anxiety and Basic Hostility.* Like Adler, Horney em-

social

phasized the _____ determinants of behavior instead of biological, instinctive ones.

sex

58. For Freud, the basic motivations were _____ and

aggression

_____; for Adler the major motivating force was striving for

perfection (superiority)

_____; and for Horney the motivating forces involved basic

anxiety/hostility

_____ and basic _____ .

59. According to Horney, the child is born into a potentially hostile world in which he or she is helpless and dependent on adults. In this situation, warm and dependable parents create security, which results in normal development. Indifferent and undependable parents, however, produce children with basic

anxiety/hostility

_____ , usually accompanied by basic _____ .

60. To deal with the conflict between basic anxiety and hostility, the individual may adopt one or more of the following three modes of behavior: moving *toward* others, moving *against* others, or moving *away* from others. If the individual adopts

normal

all three of these modes, he or she is considered to be (normal/neurotic).

61. Horney believed that all three of these modes are adopted and used in the normally functioning personality. Neurosis resulted from the use of one and only one mode. Match the following personality descriptions with the appropriate single mode by placing the words *toward, against,* or *away* in the blanks.

toward

_____ Tries to please everyone, compliant.

away

_____ Aloof, withdrawn, avoids close relationships.

toward

_____ Totally suppresses hostility.

against

_____ Dominating, strives for power over others in all situations.

62. Horney also reinterpreted Freud's Oedipal complex, emphasizing the

social

_____ relationship between parents and children rather than the sexual or aggressive aspects.

63. Horney also rejected Freud's notion that women are inferior because they lack a

superego

strong _____. Horney asserted that any feelings of inferiority

social (cultural)

experienced by women are based on _____ experiences and are not derived from penis envy, as Freud had indicated.

Learning Objectives

26. Next to the name of each theorist list the major motivating forces in his or her theory of personality.
Freud   sex & aggression
Adler
Horney

27. According to Horney, what produces basic anxiety in children? Basic hostility?

28. What is the major difference between neurotic and normal individuals, according to Horney?

29. List and describe the three neurotic modes of dealing with basic anxiety and basic hostility.

30. How is Horney's interpretation of the Oedipus complex different from that of Freud? What is Horney's view of the Freudian concepts of "female inferiority" and penis envy?

64. *Fromm's "Escape from Freedom."* Fromm distinguishes between our

animal

_____ nature, the basic biological functioning we share with

human

other animals, and our _____ nature, the ability to reason and to know ourselves.

human

65. Reason and knowledge, our _____ nature, set us apart from the animal kingdom and permit us freedom to develop in a variety of ways. But this

escape (shrink from)

freedom also produces anxieties, and people may seek to _____ the freedom.

66. While our unique freedom may lead to great accomplishments, people may at-

freedom

tempt an escape from _____. On a social level, this escape

conformity

could lead to mindless _____ to societal dictates and to the dictates of a totalitarian government. On a personal level, escape could lead to self-

psychotic

defeating behavior, including _____ withdrawal.

67. While Fromm believed that human behavior is strongly affected by society, he nonetheless asserted, in contrast to Freud's biological determinism, that it is an

human

essential part of _____ nature to take an active role in affecting the future.

Learning Objectives

31. What is the difference between our animal nature and our human nature, according to Fromm?

32. What does Fromm mean by "escape from freedom"? Name some of the negative effects of such an escape. How does Fromm differ from Freud with regard to the concept of determinism?

Erikson's Psychosocial View of Personality

68. Erikson studied with Freud, and his personality theory is clearly derived from Freudian theory. His views differ from those of Freud in several respects, how-

ego

ever, including his emphasis on the _____ over the id and his

eight

listing of _____ developmental stages rather than five.

69. In addition, while Freud asserted that personality is largely determined by early

childhood

_____ experiences, Erikson indicated with his additional stages that personality develops throughout one's lifetime. Erikson also asserted that the child does not simply accept parental values but strives to form a unique self, a

identity

separate ego _____.

70. Erikson views the task of developing a unique identity as particularly difficult in a complex society such as ours, a society with such a vast array of choices in living styles. Hence, young people in our society are likely to experience what

identity crisis

Erikson termed an _____ _____.

psychohistory

71. Erikson pioneered the field of _____, the application of psychoanalytic theory to the study of important historical figures.

Learning Objectives

33. Describe the differences between Freud and Erikson with regard to:
    emphasis on the id
    influence of early childhood
    the stages of development

34. What is an identity, and why does an identity crisis develop?

35. What is psychohistory?

EVALUATING PSYCHOANALYTIC THEORIES

Criticisms of Psychoanalytic Theory

72. As one of my old professors used to say, Freud "caught his data on both sides of the fence." By this he apparently meant that very different behaviors (e.g., displaying great love or great hatred for one's mother) could reflect the same underlying cause. Thus, many of the propositions put forth by Freud simply cannot be

tested (verified)   _____tested_____ in a scientific way.

73. While psychoanalysis may provide apparently logical explanations for behavior,

predict   it cannot _____predict_____ future behavior. This is a major failure in terms of establishing the validity of the theory.

74. In addition, those psychoanalytic propositions which do appear testable generally
have not   (have/have not) held up well under scientific scrutiny. For example, no studies have demonstrated that "oral" and "anal" personalities are formed because of critical events occurring during those developmental stages.

Contributions of Psychoanalytic Theory

75. Despite the criticisms, some studies have provided support for some of Freud's conceptions. Studies have found, for example, that people who focus on oral ac-
also   tivities (also/do not) tend to be passive and dependent. It is important to point out, however, that these correlational data do not indicate that oral activities *cause* these personality traits.

76. Freud has clearly left his mark on our culture. The way we look at art, literature, and life itself has been influenced by our general acceptance of Freud's concept

unconscious

of the _unconscious_. Although some psychologists may reject the notion of an unconscious structure, it is clear that we are not aware of many of the determinants of our behavior.

77. In addition, even clinical psychologists who reject Freud's theory are likely to use some aspects of his treatment method, aspects that emphasize the

talking/relationship

" _talking_ cure" and the individual _relationship_ between patient and therapist.

Learning Objectives

[handwritten: can't be tested / can't predict future behavior]

36. Describe some of the criticisms of psychoanalytic theory.

37. Describe some of the contributions of psychoanalytic theory.

[handwritten: - concept of the unconscious / - treatment method used on patience relationship "talking cure"]

Chapter Nineteen
Humanistic, Behavioristic, and Trait Theories of Personality

General Objectives

1. With regard to the humanistic theories of personality, discuss (a) Maslow's concepts of self-actualization, basic needs, need hierarchy, and peak experience; and (b) Rogers's concepts of the organism, the self, conditional and unconditional positive regard, and nondirective therapy.

2. With regard to the behavioristic theories, discuss (a) Dollard and Miller's contributions to contemporary psychology; (b) Skinner's radical behaviorism and his treatment of internal events; and (c) the major differences between radical behaviorism and social-learning theory.

3. For the trait approaches, describe (a) Allport's cardinal and second, common and individual traits; (b) Cattell's factor-analytic theory, with surface and source traits; and (3) Eysenck's major factors of extroversion-introversion and neuroticism-stability.

4. Discuss Mischel's view concerning the predictive validity of personality traits, whether they are stable across time or situations, and the experimental evidence relating to these questions.

Humanistic, Behavioristic, and Trait Theories of Personality

Learning Objectives appear at
the end of each major section.

HUMANISTIC APPROACHES

uniqueness
freedom

1. The "humanistic" psychologists emphasize the (sameness/uniqueness) of the individual and (determinism/freedom) in making choices.

Maslow's Humanistic Psychology

self-actualized

2. Maslow attempted to base his theory on healthy and creative people, individuals he considered to be _self-actualized_, individuals who develop their potential to its fullest.

3. Maslow classified human needs into two groups: *basic needs* and *metaneeds*.

physiological

Basic needs consist of _physiological_ needs for food and water, for ex-

psychological

ample, and certain _psychological_ needs, such as the needs for affection, security, and self-esteem. Basic needs are also called deficiency needs.

growth

4. Metaneeds, also called _growth_ needs, include the higher needs for beauty, justice, goodness, and so forth.

basic (deficiency)

5. The _basic_ needs generally take precedence over the

metaneeds (growth needs)
could not

metaneeds. Thus, if one has *not* met the needs for food and water, one (could/~~could not~~) attend to the needs for justice and beauty.

basic (deficiency)

6. In addition, the _basic_ needs are arranged in a hierarchy,

metaneeds (growth needs)

whereas the _metaneeds_ are not. Thus, one would probably meet the need for food and water before attending to the need for affection; but one

would not

(would/~~would not~~) have to attend to the need for beauty before that for justice.

7. Maslow also examined certain profound experiences during which people feel in

peak

harmony with the world, moments Maslow referred to as _peak_ experiences. Maslow assumed that during these experiences people are, for that brief period, self-actualized. For some women childbirth seems to produce a

peak experience

peak _experience_.

The Self Theory of Rogers

8. According to Rogers, most children receive only *conditional positive regard:*

conditional

love and praise are _conditional_ on the child's conformity to parental or societal standards. To maintain positive regard, children in this situation must suppress certain actions and feelings.

9. This suppression or denial of experiences leads to the development of what Rogers refers to as the *self*. The self in Rogerian theory is that portion of a person's total experiences which an individual recognizes or accepts. In contrast, the

organism

organism is the total range of a person's possible experience.

10. The concepts of the *self* and the *organism* are two major constructs in Rogers's theory. Ideally, for the fully functioning person, the organism and the self are (identical/separate) entities. Most frequently, however, the (self/organism) denies some aspect of sensory and emotional experience available to the (self/organism).

identical/self organism

11. To review, the total range of possible experience is called the

organism

Organism, while that aspect of experience accepted and allowed

self

into consciousness is called the _self_.

12. To help remedy the breach between self and organism caused by *conditional*

unconditional

positive regard, Rogers's therapy provides _unconditional_ positive regard—that is, acceptance of all that the client does or says regardless of personal or societal sanctions.

13. Rogerian therapists provide neither interpretations nor directions about the

nondirective

client's behavior. Thus, Rogerian therapy is termed _nondirective_ or client-centered therapy. Instead of directing or interpreting, Rogerian therapists attempt to reflect the client's feelings by rephrasing her or his statements.

14. In contrast to Freud, Rogers's view of human nature is primarily

optimistic

(optimistic/pessimistic). That is, rather than viewing the individual as a collection of primitive sexual and aggressive instincts, he believes that the human organism will, if unrestricted by social forces, seek self-actualization and productive relations with others.

Evaluation of Humanistic Approaches

15. The humanistic approaches to personality have been criticized for being

unscientific

unscientific and *subjective*. For example, Maslow's notion that human nature is basically "good" is untestable, and his selection of self-actualized

subjective

people is based on his own _subjective_ criteria.

16. Despite this criticism, the work of Maslow and Rogers has given impetus to the

group

group-therapy movement, to the study of altered states of con-

unconditional

sciousness, and to the use of Rogers's _unconditional_

positive

positive regard in some forms of psychotherapy.

Learning Objectives

1. Describe the following concepts from Maslow's theory:
   self-actualization
   basic needs
   metaneeds
   peak experience

2. By what other name did Maslow label the basic needs and metaneeds? Which needs are hierarchically organized, and what does this mean? *deficiency & growth needs* *deficiency needs are hierachally organized*

3. Describe the following Rogerian concepts:
   organism
   self
   conditional positive regard
   unconditional positive regard

4. Why is Rogerian therapy termed *nondirective*?

5. In what way is Rogers's view more "optimistic" than that of psychoanalytic theory?

6. Discuss some of the criticisms of the humanistic movement and some of the contributions it has made to the practice of psychotherapy.

BEHAVIORISTIC APPROACHES

17. Using concepts familiar to behaviorists of the 1940s, Dollard and Miller attempted to translate Freud's psychoanalytic theory into principles of

learning   behavioristic ___*learning*___ theory.

18. Dollard and Miller assumed that the defense mechanisms are

learned (acquired)   ___*learned*___ in much the same manner as other behaviors. Thus, they termed the defense mechanism of repression "*learned*

not-thinking   ___*not*___-___*thinking*___," learned because not thinking about particular topics reduces anxiety.

19. Dollard and Miller also demonstrated that something analogous to neurotic conflict could occur in lower animals. If a rat received both shock and food at the end of a runway, for example, it would tend to vacillate between *approaching*

avoiding   the food and ___*avoiding*___ the shock. This type of behavior was

approach-avoidance termed an ___*approach*___-___*avoidance*___ conflict.

20. Thus, while Freud asserted that conflict involved repression of wishes and thoughts, Dollard and Miller demonstrated that conflict, in this case an approach-

learned (acquired)

avoidance conflict, could be ___learned___.

21. The text indicates that Dollard and Miller's approach was important for two reasons. First, it translated psychoanalytic concepts into the terminology of

learning

___learning___ theory, thus demonstrating that psychoanalytic concepts were accessible to American researchers. Second, it helped pave the way for

behavior therapy

___behavior therapy___, a set of procedures based on learning principles for dealing with behavioral disturbances.

Learning Objectives

7. Whose theory did Dollard and Miller "translate" into principles of behavioristic learning theory? *Freuds*

8. Provide Dollard and Miller's explanation of the following concepts:
   neurotic conflict
   repression

9. List two contributions that emerged from Dollard and Miller's theory. *behavior therapy and learning theory*

Skinner's Radical Behaviorism

22. Skinner's view of human behavior is even more closely tied to observable events than was Dollard and Miller's. For example, Skinner rejected concepts about internal events (such as drive) because they cannot be directly

observed (verified)

___observed___ nor examined scientifically.

radical
internal
does not

23. Skinner's viewpoint is known as *radical* behaviorism because it focuses so much on the external environment and excludes (internal/external) events such as motivation and cognition. Skinner (does/does not) deny the existence of internal events, but he considers concepts about them not only unscientific but unnecessary to explain behavior.

24. Concepts about internal events are not needed, according to Skinner, because behavior can be adequately explained with reference to reinforcers, punishers, and a number of other environmental events. The radical behaviorists' approach is termed a *functional* analysis of behavior because, in their view, behavior may be

function

explained as a *function* of environmental events.

25. Skinner's 1949 novel *Walden Two* describes a utopian society in which people are "controlled" by reinforcement and other deliberate arrangements of the environment. While many people shy away from the word *control*, it should be pointed out that Skinner uses the word to mean (predictability/coercion). As a matter of fact, Skinner has always emphasized the use of systematic reward rather than coercion.

predictability

Learning Objectives

They used psychoanalytic Theories to support their observations

10. Discuss one major difference between Dollard and Miller's conceptions of human behavior and those of Skinner.
while skinner just observed his patients no internal events were used

11. What is meant by "internal events," and how does Skinner feel he can adequately account for human behavior without referring to internal events?

because behavior is explained

12. Why is radical behaviorism referred to as a *functional* theory?
as a function of environmental events.

13. How might Skinner respond to the comment that his utopian *Walden Two* is a totalitarian society which controls its inhabitants?
He didn't use coercion   he use's control to mean predictability   systematize rewards not coercion

---

Social-Learning Theory

26. While social-learning theory incorporates many of the views of radical behaviorism, it differs in its emphasis on the thinking or ___cognitive___ capabilities of human beings. Human behavior is partly determined by events in the environment, but it is also determined by cognitive events.

cognitive

27. *The Acquisition of Behavior*. Social-learning theorists assert that most new behaviors are acquired through ___observational___ learning, in which we watch the behavior of others. To acquire new behavior it (is/is not) necessary to be directly reinforced, as the behaviorists had indicated, but simply to observe the rewards and punishments experienced by others.

observational
is not

28. Reinforcement is an important concept in social-learning theory, but much more so for the purposes of getting people to (repeat/acquire) behavior than to learn it initially. In this sense, we may learn behavior by observing others but perform it

repeat

because we anticipate ___reinforcement___.

reinforcement

29. In addition, in the view of social-learning theorists reinforcement (does/does not) automatically strengthen a response, as the behaviorists maintain. Instead, reinforcement provides *information* and ___motivation___ which may strengthen a response.

does not

motivation

30. For example, if Ralph tells a joke and his audience laughs, the laugh functions

information   as reinforcement, which provides the _information_ that this joke may

motivation   produce laughs as well as the _motivation_ for engaging in the same
behavior again.

31. *The Regulation and Maintenance of Behavior.* Once acquired, either through observation or direct reinforcement, behaviors are regulated and maintained by

stimulus   three types of control: _stimulus_ control, reinforcement control,
and cognitive control.

32. For example, behavior that fairly automatically occurs in certain situations is said

stimulus   to be under _stimulus_ control. Behavior reflecting our history of
reinforcement, or the schedule on which we have been reinforced, is under

reinforcement   _reinforcement_ control.

33. In addition, people may provide their own reinforcements somewhat independ-

cognitive   ently of the environment through the process of _cognitive_ control.
If you operate under this type of control, then you are likely to provide

self   _self_-reinforcement when you finish a particular unit in this
book (by telling yourself that you have done a good job).

stimulus   34. Bernice stops at a red light; Bernice is under _stimulus_ control for
this behavior. Bernice smiles at Ralph, who smiles pleasantly in return as he has

reinforcement   done in the past; Bernice is probably under _reinforcement_ control for
this behavior. Bernice congratulates herself for a job which meets her own par-

cognitive   ticular standards; Bernice is under _cognitive_ control for this
behavior.

unique   35. *Social-Learning Theory as a Theory of Personality.* People react to situations in
consistent   (unique/the same) ways, and each individual's behavior is relatively
(consistent/inconsistent) over time.

36. Mischel maintains that social-learning theory can explain both uniqueness and
consistency by viewing cognitions not only in terms of past learning but also in
terms of their function as guides for the future. For example, we may value a
particular reinforcer because of our reinforcement history in the

past   _past_. In turn, such a value guides our behavior in the

future   _future_.

Learning Objectives

14. Describe the differences between social-learning theory and radical behaviorism with regard to:
the subject matter of psychology
the acquisition of behavior

— NO

15. According to the social-learning theorists, can learning occur without reinforcement? Explain. What functions does reinforcement serve?

stimulus control
Reinforcement control
cognitive control

16. Name and describe three ways in which responses are maintained or controlled.

17. Viewed as a personality theory, how does social-learning theory account for both the uniqueness and consistency of personality? *value a particular reinforcer that worked in past and will probably work in future*

by functions as guides to the future

Evaluation of Behavioristic Approaches

totalitarian

37. *Criticism of Behavioristic Approaches.* Critics of the behavioristic approaches maintain that behaviorism *oversimplifies life,* is *deterministic,* and can lead to _totalitarian_ control.

thought (thinking, cognition)

38. Radical behaviorism has been considered an oversimplification because it does not deal with _thought_ or feeling. While social-learning theory includes cognitive processes in its approach, many critics still feel that the human personality cannot be reduced to behavioral consequences and self-statements.

deterministic

39. Both radical behaviorism and social-learning theory assume that our behavior is caused, in the former case, largely by environmental events and, in the latter, by cognitive events as well. Thus, both approaches accept a (deterministic/free-will) view of human behavior. This viewpoint disturbs people who view free will as the basis of our legal, religious, and moral systems.

totalitarian

40. Finally, some critics view behaviorism as _totalitarian_ in the sense of providing a blueprint for controlling behavior. As mentioned earlier, totalitarian regimes generally rely on aversive or coercive procedures, which Skinner opposes.

treatment

41. *Contributions of Behavioristic Approaches.* The behavioristic approaches have made two major contributions: first, in the _treatment_ of personality disorders; and, second, in the objective approach to the study of human behavior.

faster

can

42. In terms of treatment, the behavioral approaches are generally _faster_, cheaper, and often more effective than treatments which have emerged from the "dynamic" theories. In terms of objectivity, the behavioral approach ensures that claims (can/cannot) be tested scientifically and either verified or discounted.

Learning Objectives

[handwritten: deterministic, oversimplifies life. lead to totalitarianism. Faster cheaper Treatment can be tested and retested to be true or false]

18. Discuss three criticisms of the behavioral approaches.

19. Discuss two major contributions of the behavioral approaches.

TRAIT APPROACHES

consistency

43. Personality traits may be conceived as a series of adjectives that describe people—such words as *friendly, aggressive, pleasant, extroverted,* and so forth. The basic characteristic of traits is that they emphasize the (consistency/inconsistency) of each person's behavior.

unfriendly

44. Traits are usually expressed on a continuum, so a series of traits may be used to describe everyone. If the continuum is quantified on a scale, with 1 being low and 10 being high, then a person described as 2 on friendliness would be relatively (friendly/unfriendly).

Allport's Classification of Traits

cardinal

45. There is an enormous number of trait words that could be used to describe people. Attempting to make this number more manageable, Allport developed three trait categories. If a trait directs a major portion of an individual's personality, it is termed a ___cardinal___ trait.

cardinal/do not

central

46. For example, someone whose every action is marked by greed would be described by a ___cardinal___ trait. Most individuals (do/do not) have such a predominant trait but are better described by a few ___central___ traits, characteristic ways they develop for dealing with the world.

secondary

47. Less influential traits, which involve tastes and preferences, are termed ___secondary___ traits.

common

individual

48. Allport emphasized the uniqueness of each individual's personality. Thus, while some traits, which he termed ___common___ traits, are held in common by all people, other traits, which he termed ___individual___ traits (or *personal dispositions*), are unique to each individual.

Factor Analysis: Cattell and Eysenck

factor

49. Through a statistical procedure called ___Factor___

analysis

___Analysis___ it is possible to take a large number of supposedly different traits, determine the extent to which they overlap, and end up with a smaller but distinct set of traits.

50. Using factor analytic techniques, Cattell arrived at two basic types of traits. The traits that correspond largely to descriptions of clusters of behavior are termed

surface

___Surface___ traits. Traits that are supposedly the underlying causes of

source

these behaviors are termed ___source___ traits.

source

51. For example, "ego strength" or "dominance" would be a ___source___

surface

trait, while "honesty" and "curiosity" would be ___surface___ traits.

52. Also using factor analysis, Hans Eysenck arrived at a different classification of traits. According to Eysenck there are two major trait dimensions:

extroversion/neuroticism

___extroversion___-*introversion* and ___neuroticism___-*stability*.

53. To understand how these two factors combine, look at Figure 19.6 in the text. Scores that show relatively high predispositions toward neuroticism *and* extrover-

psychopathic

sion, for example, are associated with ___psychopathic___ behavior. Anxiety

neuroticism

states are associated with high ___neuroticism___ and high

introversion

___introversion___.

54. Eysenck believes that these traits are related to underlying biological differences

arousal
low/intense
opposite

in cortical ___arousal___. He suggests that extroverts have a naturally (low/high) level of arousal and thus seek (mild/intense) stimulation in the environment. For introverts, the (same/opposite) relationship applies.

55. Some observations support the notion of basic biological differences between in-

introverts

troverts and extroverts. For example, ___introverts___ are more sensitive to pain and have more trouble falling asleep.

better

56. While earlier data also indicated that extroverts performed (worse/better) on ability tests when they had taken caffeine, later results found this to be true only in the morning. Evidently extroverts are helped by caffeine in the morning and

introverts

___introverts___ are helped by caffeine in the evening, a result that suggests that these two groups may not differ so much in general arousal as in pattern of arousal across the day.

Evaluation of Trait Theories

labels

57. The approach of trait theories is to provide (labels/explanations) of human behavior. While this may be useful, some may reify the labels and view them as true entities and causal agents rather than shorthand descriptions of behavior.

58. In addition, assigning traits to people may obscure the fact that traits are likely to

situations

occur in some specific _situations_ but not in others. For example, knowing that Sally is assertive in academic situations but anxious in social ones provides more information than simply calling Sally assertive and anxious.

Learning Objectives

— Allport

20. Whose approach to personality theory includes the concepts of cardinal, central, and secondary traits? Briefly describe and give examples of these concepts.

21. What distinction does Allport draw between *common* and *individual* traits?   _unique to individual_
    — held in common by all people

22. Define and give examples of surface traits and source traits. Whose theory makes use of these terms? _Cattel_

23. According to Eysenck, everyone's personality can be described in terms of two major dimensions. What are these two dimensions? _extroversion - introversion   neuroticism - stability_

24. What biological differences exist between *extroverts* and *introverts,* according to Eysenck? What effect does this have on the type of stimulation each seeks? What does the research involving caffeine and test performance suggest concerning arousal and introversion-extroversion?

25. Discuss two criticisms that may be directed at trait theory.

A CURRENT CONTROVERSY: PERSONALITY VERSUS SITUATIONAL FACTORS

The Critique

do not

59. It seems so intuitively obvious that people have different and stable personality traits that it may be difficult to understand an argument, like Mischel's, which holds that general personality traits (do/do not) exist.

poor

low

60. After reviewing a series of studies, Mischel concluded that traits measured by personality tests are very (good/poor) predictors of people's actual behavior. For example, the likelihood that a person high on a trait of *assertiveness* would behave in an assertive manner in a particular situation was quite (low/high).

do not

61. Mischel maintained that the reason the relationship between measured traits and actual behavior is low is that people (do/do not) act the same way in different situations. In other words, traits tend to be situation-specific.

do not know

62. For example, if we know that Randolph is consistently assertive at the office, we (also know/do not know) whether or not Randolph will be assertive in dealing with his family.

63. It is important to note that Mischel assumed that a person might act very consistent-

situation

ly in the same _situation_. His contention was that people would not behave the same way, or express a general trait, across different situations.

The Response

64. One group of researchers contended that Mischel had not measured behavior over a sufficient number of situations; and when they measured people's behavior over a twelve-day period, the consistency of their behavior (increased/decreased).

increased

65. Mischel responded, however, that most of the consistency revealed in the longer test period involved stability over (time/different situations). As we noted earlier, Mischel had never denied a person's tendency to act consistently in the same situation.

time

66. Another response came from Bem and Allen, researchers who maintained that some people are more consistent in their behavior than are others. In a study examining this question they found that students who rated themselves as consistently friendly did show a (low/high) correlation between friendliness in two test situations. Students who had rated themselves low in consistency of friendliness were in fact inconsistent in the two test situations.

high

67. While the study did show some consistency across situations for friendliness, there were only two situations, and no consistency was shown across

conscientiousness

conscientiousness, the second variable studied.

68. It was puzzling to both groups of researchers that students who rated themselves as highly consistent in conscientiousness across situations did not behave that way. Mischel and Peake proposed, however, that the students (and their parents and peers) were all judging the students in terms of the (temporal/situational) stability of their behavior and viewing it as if it were situationally stable.

temporal

69. Mischel had earlier pointed out other perceptual biases which may account for our tendency to perceive stable sets of traits where none exists. For example, we tend to be most influenced by our (first/later) impressions of people and are likely to dismiss behavior which conflicts with these impressions, thus supporting our mistaken impression that behavior is situationally consistent.

first

Learning Objectives

26. Data reviewed by one researcher tended to cast doubt on the trait approach. Name the researcher, and explain his findings.   _Mischel - traits measured by personality tests are poor predictors of people's actual behavior._

27. What did Mischel suggest accounts for the poor predictive power of traits?

relationship between measured traits and actual behavior is low because people do not act the same in different situations.

28. In what respect is trait behavior consistent, according to Mischel? Comment with regard to temporal versus situational differences. *- a person may act consistently in the same situation.*

29. Bem and Allen maintained, in contrast to Mischel's assertion, that some people do seem more consistent in traits. What was their finding, and what was Mischel and Peake's response?

30. Despite Mischel's data, it seems intuitively obvious that people do have traits that are consistent across a variety of situations. What perceptual bias does Mischel suggest that may account for this common impression? *First impression of a person*

After first impression of someone you always think that person acts in the same manner.

Chapter Twenty
Psychological Assessment

General Objectives

1. List and define three forms of reliability and four forms of validity.

2. Discuss the concepts of achievement and aptitude, and indicate why the distinction between these concepts is blurred.

3. Briefly describe the range of behaviors characteristic of individuals classified as retarded and of those described as mentally gifted.

4. With regard to IQ tests, define the concepts of (a) cultural bias, (b) heritability, (c) reaction range.

5. List and describe the four major procedures for measuring personality.

6. Discuss the major ethical issues involved in the use of psychological tests.

Psychological Assessment

Learning Objectives appear at
the end of each major section.

1. This chapter begins with an anecdote about a math talent search. The main point of the story is that, in this case, prediction of aptitude for mathematics was more accurate when done by (choose one):
   a. math teachers
   b. a standardized college entrance test
   c. primary-school grades
   d. the students' peers

b

REQUIREMENTS OF A TEST

Reliability

2. Suppose an individual measures a wall several times by two methods: with a carpenter's rule, and by holding his hands against the wall. Because the first method yields highly similar results every time, it is said to be more

reliable

_____reliable_____ than the second method.

3. Similarly, if each person who takes a test on Monday obtains roughly the same score when he or she takes the test (or an alternate form) again on Tuesday, the

reliable

test is said to be highly _reliable_. This type of reliability is

test-retest

termed _test_-_retest_ reliability.

4. Which of the following tests shows higher test-retest reliability, Test A or Test B?

	SCORES ON TEST A		SCORES ON TEST B	
	MONDAY	TUESDAY	MONDAY	TUESDAY
Phyllis	17	19	89	42
Xavier	97	98	75	12
Borwin	8	10	85	14
Jane	43	47	69	12
Tom	62	59	20	82

Test A (because for *each person* the scores on Monday are *highly similar* to those on Tuesday)

5. In addition to *test-retest* reliability two other types of reliability are used in psy-

consistency

chological assessment: *internal* _consistency_ reliability, the extent to

interjudge

which two halves of a test produce similar scores; and _interjudge_
reliability, the degree of agreement on scoring between different raters or judges.

internal

6. A test is said to have _internal_ consistency if the scores on two random halves of a test are similar. For example, if Phyllis has 9 items correct on one half of a test and 8 on the other, Jane has 21 items correct on one half and 22 on the other, Tom has 32 and 30, and the pattern continues for the other

internal

people tested, then the test is said to have high _internal_

consistency

consistency

7. Some tests or measurements are not scored by simply counting the number correct. For example, psychiatric diagnoses, ratings of behavior, or grading of essay examinations require the scorer to make a subjective judgment. In this case it is

interjudge

important to obtain high _interjudge_ reliability, a measure of agreement between two or more judges or observers.

Validity

8. While reliability refers to the consistency or stability of a test,

validity

Validity refers to its accuracy: Does the test really measure what it is supposed to measure?

9. If a test measures what it is supposed to measure, it will include a representative sample of the measured attribute. A test purporting to measure one's understanding of course material, for example, must adequately sample the course content. If the test does adequately sample the measured attribute, the test is said to have

content   _Content_ validity.

face   10. Content validity is sometimes confused with _face_ validity, which refers to whether or not the test *appears* valid to the people taking it. For example, if a question on a test asks "Does your mind go blank when you stand up in front of an audience?" this question might well seem to have

face validity   _face_ _validity_ for measuring the attribute of speech anxiety.

11. Quite often the purpose of a test is to predict performance. For example, if IQ tests really measure some type of intellectual ability, then they should be correlated with, or predict, grades in school. In fact, IQ tests do correlate with grades

predictive   in school, so IQ tests are said to have _predictive_ validity.

12. A test is also considered valid if it correlates with a well-established measure of the attribute. For example, if a new test purporting to measure intelligence correlates with an accepted IQ test, then the new test is said to have

concurrent   _Concurrent_ validity.

13. The broadest and most loosely defined concept of validity involves the extent to

construct   which a test measures a trait or theoretical _construct_. To demonstrate the validity of a particular construct (such as intelligence, anxiety, shyness, and so forth), a test should be related to any other behavior or measure that is also supposed to reflect that construct.

14. Thus, if a test of mechanical comprehension correlates with success in a particu-

predictive   lar job, the test has _predictive_ validity. If the test correlates with another test designed to measure mechanical comprehension, it has

concurrent   _Concurrent_ validity. If the test is also related to a capacity to understand airplane engines, dishwashers, and windmills, but is not highly related to intelligence, anxiety, and shyness, then it is likely that the test has

construct   _Construct_ validity as well.

reliable   15. To be valid, a test must be _reliable_, but a reliable test is not necessarily valid. For example, measuring head size with a tape measure is a

reliable/validity   highly _reliable_ procedure but has no _validity_ as a measure of intelligence.

Learning Objectives

1. Define the following general concepts:
   reliability *—yielding similar results all the time*
   validity *—does it test what it says it is testing*

2. Define or give examples of each of the following forms of reliability:
   internal consistency reliability *divide test in half get same amount right on each half*
   test-retest reliability *— get similar score each time you retake test*
   interjudge reliability *— different judges similar in how they correct subjective test*

3. Define or give examples of each of the following forms of validity:
   content validity *— Is content of test valid. Is it made up of stuff you learned*
   face validity *— does it appear to be valid*
   predictive validity *— how it predicts what you will do in future*
   concurrent validity *— is it valid when compared with other similar tests*
   construct validity

4. Can a test be reliable without being valid? Can a test be valid without being reliable?
   Yes   *No*

Standardization

higher

16. Suppose Phyllis answers forty out of sixty questions correctly on a test. If nothing else about the test is known, Phyllis's score alone contains little information. If you know that the *average* score of other individuals taking the test is thirty, however, you at least know that Phyllis scored (higher/lower) than average.

17. Before a test is put into general distribution, it must be given to a large and well-

standardization

defined group of people called a *Standardization* group. As an initial step

average (mean)

in standardization procedures, the arithmetic _____*average*_____ of this group is calculated.

18. A major purpose of standardization procedures is to translate a "raw" score into a score that indicates its relationship to scores obtained by others taking the same test. For example, one method of standardization indicates the percentage or proportion of people who score above or below a particular score. This is known as

percentile

the _____*percentile*_____ system.

30

19. Thus, a score at the 70th percentile indicates that _____*30*_____ percent

70

of the people taking the test scored higher and _____*70*_____ percent scored lower than this percentile.

20. The other standardization system is more complex. It indicates the distance either

standard-

above or below the average score. This is called the _____*standard*_____

score

_____*score*_____ system.

21. As shown in Figure 18.3, standard scores represent points on a bell-shaped curve. For IQ tests, raw scores are converted to standard scores with a mean of

100

_____100_____ and a standard deviation of approximately 15. With the aid of statistical tables, standard scores tell us the proportion of individuals in any area of the normal curve.

Learning Objectives

5. What is the purpose of test standardization? Name and briefly describe two procedures for translating raw scores into standardization scores.

THE MEASUREMENT OF INTELLIGENCE, APTITUDE, AND ACHIEVEMENT

22. The first reliable intelligence test was developed by Alfred

Binet

_____Binet_____ for the purpose of identifying mentally retarded children for special education in the Paris school system.

23. Scores on Binet's thirty-item test were computed in terms of "mental age" level. For example, if a five-year-old child answered questions that the average seven-year-old child could answer, then the child was said to have a mental age of

seven

_____7 seven_____.

24. Binet originally defined mental retardation as a mental-age score

two

_____two_____ years below chronological age. One problem with this definition was that a child of ten with a mental age of eight was considered as

three

retarded as a child of five with a mental age of ___3 three___.

25. A German psychologist suggested that scores on Binet's test should be expressed in terms of the following equation:

IQ

$$\frac{\text{Mental Age}}{\text{Chronological Age}} \times 100 = \text{IQ}.$$

26. Thus, a five-year-old child with a mental age of five on Binet's test would have

100

an IQ of _____100_____, and a child of ten with a mental age of eight

80

would have an IQ of _____80_____.

27. In modern intelligence tests, the ratio of mental age to chronological age is

no longer

(still/no longer) used. Instead, IQ is a standard score on a distribution with a mean of 100 and standard deviation of 15.

Learning Objectives

6. Who developed the first reliable intelligence test? *Alfred Binet*

7. What was Binet's first definition of retardation? *child with mental age two years below chrono. Age*

8. Describe the ratio of mental to chronological age with which Binet later expressed the IQ score. What is used in place of this ratio today? $\frac{mental\ A}{chrono\ A} \times 100 = IQ$

Individual Intelligence Tests

28. Tests administered by one examiner to one subject rather than to a group are

individual   called ___individual___ intelligence tests.

29. *The Stanford-Binet Test.* Binet's test was revised at Stanford University for use in the United States. Hence, the current version is known as the

Stanford-Binet   ___Stanford___-___Binet___ test.

30. The Stanford-Binet test (circle the best answer):
    a. contains items that assess verbal ability.
    b. contains performance tests—arrangement of pictures, blocks, and so on.
    c. currently may be used on preschool through adult populations.

d   (d.) all of the above.

31. *The WAIS and the WISC.* I well remember David Wechsler at a conference a few years ago saying in response to the question "What is intelligence?" that "Intelligence is not a single thing." I also remember thinking, "I traveled all this way to hear this?" But his statement was an excellent summary of the way the Wechsler tests treat intelligence—not as a single, generalized ability but as a

cluster of abilities   (cluster of abilities/unitary capacity).

32. Because the Stanford-Binet was primarily a test of verbal ability and also a poor test of adult IQ, Wechsler developed two other individually administered tests:

Wechsler Adult   the ___Wechsler___ ___Adult___ *Intelligence Scale* (WAIS)

Children   and the Wechsler Intelligence Scale for ___Children___ (WISC). The recent revisions of these tests are known as the WAIS-R and WISC-R.

WISC   33. In addition to the WAIS for adults and the ___WISC___ for schoolchil-

Preschool   dren, Wechsler developed the WPPSI, the *Wechsler* ___Pre-school___ *and Primary Scale of Intelligence* (usually pronounced something like "whipsee" by psychologists).

Wechsler tests

34. The major differences between the Wechsler tests and the Stanford-Binet are that (1) the (Wechsler tests/Stanford-Binet) provide separate scores for each subtest,

verbal

and (2) the Wechsler tests provide separate IQ scores for ___verbal___

performance

and ___performance___ abilities. This encourages the treatment of intelligence as a number of different abilities rather than as a single generalized ability.

Group Intelligence Tests

35. The major advantage of group tests is that they are economical and

convenient (easy)

___convenient___ to administer. Their major drawback is that they do not provide examiners with the additional behavioral information that may be obtained in a face-to-face testing situation.

Learning Objectives

Stanford Binet
WISC
WAIS   WPPSI

9. Name four currently used individual tests of intelligence.

10. What are the major differences between the Stanford-Binet and the Wechsler tests? *Individual Score for*
Each Task

11. List the major advantage and disadvantage of group intelligence tests. *convenient* *No Face to face interaction*

Achievement and Aptitude Tests

36. Tests constructed to assess how much a person knows about certain subjects are

achievement

termed ___achievement___ tests. Tests designed to assess talent or capacity

aptitude

for learning are known as ___aptitude___ tests.

37. One's aptitude for a particular subject depends in part on what the individual has learned or achieved in the past; and one's achievement depends in part on aptitude. Thus, the difference between aptitude and achievement tests is quite (dis-

blurred

tinct/blurred).

38. *The Scholastic Aptitude Test (SAT).* The SAT is designed to measure "aptitude

verbal

for college studies." It yields two scores, one for ___verbal___ apti-

mathematical

tude and the other for ___mathematical___ aptitude.

39. Which of the following is (are) true?
    a. The SAT is useful in predicting success in college.
    b. Other factors, such as motivation, are also important predictors of college success.

c. The combination of high-school grades and SAT scores is a better predictor of college success than SAT scores alone.

d

(d.) All of the above.

Learning Objectives

12. Briefly define and explain the differences between achievement and aptitude tests. Why is the distinction between these two types of tests said to be blurred?

13. What is the purpose of the SAT? What two major categories of ability does it test?

Variations in Intelligence

40. *Mental Retardation*. Mental retardation involves not only impaired intellectual

adaptive
greatly

functioning but deficits in ___adaptive___ behavior as well. The extent of the limitations of people classified as retarded varies ((greatly)/only slightly), however, ranging from those who are able to live relatively independent lives to those who must live in institutions.

41. *Mentally Gifted*. In 1921, Lewis Terman began the study of 1,500 children with an IQ of 140 or higher, a study that has continued over the past sixty years. The basic finding of these studies is that children who have superior IQs are

more likely

(more likely/less likely) to be taller, heavier, stronger, more mature, and to make more artistic and literary contributions than are those with lower IQs.

Learning Objectives

14. In addition to deficits in intellectual functioning, what other category of impairment is manifested by the mentally retarded? Do all mentally retarded individuals suffer roughly the same degree of limitation?

15. In general, what are the characteristics of those with IQs above 140, according to Terman's studies?

IQ Scores: Nature or Nurture?

42. While various opinions have been expressed on the issue, the bottom line is that it is impossible to determine the extent to which intellectual differences among

environment (experience)

groups are due to ___environment___ (nurture) or to

heredity

___heredity___ (nature).

43. *Cultural Bias in Testing*. The main point being made in this section is that tests that rely heavily on vocabulary items, as IQ tests do, are developed for people of a particular cultural background. Thus, such tests are clearly

biased

___biased___ against people from a markedly different background.

44. The dilemma is that, because vocabulary items provide the best single estimate of IQ, it has been difficult to develop a culture-free test with predictive validity. Even though tests may be culturally biased, IQ tests are the best single predictor

school

of success in __school__ across all socioeconomic levels.

45. *Racial Differences in IQ: The Debate.* Educational psychologist Arthur Jensen has asserted that the difference between the average IQs of black and white peo-

heritability

ple is largely attributable to the __heritability__ of IQ.

46. While Jensen indicates that genetic factors may be "strongly implicated," heritability is not a constant genetic property but an estimate that is specific to a

environment

given population in a given __environment__. Thus, if a group's environment changes, the heritability of a trait may change.

47. It is apparent that physical traits, such as height, are influenced by genetic inheritance. It is also clear, as demonstrated by the increase in the average height of

environmental

American children over recent generations, that __environmental__ factors, including nutrition, also play an important role.

48. The point is that genes do not determine a particular IQ any more than they determine a particular height: there is a *range* of IQ specified by heredity that varies with the environment. This range of possible response to the environment is

reaction

termed the __reaction__ range, and the reaction range for IQ is, in fact, not known.

49. The *main* dispute between Jensen and his critics concerns Jensen's suggestion that (circle one):
    a. there is a difference in mean IQ between blacks and whites.
    b. the black-white IQ difference is in large part due to environmental factors.

c
    c. the black-white IQ difference is in large part due to genetic factors.

50. Some of the arguments given in rebuttal to Jensen question his methods of investigating and assert that he has not taken into account some of the major

environmental

__environmental__ factors that may affect IQ.

51. In addition, a recent survey has shown that the mean IQ scores of black children adopted by white families of above-average socioeconomic status were:
    a. above average for whites.
    b. above average for blacks.

c
    c. above average for the entire population.

52. The study referred to above suggests that the reaction range for IQ is quite

broad/environment

(narrow/broad) and that __environment__ is an extremely important factor in determining IQ.

Learning Objectives

16. In what way are IQ tests culturally biased? Why are they used even though they are culturally biased? Why would it be difficult to develop a "culture-free" IQ test?

17. Briefly explain the concepts of heritability and reaction range.

18. What is Jensen's main assertion with regard to the difference between mean IQs of blacks and whites? Discuss evidence that does not seem to support his position.

THE MEASUREMENT OF PERSONALITY

Direct Assessment

53. The methods of personality measurement to be discussed in this section include direct assessment, self-report, projective tests, and physiological measures. There

interview
    are two kinds of direct assessment: the _interview_, which is essentially a conversation between the subjects and examiner; and

observation
    observation, in which a trained observer simply watches people.

54. Both interviews and observations may be conducted in either a structured or

unstructured
    unstructured manner. In structured interviews examiners use a pre-

unstructured
    arranged set of questions; in _unstructured_ interviews they do not.

55. The advantage of observation over an interview is that observation reveals what a

does
    person _does_ in a situation, his actual behavior, not just what he says he does.

56. While observation may be the best way to obtain a solution to a behavioral problem, a drawback to the method is that it consumes a great deal of

time
    time and requires the skills of a highly trained observer.

Self-Report Inventories

57. One of the quickest methods of measuring personality is with self-report inventories. Like the IQ tests, these inventories contain a specific set of items, items

factor
    selected either by the method of _factor_ analysis or by the

empirical
    empirical method.

empirical

58. Factor analysis (discussed in Chapter 19) is a statistical method for reducing a large number of items to a few underlying factors. The ___empirical___ method involves administering a series of items to people known to possess a particular trait and then selecting those items that differentiate that group from a group that does not possess the trait.

empirical

59. *The Minnesota Multiphasic Personality Inventory*. The MMPI consists of a large number of questions comprising several scales intended to reflect psychiatric diagnoses. This test was developed using the (empirical/factor analytic) method.

mental illnesses

60. The MMPI was originally intended for evaluation of (normal personalities/mental illnesses). It is still best used for its original purpose, the identification of psychopathology.

Projective Tests

have not

61. Projective tests are based on the assumption that when people are presented with ambiguous material, such as ink blots or pictures, they project something of their personalities into their interpretations of these materials. Unlike the self-report inventories, projective tests (have/have not) been carefully standardized.

d

62. *The Rorschach Ink-Blot Test*. This type of projective test consists of a series of ink blots. In scoring responses to these tests, the psychologists look for (circle the correct answer):
   a. the content of the response ("It's a bat").
   b. the amount of the ink blot used ("This small part in the middle").
   c. the form, shading, color, and activity attributed to the ink blot ("Because it's black and furry and flying up her").
   d. all of the above.

subjective

63. An advantage of the Rorschach is that it samples a broad range of behavior. A strong disadvantage is that the procedure is individualistic and

   ___subjective___, difficult to validate, and thus open to the examiner's biases.

stories

64. *The Thematic Apperception Test*. The Thematic Apperception Test (TAT) employs a set of pictures about which subjects are supposed to tell

   ___stories___.

is not

only moderately

65. There (is/is not) a single standardized scoring system used for interpreting the TAT. In fact, research indicates that clinicians agree (to a great extent/only moderately) among themselves about interpretations of the TAT.

Physiological Measures

66. The main point made in this section is that in addition to watching people behave or asking them questions, there is another way to measure personality: by moni-

physiological

toring certain _physiological_ events such as blood pressure, EEG, heart rate, skin conductance. Since these measures may indicate general arousal level or emotional reactions such as anxiety, they may be used as a check on self-report inventories.

Learning Objectives

19. In this section four categories of procedure for measuring personality were discussed. List these four categories.

20. Two methods for selecting items for self-report inventories were presented. Name and provide a general explanation of these procedures.

empirical

21. How was the MMPI devised, and for what purpose is it best used?

22. Name and describe two projective tests, indicating the criticisms of these procedures.

23. Discuss the way in which physiological measures may contribute to understanding personality.

THE ETHICS OF TESTING

67. Because psychological tests may exert such a strong influence on a person's future, it is important that the results be used properly. The potential for misuse of test scores raises certain ethical issues. First, a test must actually measure

valid

what it is intended to measure; it must be _valid_ in the specific situation in which it is used.

68. For example, a test designed to predict job success in a particular situation

validity

should have predictive _validity_ for the job in that situation.

69. The second issue concerns the proper use of test information. Who should receive this information? The person taking the test? Potential employers? College administrators? The question of how widely test scores should be distributed and

has not

to whom (has/has not) been clearly established.

IQ Tests and Special Education

70. In proportion to their numbers in the population there are four times as many blacks and three times as many Hispanics as there are whites in special education classes. These placements are made primarily by schools on the basis of

IQ

_IQ_ scores, so the possibility exists that these placements are

cultural

the result of _cultural_ bias.

are not

71. The courts (are/are not) in agreement on the cultural-bias issue. One court has declared that the tests are biased and must not be used for placement in special education classes, and another court has decided in the opposite direction.

72. The question will probably be decided only after it has been heard by the Supreme Court. In such a hearing psychologists will probably testify, as they have in past hearings, (for/against/on both sides of) the issue. The membership of the American Psychological Association is very much divided on this question.

on both sides of

Personnel Selection

73. The main issue involved in the use of tests in personnel selection concerns

discriminate

whether or not the tests __discriminate__ against different racial or cultural groups.

74. In general, courts have permitted the use of tests if test scores can be shown to correlate with job performance—in other words, if the tests have

predictive

__predictive__ validity.

75. In some instances tests that do discriminate against a group have been allowed if

predictive

the test has __predictive__ validity and if an alternative, nondiscriminatory test does not exist.

76. In addition to predictive validity, some rulings have considered

content

__content__ validity sufficient in some situations. Some psychologists have further suggested that predictive validity is useful only with jobs involving

construct

simple, repetitive tasks and that __construct__ validity should be permitted for more complex jobs. The courts have not considered this latter issue, however.

Truth-in-Testing Laws

77. Although scores on many standardized intelligence, aptitude, achievement, and personality tests are frequently not reported to the individuals who take the tests, an APA guide to the use of tests maintains that people have the right to know

career

their scores if the results are used in making __career__ decisions affecting the individual's future.

78. New York State's truth-in-testing law goes even further, requiring that people who take college admission tests such as the SAT later be permitted to obtain copies of the test and answers. Some psychologists are concerned, however, that

validity

widespread publication of the test could decrease its __validity__ in future use.

79. There is some concern that tests taken earlier may be used by employers at a much later time for a different purpose, as when an employer uses scores obtained upon hiring for consideration in promotion. One way to prevent such misuse is to destroy old scores. But an argument against this practice is the fact that

predictive   old tests may still have _predictive_ validity some years later and that old test scores may become relevant in a lawsuit concerning personnel decisions.

80. While intelligence and personality tests may be misused, as they are when used to discriminate on the basis of race, they may be used to prevent discrimination as well. That is, people may be hired or promoted on the basis of

merit   _merit_, to the extent reflected in a test score, rather than disqualified because of employer bias. Similarly, standardized tests have given some children from disadvantaged backgrounds a way out of poverty.

Learning Objectives

24. The potential for misuse of psychological tests raises two major ethical issues. What are these issues?

25. What data about the groups comprising special education classes suggest the possibility of cultural bias? What is the opinion of the courts on this issue? Of psychologists?

26. When standardized tests are used in personnel selection, what characteristic must the tests have to demonstrate that they are not being used to discriminate on the basis of racial or other group membership? Discuss the various types of validity involved.

27. According to the APA guide on the use of tests, when do people have a particular right to know their scores?

28. What does New York's truth-in-testing law require with regard to information provided test takers? What may be a drawback of this law, according to some psychologists?

29. Should test scores used in employment decisions be destroyed once they become obsolete? Present arguments on both sides of this issue.

30. Discuss a potential positive as well as a potential negative outcome of the use of standardized testing.

Chapter Twenty-One
Adjustment to Stresses

General Objectives

1. Describe what is meant by adjustment.

2. Identify the two interpretations of stress, and describe the major methods for coping with stress.

3. Explain how various kinds of life stresses affect physical functioning.

4. Explain how various kinds of life stresses affect psychological functioning.

5. Describe the various methods that have been developed to cope with stress.

6. Describe the crises of adjustment patterns for adolescents, adult men, and adult women.

Adjustment to Stresses

Learning Objectives appear at
the end of each major section.

erratic
1. The case of Karen, cited in the text, illustrates that adjustment must occur in the face of (erratic/predictable) occurrences in daily living.

cope
2. Thus when we speak of adjustment, we have in mind the ability to

_____Cope_____ with both the successes and failures of daily living. Failure to cope can result in *stress*. The text uses the term *stress* to refer to either an

stimulus
environmental event or object, a _____stimulus_____, or to the resulting

response
physical and psychological disturbances, a _____response_____.

3. Attempts to maintain adjustment through successful coping fall into three major

problem-
categories. The first category is the employment of _____problem_____-

solving
_____solving_____ skills. Development of good problem-solving skills is a critical factor in maintaining good adjustment.

accept
is not

4. The second approach is simply to _____accept_____ a difficult situation. This is likely to be an effective approach when taking positive action (is/(is not)) possible. For example, one can do little about the death of a friend or a pet; simple acceptance of the death represents a good adjustment.

5. The third approach is to employ such techniques as denial of the problem or repression of its existence in the memory. These and similar techniques are

defense mechanisms

called _____defense mechanisms_____

6. While defense mechanisms do not actually provide solutions to problems, they

anxiety

often help to reduce the _____anxiety_____ associated with stressful situations. In this respect they can be beneficial. However, overuse of them to the

disturbances

exclusion of the other approaches can result in severe _____disturbances_____

is not

7. The text concludes that there (is/(is not)) a specific formula as to how these three approaches should be applied by everyone. Which of the approaches should be

situation (problem)

employed depends on the person and the _____situation_____.

Learning Objectives

1. What does the text mean by adjustment? *How you can learn to deal with different situations at different times*

2. What two interpretations are given to the term *stress*? *environmental stimulus or a response to something*

3. Name and describe the three major methods for coping with stress. *problem-solving, acceptance, defense mechanisms*

LIFE STRESSES AND PHYSICAL FUNCTIONING

similar to

8. The physiological responses of the body when an individual experiences an exciting event—winning a large sum of money, for example—are ((similar to)/different from) the physiological responses to a tragic event, such as the breakup of a love affair. In other words, the physiological responses to emotional events, be they positive or negative, are virtually the

same

_____same_____.

The Body's Response to Stress

three

9. *Selye's Three Stages*. Hans Selye has observed that prolonged stress in any form

produces _____three_____ distinct stages in the body.

10. The initial shock reaction in the first stage, called the stage of

alarm   __alarm__, is followed by countershock. During the countershock phase, the autonomic nervous system triggers an increase of hormones by the

adrenal   __adrenal__ glands. As a consequence of the increased production, the adrenal glands begin to enlarge. Also, the thymus gland and the lymph nodes begin to shrink, and ulcers begin to appear in the stomach. Taken together, these

stress   physiological responses are called the "__stress__

syndrome   __syndrome__."

resistance
decrease   11. During the second stage, called the stage of __resistance__, the generalized reaction of the body to the stress begins to (increase/**decrease**) as more specific defenses take over. The "stress syndrome" responses begin to reverse themselves.

12. If the local defenses are unsuccessful, or if the stress continues for an extended

exhaustion   period of time, the final stage, called the stage of __exhaustion__, sets in. Once again, the "stress syndrome" responses begin to increase. If the stress

death   remains unchecked, the final outcome is __death__.

13. *Stress-Related Disease and Death.* Many diseases, such as peptic ulcers, diabetes, and cancer, are highly related to stress. While muscular overload and other physical factors may be implicated, it is generally acknowledged that

psychological   __psychological__ factors, such as anxiety and depression, are the major culprits.

has not   14. A direct relation between stress and disease, however, (has/**has not**) been estab-

correlational   lished. So far the data are merely __correlational__—no direct cause-effect relationship has been established.

15. Acute stress has also been implicated in some instances of sudden

death   __death__ that follow intense emotionally induced physiological arousal. The physiological arousal may be triggered by both negative and

positive   __positive__ emotional events. Thus winning a large sum of money can be as likely to trigger sudden death as losing a large sum of money.

rare   16. Instances of sudden death following intense emotional arousal are (**rare**/frequent),

heart   and the victims are probably people suffering from __heart__ ailments of some kind. This kind of sudden death occurs during the initial

shock   __shock__ phase of the *alarm reaction* when heart rate, blood pressure, and adrenal hormones have all rapidly increased.

nonspecific

would not

17. It is important to note that stress is the body's (specific/nonspecific) response to any demand made upon it, be it positive or negative. Therefore, the avoidance of all stress (would/would not) be a possible goal or even a desirable one.

Learning Objectives

4. What is meant when it is said that stress is the body's *nonspecific* response to demands made upon it? *Your body* *stress comes from different things*

5. List Selye's three stages that describe the body's responses to stress, and briefly describe what occurs during each stage. What is the final outcome if stress is not resolved? *Shock resistance, exhaustion*

6. What is the "stress syndrome"?

7. What appears to be a major factor in stress-related disease? Why can we not say that a direct relationship has been established here? *Psychological*

8. What kind of emotional arousal can sometimes trigger sudden death? Where in Selye's three-stage process does this *positive happy* sudden death occur? *shock phase*

9. Why is it not possible or desirable to avoid all stress? *stress is non specific - The body needs some amt of stress*

The Measurement of Life Stress

18. The Social Readjustment Rating Scale (SRRS) is a device for measuring the

stress

amount of life _____stress_____ an individual may encounter during a given period of time.

intensity

more

19. Each of the forty-three sources of stress contained in the SRRS has been assigned a mean value based on the (intensity/desirability) of stress it produces. Thus, while getting married may be a happy occasion, it produces (less/more) stress than the death of a close friend.

greater

20. When using the SRRS, a person simply indicates which of the events has occurred to him or her for a given time span. The mean values of the indicated events can then be converted into Life Change Unit (LCU) scores. The higher the LCUs, the (lesser/greater) will be the amount of stress encountered.

21. If the LCU score reaches 150, the situation is called a "life

crisis

_____crisis_____." Scores of this value and higher were found to be asso-

illness

ciated with an increased incidence of _____illness_____. Among the illnesses associated with high LCU scores were heart disease, broken

bones

_____bones_____, and cancer in children.

after

22. The SRRS has been primarily used to study persons (before/after) the onset of illness, and these kinds of retrospective studies cannot establish a causal relationship between stress and disease. However, one study did concurrently monitor both stress and throat cultures in a group of families for a period of one year and found that respiratory infections were four times more likely to occur

after

(before/after) a family crisis.

Learning Objectives

10. What does the SRRS measure? How are the scores on this scale expressed?

11. What score on the SRRS is required to reach a "life crisis"? What was found to be associated with scores in this range?

12. Why have studies with the SRRS not been able to establish a causal relationship between stress and disease?

13. What was observed in the study that monitored both stress and throat cultures for a period of one year? *After a period of stress, illness could set in*

Social Support and Physical Illness

23. One of the most common stresses that are associated with both illness and premature death arises from a lack of, or sudden loss of, close relationships with

loneliness

other human beings. For example, ___loneliness___ is said to account for the reduced longevity of persons living by themselves as compared to persons living together, such as married couples.

24. The most likely reason for the dramatic effects of loneliness on health is that the

stress

presence of others can reduce ___stress___. One study, for example, found that the increase in flow of fatty acids associated with heart disease while under a stressful situation was lowest for persons in the presence of

friends

(strangers/friends). Thus the presence of friends in this situation helped to neu-

stress

tralize the effects of ___stress___.

25. A particularly potent form of stress occurs following the disruption of a

marriage

___marriage___. It has been found that persons who are separated or divorced are much more likely to be under psychiatric care than those who are

do not

married, are widowed, or have remained single. These data (do/do not) demonstrate a causal relationship; marital breakup may have resulted in mental illness or mental illness may have resulted in marital breakup.

Learning Objectives

14. What appears to account for the increased longevity of married persons as compared to persons who are single, widowed, or divorced? *Not being lonely, having someone there*

15. It has been said that the presence of others helps to neutralize the effects of stress. What experimental evidence gives support to this view? *When people are in presence of friends stress is reduced reduced fatty acids going to Heart*

16. How do we know that the disruption of a marriage appears to be a particularly stressful event? Has a causal relationship been established here? *No*

Personality and Physical Illness

26. It is possible to place people into one of two general behavior patterns. People who are highly competitive and always appear to be working against the con-

A   straints of time are said to fit the Type _____*A*_____ behavior pattern, while people who are more relaxed and less constrained by time are said to fit

B   the Type _____*B*_____ behavior pattern.

27. A study that followed more than 2,000 male executives for a period of nine years found that the incidence of heart disease was far more prevalent among the

Type A   executives who fit the _____*Type*_____ _____*A*_____ pattern of behavior. The Type A behavior pattern strongly predicted heart disease, even after controlling for other known predictors of heart trouble.

Learning Objectives

17. Describe the difference between Type A and Type B behavior patterns. *Type A live in fastlane " B live more relaxed life*

18. What did the study of over 2,000 male executives conclude with respect to these two behavior patterns? *Type A had higher rates of heart disease*

Stress and Physical Illness: A Model

28. The *disregulation model* proposed by Schwartz is an explanation for the relation-

stress   ship between physical illness and _____*stress*_____. This model suggests

regulatory   that physical disorders result from failure in the body's _____*regulatory*_____ system. Failure can occur at any one of four stages.

29. The body's regulatory system operates upon the principle of

negative   _____*negative*_____ feedback; that is, the operation of one system slows down the operation of another system and vice versa. For example, increased body heat triggers activity in the sweat glands, which in turn reduces body heat, which in turn shuts off sweat-gland activity.

environmental

30. The initial stage in the disregulation model occurs when _environmental_ *demands* impose excessive pressures upon the body and a person is forced to ignore the resulting negative feedback. Thus an air traffic controller is likely to ignore the high blood pressure resulting from the tension of his or her job and may eventually suffer a heart attack.

31. The second stage of disregulation occurs when either heredity or learning results

information processing

in *faulty* _information_ _processing_ by the *brain*. In this case the brain mishandles negative feedback or fails to meet environmental demands. The text uses the example of children who have learned "to eat everything on their plates" and eventually become obese.

organ

32. At the third stage, some peripheral _organ_ is faulty. For instance, a jogger with a bad heart may find that her heart fails to respond and stops beating when the brain calls for increased activity.

33. The fourth stage where disregulation is possible occurs when the

negative

negative -*feedback* process itself fails. For example, pressure-sensitive cells surrounding blood vessels may be defective and fail to signal the brain that blood pressure is rising.

disregulation

34. Failure at any one of these four stages results in _disregulation_ of the entire bodily system. For example, if heart rate is disrupted, the entire

cardiovascular

cardiovascular system is also disrupted.

Learning Objectives

19. How are bodily systems regulated by negative feedback? _operation of one system slows down operation of another vice versa_

20. What does the disregulation model attempt to explain?

21. Below are listed the four stages in which disregulation can occur. Briefly describe the cause of the disregulation in each of these stages.
    a. environmental demands
    b. information processing in the central nervous system
    c. a peripheral organ
    d. the negative-feedback process

LIFE STRESSES AND
PSYCHOLOGICAL FUNCTIONING

has not

35. It has been found that stress, whether induced by positive or negative situations, can result in physical illness among some persons. A similar relationship (has/has not) been found with psychological dysfunction. Psychological

negative

dysfunction appears to be associated only with ___negative___ life events.

undesirableness

36. In reviewing a series of studies on the relationship between stress and psychological functioning, the text concludes that it is the (intensity/undesirableness) of an event that contributes to psychological dysfunction. Or, to put it another way,

body

positive or desirable events may stress the ___body___, but not the mind.

Learning Objectives

22. In what way does bodily functioning differ from psychological functioning in response to stress?

23. What does the text conclude after reviewing a series of studies relating stress to psychological dysfunction?

Life in a Stressful Environment

37. When everyday events in the environment such as loud noise, air pollution, and bad weather are found to be aversive, they may be considered to be examples of

stress
is not

environmental ___stress___. In most cases directly preventing, or even predicting, these aversive events (is/is not) possible.

38. *Predictability of Events.* Studies with both animals and human beings have consistently demonstrated that aversive events are experienced as less stressful when

predicted

they can be ___predicted___.

39. This phenomenon was further illustrated in a study in which female college students were subjected to no noise, or high or low levels of predictable noise, or

random (unpredictable)

___random___ noise while they performed verbal and numerical tasks. In this part of the experiment it was found that the groups subjected to the different levels and kinds of noise (did/did not) differ in their psychological and physical adjustment to the noise.

did not

40. In a second test these same subjects were given more complex tasks to perform,

noise

but this time without ___noise___ to distract them. In this situation it was found that the subjects who had been exposed to the loud noise at

random

___random___ intervals did not do as well as any of the other groups.

temporarily

41. It was shown, therefore, that while it was possible to (temporarily/permanently) adjust to the aversiveness of a high level of random noise, the extra effort re-

lessened

quired to adjust to this situation ___lessened___ ability on subsequent tasks.

42. *Control over Events.* A later experiment helped to explain why the random noise affects subsequent ability to perform complex tasks. In this study there were four groups of male students who were all subjected to the high level of

random/one (the first)

___random___ noise. Only ___one___ group thought that they could control the noise.

43. When later asked to perform a proofreading task, the group that believed they

better

could control the random noise did (worse/better) than the other three groups.

tension (anxiety)

This group also showed significantly less ___tension___ than the sub-jects who believed that they had no control over the noise.

44. Taken together, these studies suggest that the effect of environmental stress on

control

adjustment may be primarily attributed to the lack of ___control___ over aversive events rather than to the intensity of the stress. In other words,

control

people are less stressed when they feel they have some ___control___ over a stressful event.

Learning Objectives

24. Describe what is meant by environmental stress.   *stress you don't have control over*

25. Briefly describe the first part of the study in which female college students were subjected to different conditions of noise. What differences were noted among the groups?

26. Briefly describe the second part of the above study. What conclusions were drawn?

27. How did a second study, using male college students, demonstrate that it is primarily a feeling of lack of control that leads to the debilitating effects of environmental stress?

Learned Helplessness

45. The inability to control aversive events apparently leads to a feeling of

helplessness

___helplessness___, which in turn leads to a diminished ability to adjust.

was not

would not

46. A classic experiment demonstrated how helplessness was learned in dogs. The dogs were first placed in a sling and given electrical shocks to the feet; escape (was/was not) possible in this first phase of the study. When the dogs were later given the opportunity to escape from the aversive shocks, they (would/would not) take advantage of it. This learned helplessness was not found in a control group of dogs not previously subjected to the inescapable shock.

fewer

less well

47. In another study, human beings were subjected to a loud tone from which they could not escape while performing various assigned tasks. On subsequent tasks, when escape from the tone was made possible, these subjects made (fewer/more) attempts to escape the tone than did control subjects who had first experienced a loud tone from which they could escape. The former also performed (less well/better) on the assigned tasks.

failure

generalize (transfer)

48. It has also been demonstrated that learned helplessness could be instilled by assigning problem-solving tasks that resulted in unpredictable ____failure____. Furthermore, it was observed that helplessness learned in one situation may ____generalize____ to other situations.

not all

49. Seligman has reformulated the concept of learned helplessness to better explain observations such as the fact that (not all/all) persons demonstrate learned helplessness when subjected to the same aversive event. According to the new formulation, learned helplessness not only results from a person's belief that he or she lacks control over an aversive situation, but, more importantly, it also de-

explanation

pends upon the person's ____explanation____ for this lack of control.

permanent
internal
general

50. Seligman now believes that learned helplessness develops when people feel that their lack of control is due to causes that are (temporary/permanent), when they feel that their lack of control is (internal/external), and when they feel that their lack of control is applicable to (general/specific) areas of their lives.

cannot

51. This new formulation of the concept of learned helplessness (can/cannot) now explain all of the questions about the development of learned helplessness. For example, it cannot explain why some people blame themselves for failure while others faced with the same situation blame the environment.

Learning Objectives

28. Describe how learned helplessness was demonstrated in dogs. *shocks*

29. Describe how learned helplessness was demonstrated in human beings. What happened when people who learned to be helpless in one situation were given a different task to solve? *Noise*

30. According to the latest formulation, what is even more important than the belief that one is helpless in the development of learned helplessness?

31. Under the new formulation, what three beliefs (feelings) must people have in order to develop learned helplessness? What problem cannot be answered by this new formulation?

Gaining Control over the Environment

52. Individual members in one group of elderly adults in a nursing home were encouraged to take responsibility for personal belongings and to make their own decisions as to how they would spend their time. Individuals in a second group were encouraged to leave decisions and responsibility to the

staff   <u>staff</u>.

53. Three weeks later, it was observed that the group that appeared to be happier and

themselves   more active was the group instructed to rely on (the staff/themselves) for deci-
     sions and responsibility. An eighteen-month follow-up found that this difference

still   (still/no longer) existed between the two groups. Moreover, the death rate was
     much lower in the group instructed to rely on themselves.

54. One conclusion to be drawn from this study is that it is apparently possible both

unlearn   to *learn* and to <u>un learn</u> helplessness. It appears likely that people
     can be trained to gain control over their lives, or they can be trained to behave

helpless   as though they are <u>helpless</u> to control the conditions that dictate
     their lives.

55. It can be concluded that helplessness increases stress by increasing anxiety and

not   decreasing problem-solving ability. It can (also/not) be concluded that helpless-
     ness is always maladaptive. There are situations—the death of or rejection by a
     loved one, for example—in which acceptance represents good adjustment.

Learning Objectives

32. In what way were the two groups of patients in the nursing home treated differently? What were the results of a
    three-week follow-up? Of an eighteen-month follow-up?   <u>Still the same lower death rate</u>

33. In what way does helplessness increase stress? Explain why helplessness may not always be maladaptive.

COPING WITH STRESS

Relaxation

56. Transcendental meditation, yoga, progressive relaxation, and autogenic training

relaxation   are all techniques for producing <u>relaxation</u>. By intentionally induc-
     ing relaxation, one can reduce both the physiological and cognitive responses to

stress   <u>stress</u>.

do not   57. Researchers (do/do not) all agree that these various techniques for producing re-
     laxation all produce the same effects. However, any differences there may be are
     small, and no technique holds any specific advantage.

58. The method of *progressive relaxation* requires the tensing and subsequent

releasing (relaxing)

relaxing of different muscle groups in sequence. For example, one might start out by first tensing and releasing the muscles in the fingers, then move to the wrists, then to the arms, and so on.

59. When progressing through this sequence of tensing and relaxing sequential muscle groups, it is important for the individual to pay attention to the

differences

differences between tension and relaxation. The end goal is to teach individuals how to recognize tension and to provide them with a technique for

relaxed

returning to a _relaxed_ state whenever tension begins to be observed.

60. Another relaxation technique, called *autogenic training*, makes use of imagery

self-suggestion
herself

and _self_-suggestion to achieve a relaxed state. When using this technique, an individual suggests to (herself/another person) that her arm is getting very heavy and then imagines the arm is getting heavy.

61. This process of self-suggestion and imagery continues until one is able to make

body

the entire _body_ heavy and relaxed. The technique can also be extended into slowing heart rate and cooling and warming various parts of the body.

62. Both progressive relaxation and autogenic training achieve similar results in

autogenic

about the same amount of time. However, _autogenic_

training

training is more frequently used in conjunction with biofeedback because it does not interfere with the measurements that are a part of biofeed-

progressive

back. The tensing and relaxing of muscles required by _progressive_

relaxation

relaxation does interfere with these measurements.

Learning Objectives

34. List four techniques that can be used to produce relaxation. Are there any important differences in the results achieved by these techniques? _Meditation Yoga, progressive relaxation, autogenic training_

35. Briefly describe how to use the method of progressive relaxation. _tensing and releasing of muscles noticing difference between tensed & relaxed_

36. Briefly describe how to use the method of autogenic training. _self-suggestion and imagery_

37. Why is autogenic training, rather than progressive relaxation, the preferred technique when biofeedback is being employed?

Biofeedback

63. Biofeedback is another technique that can be used to induce relaxation. This is accomplished by electronically monitoring and feeding back

information   ~~information~~ on the current state of tension in the muscles. The immediacy of the feedback information allows one to progress slowly into deeper

relaxation   and deeper levels of muscle _relaxation_ .

64. Biofeedback has also been used to modify functioning in other physiological systems.

feedback   Again, the principle is the same: immediate _Feedback_ allows for gradually changing a physiological response in a desired direction. Biofeed-

still   back is (still/no longer) in the experimental stage.

65. It is also possible to reduce stress by actively engaging in thoughts that

counteract   _counteract_ the emotions produced by the stressful event. For example, the person waiting fearfully in a dentist's office can imagine engaging in erotic escapades and stop thinking about what might happen in the dentist's chair. Learning to use this kind of approach is known as *cognitive*

restructuring   _restructuring_

66. While there are several different cognitive-restructuring techniques, all share the same major emphasis—to change thoughts that *increase* stress to thoughts that

decrease   _decrease_ stress. In fact, cognitive restructuring is a major compo-

Lamaze   nent in the _Lamaze_ method of childbirth.

Learning Objectives

38. Describe how biofeedback can be used to induce deep muscle relaxation. _electronic monitoring to help you know what body functions to control_

39. What is the basic principle behind biofeedback that allows for its potential use in many areas of physiological dysfunction? _immediate feedback_

40. Describe how one would use the technique of cognitive restructuring to reduce the stress of an aversive event. What method of childbirth employs this technqiue?

ADJUSTMENT: A LIFELONG PROCESS

Crises of Adjustment for Adolescents and Young Adults

biological

67. Problems with adjustment during adolescence include both personality develop-ment and ___biological___ changes as adolescents become physically and sexually mature. The problems of personality development primarily revolve around the establishment of an individual identity and psychological separation

parents

from ___parents___.

ambivalent

68. As adolescents move from the dependence of childhood to the independence of young adulthood, they often experience ___ambivalent___ feelings. They are pulled between wanting the comforts and protection due them as children and desiring the freedom and independence accorded to young adults.

rarely

do

69. Research has shown that this ambivalence is (usually/rarely) accompanied by re-bellion. Nor is it necessarily accompanied by unhappiness or emotional upheav-als. Most adolescents (do/do not) like and respect their parents.

Learning Objectives

41. What two major areas pose adjustment problems for adolescents? identify psychological separation from parents

42. What is the cause of the ambivalent feelings experienced by most adolescents? What does research show regarding the potential trauma of these ambivalent feelings?

Crises of Adjustment for the Adult Man

70. Levinson and his colleagues at Yale University interviewed four groups of men with various occupational backgrounds. On the basis of these interviews they ob-served that the life structures accounts of the major periods of each man's life

were

(were/were not) characterized by a common pattern.

71. The model that Levinson and his colleagues proposed from this research divides

three

the adult years of a man's life into ___three___ major eras. The first

early

era is ___early___ adulthood. This is followed by the

middle

___middle___ adult era, which in turn is followed by the

late

___late___ adult era.

72. *Entering the Adult World*. The first, early phase of male adulthood has frequently been observed to be characterized by the lack of a full sense of

stability (permanence)

stability. Romantic relationships and vocational interests are often temporary as the young man examines the options of adulthood against the back-

stable

ground of a developing need to establish a _stable_ life structure.

73. *The Age-Thirty Crisis*. Levinson's data reveal that the ages between twenty-eight

transitional

and thirty-three represent a _transitional_ period in the lives of many men. During this period questions about satisfaction with marriage partners, vocational choices, and life goals are reviewed and new decisions are made. For many this represents a painful process, and thus Levinson termed it the "age-

thirty

thirty crisis."

has

74. *Settling Down*. During the "settling down" phase the man (has/has not) already made some firm commitments regarding family, career, and life goals. Having made these commitments, he spends his energies solidifying his position in society.

75. Levinson found that near the end of the settling-down era (between ages thirty-six and forty) there is a distinctive phase in which the man strives to become

independent

fully _independent_. Gaining independence frequently involves changing or breaking off a relationship with an older adult who has previously served

mentor (teacher)

as a _mentor_.

76. *The Mid-Life Transition*. The mid-life transition era begins around the age of

forty-five

forty and lasts until about _forty_-_five_. Once again, the man begins to question every aspect of his life, involving both his

past

future goals and his _past_ accomplishments.

77. Levinson found that approximately 80 percent of the men in his sample

did

(did/did not) experience the mid-life transition as a moderate to severe crisis. Successful resolution of this crisis was often accompanied by the man's becom-

mentor (teacher)

ing a _mentor_ for a younger man.

Learning Objectives

43. List the three major eras that Levinson and his colleagues found characterized the lives of most men.

early middle late adulthood

44. According to Levinson, what adjustment problems are characteristic of the following stages:
    a.   entering the adult world? *stability*
    b.   the age-thirty crisis? *independence*
    c.   the settling-down period?
    d.   the mid-life transition? *resolution of past & present accomplishments*

45. During which stage did Levinson find that many men strive for independence? What often results from this striving?

Crises of Adjustment for Adult Women

more

78. Although the stages of a woman's life used to be marked primarily by her capacity to reproduce (the critical stages of puberty and menopause, for instance), women today confront a much (more/less) complex set of possibilities and expectations. In fact, as work becomes central for more women, their crises of ad-

men

justment may more closely resemble those of ___*men*___.

79. *Career versus Family.* Until recently, women had to choose to have either a

career

family or a ___*career*___. Now with half of all women working many

both

women choose to have ___*both*___.

80. Some women go directly into a career and postpone marriage and children. Some women start a career or return to school only after their children no longer demand so much time and attention. Many women manage these roles

simultaneously

___*simultaneously*___

81. The woman who switches from one role to the other finds she must make a new

adjustment

___*adjustment*___. The woman who works at both roles simultaneously may find that an attempt to be superb at each means she is

overloaded (overworked, etc.)

___*overloaded*___ and takes no pleasure in either role.

82. *Physical Attractiveness in Mid-Life.* Fading attractiveness concerns both men and

female

women, but our culture values youth more in ___*female*___ beauty than in male beauty. Therefore, as a woman ages she is more likely than a man

adjust

to need to ___*adjust*___ to a different image of herself.

greater

83. In a study of women who were attractive and socially active in college, it was found that twenty years later these women had (greater/less) difficulty adjusting to routine family life than did their less attractive schoolmates. However, it may

diminished (lessened, etc.)

be more a matter of ___diminished___ social activity compared to active college years rather than difficulty in adjusting to loss of youth that is responsible for this finding.

84. *The "Empty Nest" Syndrome.* Some women whose lives have been centered on their families may find that their children growing up and leaving home precipi-

crisis

tates a ___crisis___ in their lives. This feeling of not being needed

empty nest

anymore is called the "___empty nest___" *syndrome*.

85. Occasionally when this syndrome is coupled with the physical changes of meno-

depression

pause, intense ___depression___ can result. However, most women view menopause and the empty nest as normal and natural and not as a

crisis

___crisis___. Satisfying work outside the home and a warm, supportive husband can provide important help for a woman adjusting to her changing situation.

continuing

86. The major point of this chapter is that adjustment is a ___continuing___ process. The life cycle itself creates problems of adjustment for all people.

are not

"Good" and "bad" adjustments (are/are not) permanent states. Most people experience a continuum of "bad" to "good" adjustments throughout life.

Learning Objectives

more woman are having careers and families

46. How have career and family choices for women changed in recent years? List ways women today handle the roles of career and family.

47. Why may fading physical attractiveness be more of a problem for women than for men in our culture? *youth is a sign of beauty in women*

48. What is the "empty nest" syndrome? Is this a problem for all women with children? What factors have been found to aid in adjustment to this syndrome? *when children are gone and mother doesn't feel needed anymore   supportive husband & friends*

49. Why does the text say that good or bad adjustment is not a permanent state? How does Levinson's work illustrate this point? *because things change.* *Men seem to go through many transitions — good & bad & woman .*

Chapter Twenty-Two
Psychological Disorders

General Objectives

1. Discuss the problems encountered in defining abnormality.

2. Describe the major classification system of abnormal behavior, and discuss both its strengths and its weaknesses.

3. Identify the various anxiety disorders, somatoform disorders, and dissociative disorders.

4. Describe the major affective disorders.

5. Describe the symptoms and phases that characterize schizophrenia.

6. Identify the symptoms of personality disorders, sexual deviance, and substance abuse.

7. Describe some of the major aspects of the epidemiology of mental disorders.

Psychological Disorders

Learning Objectives appear at
the end of each major section.

DEFINITIONS OF ABNORMALITY

more

1. Deciding what is normal and what is abnormal with respect to behavior is much (more/less) difficult than deciding what is normal and abnormal with respect to physical health. This is because what is considered to be normal and abnormal

changes (varies)

behavior _changes_ across cultures and even within cultures across time.

Norm Violation

2. The rules of a society that prescribe "right" and "wrong" behavior and to which

norms   a majority of citizens adhere are called _____norms_____. Since norms are
learned as part of the socialization process and seem so natural, they are usually

broken (violated)   noticed only when _____broken_____.

3. The norms in American society with respect to sexual behavior have broadened
so that many former sexual behaviors considered to be abnormal are now consid-

normal   ered to be _____normal_____. This illustrates the point that norms can

change   _____change_____ across time.

4. Norms still remain the dominant standard for defining normality and abnormality.
A major danger here is that this may serve to enforce conformity as

good/bad   _____good_____ and nonconformity as _____bad_____.

Learning Objectives

1. Why is it difficult to define what is normal and what is abnormal behavior?

2. What are norms? When are they usually noticed?

3. Provide an example that illustrates the point that norms change across time.

4. What is a major danger in using norms as the standard for defining normal and abnormal behavior? could lead to good or bad

Statistical Abnormality

5. Another way of defining normality is to say that the way the *majority* of people
act is "normal" and that persons who act very differently are "abnormal." This is

statistical   the _____statistical_____ definition of normality.

6. While a statistical definition of normality has the value of simplicity, it fails to
distinguish unusual behavior that is desirable from that which is undesirable. A
woman who plays the tuba, for example, would be considered

abnormal   _____abnormal_____ by the statistical definition. According to the statistical
definition, then, any deviation from a statistical norm, whether desirable or unde-

abnormal   sirable, is considered _____abnormal_____.

Learning Objectives

5. What is the statistical definition of normality? *way majority of people acts is "normal" other people are abnormal*

6. List one advantage and one disadvantage of using the statistical definition of normality. *Fails to distinguish unusual desirable behavior from undesirable behavior*

Personal Discomfort

discomfort

7. Another way to distinguish between normality and abnormality is to leave it up to individual judgment of *personal* discomfort. Persons who feel distressed by their own thoughts or behavior would be considered abnormal. Those not distressed by their own thoughts or behavior would be considered

normal

normal.

does not

8. Unlike the statistical definition of normality, this definition (does/does not) inhibit nonconformity and eccentricity. A major problem with this definition, however, is that the absence of personal discomfort among some persons who commit crimes against society (murderers, rapists, etc.) should not necessarily lead to

normal

the conclusion that they are normal.

Learning Objectives

7. What is the personal-discomfort definition of normality? *Persons who feel distressed by their own thoughts and feelings*

8. List one advantage and one disadvantage of using personal discomfort as a definition of normality. *case of rapist*

Impairment of Functioning

9. A somewhat similar method for distinguishing between normality and abnormality is to say that those people who cannot carry out the simpler tasks of daily living are to be considered abnormal and in need of psychological help. This

impairment/functioning

definition is based upon impairment of functioning.

10. Although this approach is simple and may work well for persons who have lost

reality

all contact with reality, many people may show only a slight impairment in daily living skills and yet may be suffering from intense psychological disturbance.

Learning Objectives

9. How is abnormality defined in terms of impairment of functioning? *people who can't carry out simple tasks of daily living*

10. List one advantage and one disadvantage of using impairment of functioning as a definition of normality.

Deviation from an Ideal

11. A fifth and final way of defining normality is to define as normal an ideal model of the well-adjusted person and then define as abnormal any

deviation
abnormal

deviation *from the ideal*. Unfortunately, this definition leaves most persons in the (normal/abnormal) category.

12. Categorizing most people as abnormal poses at least two major problems. One is that any less-than-perfect human being may feel that he or she has a serious

adjustment (psychological)

adjustment problem in spite of evidence of successful living in many areas of his or her life. Another problem is that the definition of the ideal per-

culture

sonality is relative to the _culture_ that defines it. Such a definition would change from culture to culture and across time within cultures.

13. Among the five ways of defining abnormality, _none_ of them provides an entirely satisfactory solution for distinguishing between adjustment and maladjustment.

Learning Objectives

11. How is abnormality defined in terms of deviation from an ideal? *ideal model of the well adjusted person abnormal any deviation from that*

12. List two disadvantages of using deviation from an ideal as a definition of normality. *change over time and across cultures*

CLASSIFICATION OF ABNORMAL BEHAVIOR

14. *The Diagnostic and Statistical Manual of Mental Disorders*, 3rd ed. (*DSM III*),

classification

provides a _classification_ of psychological disturbances into various categories. It is the system used by most mental health professionals.

15. The *DSM III* approaches psychological disturbances in the same manner physicians approach physical ailment. They are thought to be analogous to

diseases

___diseases___ with specific symptoms and causes which need to be diagnosed and treated according to the diagnosis. This view of psychological dis

medical
is not

turbances is called the ___medical___ model. The medical model (is/is not) supported by all mental health professionals.

Advantages of Classification

16. There are some advantages to using a classification system such as that offered by the *DSM III*. One advantage is that it allows mental health professionals to

language

communicate with one another using the same special ___language___. A second advantage is that it makes possible the collection and advancement of

disturbances (illnesses, etc.)

knowledge regarding specific psychological ___disturbances___

Criticisms of Psychiatric Diagnosis

17. There are also several criticisms of basing a classification system for psychological disturbances upon the medical model. One such criticism is that labeling people with psychological disturbances as being "sick" and treating them as such

role

causes them to act out the ___role___ expected of them.

18. Another criticism is that the diagnostic labels give the illusion of

explaining
does not

___explaining___ psychological disorders when in fact they do not. Thus labeling a particular disturbance as being a phobia (does/does not) contribute an answer as to what caused the disturbance.

detract from

19. A third criticism of such labels is that they (add to/detract from) the character and reputation of the persons to whom they are applied. This can result in unintended social and personal consequences for individuals so labeled, such as jeopardizing their employment and loss of civil liberties.

20. A fourth and final criticism is that all too frequently the same patient might receive different diagnoses when examined by different professionals. This illus

unreliable

trates the point that the classification system can be ___unreliable___.

21. While many of these criticisms are justified, for now at least a classification system is needed and the *DSM III* represents the best one available. One indication that it is not too far off the mark is that patterns of psychopathology classified in

world

the *DSM III* are found ___world___-wide.

Learning Objectives

13. What is the *DSM III*? What does the *DSM III* have to do with the medical model?

14. List two advantages of using a classification system such as the *DSM III*.

15. List four criticisms of psychiatric classifications such as the *DSM III*.

16. What finding indicates the *DSM III* system may not be too far off the mark? *The classification of its mental disorders seem to appear world-wide*

ANXIETY DISORDERS

anxiety
is not

22. A feeling of apprehension or fear that is accompanied by physiological arousal is called _anxiety_. The presence of anxiety from time to time (is/is not) considered to be abnormal. Rather, occasional anxiety is a necessary component in the lives of all people.

anxiety disorder

23. When anxiety becomes too extreme and begins to interfere with everyday functioning, then the anxiety is no longer considered to be normal and is instead classified as an _anxiety disorder_.

Generalized Anxiety Disorder and Panic Disorder

generalized anxiety

free-

floating

24. Diffuse and generalized anxiety which is impossible to control by avoiding specific situations is called _generalized anxiety_ disorder. Individuals suffering from this disorder cannot specify what is generating the pervasive anxiety, which led Freud to label it "_free_-_floating_" anxiety.

panic

phobic disorder

25. Persons suffering from generalized anxiety disorder will sometimes experience periods in which the generalized anxiety suddenly mounts to overwhelming intensity. Such episodes are called _panic_ attacks. When the panic attack is not precipitated by a specific stimulus or situation, it is called a _phobic disorder_.

Phobic Disorder

phobia

agoraphobia

26. When intense anxiety is triggered by a specific stimulus or situation that is not particularly dangerous, it is called a _phobia_. The most common phobia is a fear of being in public places and is called _agoraphobia_

27. There are two distinct problems associated with phobic disorders. One is the desire to control the anxiety generated by the feared stimulus or situation, which

avoidance

means the consequent _avoidance_ of these stimuli or situations. The other problem is that the active avoidance of these situations may result in other

problems (complications)

problem's in a person's daily life. For example, a person who develops a phobia of being in elevators will find many inconveniences associated with this fear.

Learning Objectives

apprehension or fear accompanied by physiological arousal

17. Define what is meant by anxiety. When is the presence of anxiety likely to constitute a serious problem?

18. Explain what is meant by the following disorders:
    generalized anxiety disorder
    panic attacks –
    phobic disorder (or phobia)

19. What was Freud's term for the kind of anxiety experienced in a generalized anxiety disorder? *free-floating anxiety*

20. What two distinct problems are associated with a phobic disorder? *avoidance, problems in life*

Obsessive-Compulsive Disorder

28. An irrational thought that repeatedly occurs without conscious effort is called an

obsession/are not

obsession. Obsessions (are/are not) always indicative of psychological disturbance. It is only when they become so persistent that they

interfere

interfere with daily life that they are considered to represent a psychological dysfunction.

29. A ritualistic action that is performed again and again for no apparent benefit is

compulsion
is not

called a _compulsion_. The anxiety associated with compulsive behavior is found when an individual (is/is not) allowed to perform the ritualistic behavior.

30. There are two general categories of compulsions. One category is illustrated by the person who is constantly looking for unlocked doors or windows; these kinds

checking rituals

of behaviors are called _checking rituals_. The other category is illustrated by the person who is constantly emptying ashtrays or wiping the dust from furniture; these kinds of behavior are called

contamination compulsions

Contamination compulsions

31. In many cases a person exhibiting these ritualistic behaviors may have both *com-*

obsessive

pulsive and ___obsessive___ elements involved in the behavior. For example, the compulsion to repeatedly wash one's hands may result from an

obsession

___Obsession___ with germs.

Learning Objectives

irrational thought that repeatedly occurs without conscious effort.

21. What is an obsession? When do obsessional thoughts represent a psychological disturbance? *when they interfere with daily life*

22. What is a compulsion? At what point is anxiety most likely to be exhibited in compulsive behavior? *ritualistic action that is performed again and again — when a person is not allowed to express their compulsion*

23. Name and give examples of the two general categories of compulsions.

24. Give an example of a ritualistic behavior that involves both obsessive and compulsive components. *obsession with germs always washing hands*

SOMATOFORM DISORDERS

32. Persisting somatic (bodily) symptoms in which there is no physiological

somatoform
different from

malfunctioning are called ___somatoform___ *disorders*. Somatoform disorders are (similar to/different from) psychosomatic disorders in that the latter involve actual physiological damage or disease.

Hypochondriasis

33. The preoccupation with bodily symptoms as indicators of possible serious illness

hypochondriasis

is called ___hypochondriasis___. The diagnosis of hypochondriasis is applied

healthy

only to persons who are perfectly ___healthy___, since in the presence of ill health such concern might well be justified.

Conversion Disorders

34. When an individual develops a physical dysfunction (blindness, deafness, paralysis, etc.) that has no organic basis, he or she is said to have a

conversion disorder

___Conversion disorder___. Since the physical dysfunctions found in conversion disorders have no organic basis and since they often appear

disappear/cures

or ___disappear___ suddenly, "miraculous ___cures___" are often found in persons suffering from conversion disorders.

is not

35. Distinguishing between conversion disorders and the early stages of actual neuro-logical disease (is/is not) always without error. For example, one study found that organic brain disorders were much more likely to be later found among per-

conversion disorders

sons previously diagnosed as having (anxiety or depression/conversion disorders).

Learning Objectives

problems associated with body

25. What are somatoform disorders? How do they differ from psychosomatic disorders? *No organic basis for problem*

26. What is hypochondriasis? *a healthy person who thinks he has something with himself all the time*

27. What are conversion disorders? Why are "miraculous cures" possible with conversion disorders?

28. What research evidence casts some doubt on the ability to always accurately diagnose conversion disorders?

neurological disorders

DISSOCIATIVE DISORDERS

dissociative

36. Psychological dysfunctions characterized by a dissociation or breaking apart of normally integrated behaviors are called *dissociative*

disorders

disorders. A common feature in all dissociative disorders is the

memory

loss of *memory* for some aspects of present or past experience. Three of the more common dissociative disorders discussed by the text are amnesia, fugue, and multiple personality.

37. The partial or total loss of memory of past experiences is called *amnesia*. When this loss of memory is *not* due to organic factors, it is called psychogenic

amnesia/can

amnesia. Psychogenic amnesia (can/cannot) be distinguished from organic amnesia. For example, the disappearance and reappearance of memory

psychogenic

may occur quite suddenly with *psychogenic* amnesia. Moreover, the forgotten material can often be recovered under hypnosis. This is not true of or-ganic amnesia.

fugue

38. In the dissociative disorder called *fugue* ("flight"), the person flees from both the immediate environment and the self to take up an entirely

does not

new life. After recovering from a fugue state, the person (does/does not) remem-ber what happened during the fugue state.

39. Still another type of dissociative disorder occurs when the personality becomes divided into two or more separate personalities, a condition called

multiple personality

multiple personality. The separate personalities that

extreme

evolve in multiple personality often take opposite and _extreme_ forms—one naughty and one nice, one dominant and one submissive, for instance. These extremes found in multiple personality appear to be exaggerations

normal

of _normal_ conflicts found in all persons.

Learning Objectives

29. What are dissociative disorders? What is a common feature in all dissociative disorders?

30. What is psychogenic amnesia? How can it be distinguished from organic amnesia?

31. What occurs in the dissociative disorder called fugue? What is observed when a person returns from a fugue state?

32. What is multiple personality? What forms do the multiple personalities often take? From what do these forms appear to derive?

MAJOR AFFECTIVE DISORDERS

40. The major affective disorders are characterized by extreme or exaggerated

mood

disturbances of _mood_. Major affective disorders differ from mood changes experienced by everyone in that they are more exaggerated and inappropriate and often include instances of delusions or hallucinations. They

reality

may also result in the loss of contact with _reality_.

Major Depression

intensity

41. The symptoms found in major depression differ drastically in (kind/intensity) from the symptoms found in the normal depressions experienced by everyone. Thus major depression is a much more intense form of the kinds of depressions we all occasionally experience.

gradually
gradually

42. The onset of major depression occurs (suddenly/gradually) and the depressive episode ends (suddenly/gradually) with a period of several months or more between onset and offset. In addition to drastic changes in mood, persons suffering from major depression also exhibit changes in motivation, thinking, and

physical (motor)

physical functioning.

43. Major depression constitutes a significant health problem in that

20/10

_____20_____ percent of women and ____10____ percent of men are likely to experience at least one major depressive episode during their lives. Only about 6 percent of the women and 3 percent of the men will actually require hospitalization for this depressive episode, however.

Bipolar Disorder

44. Bipolar disorder is characterized by cyclical and extreme changes in

mood

____mood____. Bipolar disorder usually begins with intense excitement

manic

and hyperactivity, called the ____manic____ episode or phase, which is

depressive

then frequently followed by a ____depressive____ episode.

45. The hyperactivity and excitement commonly found in the manic episodes of bi-

are not

polar disorder (are/are not) generally put to constructive use. Rather, the increased energy fuels erratic pursuits that are often detrimental to the individual. The cyclical episodes found in bipolar disorder are generally much

shorter

(longer/shorter) than the episodes of depression found in major depression.

twice

46. Unlike depression, which is (half/twice) as common in women as in men, bipolar

equally

disorders affect both sexes ____equally____, with the first episode gener-

before

ally occurring (before/after) thirty years of age. Both bipolar disorders and

genetic

depression appear to have a ____genetic____ link or predisposition, since both are most likely to occur in persons whose relatives have also been afflicted.

Learning Objectives   _extreme or exaggerated disturbances of mood_

33. What is the primary feature that characterizes major affective disorders? In what way do persons suffering from these disorders differ from normal persons? _—more exaggerated and inappropriate accompanied by delusions and hallucinations_

34. Describe the sequence of events that accompanies major depression. In what way does this disorder differ from the depressions experienced by everyone?

35. What percentage of women and what percentage of men are likely to suffer from major depression at least one time in their lives? _20% of women   10% of men_

36. Describe the symptoms that accompany bipolar disorder. What is the manic phase like? _cyclical and extreme changes in mood.   —consists of Euphoria and excitement_

37. What are the facts regarding:
    a. the frequency of bipolar disorder in men and women? _occurs equally the same in both_
    b. the age of onset of bipolar disorder? _before thirty_
    c. the possibility of a genetic predisposition in both depression and bipolar disorder? _positive_

SCHIZOPHRENIA

47. Schizophrenia, which means a "psychic split," is primarily characterized by a

dissociation (separation)   _dissociation_ of the normally integrated components of the **personality**. For example, there is a separation between ideas and emotions or between emotions and behavior.

48. The most prevalent mental disorder in the United States is

depression   _depression_, but the most common cause of hospitalization for men-

schizophrenia   tal disorders is _schizophrenia_

Symptoms of Schizophrenia

49. _Disorders of Thought_. The schizophrenic person may display a variety of abnormalities, including motor, perceptual, and emotional disorders, but

thought   _thought_ disorders are the predominant symptom. All schizo-
some/some   phrenics will display (some/all) of these symptoms (some/all) of the time.

50. The thought disorders that characterize schizophrenia primarily involve a split or

association (relationship)   lack of _association_ between ideas or between ideas and emotions. For example, instead of linking together the words in a sentence to express a logical thought, the thought-disordered person may link words together on the basis of sound or rhyme. Words linked together in this manner are called

clang   _clang_ associations.

51. Another kind of thought disorder is characterized by a tendency to continue to dwell on a primary association to a particular stimulus (green grass, blue skies,

perseveration   dark closets, and so forth), a condition called _perseveration_

52. Still another kind of thought disorder involves a tendency to generate each sentence from some mental stimulus in the preceding sentence, thus losing any connection with a central idea to be expressed. This behavior is called

overinclusion   _overinclusion_

53. One of the most common thought disorders found among schizophrenics is the presence of an irrational belief in spite of overwhelming evidence that the belief has no basis in reality. These irrational beliefs are called

delusions   _delusions_.

distorted

54. *Disorders of Perception.* One of the most distinguishing features of schizophrenia is the tendency to perceive the external world in a (distorted/realistic) manner. Schizophrenics frequently experience sensory perceptions that are unrelated to any external stimuli. These false perceptions are called

hallucinations

hallucinations

55. Hallucinations are most commonly found among three of the sense modalities—

auditory

somatic, tactile, and _auditory_. Hallucinations involving vision,

smell

taste, and _smell_ are far less common and may not be related to the schizophrenic process when they do occur.

56. In addition to hallucinations, schizophrenics show other perceptual disturbances,

attention

such as the inability to focus or maintain _attention_ and an exag-

stimuli
do

gerated sensitivity to certain _stimuli_, such as odors. Standard laboratory tests (do/do not) confirm these perceptual disturbances, but their cause remains unknown.

57. *Disorders of Affect.* Disturbances are also frequently encountered in the emotional responses, or *affect,* of schizophrenic patients. The complete absence of an emotional response and an entirely inappropriate emotional response are examples of this disturbed

affect

ples of this disturbed _affect_. The central feature here is that the

emotional

external situation does not trigger the appropriate _emotional_ response.

58. *Disorders of Motor Behavior.* Another area in which schizophrenic patients fre-

motor

quently exhibit disturbances involves their _motor_ behavior. They often endlessly repeat an inappropriate motor response, engage in such bizarre behaviors as banging their heads, or remain for hours without exhibiting

catatonic

any motor behavior, a condition referred to as a _catatonic_ stupor.

59. *Disorders of Identity.* Schizophrenics may often lose their sense of individuality and become confused as to who they are. In other words, they have a disorder of

identity

Identity.

60. *Disorders of Volition.* Schizophrenics usually display an inability to either initiate or follow through with purposeful activity leading to some useful outcome. This inability to initiate and maintain willful control over their behavior is called a

volition

disorder of _volition_.

61. *Disorders of Relationship to the World.* Finally, schizophrenics often become preoccupied with their own thoughts and may totally withdraw from any mean-

world   ingful relationship with the ___world___.

Learning Objectives ~~dissociation of normally integrated components of personality~~

38. What is schizophrenia? How does schizophrenia compare with depression as a serious health problem? *to schizophrenia, compares with it in that most people are hospitalized due*

✳ 39. Thought disorders are the predominant symptom found in schizophrenia. Describe what is meant by thought disorders, and identify each of the following types: *lack of association between ideas*
    delusions *- irrational*
    clang associations *saying words in a sentence because they rhyme not because they mean anything.*
    perseveration *- tendency to dwell on a primary association*
    overinclusion *- generating sentences from some mental stimulus in preceding one*

40. What are hallucinations? In what three senses do schizophrenics most frequently experience hallucinations? *false perceptions. tactile, auditory somatic.*

41. What are two other disorders of perception frequently found in schizophrenia? *Inability to focus or maintain attention. exaggerated sensitivity to certain stimuli.*

42. Describe each of the following disorders that are also commonly found in schizophrenia:
    disorders of affect *- giving inappropriate emotional response or none at all*
    disorders of motor behavior *repeating inappropriate motor response banging head.*
    disorders of identity *- lose sense of individuality*
    disorders of volition *inability to maintain willful control over behavior*
    disorders of relationship to the world *- preoccupied with own thoughts withdraw from world*

The Course of Schizophrenia

62. There are five major subtypes of schizophrenia, and while there are many differences in the kinds of symptoms manifested by individual schizophrenics, the schizophrenic process generally follows a course that moves through

three   ___three___ distinct phases.

63. The initial phase, which may be brief or last for years, is characterized by a slow deterioration of behavior and a withdrawal from active participation in daily life.

prodromal   This period is called the ___prodromal___ phase. In the second phase, which is frequently triggered by a stressful event while in the prodromal phase, some or many of the psychotic symptoms described above begin to appear. This

active   period is called the ___active___ phase. In the final phase, the schizophrenic's behavior becomes less bizarre and often returns to the pattern seen in

residual   the prodromal phase. This period is called the ___residual___ phase.

some

64. A longitudinal study of more than a thousand schizophrenics showed that (most/some) do recover from this disorder. In fact, about 25 percent did so. A majority of these persons (between 50 and 65 percent) continued to alternate be-

active

tween the residual and ___active___ phases, while approximately 10

active

percent remained permanently in the ___active___ phase.

Learning Objectives

43. Name and briefly describe the three phases that characterize the schizophrenic process.

prodromal = dormant
active - oscizophrenia is brought out
residual - back in dormancy

44. What did the data from a longitudinal study of more than a thousand schizophrenics show?

some recover
majority stay in residual and active phase

OTHER DISORDERS

Personality Disorders

gradual

65. Personality disorders are characterized by the (sudden/gradual) development of deviant behavior patterns that often begin during childhood. The deviant behavior patterns are usually less problematic to the individual with the personality disor-

others (society)
is not

der than they are to ___others___. The behavior of personality-disordered persons (is/is not) considered to be psychotic.

66. A person who is virtually indifferent to the effect his or her behavior may have

antisocial

on other persons is said to have an ___antisocial___ personality, and such

sociopath

a person is labeled a ___sociopath___. To be diagnosed as a sociopath an individual must display at least four of nine possible antisocial symptoms, but the most striking feature of this disorder is the absence of

emotion

___emotion___ in social relationships.

Sexual Deviance

can be

67. The text lists ten of the most common behaviors that (are always/can be) considered "abnormal" in our society. Sexually "normal" individuals may engage in some of these behaviors in mild forms. These behaviors are only considered to

only (sole, major)

be deviant when they become the ___only___ means of achieving gratification.

68. In other words, sexual behaviors are no longer considered to be deviant unless the deviation from standard sexual conduct seriously impairs the capacity for af-

adult

fectionate sexual activity between ___adult___ human partners.

Substance Abuse

69. The use of a drug or drugs is not considered to be a psychological problem un-

centered (directed)

less one's life begins to be ___centered___ around getting and using a

abuse

drug or drugs. Drug use is not considered drug ___abuse___ unless it gets out of control and begins to dominate one's life.

alcohol

70. The most abused drug in the United States today is ___Alcohol___. Ap-

10

proximately ___10___ percent of the American population is considered either to be alcoholic or to have a severe drinking problem.

depressant

71. Alcohol is a ___depressant___ of the central nervous system. Taken in large quantities, alcohol causes disorders of sensation, perception, and thinking. If a large quantity is consumed over a short period of time, it can produce

coma

___coma___ and even death.

72. Persons who continue excessive drinking begin to build up a

tolerance

___tolerance___ for alcohol, making it necessary to increase the dosage to achieve the same effect. The increased tolerance is also accompanied by an

psychological

increased ___psychological___ dependence in which life is bearable only when intoxicated.

73. Prolonged and heavy use of alcohol is often accompanied by

malnutrition

___malnutrition___. The toxic effects of the alcohol along with malnutrition have been found to produce several diseases affecting the liver, brain, and nervous system.

Learning Objectives

45. Explain what is meant by the following disorders:
personality disorder - *gradual development of deviant behavior in childhood*
antisocial personality - *someone indifferent to how his behavior effects other people*
sociopath - *antisocial person must have 4 of 9 antisocial symptoms*

46. When is a sexual deviance considered to indicate a psychological disturbance? *when they become the only means of achieving gratification*

47. What is the most abused drug in the United States today? Approximately what percentage of Americans does it affect? *Alcohol 10% of Americans affected by Alcoholism or drinking problems.*

48. What effect does alcohol have on the central nervous system? What is meant by an increased tolerance for alcohol? *depressant lovers inhibition* *need more* What other kind of dependency is associated with this drug? *psychological* *alcohol to get same eff*

49. What frequently accompanies prolonged and heavy use of alcohol? What is the end result of this combination of factors? *Death* *—many diseases liver etc*

ORGANIC DISORDERS

organic

74. Mental disorders that are directly traceable to destruction of brain tissue or to biochemical imbalances in the brain are called ___*organic*___

brain

___*brain*___ syndromes. The organic brain syndromes have a separate classification in the *DSM III*.

is not

75. It (is/is not) always easy for professionals to determine whether a particular behavioral disturbance is caused by organic disorders or emotional factors. Many of the common impairments found in organic disorders are also found in persons suffering from schizophrenia, conversion disorder, and even

depression

___*depression*___

Learning Objectives

destruction or biochemical imbalances in brain

50. What are organic brain syndromes? Are these disorders easy to distinguish from mental disorders resulting from nonorganic factors? *No*

51. What three other disturbances can produce symptoms similar to those found in organic brain syndromes?
depression, conversion disorder schizophrenia

EPIDEMIOLOGY OF MENTAL DISORDERS

epidemiology
are not

76. The study of the incidence, distribution, and control of illness in a population is called *epidemiology* (the study of epidemics). Accurate figures for mental illness (are/are not) easy to come by, but it has been estimated that

6/10

between ___*6*___ and ___*10*___ percent of the population of the United States will be treated for some kind of mental disorder during their lives. Many more people will also develop symptoms of mental illness for which they will not be treated.

Demographic Variability

77. *Sex.* The overall incidence of psychological disturbances is higher in

women

_____women_____ than in men, but drug dependence, organic brain syn-

men

drome, and sexual deviation are more frequent in ___Men___. Studies have consistently found that women are more prone to

depression

___depression___ than men.

78. *Marital Status.* Your text describes the incidence of psychological disturbances among marital status groups. After reading this material you should be able to rank-order the following groups from highest to lowest with respect to the *incidence* of psychological disturbances.

INCORRECT RANK ORDER	CORRECT RANK ORDER
married	single
divorced/separated	divorce/seperated
single	widows/widowers
widows/widowers	married

single

divorced/separated

widows/widowers

married

79. The lower frequency of psychological disturbances among married persons

cannot

(can/cannot) be attributed to marriage itself. It may be that disturbed persons are more likely to remain single or fail at marriage.

80. *Social Class.* A majority of studies have found that the incidence of serious psy-

lower

chological disturbances is highest among the ___lower___ social classes. There are two explanations for this finding. One is that life in the lower

stressful

social classes is more ___stressful___, and this produces the greater incidence of psychological disturbances. The other explanation is that persons who

drift

develop psychological disturbances tend to ___drift___

downward

___downward___ into the lower social classes as they develop serious psychological disturbances.

Cross-Cultural Variability

81. Perhaps the major point made in the section of the text dealing with cross-cultural variability is that people in most cultures exhibit some form of the most common mental disorders, but that the syndromes, or collections of

symptoms   _symptoms_____ , may differ as a function of differences in

cultures   _cultures_____ . For example, it has been observed that Christians and Moslems have delusions of destruction and delusions revolving around

religious   _religious_____ themes. Asian peoples, on the other hand, most frequently exhibit delusional

jealousy   _jealousy_____ .

Learning Objectives

52. What is epidemiology?   _Study of incidence, control, and distribution of illness in a society_

53. What percentage of the population in the United States will be treated for some form of psychological disturbance during their lives?   _6% to 10% of pop_

54. What kinds of psychological disturbances are more common to men than to women? What kind of disturbance is far more common to women? Which of the sexes is more likely to suffer from a serious psychological disturbance?   _sexual deviance, drug dep_   _depression_   _women_

55. Rank-order marital status groups on the basis of incidence of psychological disturbance.   _single, sep/div, widow, married_

56. Why can it not be concluded that marriage by itself contributes to a lower frequency of psychological disturbances?   _Because single people with psycho problems may not get married or only people with psycho problems end their marriages_

57. What social class has the highest frequency of serious psychological disturbances? What two explanations have been given for this finding?   _lower class_   _stress   downward mobility_

58. How do the delusions of Christian and Moslem peoples differ from the delusions of Asian peoples? What point is illustrated by this difference?   _religious_   _jealousy_

cross cultural difference in variability of mental disorders

Chapter Twenty-Three
Theories of Abnormality

General Objectives

1. Describe some of the early historical theories of abnormality.

2. Distinguish between the biogenic and psychogenic approaches to abnormality.

3. Describe the relatively recent historical origins of modern theories of abnormality.

4. Explain and contrast the following perspectives of abnormal behavior:
   a. the psychoanalytic perspective
   b. the behavior perspective
   c. the humanistic-existential perspective
   d. the family perspective
   e. the sociocultural perspective
   f. the biological perspective

Theories of Abnormality

Learning Objectives appear at
the end of each major section.

SOME THEORIES FROM THE PAST

Demonology

1. Throughout history human societies have developed many different theories to explain abnormal or deviant behavior. These theories have reflected the philo-

religious   sophical and ___religious___ outlooks of the societies as well as their scientific advancement.

2. For example, Stone Age people and many early societies believed that deviant behavior was caused by gods or demons who had taken possession of the deviant

body

person's __body__. Among many Stone Age societies the solution to this problem was to drill a hole in the victim's skull, thus allowing the evil

trephining

spirits to escape. This treatment is called __trephining__.

3. Similar ideas of spirit possession were held in early Chinese, Egyptian, Hebrew,

was not

and Greek societies. Spirit possession (was/was not) always considered to be an undesirable circumstance. For example, the priestesses at Delphi, who were thought to be possessed, were sought out for their prophecies by the

Greeks

__Greeks__.

Greeks

4. It was also the early __Greeks__ who first proposed a natural, rather than a supernatural, explanation of deviant behavior. Hippocrates developed the

natural

first organic theory, or __natural__ explanation, of deviant behavior. He assumed that it resulted from a deficiency or overabundance of one of the

humors

four __humors__ that were thought to compose the body.

5. During the Middle Ages, Western societies, under the strong influence of religion, returned to explaining deviant behavior in terms of possession by

demonic (supernatural)
gently
much harsher

__demonic__ forces. Persons thought to be unwillingly possessed by evil spirits were generally treated (gently/harshly). The deviant people thought to be in league with the devil were given (much harsher/similar) treatment. In the latter cases, execution by strangling, beheading, and burning was not unusual.

Learning Objectives

Demon's possesing the body

1. How did Stone Age societies explain deviant behavior? What treatment technique did they frequently employ?
   They used trephining - drill a hole in victims head to let evil spirit out

2. What other early societies also believed that spirit possession caused deviant behavior? Cite an example to show that spirit possession was not always considered to be an undesirable circumstance. _Chinese, Egyptian Greek and Hebrew The Greeks liked it because tnestesses would give prophecies_

3. Who developed the first natural theory of deviant behavior? To what did he ascribe deviant behavior?
   Hippocrates   He ascribed deviant behavior to humors

4. Describe how Western societies explained deviant behavior during the Middle Ages. In what way were people who were thought to be unwillingly possessed by evil spirits treated differently from people thought to be willingly possessed? _They thought it was possesion by demonic forces._

People unwillingly controlled by demons were treated gently People willingly possesed were treated harshly. They were killed.

Biogenic Theory

eighteenth

natural

Kraepelin

brain

6. During the Middle Ages there were a few protests against demonology as an explanation of mental disturbances, but it was not until the _eighteenth_ century that deviant behavior was again widely believed to result from _natural_ forces.

7. *The Textbook of Psychiatry*, written by Emil _Kraepelin_ and published in 1883, represented the first firmly established biogenic theory of mental disturbance since Hippocrates' time. Kraepelin asserted that deviant behavior resulted primarily from _brain_ pathology.

classifying

Kraepelin's

8. Kraepelin also furnished psychiatry with the first system for _classifying_ psychological disturbances. The series *Diagnostic and Statistical Manuals of Mental Disorders (DSM I–III)*, published by the American Psychiatric Association, are all descendants of _Kraepelin's_ system.

brain

syphilis

9. At the beginning of the present century, neurological research began to uncover the _brain_ pathology that was found to underlie many kinds of mental disorders. For example, it was discovered that general paresis is actually an advanced stage of _syphilis_.

Learning Objectives

Emil Kraepelin   1883

5. Who wrote *The Textbook of Psychiatry?* What was its publication date? What were the two important contributions to come out of this work? _classification of psychological disorders and DSM I - III_

6. What was eventually discovered to be the cause of general paresis? What is the significance of this finding? _syphilis_ _Show that it doesn't come from psychological disorders_

Psychogenic Theory

emotional

10. Biogenic theory assumes that mental disturbances result from some form of brain pathology or brain dysfunction. Psychogenic theory, on the other hand, assumes that mental disturbances result primarily from _emotional_ stress.

11. Psychogenic theory began with Mesmer and his theory of "*animal*

magnetism   _magnetism_." While his theory was incorrect, Mesmer's technique was effective in many cases. This technique, called "mesmerism," was actually a

hypnosis   form of _hypnosis_. Thus, Mesmer's major contribution to psychogenic theory was that his work led to the discovery that the power of

suggestion (hypnosis)   _suggestion_ _hypnosis_ can cure, and perhaps cause, mental disturbances.

12. Two French physicians, Ambroise-Auguste Liebault and Hippolyte Bernheim, used Mesmer's hypnosis technique more systematically in treating mental dis-

Charcot   turbances and introduced the technique to Jean-Martin _Charcot_. Charcot's major importance lies in the fact that he introduced one of his stu-

Freud/hypnosis   dents, Sigmund _Freud_, to the use of _hypnosis_ as a treatment for psychological disturbances.

13. It was from this beginning that Freud later developed his theory and technique of

psychoanalysis   _psychoanalysis_. Psychoanalysis is both a general theory of personality

abnormal (deviant)   and a detailed theory of _abnormal_ behavior.

Learning Objectives   Biogenic says that mental disorders are due to problem with the brain. Psychogenic says it has to do with emotional stress

7. Distinguish between the biogenic and psychogenic theories of abnormal behavior.

8. What theory did Mesmer propose as an explanation for mental disturbances? What was Mesmer's major contribution to psychogenic theory? "animal magnetism" "hypnosis" "suggestion"

9. Describe how Mesmer's use of "mesmerism," or hypnosis, eventually influenced Sigmund Freud. His teacher Charcot taught him how to use hypnosis to treat people with psychological disturbances

THE PSYCHOANALYTIC PERSPECTIVE

Freud's general theory of psychoanalysis was extensively covered in Chapter 18, and only a brief review of some important terms will be provided here.

14. Freud believed that the personality could be divided into three forces: the

id/ego/superego   _ID_, _Ego_, and _Superego_. It was the interaction among these three forces that determined human behavior and emotion, according to Freud. Mental disturbances arise when the

ego   _Ego_ is unable to maintain a balance between the other two opposing forces and conflicts go unresolved.

15. Freud further assumed that there are three types of anxiety. Identify each type from the following descriptions:

Reality

a. ___Reality___ anxiety occurs when a person is confronted with a realistic danger.

Moral

b. ___Moral___ anxiety occurs when a person violates some moral code contained in the superego.

Neurotic

c. ___Neurotic___ anxiety occurs when a person's ego is in danger of being overwhelmed by demands being made by the id.

neurotic

16. When the ego is unable to meet the demands of the id, ___neurotic___ anxiety begins to rise and the ego may then resort to a variety of

defense

___defense___ mechanisms in order to reduce the neurotic anxiety.

17. The defense mechanisms employed by the ego are usually symbolically disguised

aware (conscious)

so that an individual is not ___conscious___ *aware* of the nature of the conflict or the connection between the symptoms and the real problem.

18. The form that neurotic behavior takes is determined by the particular defense

ego

mechanism employed by the ___ego___. For instance, the panic attacks that characterize anxiety disorders are said to result from the use of

repression

___repression___ as the defense mechanism, while obsessive-compulsive

reaction

behaviors are said to result from the use of ___reaction___ *formation* as the defense mechanism.

19. When the ego is so severely deficient that it cannot make use of defense mecha-

psychotic
is not

nisms, then ___psychotic___ behavior is said to result. According to Freud, psychosis (is/(is not)) simply a severe form of neurosis. Being unable to employ defense mechanisms to ward off unacceptable impulses, the psychotic person retreats to earlier stages of psychosexual development and away from

reality

___reality___.

defense

20. While neurosis is characterized by an overuse of ___defense___

mechanisms

___mechanisms___ to control id impulses, psychosis is characterized by a

defense

weakened ego that has no ___defense___ against the id impulses. In contrast to neurotic and psychotic individuals, the normal individual has developed an ego that effectively functions to meet the conflicting demands of the id

defense

and superego without excessive use of ___defense___

mechanisms

___mechanisms___.

Learning Objectives

when Ego can not mediate between Id an Superego

10. What is the basis of mental disorders according to Freud?

11. Distinguish among reality anxiety, moral anxiety, and neurotic anxiety.
    realistic danger   Superego dominates   Id takes control

12. What is the basis of neurotic behavior according to Freud? What determines the form neurotic behavior will take?
    when ego is unable to meet demands of ID   Type of def. mech. Ego takes

13. What is the basis of psychotic behavior according to Freud? How does it differ from neurotic behavior?
    when ego can't use def. mech.   Person retreats to early stages of Psychosexual dev and moves away from reality

14. What distinguishes the neurotic individual from the normal individual according to Freud?
    excessive
    Person learns to control the id and Superego without use of def mech

– BEHAVIORAL PERSPECTIVE –

rejects

21. The behavioral approach to abnormal behavior (accepts/rejects) most Freudian concepts. The basic premise of the behavioral theories of abnormality is that

learned

   "abnormal" behavior is ___learned___ in much the same manner as is "normal" behavior, through the processes of modeling, classical conditioning, and operant conditioning.

22. Below are several examples of abnormal behavior that have resulted from learning. Identify which kind of learning is operating in each of these cases.
    a. Sweet Alice develops an intense fear of thunderstorms from viewing her mother cowering under the bed during such occasions.

modeling

   ___modeling___

   b. Joe Cool develops an intense fear of dark streets after being severely beaten

classical

   while walking down a dark street. ___classical___

conditioning

   ___conditioning___

   c. Mary Coed finds she gains a lot of sympathy and attention from her roommates whenever she complains of depression. Her depression grows steadily

**operant conditioning
(direct reinforcement)**

   worse. ___operant___ ___conditioning___

23. Many of the behaviors observed in persons suffering from depression may in part result from a combination of reinforcement and extinction. In this case, behav-

reinforced

   iors associated with depression are ___reinforced___ by undue attention from other persons, while more adaptive behaviors are subjected to

extinction

   ___extinction___ through lack of sufficient attention from others.

24. Depression may also result from the sudden reduction of positive reinforcement—for instance, from the death of a loved one or the loss of a satisfying job. Moreover, the amount of positive reinforcement available to an individual depends on three broad factors: (a) the number and range of stimuli found to be

reinforcing

reinforcing, (b) the availability of such reinforcers in the

environment/skill

enviornment, and (c) the individual's _skill_ in obtaining reinforcement. The lack of reinforcement because of failure in any one or more of these systems can result in depression.

25. The way an individual interprets a particular event may be as important as the

cognitive

event itself. Thus _cognitive_ factors are thought to play an important role in the development of maladaptive behavior. For example, depression is

interprets

likely to develop when a person consistently _interprets_ daily events in a negative manner.

is not

26. From the behavioral viewpoint maladaptive behavior (is/is not) symptomatic of illness as postulated by the medical model. Nor is it indicative of underlying un-

psychoanalytic

conscious conflict as postulated by the _psychoanalytic_ model. Rather,

maladaptive

the problem is the _maladaptive_ behavior itself.

Learning Objectives

abnormal behavior is learned

15. What is the basic premise of the behavioral approach to abnormal behavior?

16. Cite examples of how modeling, classical conditioning, and operant conditioning can be mechanisms for learning abnormal behavior. _watching other people_ _associating scary ordeal with certain places_ _do things you are reinforced for time after time_

17. In what way can positive reinforcement and extinction be causal factors in depression? _it get reinforcement_ _people get reinforced for bad things or feelings and they don't for good things — extinction_

18. What three broad factors determine the amount of positive reinforcement available to an individual? What can result from failure in any one or more of these factors? _# of stimuli found to be reinforcing, availibility of them in environment, skill in getting reinforced. Depression._

19. In what manner can cognitive factors contribute to abnormal behavior? _If you interpret things in a wrong or negative way it can lead to abnormal behavior._

20. How does the behavioral approach differ from the medical model regarding abnormal behavior? How does it differ from the psychoanalytic approach?

Abnormal behavior is not considered a symptom of illness. It doesn't say it is due to underlying unconscious conflicts it is just due to the maladaptive behavior itself

HUMANISTIC-EXISTENTIAL PERSPECTIVE

psychogenic

27. The humanistic-existential perspective is a third (biogenic/psychogenic) approach to abnormal behavior. While there are differences between humanistic and existential theorists, there are certain general principles on which they can agree. These are (a) a *phenomenological* approach is taken in which the

individual's

(individual's/therapist's) perception of events is stressed; (b) the

uniqueness

uniqueness of each individual is emphasized; (c) great emphasis is

potential

placed on human _potential_; and (d) individual freedom and

responsibility

personal _responsibility_ are emphasized.

28. The humanists and the existentialists do differ somewhat in the causes to which they attribute maladjustment. Lack of self-actualization because of a constricting family and society is the major factor leading to maladjustment according to the

humanists

humanists.

29. The existentialists, on the other hand, believe that maladjustment results more

authenticity

from the failure to establish a personal _authenticity_, in which an individual establishes his or her own values and then lives by them.

30. An even more radical existentialistic view is that of R. D. Laing, who assumes that family and society constrictions represent the primary cause of

maladjustment (mental illness)/good

maladjustment. For example, Laing believes that schizophrenia represents a (good/bad) adjustment to the constrictions of family and society. According to Laing, the schizophrenic has escaped from the mad world of reality im-

authentic

posed by society and found a much more _authentic_ identity in his or her own unique world.

Learning Objectives _Individual perception of events stressed, uniqueness of individual emphasis on human Potential, personal responsibility emphasized_

21. What are the four general principles that theorists of the humanistic and existentialistic approaches can agree upon?

22. What is the primary cause of maladjustment according to humanistic theorists? According to existentialistic theorists?

Lack of self actualization due to family and society   _Failure to establish personal authenticity in establish his or her own values._

23. What is Laing's view as to the cause of maladjustment? Why does Laing feel that schizophrenia represents a form of good adjustment? _family and societal constrictions are the main cause of maladjustment._

Because person is being authentic in escaping from the mad world of reality posed by society.

FAMILY PERSPECTIVE

31. All three of the psychogenic perspectives discussed so far are in agreement that

    family   the _family_ plays an important role in the development of abnormal behavior. However, although each of these perspectives emphasizes different aspects of family relationships, their primary emphasis is on the

    individual   psychological processes of the _individual_. Other psychogenic perspectives have placed the primary emphasis on the processes of the

    family   _family_ as the primary determinant of abnormal behavior.

32. A long-term study of the families of schizophrenics conducted by Lidz concluded

    two   that there appear to be _two_ general types of families with schizophrenic children. One type was characterized by constant discord between the parents, with each parent constantly "undercutting" the worth of the other to

    schism   the children. Lidz called this pattern _marital_ _schism_.

33. The other pattern Lidz observed was characterized by one strong parental figure and a spouse who played a dependent role, often supporting even the pathological behavior of the dominant spouse. Lidz called this pattern _marital_

    skew   _skew_.

34. Lidz concluded that the children in both types of marital patterns develop ways

    coping (adjusting)   of _coping_ that interfere with good adjustment in later life.

35. Another psychiatrist, Frieda Fromm-Reichman, observed that the mothers of schizophrenic persons are often cold and domineering women who reject their

    overprotecting   children while simultaneously _overprotecting_ them. Fromm-Reichman

    schizophrenogenic   called such women "_schizophrenogenic mothers_" and theorized that these schizophrenogenic mothers in conjunction with weak and yielding fathers could produce schizophrenic children.

36. Bateson and Jackson also examined the family environments of schizophrenics. They observed that frequently the schizophrenic's parents give

    conflicting (mixed)   _conflicting_ messages to the child. For example, a verbal message implying love and affection may be accompanied by facial expressions and postural behavior that imply rejection. According to Bateson and Jackson, the child

    double   receiving these conflicting messages is caught in a _double_

    bind   _bind_.

37. Thus the double-bind hypothesis of schizophrenia assumes that the

conflicting (mixed)

conflicting parental messages received by the preschizophrenic child interfere with learning the meaning and distinctions expressed in normal language and behavior. Instead, the child later develops the bizarre language and ineffec-

schizophrenia

tive social behavior characteristic of _schizophrenia_

38. Many additional studies have since found that the families of schizophrenics of-

communication/does not

ten show deviant _communication_ patterns. This (does/does not) prove that deviant and bizarre communication in families causes schizophrenia. It may

disturbed (schizophrenic)

well be that it is the presence of the _disturbed_ child that causes the deviant communication patterns.

Learning Objectives

24. In what way do theorists who follow the family perspective differ from the three previous psychogenic perspectives?
    They concentrate on the family as the problem and not just the individual

25. Explain what Lidz meant by the "marital skew" and "marital schism" that he frequently observed in the families of schizophrenics. How did these types of families affect the development of children according to Lidz?
    marital skew one parent dominated
    marital schism - parents were divided and in constant conflict   child didn't know how to cope with
    world

26. What did Frieda Fromm-Reichman mean by "schizophrenogenic mothers"? What combination resulted in schizophrenic children according to Fromm-Reichman?   _mother who was cold and over protecting but didn't_
    schizophrenogenic mothers and passive fathers resulted in schizophrenia in children   _show her children love_

27. What is Bateson and Jackson's double-bind hypothesis for the origin of schizophrenia?
    If you give children conflicting messages they won't know how to use them in the
    real world   small language and ineffective social behavior

28. What is a typical finding with respect to communication patterns in families of schizophrenics? Why can it not be said for certain that deviant communication patterns cause schizophrenia?   _Deviant_

    Because if the child is already schizo. he
    may be causing the problems with comm.

SOCIOCULTURAL PERSPECTIVE

39. This final psychogenic view of abnormal behavior, the sociocultural perspective,

society

emphasizes the role of the entire _society_ as the primary causative factor in abnormal behavior. According to this perspective, two interrelated

stress/labeling

social factors, social _stres_ and social _labeling_, play a major role in the production of abnormal behavior.

40. It is well documented that psychological disturbances are more frequently found

lower

among the _lower_ social classes. The sociocultural perspective assumes this is because the lower social classes are subjected to greater social

stress

stress than the other social classes; they suffer more from the effects of poverty, discrimination, and so on.

41. In addition to suffering from greater social stress than the other social classes, persons from the lower social class are also more likely to be

labeled (diagnosed)

labeled as mentally ill should any problem bring them in contact with the mental health establishment. This is what is meant by *social*

labeling

labeling.

42. Moreover, a person from the lower social class who seeks help from mental

psychotic

health professionals is much more likely to be labeled as _psychotic_ for the same kind of disturbance that would be labeled as *neurotic* in a person from a higher social class. Being diagnosed as psychotic rather than neurotic

recovery (improvement)

greatly affects the chance of eventual _recovery_. Thus social labeling may affect both diagnosis and recovery.

Learning Objectives

29. Where does the sociocultural perspective place the blame for abnormal behavior? _Places the blame on society._

30. Describe how social stress and social labeling may lead to a greater incidence of abnormal behavior among the lower classes. _social stress will lead to abnormal behavior because life for these people is generally hard. Social labeling stygmatizes them and they can't get out of that role_

31. Describe how social labeling may affect both diagnosis and eventual recovery. _when someone is labeled they are usually look upon as always being that way so this usually affects the chance of recovery_

32. As a brief review, list the five psychogenic perspectives on abnormal behavior. _Psychoanalytic Perspec. Family Per Behaviorist Pers sociocultural Peis Humanist-Existential_

BIOLOGICAL PERSPECTIVE

43. Both research and theory for the less severe kinds of psychological disturbances,

psychogenic

such as anxiety disorders, have primarily emphasized _psychogenic_ origins. However, theory and research for the more severe kinds of mental disturbances, such as schizophrenia, have in a large part tended to emphasize

biogenic (biological)

biogenec origins.

Genetic Theories of Disorder

44. While the genetic transmission of a mental disorder would allow for clear evi-

biological

dence of its _biological_ origin, few mental disturbances have been directly traced to genetic defects. Down's syndrome and Turner's syndrome are

genetic

two exceptions in which a _genetic_ defect has been clearly identified as the causal agent.

45. It has proven extremely difficult to determine whether or not schizophrenia has a biological origin since it is virtually impossible to separate biological variables

environmental from _environmental_ variables.

does 46. Nevertheless, evidence is clear that schizophrenia (does/does not) tend to run in families that live together. For example, the brother or sister of a schizophrenic is more likely also to have schizophrenia than is a more distant relative, and

an identical (a fraternal/an identical) twin is more likely to have schizophrenia if the other twin has it.

does not 47. The above evidence (does/does not) prove a genetic origin for schizophrenia. It

environmental is possible, for example, that _environmental_ factors were responsible since the people in these studies shared a common environment.

48. In order to rule out environmental factors some researchers have studied children who have been adopted from schizophrenic parents and reared in environments away from their natural parents. These studies can be summarized by saying

do that, in general, they (do/do not) support a genetic basis for schizophrenia. For example, children who are adopted away from schizophrenic parents are

more (less/more) likely to develop schizophrenia than children adopted from non-schizophrenic parents.

heredity 49. Even though the evidence indicates that _heredity_ may be one of the causative factors in schizophrenia, environmental factors cannot be ruled out. For instance, if schizophrenia primarily resulted from heredity, the incidence

higher should be much (higher/lower) than is the case.

50. This has led many researchers to the conclusion that heredity sets up a predispo-

diathesis/stressful sition or _diathesis_ for schizophrenia, but a _stressful_ environment is required to activate the predisposition. This is known as the

diathesis-stress _diathesis_-_stress_ model of schizophrenia.

Learning Objectives

less severe disorders anxiety

33. What kind of disorders have been the primary interest of psychogenic theories and research? What kind have been the primary interest of biogenic theory and research? – More severe kinds like schizophrenia etc

34. What two mental disturbances have been traced to genetic defects? Down's syndrome & Turner's Syn

35. Describe the evidence in favor of a genetic origin for schizophrenia. If a member in the same family has schizophrenia someone else is likely to have it. hereditary

36. Why can it not be safely concluded that schizophrenia has a genetic origin? – Because the environment plays a big part in people's lives It influence, them a great deal

37. What is the diathesis-stress model of schizophrenia? also the diathesis-stress model

heredity sets up a predisposition for schizophrenia but a stressful situation is needed to set the predisposition off.

Biochemical Theories of Disorder

51. In the search for specific biochemical causes of mental disturbances—schizophrenia, for example—researchers have selected a group of patients with this disorder

control

and compared their biochemistry with that of a _control_ group of normal persons. The problem here, however, is that it is extremely difficult to

environmental

find persons for the control group who have experienced _environmental_ conditions similar to those of the patients. Many factors unrelated to specific mental disorders, including diet, activity level, smoking, previous drug history,

biochemistry

and so on can influence the _biochemistry_ of an individual.

52. One of the most promising biochemical leads involves the neurotransmitter *dopamine*.

dopamine

According to the _dopamine_ hypothesis, schizophrenia may be related to excessive activity in those brain neurons that use dopamine as a

neurotransmitter

neurotransmitter

53. Evidence for the dopamine hypothesis comes from two sources. First, it has been found that the "antipsychotic" drugs that reduce the primary symptoms of schizo-

dopamine

phrenia do so by reducing the absorption of _dopamine_ in neurons that use this neurotransmitter. Second, drugs known to increase dopamine activ-

increase

ity produce an _increase_ in the primary symptoms of schizophrenic persons.

cannot

gradual

54. The dopamine hypothesis (can/cannot) fully explain the schizophrenic process. For instance, not all patients respond to the dopamine-blocking antipsychotic drugs. Moreover, these drugs reduce the symptoms in a very (gradual/rapid) manner, whereas the direct effect of the drug on the brain is relatively rapid.

55. Another neurotransmitter, *norepinephrine*, has been implicated as a causative

depression

factor in _depression_. Norepinephrine belongs to a group of neurotransmitters called the *catecholamines*, and this biochemical theory of depression

catecholamine

is called the _catecholamine_ hypothesis.

56. Evidence for the catecholamine hypothesis is again based on drug effects. Drugs

decrease

that increase norepinephrine levels _decrease_ the symptoms of depression or produce mania (unrealistic elation). On the other hand, drugs that

increase

decrease norepinephrine levels _increase_ the symptoms of depres-

mania

sion and decrease the symptoms of _mania_.

57. Recent evidence suggests that the effect of norepinephrine on mood may result from an interaction of this neurotransmitter with excess hormones produced by

thyroid

the ___thyroid___ *gland*. It is the interaction of these two biochemical

depression

factors that together produce symptoms found in both ___depression___

mania

and ___mania___.

psychogenic

58. At the present time it requires both *biogenic* and ___psychogenic___ theories to explain the many facets of abnormal behavior. In fact, there is no reason to

complementary (compatible)

assume these two approaches cannot be ___complementary___. Many kinds of abnormal behavior probably result from a combination of biological and environmental factors.

Learning Objectives

38. Why is it difficult to find appropriate control groups for biochemical comparisons with schizophrenic patients?

hard to find undisturbed people who have experienced similar environmental conditions

39. What is the dopamine hypothesis of schizophrenia? What two kinds of evidence support this hypothesis? What two kinds of findings suggest that this hypothesis cannot alone explain schizophrenia?

excessive activity in brain neurons that use dopamine as a neurotransmitter
— Two drugs that help elicit and stop the prod of dopamine
Not all people react in the same way to the drugs. It happens to gradually → Drugs

40. What is the catecholamine hypothesis of depression and mania? What two kinds of evidence support this hypothesis?

neurotransmitter that supposedly causes depression in people.

41. What additional factor has recently been found to interact with norepinephrine in the production of depression and mania?

Interaction of this neurotransmitter and the hormones produced by the thyroid gland.

42. What conclusion was reached as to the superiority of biogenic or psychogenic theories in explaining abnormal behavior?

Neither is superior. These two approaches can be seen as complementary

Chapter Twenty-Four
Approaches to Treatment

General Objectives

1. Define the term *psychotherapy,* and identify the various professional groups that engage in the practice of psychotherapy.

2. Describe the general theory of psychoanalysis, and explain its approach to psychotherapy.

3. List the various kinds of psychoanalytically oriented psychotherapy, and describe how they differ from psychoanalysis.

4. Describe the various forms and techniques of behavior therapy.

5. Describe the various forms and techniques of humanistic therapies.

6. Discuss the group and family approaches to psychotherapy.

7. Describe the conclusions of the studies that have attempted to evaluate the effectiveness of psychotherapy.

8. Describe the major organic approaches to psychotherapy.

9. List the major kinds of community mental health services.

Approaches to Treatment

Learning Objectives appear at
the end of each major section.

THE NATURE OF PSYCHOTHERAPY

interactions

1. The text defines psychotherapy as a systematic series of <u>interactions</u> between a specially trained therapist and a person who is either troubled or who

troubling

is <u>troubling</u> others.

2. There are five different professional groups trained in the area of psychotherapy. Identify each of these groups from the descriptions given below.

psychiatrist

a. A _psychiatrist_ is a medical doctor who has completed three years of residency training in psychiatry.

psychoanalyst

b. A _psychoanalyst_ is usually a psychiatrist who has had additional training in psychoanalysis and who has been psychoanalyzed.

clinical psychologist

c. A _clinical psychologist_ is a person who holds a doctorate in clinical psychology and who has completed a one-year internship in psychotherapy.

psychiatric social worker

d. A _psychiatric social worker_ is a person who has a master's degree (two years of postgraduate training) in psychotherapy for individuals with psychological problems related to family and social situations.

psychiatric nurse

e. A _psychiatric nurse_ is a registered nurse who has specialized in psychiatric nursing.

Learning Objectives _systematic series of interactions between a specially trained therapist and a person who's either troubled or troubling someone_

1. How does the text define psychotherapy?

2. Name and describe the training of each of the five professional groups who engage in psychotherapy. _Psychiatrist Psychoanalyst clinical psychologist Psychiatric social worker psychiatric nurse_

PSYCHODYNAMIC THERAPIES

Freudian Psychoanalysis

3. Psychoanalysis is a general theory of personality, a theory of psychopathology,

psychotherapy

and a form of _psychotherapy_. The originator of psychoanalysis was

Freud

Sigmund _Freud_.

4. Freud believed that neurosis was caused by the unacceptable unconscious demands of the id threatening to break through the constraints set by the

ego

ego. This threatening situation was said to lead to the arousal

anxiety

of _anxiety_, which in turn caused the ego to employ

defense mechanisms

defense mechanisms to alleviate the anxiety. It is the overemployment of defense mechanisms that constitutes the neurotic behavior, according to Freud.

repression

5. Perhaps the most frequently used defense mechanism is __repression__.
In this case the ego prevents the unacceptable material from coming into the

conscious

__conscious__, but this extracts strength and energy from the ego and
continues to provoke anxiety.

6. Thus Freud believed that the proper treatment for neurosis was for the patient to

conscious

allow the repressed material to become __conscious__. The patient

ego

could then learn to confront the newly conscious material and thus allow the
(id/ego) freedom and energy to engage in more productive pursuits.

7. One of the major techniques Freud developed to bring repressed material into
consciousness was to have patients lie quietly on a couch and verbalize whatever

free

thoughts came to mind. He called this technique __Free__

association

__association__.

8. Freud also believed that clues to the sources of anxiety could be found in the

dreams

content of __dreams__. According to Freud, the obvious or

manifest

__manifest__ *content* of a dream was its plot or story line while the
hidden, real meaning was contained in the *latent content* of the dream. Freud
further assumed that a trained psychoanalyst could interpret the

latent

__latent__ *content* of dreams, thus exposing unconscious demands
and conflicts.

9. Psychoanalysis assumes that as the repressed material is brought to the conscious
through free association and dream analysis, it will meet with

resistance

__resistance__ in the form of denial, avoidance of further therapy sessions, and so forth. It is then the psychoanalyst's task to interpret this

resistance

__resistance__ to the patient so that he or she may accept and analyze
these painful thoughts.

10. Psychoanalysis further assumes that as therapy progresses, the patient will begin
to *transfer* feelings of love, hostility, and so on originally directed at parents or

psychoanalyst (therapist)

other important people from childhood onto the __psychoanalyst__. In order
for treatment to be successful, the patient must pass through this stage of treat-

transference

ment, which Freud called __transference__ *neurosis*.

years

11. Psychoanalytic treatment is typically very lengthy, often lasting for several (months/years). During this time the patient supposedly becomes conscious of the repressed material that is the true source of anxiety, breaks through resistance to

transference neurosis

treatment, and resolves the ___transference neurosis___ . The

anxiety

end result is that ___anxiety___ and the self-defeating behaviors are eliminated.

Learning Objectives

3. List the three areas that are encompassed by the term *psychoanalysis*. *personality, psychopathology psychotherapy*

4. Describe Freud's theoretical explanation of neurosis. *unconscious demands of id trying to break through constraints of Ego*

5. What defense mechanism did Freud believe was most commonly employed by neurotics? *— repression*

6. What two techniques did Freud employ to reveal the patient's repressed demands and conflicts? *— Free association & content of Dreams*

7. What did Freud mean by the manifest content of dreams? What did he mean by the latent content of dreams? *The dreams plot or story line   underlying meaning what it was symbolic of*

8. What forms does resistance take in patients during psychoanalysis? How does the psychoanalyst treat this resistance? *denial and avoidance of further therapy*

9. According to Freud, what causes transference neurosis? *conflict with parents as a child*

10. What does psychoanalysis hope to achieve for the patient? *elimination of anxiety and self defeating behaviors*

Other Psychodynamic Therapies

12. An informal group of theorists who broke away from Freud and his psychoanaly-

ego

tic theory are collectively known as ___ego___ *psychologists*. The primary difference between the ego psychologists and the more traditional psychoanalysts is that the ego psychologists place greater emphasis and importance

ego

on the ___ego___ . Freud assumed that the ego derived all of its en-

id

ergy from the ___id___ ; ego psychologists assume that the ego has substantial energy of its own.

13. Another group of psychodynamic theorists who broke away from Freud emphasize social influences and interpersonal relationships as important determinants of maladjustment—in contrast to Freud's emphasis on the instinctual impulses of

id

the ___id___ . This group of theorists is known collectively as

neo

___Neo___-Freudians.

14. The many variations of psychoanalysis are collectively called

psychoanalytically
present
more

psychoanalytically oriented psychotherapy. Modern psychotherapists with this orientation tend to place greater emphasis on (past/(present)) situations than did Freud. They also generally take a ((more)/less) active role in the therapy and seek to achieve a briefer period of treatment.

Learning Objectives

these psychologists place greater emphasis on ego; while Freud placed great influence on the Id

11. In what way do the ego psychologists differ from the traditional theory of Freud? In what way do neo-Freudians also differ? _Greater emphasis on social influences and interpersonal relationships as impt determinants of maladjustment_

12. What is the collective name given to the many variations of psychoanalytic therapy? In what ways do therapists of this persuasion differ from traditional psychoanalysts? _psychoanalytically oriented psychotherapy place greater emphasis on present situations and take a more active role in the therapy, to seek briefer treatment time._

BEHAVIOR THERAPIES

15. Behavior therapists assume that all behavior, including deviant or problem

learned/do not

behavior, is _learned_. Behavior therapists (also/(do not)) believe that unconscious conflicts are the cause of problem behavior; rather they feel that

problem

the deviant or maladaptive behavior itself is the _problem_.

16. Behavior therapists also assume that, to a large extent, behavior is controlled by

environmental

environmental events. This means that a particular problem behavior is

specific (certain)

likely to occur only in _specific_ environmental situations.

are not

17. Moreover, emotions and cognitions (are/(are not)) felt to be clues to unconscious

unobservable (hidden)

conflicts; rather, they are simply regarded as _unobservable_ responses that are subject to the same laws of learning as are observable responses. Moreover, they are equally open to change.

Learning Objectives

13. What do behavior therapists assume with respect to:
    a. the cause of problem behavior? _— it is learned_
    b. the role of unconscious forces in problem behavior? _they do not play a role_
    c. the role of environmental factors in problem behavior? _plays a big role_
    d. the significance of emotions and cognitions in problem behavior? _they do not create problems_

Therapies Based on Classical Conditioning and Extinction

18. Behavior therapy techniques based on classical conditioning and extinction at-

emotion

tempt to change behavior by changing the _emotion_ evoked by particular events or stimuli. For instance, if Beauford is made extremely anxious (emotional) by public speaking, then a behavior therapist would set about reduc-

anxiety

ing Beauford's _anxiety_ when he engages in public speaking.

19. Classical conditioning and extinction are also used to change emotions in a nega-

aversions

tive direction by producing _aversions_ to events or stimuli that may be overattractive or too appealing. For example, an intense liking for chocolate

aversive (noxious)

may be dramatically reduced by pairing chocolate with _aversive_ stimuli.

20. *Systematic Desensitization*. Systematic densensitization was developed by Joseph

Wolpe

Wolpe. The primary emphasis of this technique is to

gradually

gradually reduce unrealistic anxiety evoked by particular environmental stimuli.

21. Systematic desensitization is a three-step process. The first step consists of train-

relaxation

ing the client to self-induce a state of deep _relaxation_. The second step consists of arranging the anxiety-producing situations into a *hierarchy* of

most

imagined scenes, ranked from the *least* to the _most_ feared scenes. In the final step, the actual desensitization, the client, while in a state of

imagines

deep relaxation, _imagines_ the scenes in the hierarchy.

22. During the actual desensitization process, the therapist begins with the

least

least-feared scene and instructs the client to imagine it while

anxiety

relaxing until he or she no longer experiences any _anxiety_. This process continues up the hierarchy until the client can imagine the most-feared scene without any undue anxiety.

23. *Flooding*. Flooding is based on principles similar to systematic desensitization,

actual

but unlike desensitization, flooding requires (actual/imagined) exposure to the feared stimulus until it no longer evokes undue anxiety. Furthermore, the flooding procedure does not require that the client first be placed in a state of deep

relaxation

relaxation.

24. Flooding has been found to be particularly useful for treating obsessive-compul-

anxiety (fear)

sive behavior motivated by ___Anxiety___ when the compulsive act is not performed. In this case the client is directly exposed to the feared object or

is not

situation and then (is/is not) permitted to perform the compulsive act. Eventually, the anxiety aroused by not performing the ritualistic act will

extinguish (disappear)

___extinguish___.

25. *Aversive Conditioning.* Aversive conditioning is based upon

classical

___classical___ *conditioning.* This technique pairs an aversive stimulus, such as mild electric shock, with some object or event, such as cigarette smok-ing, in order to transfer the aversive properties of the electric shock onto the

cigarettes

object, in this case ___cigarettes___.

26. A similar technique, called *covert sensitization,* replaces the aversive external stimulus (electric shock, for example) with an unpleasant or aversive scene that

imagined

is merely ___imagined___ (covert). Again, the principle is the same as with aversive conditioning. The aversive properties of the imagined scene will be

transferred

___transferred___ in the manner of classical conditioning to the previously appealing object or event with which it is paired.

27. Both aversive conditioning and covert sensitization are usually combined with

behaviors (responses)

teaching new ___behaviors___ that can be used to replace the maladaptive behaviors being eliminated. For example, the person who drinks too much when

social

at social gatherings will be given additional training in ___social___ skills to replace the excessive drinking behavior.

Learning Objectives

14. What is the primary purpose of the techniques based on classical conditioning and extinction? What two directions can this purpose take? *attempt to change behavior by changing emotion evoked by a particular event or stimuli   reducing anxiety or producing aversions*

15. Who developed the technique of systematic desensitization? What is the primary emphasis of this technique? *Joseph Wolpe   gradually reduce unrealistic anxiety*

16. Describe the three-step process of systematic desensitization. *relaxation, arrange anxieties in a hierarchy from least to most feared, imagine scenes in hierarchy*

17. Briefly describe the flooding procedure. Point out how it differs from systematic desensitization. *actual exposure to feared stimulus*

18. How would the flooding procedure be employed to treat a client who complains of excessive hand-washing because of a fear of dirt? What is the principle behind the lessening of fear in this instance? *the client would have to be exposed to the feared object dirt and then not be permitted to perform compulsive act. extinguish anxiety of not performing the ritualistic response.*

19. Describe how aversive conditioning would be employed to reduce the appeal of cigarette smoking. How would covert sensitization be employed in this situation? *When someone has urge to smoke they'll get a mild electric shock — use an imagined scene that is very aversive*

20. What is the basic learning principle behind both aversive conditioning and covert sensitization? What additional technique usually accompanies these two forms of therapy? *classical conditioning — training in social skills*

Therapies Based on Operant Conditioning

28. Therapies based on classical conditioning are generally used to replace

maladaptive   *maladaptive* emotional responses elicited by environmental stimuli

adaptive   with more *adaptive* emotional responses. However, the responses themselves, whether they be adaptive or maladaptive, have no direct effect on the environment.

29. Therapies based on operant conditioning are used when the goal is to increase or

frequency   decrease the *frequency* of a specific behavior rather than to change the emotional response elicited by a given environmental stimulus. The increase in the frequency of a desired behavior is brought about by

reinforcement   *reinforcement*, while the decrease in the frequency of an undesired be-

punishment   havior is brought about by extinction or *punishment*.

30. *Behavioral Contracts.* Behavioral contracts are usually agreements between two or more persons stating which behaviors are desired, which behaviors are unde-

consequences   sired, and the *consequences* for emitting either the desired or undesired
all   behaviors. As a general rule, behavioral contracts contain benefits for (all/some) of the persons who sign the contract.

31. Behavioral contracts have also been successfully employed to help individuals

self-control   attain personal goals involving *self-control*, such as weight loss. One study compared dieters using behavioral contracts with dieters using drugs to control eating. A one-year follow-up revealed that the diet-
behavioral contracts   ers using (behavioral contracts/drugs) showed better overall weight loss.

32. *Token Economies.* Token economies are used primarily in

institutions   *institutions*. A wide range of desirable behaviors are specified, and

reinforced   the residents are *reinforced* with tokens whenever they exhibit these desired behaviors. The tokens can then be exchanged for either items in a canteen or for special privileges. The primary goal of token economies is to make the residents of these economies more independent and self-reliant.

Learning Objectives

21. What is the usual goal of therapies based on operant conditioning? How does this goal differ from therapies based on classical conditioning? *replace maladaptive with adaptive behavior classical cond tries to change emotion evoked by certain stimuli*

22. How do operant conditioning techniques increase the frequency of a specific behavior? How do they decrease the frequency of a specific behavior? *reinforcement Punishment*

23. What are behavioral contracts? Whom are they intended to benefit? *agreement made between one or more persons stating which beh are desired and which are undesired and consequences for desired and undesired behavior → everyone all people involved*

24. Give an example of how behavioral contracts can be used to attain personal goals. *self-control in dieting* *to make people more independent and self reliant*

25. What are token economies? What is the intended purpose of these token economies? *token economies to get people to do desired things as a result they get reinforced in the form of a token*

Therapies Based on Modeling and Cognitive Restructuring

33. In addition to employing the principles of classical and operant conditioning, therapies based on modeling and cognitive restructuring also emphasize

cognition   _cognition_ as an important adjunct to therapy.

34. *Modeling*. Learning a behavior by watching others perform it is called

modeling   _modeling_ . When learning through modeling, it is assumed that the

information   behavior of the model furnishes _information_ to the observer.

35. For example, a child who is frightened of dogs can eliminate this fear by watching a model fearlessly playing with dogs. In this case the model's behavior sup-

information   plies _information_ to the child that the dogs are not only harmless but fun. As is illustrated by this example, modeling has been found to be particularly

phobias (phobic behavior)   effective in treating _phobias_ .

36. An even more effective technique is to combine modeling with the active *participation* of the observer, who confronts and masters a graduated series of threaten-

participant   ing activities. This procedure is called _participant_ *modeling*. When this technique is used in the training of social skills, such as learning to be more

behavior   assertive without becoming aggressive, it is called _behavior_ *rehearsal*.

37. Albert Bandura has theorized that cognition is a major component in the effectiveness of any behavior change technique. Particularly important here are the

expectations   _expectations_ that people have in their ability to execute a particular behavior (their efficacy). Thus participant modeling and behavior rehearsal are effective techniques for inducing behavior change because both offer a potent

efficacy expectations   means of changing _efficacy_ _expectations_ in people.

38. By actively engaging in and successfully carrying out a previously feared behavior, people learn that they have the _efficacy_ to successfully per-

efficacy (ability)

expectations   form a particular behavior. Furthermore, their _expectations_ will be that they can successfully perform this behavior whenever it is required on future occasions.

39. *Cognitive Restructuring.* Many behavior therapists believe the self-defeating behaviors commonly found in many clients seeking psychotherapy result from their

false (irrational)   _false_ assumptions. For example, a person may expect too much from social relationships and overreact to mild social rejections. In this

cognitive restructuring   case treatment might consist of _cognitive_ _restructuring_, in which the client is persuaded to replace the irrational beliefs with more sensible beliefs. This is the approach taken by Albert Ellis in his technique called

rational-emotive   _rational_-_emotive_ therapy.

40. Another effective technique for changing false assumptions that lead to problem behavior has been developed by Donald Meichenbaum. In this technique, called

instructional   *self-*_instructional_ *training,* clients learn to give up self-defeating assumptions by actively engaging in learning more positive and rational attitudes through *"self-talk."* That is, they learn by modeling the therapists' positive state-

self-   ments and applying these to themselves through "_self_-

talk   _talk._"

41. A third method of cognitive restructuring was developed by Aaron Beck, who

cognitive   calls his technique _cognitive_ *therapy.* Beck also assumes that many

faulty   emotional disorders are the result of _faulty_ assumptions about oneself. As with the other two methods of cognitive restructuring, this method also puts major emphasis on changing unreasonable or faulty

assumptions   _assumptions_ through active advice and guidance by the therapist.

Learning Objectives

26. In what important way do therapies based on modeling and cognitive restructuring differ from behavior therapies based on classical and operant conditioning? *They emphasize cognition is important in therapy*

27. Describe how modeling and participant modeling would be used to eliminate a child's fear of dogs. Why is information said to be an important component of these two techniques? *A child would watch another person acting fearlessly toward a dog. models behavior supplies infor to observer reduces phobias*

28. Distinguish between participant modeling and behavior rehearsal. *mastering threatening activities.* *help overcome social anxieties learning social skill*

29. Explain what Bandura means by "efficacy expectations." *ability to perform successfully* *ability to do something in certain situations*

30. What is the basic assumption underlying the various kinds of cognitive restructuring therapies? *False assumptions on the part of the client*

31. Briefly describe the methods used by the following cognitive restructuring therapies:
    a. Albert Ellis's rational-emotive therapy *replace irrational beliefs with sensible ones*
    b. Donald Meichenbaum's self-instructional training *engage in learning more positive and rational attitudes through self talk.*
    c. Aaron Beck's cognitive therapy *changing unreasonable or faulty assumptions through active advice and guidance by the therapist*

HUMANISTIC THERAPIES

growth

42. Humanistic therapies view psychotherapy as a __growth__ experience. These therapies see no need for the concept of mental illness, nor do they view the traditional role of doctor and patient as pertinent to the psychotherapeutic relationship.

Client-Centered Therapy

Rogers

43. Client-centered therapy originated with Carl __Rogers__, who be-

innate (natural)

lieves that clients in psychotherapy have a(n) __innate__ *motivation* to fulfill their own individual potential.

44. Rogers believes that the effective psychotherapist must possess three abilities or capacities. First, the therapist must be able to share his or her own deepest feel-

congruence

ings with the client. Rogers calls this capacity __congruence__.

45. Second, the therapist must be able to communicate a completely nonjudgmental

unconditional

acceptance of the client. Rogers calls this capacity __unconditional__ *positive regard.*

46. Finally, according to Rogers, the therapist must have the ability to enter into the client's inner world as if it were the therapist's own. Rogers calls this capacity

empathic

__empathic__ *understanding.*

helps

47. Using these three capacities, the client-centered therapist (helps/directs) the client to clarify feelings and to begin to value his or her own personal experience of the world, or, as Rogers would say, to develop an *unconditional positive*

self-regard

self-_regard_.

are not

48. In spite of Rogers's contention that empathy, warmth, and sincerity are necessary characteristics of an effective therapist, research shows that these qualities (are/are not) highly related to the success of therapy.

Learning Objectives *they view psychotherapy as a growth experience*

32. What is the view of humanistic psychotherapists with respect to psychotherapy?

33. Who developed client-centered psychotherapy? What is one of the major assumptions of this form of therapy? What is the expected outcome for the client? *Carl Rogers client centered — innate motivation to fulfill their own individual potential*

34. List and describe the three capacities that Carl Rogers feels are essential in the effective psychotherapist. *congruence between client and Doctor, unconditional-positive regard and empathy*

35. What does research show with respect to the qualities of empathy, warmth, and sincerity on the part of the therapist? *they are not related to success of therapy*

Gestalt Therapy

Perls

49. Gestalt therapy was developed by Fritz _Perls_. Its ultimate goal is for the client to achieve balance and integration through

awareness

awareness of imbalances and by integrating various aspects of his or her personality.

now

50. The three major values of gestalt therapy are emphasis on the (past/now/future);

present

focus on the *spatial*, what is _present_ rather than absent; and con-

act

centration on the *substantial*, the _act_ rather than the fantasy.

inherent

51. Gestalt therapists employ several techniques and exercises to help the client utilize his or her (inherent/learned) capacity for growth. The gestalt therapist sees

equals

the client-therapist relationship as one of _equals_ in helping the client to achieve balance and integration of the personality—or, as Perls calls it, "*organismic self-regulation.*"

Learning Objectives

36. Who developed gestalt psychotherapy? What is the ultimate goal of this form of therapy?

Fritz Perls — balance and integration through awareness of imbalances and by integrating various aspects of his or her personality

37. List and describe the three major values of gestalt therapy.

emphasis on now; what is present and the act rather than fantasy

38. Do gestalt therapists believe that clients have an inherent capacity for growth, or must this capacity be learned?

They believe clients have an inherent capacity for growth.

39. How do gestalt therapists view the client-therapist relationship?

in helping client achieve relationship as one of equal balance and integration of personality

GROUP AND FAMILY APPROACHES

Group Therapy

interpersonal/less

52. Perhaps the major advantage of group psychotherapy is that it emphasizes and promotes improved __interpersonal__ relationships. It is also (less/more) expensive for the client than individual psychotherapy.

common (particular)

53. Group psychotherapy appears to be particularly effective when the group members share a __common__ problem. For example, the mutually supportive role of group membership has been useful in treating alcoholism, obesity, and various kinds of drug addictions.

transactional analysis

decreased

54. A group therapy that is often used with groups of couples was originated by Eric Berne and is called __transactional analysis__. Berne's basic assumption is that marital partners often set up rules for each other (play games) that satisfy their own neurotic needs. Unfortunately, these rules or games usually result in (increased/decreased) marital harmony.

parent-

child

55. In Berne's view, marriages often consist of __parent-child__ relationships instead of adult-adult relationships. In this case one partner plays the role of a dictatorial adult and the other the role of a

child

rebellious __child__.

transactions

56. The goal of transactional analysis is to help couples see these antagonistic roles they have assigned to themselves and the interpersonal __transactions__ that result from these roles. Through analyzing these transactions, couples try to uncover unproductive transactions and change the rules of the game to promote

mutual

__mutual__ satisfaction in an adult-adult relationship.

Learning Objectives

increases interpersonal relationships

40. What is a major advantage of group therapy? What is a minor advantage? *— less expensive*

41. For what kinds of members has group therapy been found to be particularly effective? *members who have something in common*

42. What form of group therapy was originated by Eric Berne? What is the cause of most marital conflict according to Berne? *transactional analysis   Marital partners play games that decrease marital harmony*

43. How does transactional analysis attempt to accomplish its goal? *by showing couples antagonistic roles they have setup and interpersonal transactions that take place*

Family and Marital Therapies

57. Family and marital therapies are directed toward improving relationships that exist within a marital or family group. A basic assumption of these forms of therapy is that (circle the correct answer):

    a. family and marital problems usually arise because one of the family or marital members is at fault or is mentally disturbed.

b
    b. all members of a marital or family group usually contribute to the problems within the group, even if only one member seems to be especially disturbed.

58. While there are several types of family therapy and each accentuates different aspects of family relationships (reinforcement, communication patterns, expected roles, and so on), the major emphasis of all these therapies is to point out the

influence
    influence each member has on other members of the family. In this way ineffective reinforcement, poor communication patterns, and unrealistic

changed (improved)
    expectations can be _changed_ to promote a more satisfactory family relationship.

Learning Objectives

all members contribute to problems within the group

44. What is a basic assumption of practitioners of marital and family therapies? Where do these forms of therapy place their major emphasis? *major emphasis of therapies is to point out the influence each member has on other members*

THE EFFECTIVENESS OF PSYCHOTHERAPY

59. H. Eysenck reviewed the published material from numerous research studies evaluating the success of psychotherapy and concluded that psychotherapy is

no more
    (no more/more) effective than no treatment at all.

60. Bergin's more recent review of similar studies concluded that the improvement

higher
lower
    rate from psychoanalytic treatment was (higher/lower) than Eysenck had originally reported and the improvement rate from no treatment was (higher/lower) than Eysenck had originally estimated. However, Bergin's conclusions are based

different
    on (different/similar) assumptions from those used by Eysenck.

61. A recent analysis designed to surmount some of the difficulties arising from these differences in assumptions was conducted by Smith, Glass, and Miller. These researchers found that (treated/untreated) patients were more likely to show improvement. In analyzing the difference in success rates among various schools of psychotherapy, the researchers found that the differences in success rate were (small/large) across different forms of psychotherapy, including group therapy.

treated

small

62. Unfortunately, many of the studies included in the Smith, Glass, and Miller survey had serious methodological problems. For example, improvement was judged by either the patient or _therapist_ rather than an independent source, as would be required for scientific validity.

therapist

63. A review of sixteen methodologically strong studies by Kazdin and Wilson found that in nine of these sixteen cases _behavior_ therapy was the most effective; the other seven showed no difference in effectiveness between behavioral and other treatments. Moreover, a survey of a wide range of additional studies again showed _behavior_ therapy to be the superior form of treatment.

behavior

behavior

Learning Objectives

45. What did Eysenck conclude from his review of studies of psychotherapy? _psychotherapy is no more effective than no treatment at all_

46. What did Bergin conclude from his review of outcome studies? _improvement rate from psychoanalytic treatment was higher than Eysenck reported and improve rate from no treatment was lower_

47. What were Smith, Glass, and Miller's two conclusions with respect to the effectiveness of psychotherapy? _treated patients more likely to show improvement, success rates across therapies were small_

48. What was a major flaw in the Smith, Glass, and Miller survey? What two conclusions were reached by Kazdin and Wilson? _methodological problems, 9 of 16 cases behavior therapy most effective, in other studies behavior also found to be best treatment_

ORGANIC APPROACHES TO THERAPY

64. While organic approaches to therapy include psychosurgery and electroconvulsive shock, by far the most frequently employed organic approach is _drug_ therapy. In fact, drug therapy is often used along with _psychotherapy_ in the treatment of emotional disturbances.

drug

psychotherapy

Antianxiety Drugs

65. Antianxiety drugs are primarily used to treat persons with relatively minor disor-

anxiety

ders in which _anxiety_ is a major symptom. Extended use of

dependency

these drugs can result in _dependency_ on the drug, and heavy doses

death

taken along with alcohol can result in _death_.

Antipsychotic Drugs

66. As the name implies, antipsychotic drugs are used to treat the extreme symptoms (agitation, hallucinations, delusions, and so on) that are found in

psychotic/very
do not

psychotic patients. They have proven to be (very/somewhat) effective in this role. Antipsychotic drugs (do/do not) affect anxiety.

67. However, there are serious drawbacks to the use of antipsychotic drugs. One is that they have unwanted side effects, the most serious being

tardive dyskinesia

tardive _dyskinesia_, a disorder of the facial and tongue muscles. Another drawback is that psychotic symptoms

return (reappear)

return shortly after the antipsychotic drugs are withdrawn.

Antidepressant Drugs

mood

68. Antidepressant drugs are used to produce _mood_ elevations in persons suffering from depression. There are three major types of antidepressant drugs: *MAO inhibitors, tricyclics,* and *lithium.*

Learning Objectives

drug

49. What is the most frequently used organic approach to therapy? With what is it often combined? _psychotherapy_

50. What is the major use for the antianxiety drugs? What can result from extended use of these drugs?
reduce anxiety   _dependency and death_

51. What is the major use for the antipsychotic drugs? What two drawbacks do these drugs have? _side effects_
treat psychotic patients   tardive dyskinesia and return of symptom when stopped being used

52. What is the major use for the antidepressant drugs? What are the three major types of antidepressant drugs?

produce mood elevations   _MAO inhibitors, tricyclics, and lithium_

Electroconvulsive Therapy

69. While no one is certain why it works, electroconvulsive therapy has proven quite

depression

drastic

useful in the treatment of _depression_ . In fact it usually works faster than the antidepressant drugs. However, this is a (drastic/benign) form of treatment, and it is often accompanied by a temporary loss of

memory

_____memory_____ —which in some cases lasts for an extended period of time.

Psychosurgery

70. Psychosurgery, as performed in the United States at the present time, is a

last choice

massive

(preferred/last choice) method of treatment. It is used only when all other methods have failed. While psychosurgery operations formerly involved rather (limited/massive) destruction of brain tissue, these operations have been abandoned in favor of fractional operations involving small, selected areas of the brain. Modern psychosurgery has been found beneficial in cases of

depression

depression and in cases of depression associated with intractable pain.

Learning Objectives

treat depression not sure

53. What is the major use for electroconvulsive shock? Why does it work? What is an unwanted side effect of this form of treatment? _loss of memory for unknown amount of time_

54. When is psychosurgery performed? In what ways has psychosurgery evolved in recent times? What kind of mental disturbances have been found to benefit from psychosurgery? _last choice\fractional operations._ _depression and depression associated_ _parts of the brain are only small_ _with a operated on_ _lot of pain_

COMMUNITY MENTAL HEALTH

71. The paragraphs that follow describe three types of mental health services. Read the descriptions, and then place the appropriate names in the blanks that follow each description.

a. A community-based clinic that provides psychological services directly to clients, thus allowing them to remain in the community. These clinics also train other community workers in the principles of preventive mental health, they train paraprofessionals, and they carry out research.

community mental health

centers

community mental health _centers_

b. Temporary residences where individuals with common problems can live together until they are able to function independently. Residents are often in a state of transition from institutional living to independent living.

halfway houses

halfway houses

c. A service that provides emergency relief for persons suffering from psychological stresses. In addition to offering sympathy, this service also provides information about community agencies that are available for more thorough

crisis intervention   aid. _crisis_   _intervention_ *(hotline)*

Prevention

72. The basic goal of community psychology is the prevention of psychological dis-

primary   turbances at three different levels. The first level, called _primary_ prevention, is to prevent the initial occurrence of psychological disturbances. The

secondary   second level, called _secondary_ prevention, is to prevent the worsen-

tertiary   ing of disorders. The third level, called _tertiary_ prevention, is to prevent the severe effects of psychological disorders from carrying over to the community and the victims.

Learning Objectives   Comm Mental Health center, Halfway houses   crisis intervention; (hotline)

55. List and describe the services of three different kinds of community mental health facilities.

56. List and describe the three different levels of prevention which are the goals of community mental health services.

Primary prevention - prevent initial occurrence of psychological problems

Secondary prevention - prevent worsening of disorders

Tertiary prevention - stop severe side effects of psy problems from carrying over to community and victims

Chapter Twenty-Five
Attitudes and Attitude Change

General Objectives

1. List and define the two components of an attitude.

2. Describe the effects of repeated exposure, classical conditioning, and operant conditioning on attitude formation.

3. Describe the circumstances that tend to produce a "dissonance effect" versus those that are more likely to produce a "reinforcement effect" in attitude change.

4. Describe the characteristics of the source, the message, and the audience that influence acceptance of a persuasive appeal.

5. Explain how *inoculation* and *forewarning* may affect resistance to persuasion.

6. Discuss some inconsistencies found between attitude measures and behavior, and explain why such inconsistencies may not be so unreasonable.

Attitudes and Attitude Change

Learning Objectives appear at
the end of each major section.

cognitive/affective

1. An attitude may be viewed as consisting of two components: a _____cognitive_____ component and an _____affective_____ component.

cognitive

2. The term _____cognitive_____ refers to knowing, thinking, and believing. The

affective

term _____affective_____ refers to emotion, feeling, and attraction or aversion. Attitudes consist of both components.

3. For example, you may know that cottage cheese is a nonfattening dairy product and a fair source of protein, and you may even think about these things once in a

is not

while. Your rumination about the characteristics of cottage cheese (is/is not) an

affective

attitude, however, because it lacks feeling, the _____affective_____ component.

355

4. Which of the following is an attitude?
   a. You think your roommate is an excellent student.
   b. You briefly become angry after an argument.
   c. You know how socialized medicine works, and you strongly favor it.

c

5. The cognitive component of an attitude has less stability than the affective component. For example, we may change our thoughts about cottage cheese while

affective

still maintaining a feeling of disgust, the _affective_ component of our attitude toward the substance. Similarly, we may know that we dislike a certain politician but be unable to recall the reasons why.

Learning Objectives

affective
cognitive

1. Name and describe the two components of an attitude.

2. Why is the cognitive component said to have less stability than the affective component?

EXPLAINING ATTITUDE FORMATION AND CHANGE

The Effects of Repeated Exposure

not necessarily

6. From what we have just said it is clear that our attitudes are (usually/not necessarily) formed because of what we know about objects or events. Attitudes are affected by a number of very subtle factors, including some of which we may be only vaguely aware.

more

7. One of the factors that influence our attitudes toward an object is the number of times we are exposed to it: other things being equal, the more we encounter something, the (more/less) we like it. This phenomenon is referred to as the

exposure

exposure effect.

also

8. The exposure effect has been demonstrated for such objects as nonsense words, Chinese ideographs, and photographs of faces. The effect has (also/not) been demonstrated with lower animals. Rats reared listening to Mozart preferred Mozart to Schönberg; vice versa for rats reared listening to Schönberg.

9. At one time it was thought that the exposure effect might be due to the pleasantness associated with recognizing familiar objects. By presenting stimuli so briefly (one millisecond) that subjects could not possibly recognize them, however, re-

recognition

searchers demonstrated that _recognition_ is not essential for the exposure effect.

Reinforcement Theories

10. Repetition or exposure is just one of the ways in which we acquire attitudes, and the effect is limited to the formation of positive attitudes. In addition, we learn attitudes in much the same way that we acquire other behaviors, through the proc-

classical/operant
esses of _classical_ and _operant_ conditioning (discussed in Chapter 8).

11. *Classical Conditioning.* In one study involving conditioning of attitudes, the

shock
words "light" and "dark" were followed either by a _shock_ or else by termination of shock. When the words were later rated by the subjects, those words paired with shock were evaluated less favorably than those words paired with termination of shock. The procedure described here involved

classical
classical conditioning.

12. The subjects also generalized to similar word stimuli. For example, subjects who were shocked just after they saw the word "light" also evaluated similar words,

white
such as the word "_white_," more negatively.

13. Thus, through classical conditioning we may attach a positive or negative emotional reaction to some object without necessarily acquiring a corresponding set

cognitions (beliefs, thoughts)
of _cognitions_ about the object.

14. *Operant Conditioning.* One of the factors that frequently (but not always) distinguishes between classical and operant behavior is that operant behavior is said to

voluntary
be (voluntary/reflexive). More specifically, operant behavior generally involves movement of the skeletal muscles (talking, walking, and so on) rather than behaviors associated with the autonomic nervous system.

15. In operant conditioning, a reinforcer is defined as a stimulus that increases the frequency of a behavior that it follows. Thus, if others respond to the attitudes we express with such comments as "I agree" or "good idea," we may tend to repeat our attitude statements. In this case the comments by others are the

reinforcers
reinforcers.

16. For example, in a telephone interview, some students at the University of Hawaii were reinforced with the word "good" whenever they responded favorably to the idea of an Aloha Week festival. One week later, when these same students were asked to express their opinions about holding an additional Aloha Week in the

reinforced
spring, those students previously _reinforced_ for their comments expressed more favorable attitudes toward the festival than did those not previously reinforced.

17. In the "Aloha Week" study the reinforcer was delivered by an experimenter who was unknown to the subjects. The text makes the point that reinforcers delivered

parents

by one's ~parents~ are probably powerful shapers of young children's attitudes. It is partly for this reason that children tend to have the same prejudices, religious beliefs, and political affiliations as do their parents.

Learning Objectives

3. What are the effects of repeated exposure on attitude toward a stimulus? Give examples with regard to both human behavior and the behavior of rats. What evidence suggests that recognition is not essential for the exposure effect to occur?

4. Attitudes may be acquired both through classical conditioning and through operant conditioning. Illustrate these processes by describing the "light-dark" word study and the "Aloha Week" study.

18. *Reinforcement and Attitude Change.* In some situations, as discussed in Chapter 15, people tend to value more highly (have more favorable attitudes toward) behaviors that produce less payoff. For example, in the Festinger and Carlsmith study previously described, the group that was paid (twenty dollars/one dollar) reported liking the "boring" experiment more than the other group.

one dollar

19. It may be that effects like those just described are attributable not to dissonance but to the fact that we are observers of our own behavior. For example, if you saw yourself accepting a large amount of money for saying something, you might infer that you were saying it because (of the money/you believed it).

of the money

20. On the other hand, if you were given only a small amount of money, that would be insufficient reason for saying something you did not believe. So in this case you might infer from your behavior that you (believed/did not believe) what you were saying.

believed

21. Thus, one explanation for why small rewards may produce greater attitude change is not that we behave in a particular way because of our attitudes, but

attitudes

that in some cases we form our _____ only after observing our

behaviors

_____ .

22. More recent investigations have also demonstrated that whether a dissonance or a reinforcement effect occurs depends on one crucial aspect of the situation:

choice

whether or not the individuals feel they have a _____ between performing or not performing the requested behavior. If subjects are led to believe that they *must* perform the task, then it is likely that a

reinforcement
more

_____ effect will occur. In this case, the group given the large monetary incentive will like the task (less/more) than the group given the small monetary incentive.

a choice

23. Thus, for the dissonance effect to occur, it is essential that subjects feel that they have (a choice/no choice) about performing the task. A reinforcement effect is more likely to occur if subjects feel they must comply with the experimenter's instructions.

Learning Objectives

5. Explain how some of the results of the dissonance experiments may be explained by assuming that some of our attitudes are formed because we are observers of our own behavior.

6. In a situation involving large and small rewards, under what circumstances is a "dissonance effect" more likely to occur? A "reinforcement effect"?

PERSUASIVE COMMUNICATION

Influences on Persuasiveness

24. *The Characteristics of the Source.* The source of a communication is the person who delivers it. Most people are more likely to be influenced by a source they

knowledgeable

consider _____—perhaps someone they assume is an expert on the topic being presented.

25. In addition to expertise, sources are more persuasive if they are viewed as honest

trustworthy

or _____. For this reason people may be more influenced by a

overhear

message they _____ than one they hear directly. Since an over-heard message is usually not intended to persuade the person who overhears it,

trustworthiness (motives)

there may be less reason to question the _____ of the source.

26. A third factor that influences the persuasiveness of the source is the degree to

attractive

which the source is _____ and likable. Thus, advertisements use testimonials by attractive, likable individuals presented in pleasant situations.

27. So far we have discussed three factors that influence the persuasiveness of the

attractiveness

source: knowledgeableness, trustworthiness, and _____. In ad-

nonverbal

dition, people also pay attention to the _____ behavior of the source—his or her posture, extent of eye contact, and so on. Some people believe that this nonverbal factor may have contributed to Nixon's defeat by Kennedy in the presidential election of 1960.

distance

28. Finally, the text mentions the physical _____ between the speaker and the person receiving the message. For example, one study found that speakers were more likely to influence attitude change when they stood:
    a. close to the audience (one or two feet away).
    b. farther away from the audience (fourteen or fifteen feet away).

b

is not

29. Future research will probably find that there (is/is not) a single optimal distance at which to deliver all messages and that the most effective distance will depend

message

on both the type of _____ and the type of relationship between speaker and listener.

30. *The Characteristics of the Message.* In attempting to persuade an audience, should you present both sides of the issue or only the side you favor? Research has indicated that the answer to this question depends on the characteristics of

audience

the _____ for whom the message is intended.

favors

31. A one-sided message is effective for an audience that initially (favors/opposes) the content of the message. It is also effective for an audience that is

not well educated

(not well educated/well educated).

both sides
well educated

32. If the audience initially opposes the point of view of the message, it is better to present (one side/both sides). A two-sided appeal is also more persuasive for an audience that is (not well educated/well educated).

33. Another factor that influences the persuasiveness of a message is the situation in

pleasant

which it is presented. If the message is linked with a _____ emotional state, it is more likely to be accepted. For example, several studies have demonstrated that people are more likely to be persuaded by messages pre-

eating

sented when they are _____.

34. Fear appeals may also be used to persuade, but the intensity of the fear induced seems to be an important factor. In the dental-hygiene study described in the text, the most persuasive message was the one associated with the

lowest

(lowest/highest) level of fear.

35. If the audience hearing a fear appeal is given specific directions on how to carry out preventive action, and if they believe the actions are possible and effective,

is

then a high fear appeal (is/is not) likely to be persuasive. When preventive actions are difficult to carry out or unlikely to be effective, then a

low

_____ fear appeal is most effective.

36. *The Characteristics of the Audience.* There are apparently differences between people in the degree to which they are susceptible to persuasion. Some studies

approval

have found that people with a strong need for social _____ are easier to persuade than those with a weak need.

37. Other aspects of the audience's needs or motivations may also be important. For example, in an attempt to increase blood donations by men, one motivational researcher emphasized the masculinity and pride that men could feel in their act of donating. His underlying assumption was that men have unconscious anxieties

virility (masculinity)
about giving away their strength and _____, and he felt that his technique would counteract these fears.

38. Early studies supported the notion that women are more susceptible to persuasion than men. The differences found, however, apparently reflected the issues involved rather than sex differences in susceptibility to persuasion. In more recent studies, men have been found to be more easily persuaded with regard to

female
_____-oriented issues and women with regard to

male
_____-oriented issues.

Learning Objectives

7. The following characteristics of the source of persuasive communication are likely to influence its acceptance. Briefly explain the effects of these factors:
   expertise or knowledgeableness
   trustworthiness
   attractiveness
   nonverbal behavior
   physical distance

8. The message may include either one or both sides of an issue. What characteristics of the audience tend to make the one-sided message more persuasive? What characteristics of the audience tend to make the two-sided message more persuasive?

9. In one study the message was presented while people were eating and drinking. What was the point of this study?

10. Under what circumstances is it likely that a strong fear appeal will be more effective than a weak one? When is the weak fear appeal likely to be more effective?

11. Name an individual trait or personality characteristic that is related to susceptibility to persuasion.

12. Describe the "motivational" approach used in an attempt to increase blood donations from men.

13. Are women generally more susceptible to persuasion than men? For what types of issues are women more susceptible to persuasion? What types of issues affect men more?

Resistance to Persuasion

39. *Inoculation*. Some of our attitudes may never have been exposed to attacks from the opposite point of view. Once they are attacked, however, they may be particularly (susceptible/resistant) to the opposing arguments.

susceptible

40. According to McGuire, the reason for this susceptibility is that people who have never heard the opposing views do not develop counterarguments, or resistance, to the attacks. Such an effect may be lessened by exposing people to an

inoculation

_____ in the form of opposing arguments followed by a refutation of the opposing arguments.

41. An inoculation against persuasion involves two phases. First, individuals are exposed to the challenging argument; then they are exposed to statements that

attack (oppose)

_____ the challenging argument.

42. *Forewarning*. In some cases the persuasiveness of a message may be lessened

forewarning

simply by _____ people that their point of view will be challenged. In one study, for example, one group of teenagers were forewarned that they would hear a speech opposing teenage driving. Results indicated that teenagers who were forewarned about the opposing arguments tended to be more

resistant to

(accepting of/resistant to) the arguments than the group that had not been forewarned.

43. In another study, however, in which the persuasive speech asserted that an economic recession was likely, those who were forewarned were more

accepting of

(resistant to/accepting of) the arguments than those who had not been forewarned.

44. The text discusses two ways in which these apparently contradictory results may be reconciled. First, it may be that resistance increased for the teenagers in the

very strongly

first study cited because they were (very strongly/only moderately) committed to their beliefs about driving. This explanation assumes that the subjects in the second study who listened to the discussion of economic recession were

only moderately

(very strongly/only moderately) committed to their views.

45. Second, it may be that the subjects' knowledge of the issues is important. This explanation would assume that the teenagers who were strongly committed to

well

their beliefs were relatively _____ informed, and that subjects

poorly

who heard the discussion of economics were relatively _____ informed.

Learning Objectives

14. According to McGuire, what types of attitudes are particularly susceptible to persuasive arguments? Describe the procedures used to produce inoculation against opposing arguments.

15. Suppose people are forewarned that they will hear an appeal that challenges their point of view. What may be the effect of such forewarning? When is it likely to increase and when is it likely to decrease resistance to persuasion?

Can Attitudes Predict Behavior?

may not be

46. As illustrated by the experience of LaPiere in his travels with a Chinese couple in the 1930s, attitudes (are always/may not be) good predictors of behavior.

47. Only once, in 10,000 miles of travel, were LaPiere and the couple refused food and lodging. However, when the innkeepers were later asked in a letter if they

90

would serve a Chinese couple, more than _____ percent of them said that they would not. Thus, what the innkeepers *said* they would do was not a good predictor of their behavior when confronted with the real situation.

48. Similarly, in a study examining the attitudes of church members toward their church, it was found that those who expressed the most favorable attitudes to-

not necessarily

ward the church were (also/not necessarily) those who attended regularly or contributed and participated the most. Again, attitudes were not highly related to behavior.

49. It is important to point out, however, that in some situations attitudes and behavior are quite consistent. In addition, the inconsistencies may appear

reasonable

(reasonable/unreasonable) under close scrutiny. For example, the innkeepers' stereotypes of Chinese people probably did not fit the characteristics of the couple they actually encountered.

50. In addition, some individuals appear to have greater consistency between their attitudes and behavior than do others. This is one of the points being made in the

differences

last section, that there are individual _____ in consistency, dif-

self-

ferences that appear to be tapped by Snyder's test of _____-

monitoring

_____.

Learning Objectives

16. Describe LaPiere's experience in the 1930s. What is the main point of this episode as it relates to attitudes? How does the study of attitudes of church members reflect on this problem?

17. Explain why some of the inconsistencies found between attitude measures and behavior may not be so unreasonable. Explain the way in which individual differences may influence attitude-behavior consistency.

Chapter Twenty-Six
Interpersonal Perception and Attitudes

General Objectives

1. Discuss the positive and negative aspects of our use of social categories.

2. Understand the extent to which physical appearance affects perceptions and relationships between people.

3. Describe the *primacy effect* in person perception. Illustrate the effect of central traits.

4. Describe the circumstances that lead us to attribute behavior to enduring traits versus situational factors.

5. Describe the reciprocal causal relationships between proximity, similarity, and friendship.

6. Explain Toman's duplication hypothesis, and discuss the evidence relating social skills to birth order.

7. Describe the two-factor (attributional) view of love.

Interpersonal Perception and Attitudes

Learning Objectives appear at
the end of each major section.

INTERPERSONAL PERCEPTION

1. The major advantage of using categories is that they help us *organize* and
predict. For example, last evening I selected tomatoes that I categorized as
home-grown rather than *hothouse,* a classification that permitted me to

predict

_____ aspects of taste, texture, and pleasantness of the eating
experience.

2. If we were to treat each aspect of our environment and experience as a unique event, we would be unable to behave at all. The table I write on today is not, in fact, exactly the same as it was yesterday (it is one day older, slightly warmer, etc.). But I have made an assumption about a category called tables, a classifica-

organize

tion that helps me _____ my experience and

predict

_____ my future relationship to it.

3. We categorize or classify not only objects but people, and it is clear that such a

some good

classification has (<u>some good/only bad</u>) aspects. Classifying a person as fun-loving or intellectual or obnoxious frees us from the burden of attending to all aspects of an individual's behavior each time we meet. A bad aspect, of course,

prejudice

is that classification may result in _____ against an individual in which we blindly assign a person all of the attributes of a particular category.

The Consequences of Social Categorization

4. The way we categorize others may profoundly affect not only our behavior but the behavior of those we categorize. For example, attractive children tend to be sensitive and kind to others, behavioral characteristics that probably result from

stereotypes

(<u>stereotypes/innate traits</u>) of attractive children.

5. If we assign another person to the category *attractive,* then our behavior toward

will also

that person is likely to be affected, which (<u>will also/will not</u>) affect the behavior of that person in response.

6. Thus, the behavior of men who thought they were talking to an attractive woman on the phone was rated to be more sociable, sexually warm, humorous, and confident than that of men who thought they were talking to an unattractive woman. And the behavior of the women to whom the men were talking was also affected: the women were more friendly, confident, and sociable in response to the

attractive

men who held photographs of _____ women.

7. The effect of segregation on the basis of an arbitrary category is dramatically illustrated in the behavior of bees. When bees in a single hive were divided into halves by a glass partition, bees from both halves behaved in a friendly manner

one day

if the partition was removed (<u>one day/four days</u>) later.

four

8. However, when the partition was left in place for _____ days, each group tried to exterminate the other. By the end of four days, the passing of food had led to identifiable odors in the two groups.

9. In many situations, categorizing people on trivial grounds has a similar effect. For example, subjects in one study were divided into two groups, and members of one group were given transistor radios based on the flip of a coin. When asked to rate each other, subjects rated members of the other group more negatively than members of their own group, despite the fact that assignment to

at random

groups had been (<u>at random/based on similarity</u>).

Learning Objectives

1. Discuss both the positive and negative aspects of our use of categories, especially social categories.

2. What point was made in the study involving the photographs and telephone conversations?

3. Describe the study involving the glass partition and beehive. On what basis did the bees categorize other bees? Describe an analogous study with human beings.

Clues to the Personalities of Others

10. There are two major categories we use in forming impressions of others: the

appearance

_____ of the person and his or her behavior.

11. *Expectations Based on Appearance.* When we first meet people, we tend to cate-

appearance

gorize them on the basis of their _____. For example, we might guess that a man with a flat-top crew haircut is politically

conservative

(conservative/liberal).

12. Although we have always heard that "beauty is only skin deep," research indicates that attractive people are perceived more favorably than unattractive people on a wide range of personality traits. Adults view attractive children as

smarter/better

(smarter/less smart) and (better/worse) behaved than unattractive children, and an unattractive child who misbehaves is more likely to be judged "bad" or "cruel" than an attractive child who commits the same act.

13. *Inferring Traits from Behavior: Attribution Theory.* Although initial impressions may be formed on the basis of appearance, these impressions may be altered

behavior (actions)

when we observe the actual _____ of people. We tend to *attribute* traits to people based in part on the way they behave.

14. Theories that attempt to identify those factors which influence the way we attrib-

attribution

ute personality traits to others are known as _____ theories.

15. Suppose you wish to purchase a sewing machine (or radial arm saw or windmill), and you tend to favor brand X, which costs about $300. In the store you notice brand Y, which costs about $200. Assuming that the salespeople work on commission, who do you think would be more likely to be telling the truth:

(Based on attribution theory, we guess that most would pick b.)

   a. a salesperson who says the $300 machine is far superior to the $200 machine.
   b. a salesperson who says the $200 machine is slightly better than the $300 machine.

16. If you selected *b* above, you behaved much like subjects in the attribution experiments described in the text: you attributed honesty to the person whose behavior

unexpected/one

was (unexpected/expected) and could be explained by (one/more than one) motive.

expected
more than one

17. The behavior of the salesperson urging us to buy a more expensive machine is (unexpected/expected), and his or her behavior could be explained by (one/more than one) motive: the salesperson could be telling the truth or simply trying to make a larger commission. Thus, it is more difficult to make an attribution in this case than in the case of the salesperson in *b*.

18. *Biased Inferences*. In making judgments about "Tom," 95 percent of the graduate

computer

students said they thought Tom's graduate specialty was _____ science. This was a rare specialty at the time of the study, and the interesting aspect of this example is that the students had ignored important background information on enrollments in the large specialties in education and the humanities. Students were so impressed with the stereotypical illustration that they made

biased

_____ rather than more reasonable inferences.

19. The same biases that affect problem solving also affect our inferences about people. When a series of descriptive traits has a compelling pattern which resembles

stereotype

a _____ of a particular group, people will tend to show biased inferences, discarding information that might lead to more accurate judgments.

Integrating Impressions of Others

20. *Central Traits*. People's personality traits may be considered as a set of adjectives: an individual may be described as considerate, humorous, cooperative, as-

do not

sertive, and so forth. All such descriptive traits (do/do not) have the same power to influence impressions, however. Those with the strongest influence are termed

central

_____ traits.

21. For example, a person described as "cold, industrious, critical, practical, and de-

less

termined" is evaluated much (less/more) favorably than one described as "warm, industrious, critical, practical, and determined" even though only one word in the two lists is different.

central

22. Asch referred to trait words such as *warm* and *cold* as _____ traits. These traits have a very marked influence on our perception of other traits, and in fact we tend to organize our other impressions around these central traits.

23. *The Primacy Effect*. Evidently, first impressions do count—at least in some situations. The observation that the first in a list of traits has more influence than

primacy

later traits is known as the _____ effect.

24. Consider the following list of traits: *cooperative, assertive, informal, warm, intelligent*. Of these, the words that would probably tend to have the strongest impact would be the words *cooperative* and *warm*, the former because of the

primacy   _____ effect and the latter because it is a

central trait   _____ _____ .

Learning Objectives

4. What types of traits are generally attributed to physically attractive people? Cite examples of the way this affects relationships among children and between children and adults.

5. What is attribution theory? On the basis of what type of behavior is one likely to infer a single trait, such as truthfulness?

6. Discuss the way in which people tend to make biased inferences when presented with compelling stereotypes. Cite a study that indicates the extent to which people, even highly intelligent individuals, are susceptible to this bias.

7. Briefly describe and illustrate the concepts of *central trait* and the *primacy effect*.

SELF-PERCEPTION

25. We have said that we infer the personality traits of others by observing their behavior. Self-perception theory maintains that we also infer our own traits by

behavior   observing our own _____ .

26. As we observe ourselves behave, we build up clusters of generalizations about

schemata   the self referred to as *self-_____* . These generalizations derive from two sources: observations of past incidents of our behavior and generalizations about our behavior made both by ourselves and others.

27. We do not all have the same self-schemata. For example, while Mary has a

aschematic   schema relating to creativity, Ralph does not. Ralph is "_____" with regard to creativity.

28. Knowing that Mary has a schema for creativity, we also know that she will ab-
more   sorb new information relating to creativity (less/more) rapidly than will Ralph. Once a schema is developed, a person uses it to decide what information to attend to and how to evaluate it.

29. While the processes involved in attributing traits to others and to ourselves are probably similar, there appear to be important differences. For one thing, we tend to explain other people's behavior in terms of enduring

traits   _____ but account for our own in terms of

situational   _____ demands.

30. For example, a student obtaining failing marks in school is likely to attribute his or her difficulty to (<u>enduring traits/external factors</u>), such as sickness or stress. Another person, however, is more likely to attribute the student's behavior to

external factors

traits   relatively stable personality _____.

31. An exception to our tendency to attribute our own behavior to situational factors is when we obtain success or achievement. In this case, we are likely to attribute

traits   our behavior to _____.

32. Thus, in the experiment involving games, the winners were likely to attribute their winning behavior to (<u>skill/luck</u>) and the losers' behavior to (<u>poor skills/bad luck</u>). Not surprisingly, the opposite viewpoint was held by the losers.

skill
poor skills

Learning Objectives

8. According to self-perception theory, on what basis do we infer our own traits?

9. Define the terms *self-schemata* and *aschematic*. Explain how the schemata are acquired and how they function in self-perception.

10. Describe the circumstances under which we tend to attribute our own behavior and other people's behavior to enduring traits or to situational demands.

INTERPERSONAL ATTITUDES

33. Interpersonal perception is rarely neutral. When we meet others, we not only classify them but we have positive or negative affective reactions toward them. In other words, interpersonal perception is usually accompanied by interpersonal

attitudes   _____.

INTERPERSONAL ATTITUDES AND FRIENDSHIP FORMATION

The Effects of Proximity

34. If you live in a college dormitory, the chances are that your best friends live on the same floor, perhaps in an adjacent room; and it is unlikely that you are good friends with most of the individuals who live on different floors. This illustrates the single most important factor in friendship formation, the effects of physical

proximity   _____, how close to one another people live and work.

35. One of the explanations of the power of proximity involves the

exposure   _____ effect, the fact that we interact more frequently with those near us. But proximity is related to other factors as well, including the fact

similar   that people who live close to one another also tend to be _____ in socioeconomic status, ethnic background, political leanings, and a number of other factors.

The Effects of Similarity

36. *Similarity in Appearance.* In general, people similar in physical attractiveness tend to pair off. Some data suggest that this occurs because people calculate not

rewards   only the _____ available from an attractive partner but the risk

rejection   of possible _____.

37. Other studies, however, have contradicted this finding. One study, for example, found that men who rated themselves low in physical attractiveness selected

as attractive   dates who were (less attractive/as attractive) as did men who rated themselves high in attractiveness.

38. It may be that the men with a low evaluation of their appearance were relatively less sensitive to rejection or perhaps that people try to develop relationships with the most attractive partner but are rejected until they are paired up with a partner

similar   of _____ attractiveness. In any case, it is clear that there is a "matching process" with regard to attractiveness.

39. *Similarity in Social Background.* The study with red and green chicks found the chicks preferred their cagemates over other chicks, but among other chicks they

their cagemates   preferred ones who were the same color as (themselves/their cagemates). In this

exposure   study, _____ was clearly more important than

similarity   _____ of color.

40. There is a rich interplay among friendship, proximity, and similarity. Which of the following is the best summary of that interplay?
    a. Friendship produces both proximity and similarity, as when good friends become like one another and seek to remain close.
    b. Proximity, due largely to the exposure effect, is the source of both similarity and friendship.
    c. Similarity is the major cause of friendship, which in turn produces the desire to remain close.
    d. A reciprocal relationship exists between all three factors, such that any one seems both to produce the other two and to be produced by the other two.

d

Learning Objectives

11. What is the usual relationship between interpersonal perception and interpersonal attitudes?

12. Briefly describe two possible explanations of why *proximity* leads to *liking*.

13. Explain what is meant by the "matching process" in partner selection—that is, matching with regard to what? Discuss a possible explanation of why the matching process occurs.

14. Describe the likely causal relationships between proximity, similarity, and friendship.

Attraction and Attribution of Similarity

41. Think of an attractive person of your gender, perhaps a movie star. Do you think that you are similar to that person in terms of the personality traits that you have in common? This was the question of a recent study, and the findings were that

similar

college students assumed that they were _____ to physically at-

dissimilar

tractive strangers and _____ to physically unattractive strangers.

42. Further, the students assumed that they possessed both the positive and negative traits of the attractive stranger. With regard to the unattractive stranger, they maintained that they possessed:
    a. only the stranger's negative traits.
    b. only the stranger's positive traits.
    c. neither the positive nor the negative traits of the unattractive stranger.

c

The Effects of Approval

43. It may seem reasonable to suppose that the more approving people are, the more we tend to like them. A study by Aronson and Linder, however, suggests that in some circumstances people are attracted to others who initially make

derogatory

(complimentary/derogatory) remarks.

44. In that study, subjects were divided into four groups. One group heard a confederate of the experimenters make only complimentary remarks about them; a second group heard only derogatory remarks; a third heard first derogatory and then

complimentary

derogatory

complimentary remarks; and a fourth heard _____ and then

_____ remarks.

45. The four roles played by confederates in this experiment are designated below. Rank-order these roles from best-liked confederate to least-liked confederate by assigning them numbers (use a scale of 1 to 4, with 1 equal to best-liked and 4 equal to least-liked).

2

_____ only complimentary

3

_____ only derogatory

1

_____ derogatory then complimentary

4

_____ complimentary then derogatory

more

46. Thus, the subjects who first heard a confederate make derogatory and then complimentary remarks liked that person (less/more) than the confederate who made only complimentary remarks. Evidently, the initial derogatory remarks estab-

credibility (genuineness, believability)

lished the _____ of the confederate. (You should be aware, however, that these results are not general across all variations of this experiment.)

The Effects of Complementary Needs

47. While much research on attraction has concentrated on the effects of similarity,

complement

some psychologists have suggested that individuals who _____ one another's needs are attracted.

48. For example, a person who is highly dependent may be attracted to someone with a need to nurture. In a sense, one need completes the other, and in Winch's

complementary

terms the needs are said to be _____ .

compatibility

49. More recent research suggests, however, that _____ of needs may be a better predictor of friendship than complementarity. Compatible needs may include similar, as well as complementary, needs. But most research involving married couples supports the notion that it is primarily

similarity

(similarity/complementarity) of needs that makes for a harmonious marriage.

Learning Objectives

15. Ralph assumes that an attractive person shares his political and philosophical beliefs and that an unattractive person does not. Discuss a study that indicates that Ralph's perceptions may be biased.

16. Describe Aronson and Linder's study of the effect of approval on attraction, indicating the four sequences of approving and disapproving statements and the results.

17. Briefly discuss the concepts of complementarity and compatibility of needs.

The Effects of Birth Order

later-

50. Some relatively recent research has suggested that birth order is related to sociability, with (first-/later-) borns apparently developing greater social skills.

51. The difference may involve the fact that first-borns have their

parents

_____ to themselves. Later-borns do not, and much of their experience is dominated by the fact that they must learn to live with and around an older sibling.

52. In a study concerned with this issue, schoolchildren were asked to choose from among their classmates the child they would like to play ball with during

recess/first-

_____. Results indicated that _____-

born

_____ children were picked more often.

53. Walter Toman has developed a theory which maintains that marriage partners seek to *duplicate* their childhood sibling relationships and are happiest when they do so. Thus, a later-born woman with an older brother would be happiest mar-

first-born

ried to a _____-_____ man with a younger sister.

duplication

54. Toman's theory, which he terms the _____ hypothesis, has received some support in predicting probability of divorce, but more recent research has failed to support his predictions.

more

55. One new study has found, however, that both later-born men and later-born women were rated (more/less) sociable than first-borns. Ratings were by opposite-sex partners based on brief (five-minute) meetings, so it would be difficult to generalize to marriage. Nonetheless, the study does support the notion that later-

social

borns have an edge in _____ situations.

Learning Objectives

18. What evidence with schoolchildren suggests that first-borns are more socially skilled than later-borns?

19. What is Toman's duplication hypothesis with regard to sibling relationships and marriage? Does the evidence provide consistent support for his position?

20. Describe the study involving brief encounters between men and women and the relationship of the subsequent ratings to birth order.

INTERPERSONAL ATTRACTION AND LOVE

56. In an attempt to understand the nature of romantic love, one psychologist asked several hundred students to select from a long list of statements the ones that best expressed their feelings toward their boyfriends or girl friends. Two

liking

categories of affection emerged: _____ and

loving

_____ .

57. It was also found that answers to the questionnaire predicted behavior: those couples who obtained high scores on the "loving" scale spent more time looking into

eyes

each other's _____ than did those who scored high on the "liking" scale.

58. Love has also been interpreted in terms of the two-factor (attributional) theory of emotion discussed in Chapter 16. According to this theory, emotion is deter-

arousal

mined both by general _____ and by situational factors which influence our interpretation of the arousal.

59. In many situations arousal and attribution are caused by the same thing. For example, the sight of an approaching bear would produce both arousal and an

attribution (interpretation)

_____ that it is the bear that is causing the arousal.

60. In some cases, however, the arousal may be *misattributed* to another source. For example, arousal that may in fact have been caused by fear may be

misattributed

_____ to sexual excitement or romantic attraction.

61. Support for the notion that misattribution may increase romantic attraction comes from a study in which male subjects met an attractive female on either a rickety (and fear-producing) bridge high above a canyon or on a solid bridge a few feet above shallow water. It was found that subjects who met the female on the

rickety

(rickety/solid) bridge expressed more sexual imagery in the brief stories they were requested to write than did those who met the woman on a solid bridge.

62. In addition, the subjects who met the female on the rickety bridge were more likely to telephone her later. In terms of the two-factor theory of emotion, these

fear

results suggest that subjects relabeled arousal due to _____ as arousal due to sexual attraction.

Learning Objectives

21. What two categories of affection emerged from the study of romantic love? What behavior did the type of affection successfully predict?

22. Briefly explain the two-factor (attributional) view of love and its use in accounting for the results of the "bridge" study.

Chapter Twenty-Seven
Social Influence and Group Processes

General Objectives

1. Describe the circumstances under which social facilitation occurs.

2. Present the conclusions of the autokinetic effect and line-judging studies of conformity.

3. Discuss the factors that influence obedience in the Milgram studies.

4. Discuss the biological, social-learning, and situational factors that affect aggression.

5. Present the text's definition of altruism.

6. Describe the factors that influence helping in emergencies and those that influence giving and sharing.

7. Discuss the "human dilemma" and the factors that affect cooperation and competition.

8. Discuss the "tragedy of the commons," its implications in terms of immediacy of reward, and the direction of possible solutions.

Social Influence and Group Processes

Learning Objectives appear at
the end of each major section.

SOCIAL FACILITATION

1. The mere presence of other people affects our performance, sometimes to improve it and sometimes to make it worse. If the presence of others improves

social

our performance, the effect is referred to as _____

facilitation

_____.

2. Social facilitation seems to occur when the task is either quite

simple _____ or when it has already been thoroughly

learned (mastered) _____ .

3. Social facilitation does *not* occur when the task is either very

complex (difficult) _____ or when it is a new task that requires an individual to

learn (master) _____ new skills.

4. For example, if one is just beginning to learn a finger maze, the presence of an
interfere with audience or of others working on the same task will (improve/interfere with)
one's performance. However, after one has mastered the maze, the presence of

improve others will _____ both the speed and accuracy of one's
performance.

5. Social facilitation seems to occur because the presence of others increases

dominant *arousal*, which in turn increases our tendency to perform _____
responses. Dominant responses are responses that are most likely to occur in a
situation—generally, the simple or well-learned responses.

Learning Objectives

1. Define the concept *social facilitation*.

2. Under what circumstances does social facilitation occur? When does the presence of an audience seem to disrupt
performance? Explain these effects in terms of the concepts of *arousal* and *dominant responses*.

CONFORMITY

6. The point being made in the introductory comments for this section may best be
summarized as follows:
a. The world is made up of two types: conformers and nonconformers.
b b. We conform to some degree in almost every aspect of our lives, from the
things we believe in to the manner in which we eliminate waste.
c. Conformity is a negative aspect of human behavior that may, with persever-
ance, be overcome.

Individual Conformity to Norms

7. *Sherif's Experiments*. If a pinpoint of light is viewed in total darkness, the light

autokinetic will appear to move. This illusion is known as the _____
effect.

never moved

8. In an experiment making use of this illusion, Muzafer Sherif asked subjects to view the lights and then to indicate how far the lights had moved. In fact, the lights (never moved/moved short distances).

converge

9. When individuals who had made several judgments alone were then placed in a group and asked to make judgments, their judgments tended to (diverge/converge) until they resembled one another closely.

the same as

10. Judgments were also taken from individuals who first viewed the lights in a group. When they viewed the lights by themselves, they tended to make estimates that were (the same as/different from) those developed by the group.

conformity

11. Sherif's experiment with the autokinetic effect was an early one demonstrating

_____ to norms, in this case norms of judgment about the illusory movement of a point source of light.

12. *Asch's Experiments*. Look at Figure 27.1 in the text. Assume that the first six subjects (actually "bogus" or confederate subjects) selected line 1 as the closest

2

match for the standard line. In fact, of course, line _____ is the

two-

closest match; but Asch found that approximately _____-

thirds

_____ of the real subjects in the study conformed on at least *half* of the critical trials.

13. *Factors Influencing Conformity*. Unless the confederates are unanimous in their judgments, conformity in the Asch experiment is greatly reduced. In a variation of this type of study, Asch found that conformity dropped from 32 percent to 5

one
correct

percent when _____ of the confederates gave the (correct/incorrect) answers rather than those of the majority.

14. A second factor that affects conformity in this situation concerns whether or not subjects' judgments are made anonymously. In the Asch studies the judgments were made on a face-to-face basis; in studies in which judgments are made anon-

decreases

ymously, conformity (increases/decreases).

15. The social pressure to conform also diminishes once the source of the misinformation has been removed, as demonstrated in the experiment involving "generations" of subjects. In that experiment, social pressure was initially introduced by

confederates

two _____ of the experimenter, who announced that the light moved fifteen or sixteen inches.

16. The first experimental group was made up of two confederates and one real subject; the second of one of the confederates, the previous subjects, and one new subject; the third of the first two real subjects and one new subject. Thus, after

none

the first two groups, _____ of the subjects included confederates.

17. As shown in Figure 27.2, the initial influence of the confederates was strong but gradually diminished, so that by the time the tenth group of three had been run, the social influence of the confederates had been reduced to

nothing   (nothing/a moderate amount).

18. *Zimbardo's Prison Experiment.* Several years ago Philip Zimbardo conducted an experiment involving a mock prison housed in the basement of the psychology building at Stanford University. Subjects were paid volunteers who were as-

guards/prisoners   signed roles as either _____ or _____ .

19. After only a few hours the guards began to act in a way we have come to expect prison guards to act, becoming abusive and aggressive. The prisoners also responded to stereotypical social norms, becoming passive, depressed, and enraged at the guards. It is important to note that subjects had been assigned to their roles:
    a.   on the basis of personality test scores.
    b.   on the basis of Zimbardo's clinical judgment.
c   c.   at random.

norms   20. Zimbardo's prison experiment demonstrated that social _____ controlled the behavior of both groups. Although they had been assigned to

random   groups at _____ , both groups conformed to the behaviors they had come to associate with their respective roles in the outside society.

Learning Objectives

3. Describe the autokinetic effect and Sherif's use of it in his studies of conformity. Specifically, how did first judging the lights individually affect later judgments in a group? How did first judging the movement as part of a group affect later individual judgments?

4. Describe the general procedure of the line-judging studies. How much conformity was found in the original studies? What two factors seem to reduce dramatically the amount of conformity?

5. What was the conclusion of the autokinetic-effect study that employed "generations" of subjects?

6. What is the main point of the Zimbardo mock-prison study?

Obedience to Authority

21. *Milgram's Experiments.* In Milgram's studies two individuals participated at a time, but only one of them was a real subject. The real subject was assigned the role of teacher, and the accomplice was assigned the role of

learner   _____ .

22. The subject's task was to manipulate switches that supposedly increased the in-

shock
was not

tensity of _____ given to the learner. In actuality, shock (was/was not) given. The learner merely acted out the part of someone in pain.

23. Each time the learner made a mistake in a word-memorization task the subject

increase

was supposed to _____ the amount of shock given, ranging from 15 volts at the beginning of the session to as much as 450 volts at the end.

24. The majority of the students, psychologists, and others whom Milgram consulted believed that most subjects would refuse to deliver a dangerous shock. In the

65

experiment, however, approximately _____ percent of the subjects administered what they thought was a shock of 450 volts. Despite the obvious distress they exhibited, the subjects continued to obey the commands of the experimenter.

25. *Factors Influencing Obedience.* One of the factors that seems to influence obedience concerns whether or not the person giving instructions is viewed as a

legitimate authority

_____   _____.

26. As demonstrated in one study, a uniform may be enough to identify an individual as a legitimate authority. In that study people were more obedient in picking up a paper bag or giving a dime to a stranger when the researcher who was

guard

giving the orders was dressed as a (guard/civilian).

27. In addition to the legitimacy of the authority, several other factors affected obedience in the Milgram situation. In one version of the study the experimenter was either physically present or else absent from the room in which the teacher (the real subject) was located. While about 65 percent of the subjects obeyed the

present

experimenter when he was _____, only 22 percent obeyed

absent

when he was physically _____, giving instructions by telephone.

28. In another study, the closeness of the teacher to the victim was manipulated. Rank-order the following conditions, giving a rank of 1 to the condition that produced the *least* obedience.

2

_____ The teacher was in the same room as the learner.

1

_____ The teacher was required to force the victim's hand onto a shock plate.

3

_____ The teacher heard the victim's screams in an adjacent room.

29. It was suggested that the farther the subject was from the victim, the easier it

deny
was for the subject to _____ that he or she was inflicting pain. Similarly, killing from long-range bombers may be less discomforting than killing in hand-to-hand combat.

30. In another version of the Milgram situation there were three teachers, two of whom were confederates of the experimenter. It was found in this case that when the two confederates refused to continue shocking the learner, most of the true

also refused
subjects (continued/also refused) to deliver further shocks.

31. The study just described involved a subject's choice between

obedience/conformity
_____ to the authority and _____ to his peers. The text points out, however, that in real life penalties for disobedience may be far more severe than the disapproving remarks of an unknown experimenter.

Learning Objectives

7. Describe the tasks of the learner and the teacher (the real subject) in the original Milgram shock study. Did the learner actually experience shock?

8. What proportion of the subjects tended to obey the experimenter throughout the experiment in the original version? How intense was the maximum voltage they thought they had delivered?

9. Describe the way in which the physical presence or absence of the experimenter influenced obedience in the Milgram studies.

10. In addition to the condition in which the learner's (accomplice's) voice could be heard, three other conditions were used that varied the physical closeness of the teacher to the learner. List and describe each of these conditions. What effect did increasing the physical closeness of the feedback from the learner have on the subject's administration of what he thought to be shock?

11. What happens to obedience in the Milgram situation when two confederates defy the experimenter?

AGGRESSION

32. The key attributes that define an act as aggressive are the *target* and the *intention*. Aggression is a deliberate act directed against a person with the

intention
_____ of doing harm.

would not
33. Thus, intentionally damaging a tree (would/would not) be considered an act of aggression, nor would accidentally running into a pedestrian.

verbal

34. Aggressive acts include both physical and _____ behaviors. Attempts to explain why human beings are so aggressive fall into three categories:

learning

biological explanations, social-_____ explanations, and situational explanations.

Biological Influences

35. Freud postulated that human beings pursue aggressive and self-destructive acts

death

because of a _____ instinct, which is for the most part evenly

life

balanced with a _____ instinct.

36. Although today's psychologists consider Freud's notion of a death instinct as

speculative

being highly (accurate/speculative), there is some support for the underlying idea

biological (instinctual, genetic)

that aggression may have a _____ basis.

37. While specific gene locations for aggression have been isolated in lower animals,

does not

such evidence (does/does not) exist for human beings. One genetic abnormality that has been suspected of contributing to violence, however, is the presence of

XYY

an extra Y chromosome in males, the so-called _____ chromosomal pattern. Another suspected biological factor is brain

damage (injury)

_____ resulting from infection, tumors, or injuries.

unlikely

38. It is (unlikely/likely) that these two kinds of biological abnormalities account for much of the widespread aggression found in most human societies. First, the

rare

presence of an extra Y chromosome is quite (rare/frequent), and a study of 4,000 Danish men has failed to find a connection between this chromosomal pattern and violent behavior.

39. Second, although it is estimated that between 10 and 15 million Americans suffer from some form of brain damage, there is no evidence to suggest that most of these persons are any more aggressive than anyone else. Moreover, the majority

do not have

of people with a history of violent behavior (do not have/have) some form of brain damage.

40. Even when brain damage is found to be a factor in a violent person, the case of

learning

Paul M suggests that social _____ may still play an important role.

Social-Learning Mechanisms

41. *The Importance of Models.* According to social-learning theory, we learn how to

observing (modeling)   perform specific aggressive skills by _____ the behavior of others. Two of the most powerful models are family members and characters

television   portrayed in films and on _____.

42. Although many parents are physically aggressive toward their children, many

words (attitudes)   others model aggression in their _____ rather than in actual violent acts.

43. One study demonstrated that violent films shown to a group of delinquent boys

increase   resulted in a clear (increase/decrease) in verbal and physical aggression. Studies of delinquent girls and nondelinquent college students have reported

similar   (similar/opposite) findings.

44. Although individuals may learn aggressive behavior by watching movies and television, whether or not they will later display this aggressive behavior depends to

rewards (reinforcement)   a large extent on the _____ they expect to receive.

is   45. In most societies, including our own, aggressive behavior (is/is not) frequently rewarded. The rewards may be *tangible,* as when aggression results in the acquisition of goods or territory; *social,* as when soldiers are treated as heroes for being aggressive; or *internal.* Aggressive behavior that serves as a source of

internal   pride and self-esteem is said to provide _____ rewards for the individual.

Situational Factors

46. John Dollard hypothesized that frustration, which he defined as interference with any form of goal-directed behavior, always leads to some form of

aggression   _____; and, conversely, aggression is always the consequence

frustration   of _____.

47. Although experiments have demonstrated that frustration frequently does lead to aggression, it is clear that aggression is only one of many possible responses to

is not   frustration. It is also clear that all aggressive behavior (is/is not) caused by frustration.

48. In one study, for example, the experimenter *frustrated* students in one condition and *angered* those in another; a third group, which completed the experimental tasks without interruption or insult, functioned as the control group. Results indi-

angered (insulted)   cated that only the students who had been _____ showed an increase in physiological arousal and a tendency to behave aggressively toward the experimenter (by delivering ostensive shocks).

49. In support of Berkowitz's view of aggression, this study demonstrated that anger produced by insults may be a more important source of aggression than

frustration   _____ produced by interrupting a task. It further demonstrated that frustration does not always lead to aggression, nor is aggression always the consequence of frustration.

50. There are other situational factors that seem related to aggression, including *noise* and *heat*. For example, in one study subjects working in rooms heated to

shocks   93 degrees Fahrenheit delivered more _____ to a confederate than did subjects working under more normal temperature conditions.

Learning Objectives

12. What are the two key aspects of the text's definition of aggression? Are verbal acts included in this definition?

13. What are the three major categories of explanation for aggressive behavior?

14. How did Freud explain aggression?

15. What evidence indicates that the XYY chromosomal pattern is not a determinant of violent behavior? Does brain damage seem to be a major cause of violence?

16. With regard to the social-learning-theory view of aggression:
    a. how are aggressive behaviors acquired?
    b. who are some of the most important models for training aggression?
    c. what is the function of reinforcement with respect to aggression?
    d. aside from tangible rewards, what other types of rewards support aggressive behaviors?

17. Explain Dollard's frustration-aggression hypothesis. Does research tend to support the theory? What other factors are important in producing aggression?

HELPING

51. A behavioral act that is intended to help someone in need and that is done

altruistic   without expectation of external rewards is referred to as _____ behavior.

52. There are two key aspects of our definition of altruistic behavior: the act must be

intended

_____ to help someone in need, and there must be no

rewards

_____ involved other than personal satisfaction.

53. According to the sociobiologists (discussed in Chapter 7), human beings are

genetically

_____ programmed to help one another, a concept referred to
as *inclusive fitness*. Many social scientists reject the genetic theories, however, in
favor of factors that are of known importance in the acquisition of altruistic be-

modeling

havior, the factors of _____ and reinforcement.

Bystander Intervention in Emergencies

54. Thirty-eight neighbors witnessed the murder of Kitty Genovese without coming
to her aid or even calling the police. Later investigation revealed that these wit-

were not

nesses (were/were not) indifferent to the murder, however.

55. *The Presence of Other Bystanders.* In an attempt to understand the factors that
operate in situations like the Genovese murder, Latané and Darley conducted a
series of experiments in which "emergency" situations were staged. They found
that a key factor preventing people from helping in these staged situations was

others

simply the presence of _____ .

56. Latané and Darley offered three possible explanations for this response. The first

inhibits

is that the presence of others _____ intervention because people
fear looking foolish in front of an audience. Latané and Darley refer to this fac-

audience

tor as _____ *inhibition*.

57. The second possible explanation is that bystanders watch each other for cues
concerning whether or not the emergency is genuine, and each bystander attempts to look calm and collected during this process. The group calmness acts

a nonemergency

to define the situation as (an emergency/a nonemergency). This factor is termed

influence

the *social-*_____ factor.

58. The third possible explanation is that the presence of many other bystanders in
an emergency situation diminishes the need for any individual to feel personally

responsibility

responsible. Thus, there is a *diffusion of* _____ when other observers are present. The onlooker may leave the scene without feeling so guilty.

59. In a study evaluating the differential and combined effects of the three explanations, Latané and Darley found that the presence of only one or two factors

decreased

(decreased/did not decrease) helping behavior, but that helping was least likely to
occur when all three factors were present.

60. Additional studies have demonstrated that the presence of bystanders does not always inhibit individual action. For example, when there is clear evidence that

emergency

there is an _____, as when observers can gauge one another's immediate reaction through nonverbal cues, then the bystander effect is less likely to occur.

61. *The Assessment of Costs*. Further research on bystander intervention has shown that individuals are more likely to offer aid when the cost of intervening is

low

_____ and the cost of not intervening is

high

_____.

62. For example, it was found that the bystanders in a subway were more likely to

a man with a cane

come to the aid of (an apparent drunk/a man with a cane) who had staged a collapse. Evidently the bystanders in this situation assessed the cost of helping

low

the man with the cane as being _____ because he was unlikely to be abusive; the opposite was true in the case of the man who appeared to be drunk. Moreover, the cost of not helping, in terms of guilt and self-recrimina-

man with the cane

tion, was much higher for the (apparent drunk/man with the cane).

63. When the researchers placed a man in a white hospital uniform near the scene of

reduced

the staged collapse, intervention by bystanders was (reduced/increased). Evidently the presence of a person who appears to be qualified to act in an emer-

responsibility (obligation)

gency situation reduces the _____ felt by bystanders to intervene.

Learning Objectives

18. What are the two key aspects of our definition of altruistic behavior?

19. Why does the presence of others tend to inhibit helping in emergencies? List the three possible explanations offered by Latané and Darley.

20. Under what conditions is the bystander effect less likely to occur? In your answer discuss:
    a. the "clear emergency" aspect.
    b. costs and rewards, as illustrated in the study of the man who collapsed in a subway.
    c. the presence of someone apparently qualified to act in an emergency.

Giving and Sharing

64. Donating to charities is another form of altruistic behavior that is clearly different

less

from helping in emergencies. Giving and sharing involve much (more/less) risk,

ambiguous

and the situation is usually less _____ than is frequently the case in emergency situations.

norms

mood

increase

c

norm

positive

decrease
increase

65. Thus, some of the costs involved in emergency situations do not apply to giving and sharing behaviors. The two factors that seem to have the greatest impact on

giving and sharing are social _____ and the

_____ of the giver.

66. *The Influence of Norms*. In an experiment involving donations to a Christmas charity, donations were found to (increase/decrease) when a costumed Santa Claus was stationed near the donation box, apparently because he called attention to a need. In a further aspect of this study, a behavioral model passed by the box, sometimes giving and sometimes stating that she did not want to give. Donations by others increased when the model:
    a. donated.
    b. did not donate.
    c. either of the above.

67. Regardless of whether the model donated or did not donate, the presence of the model increased donations from others, quite possibly because even when she

turned away, her action reminded people of the _____ of giving.

68. *The Influence of Moods*. Research with young children has shown that they are more willing to share with others when they are in a (positive/negative) mood. Positive moods also increase giving by older children and adults, but the effect of negative moods is more complicated.

69. For younger children, negative moods have been found to (increase/decrease) giving; for older children, negative moods seem to (increase/decrease) giving. It was suggested that this difference results from the process of socialization, in which children acquire empathy and an understanding of the link between altruism and social approval.

Learning Objectives

21. What are the two most important factors that affect giving and sharing?

22. In the study involving charity donations, what behaviors of the model increased giving? What explanation of this effect was presented?

23. What are the effects of *moods* on giving and sharing? Discuss the apparently different effect of bad moods on giving by younger versus older children. What may account for this difference?

THE HUMAN DILEMMA: COOPERATION VERSUS COMPETITION

competitive

70. In going about our daily lives, we are frequently forced to choose between being

    cooperative and being _____ in our exchanges with other people. The choice between cooperation and competition is a persistent human dilemma.

Studying the Human Dilemma

cooperation

71. Psychologists have studied the conflict between cooperation and competition by means of an experimental situation called the prisoner's dilemma game (see Figure 27.11 in the text). The behavior that maximizes the benefits for *both* prisoners in this game is (cooperation/competition).

compete

72. Despite the greater benefits of cooperation, most subjects choose to (cooperate/compete). One of the reasons for this reflects the dilemma of the game, the fact that the cooperative response is not beneficial unless both parties use it, which in part depends on the factor of trust.

Factors Influencing Two-Person Cooperation

cooperative

difficult

73. *The Use of Threats*. Deutsch and Krauss conducted an experiment in which pairs of subjects were asked to play a "trucking game" in which they acted as owners of a trucking company that shipped goods over one of two prescribed routes (see Figure 27.11 in the text). The procedures of the game allowed for (cooperative/competitive) behavior to generate the maximum gain for *both* players. Under the initial conditions, without any potential threats, cooperative behavior was (easy/difficult) to achieve.

a further decrease

74. Giving one of the subjects a unilateral threat—a gate that could be locked to prevent the other player from using the main route—resulted in (an increase/a further decrease) in cooperation between the two subjects.

a further decrease

may not be

75. Providing a bilateral threat, in which both subjects had a gate, resulted in (an increase/a further decrease) in cooperation between the two subjects, so that cooperation became almost impossible. It should be pointed out that these results (are/may not be) generalizable to real-life situations, however.

b

76. *Observation and Experience*. Braver and Barnett allowed subjects first to view the consequences that result from various combinations of cooperation and competition when players engage in games like the two previously described. They found that only one of the three combinations produces cooperative behavior. This was the condition in which (choose one):
    a. one player was cooperative and the other was competitive.
    b. both players were competitive.
    c. both players were cooperative.

77. Apparently, viewing a highly competitive situation inhibits the observer from becoming involved in a similar situation. The answer as to why this is true may lie

attribution

in _____ *theory*.

Learning Objectives

24. What is the "human dilemma" discussed in this section?

25. What strategy will maximize the payoff to both players in the prisoner's dilemma game? What strategy do most players tend to follow (especially in the initial stages of the game)?

26. What were the results of the trucking game when neither player had a potential threat? When there was unilateral threat? Bilateral threat?

27. How does observation of other players affect cooperation in the trucking game?

Promoting Social Cooperation

greater
greater

former

78. *Tragedy of the Commons*. The "tragedy of the commons" refers to the fact that when a group of people share a common resource, an individual's personal benefits will be (greater/lesser) when he or she consumes the resource as quickly as possible. The *long-term* benefits for the group as a whole will be (greater/lesser) when each individual curtails his or her consumption of the resource. In real-life situations people tend to follow the (former/latter) practice. The end result is a self-accelerating social trap in which the resource is consumed without an effective alternative becoming available.

79. Psychologists have demonstrated many times that *immediate* consequences have a

long-

term/against

far greater influence on behavior than do _____-

_____ consequences. This works (for/against) large-scale social cooperation over an extended period of time.

coercion

80. *Breaking Out of Social Traps*. Hardin has argued that the solution to the tragedy of the commons is the imposition of mutually agreed-upon (coercion/appeals to conscience). In other words, it is necessary to make it increasingly difficult and expensive for individuals to exploit a commonly held resource.

communication

81. Some research indicates that there may be other solutions. In games simulating the commons dilemma, subjects have been found to increase cooperation when

_____ among players is facilitated.

a

b

c

nuclear

population

birth rates

nuclear

82. The text suggests that communication facilitates long-term cooperation because it allows people to (circle the correct answer[s]):
   a. develop acquaintances and increase concern for one another.
   b. exchange information relevant to a cooperative decision.
   c. state their intentions and assure others that these intentions are sincere.

83. In 1970 futurist John Platt identified _____ annihilation, eco-logical imbalance, and the _____ explosion as the most serious threats to humankind, and he estimated that we had at most twenty to fifty years to reverse the current trends.

84. By 1982 there were at least two hopeful signs that such a reversal might be possible: the dramatic plunge in _____ _____ in America, and the widespread support for _____ disarmament. Although these events indicate that human behavior can change, the short-term rewards make the long-term solutions difficult to obtain.

Learning Objectives

28. What is the "tragedy of the commons"? Why does it occur?

29. What solution does Hardin offer? What seems to help in games that simulate the commons dilemma?

30. List the three most serious threats to humankind discussed by futurist John Platt. What are the "hopeful signs" that we may be able to reverse these threats?

Chapter Twenty-Eight
Environmental Psychology

General Objectives

1. Define the concept of personal space, and describe the four zones of interpersonal distance.

2. Compare the concepts of personal space and territoriality.

3. Describe the three types of human territories identified by Altman.

4. Describe the differences between human territoriality and the territoriality of lower animals.

5. Compare the views of the ethologists, sociobiologists, and sociocultural theorists concerning the relationship between defense and territoriality.

6. Define the term *privacy,* discuss the relationship between privacy and self-disclosure, and list the factors that affect self-disclosure.

7. Differentiate between density and crowding. Discuss the effects of crowding on interpersonal interaction.

8. Explain Altman's concept of microinterpersonal behavior.

9. Give examples of the way in which environmental design may influence interpersonal behavior.

Environmental Psychology

Learning Objectives appear at
the end of each major section.

THE NATURE OF ENVIRONMENTAL PSYCHOLOGY

1. Some aspects of the relationship between the environment and individual behavior were examined in Chapter 21. This chapter will emphasize the effects

social

of the environment on _____ behavior.

an interdisciplinary field

2. The field of environmental psychology may best be described as (a branch of social psychology/an interdisciplinary field). In fact, it has evolved from the collaborations of psychologists, sociologists, anthropologists, geographers, and architects.

PERSONAL SPACE

personal

3. The invisible bubble that surrounds each of us and creates a boundary between each of us and potential intruders is known as our _____ space.

a

4. Personal space changes, becomes larger or smaller, depending on such factors as gender, age, culture, and degree of familiarity. For example, in our culture distance is generally greatest for interactions between:
   a. two males.
   b. two females.
   c. a male-female pair.

Interaction Distances

eighteen

5. *Intimate Distance.* Hall has classified personal space in terms of four distinct zones: intimate, personal, social, and public distances. The intimate distance extends from physical contact to _____ inches. Interaction within

emotion

this space is reserved for the expression of deep _____, such as love and intense hostility.

intimate

6. Dolores shakes her fist in Marjorie's face; Ralph kisses Bruce tenderly. These individuals are in the zone referred to as _____ distance.

personal

7. *Personal Distance.* The zone reserved for close friends or acquaintances discussing personal matters is referred to as the _____ distance. It ex-

four

tends from one and one-half to _____ feet around an individual.

twelve

8. *Social Distance.* The social distance, which extends from four to _____ feet around an individual, is used for casual acquaintances and formal business and social dealings.

9. *Public Distance.* Individuals interacting within the range of twelve to twenty-five

public

feet or more are in the zone of _____ distance, generally used by actors, politicians, or teachers. At this distance words are more clearly enun-

voice

ciated, gestures are exaggerated, and the _____ becomes louder.

Learning Objectives

1. What is personal space, and what factors affect its size?

2. List the names and the approximate sizes of the four personal distance zones proposed by Hall. Describe the types of interaction that take place in each.

The Protective Function of Personal Space

buffer

10. One of the functions of personal space is as a "body-_____ zone," which protects against physical or emotional threats from others. Violent

larger-

individuals and people under stress have (larger-/smaller-) than-average zones of personal space.

11. In a series of studies Robert Sommer has found that people react to an invasion of their zones of personal space by showing increased signs of

stress (discomfort)

_____. For example, when a female experimenter sat next to or across from female students in a library, most of the students left within a period of thirty minutes.

12. When two people are interacting, a zone of personal space surrounds the pair, and others feel awkward about invading that space. In one study, subjects forced to walk between people in conversation showed increased signs of

stress

_____, including facial expressions in which the lips were pursed or twisted.

13. In another study, more subjects avoided walking through a group of four people

size

talking than between a pair of individuals. Thus, the _____ of the group appears to affect the amount of stress felt by the intruder.

14. In addition, a pair of talkers who appeared to be faculty members blocked as many passersby as did four students. Thus, the _____ of the

status

group members also appears to affect intrusions into personal space.

Personal Space and Interpersonal Attraction

smaller

15. In a study in which students were asked to pretend to be interacting with others whom they liked or disliked, it was found that the friendlier the supposed relationship, the _____ the zone of personal space between them. The relationship between liking and interpersonal distance has frequently been observed in the natural environment as well.

Learning Objectives

3. How does personal space function as a "body-buffer zone"? How is this zone affected by individual differences in aggressiveness or by stress?

4. What evidence is there that supports the notion that invasion of personal space produces stress?

5. How do the factors of the size and status of groups affect invasion of the personal space surrounding a group?

6. What is the relationship between personal space and attraction?

TERRITORIALITY

The Nature of Territoriality

territory

16. Territoriality differs from personal space in that it is linked to a specific geographical area. Personal space accompanies an individual wherever he or she goes; a _____, however, is stationary.

invisible

17. In addition, the boundaries of a territory are usually visible, whereas the boundaries of personal space are always _____.

primary

secondary

18. Altman has identified three types of territory. Territories that are central to their users' lives and that help to regulate privacy are termed _____ *territories*. Semipublic places, where acquaintances and neighbors regularly interact, are termed _____ territories.

primary

secondary

19. For example, one's home is a _____ territory, while country clubs, neighborhood bars, and backyards are _____ territories. Since a secondary territory is not always clearly identified,

conflict

_____ may arise over its possession and boundaries, as when outsiders enter a neighborhood bar.

20. Altman classifies territories to which there is free access as

public   _____ territories. Included in this category are streets, parks, tables in restaurants, and in general any area that may be occupied temporarily by anyone.

Territoriality and Defense

21. When the ethologists originally developed the concept of territoriality, they as-

defense
genetic   sumed that it necessarily involved _____ against invaders. They also assumed that both territoriality and defense have a (genetic/environmental) basis.

sociobiologists   22. Like the ethologists, the _____ emphasize the biological basis of territoriality and the importance of defense. Unlike the ethologists, however, these theorists indicate that the expression of defense in human beings is heavily

environmental   influenced by _____ factors, as illustrated by the nomadic hunter-gatherers who have no concept of land ownership.

ethologists'/sociobiologists'

environmental   23. In contrast to the _____ and _____ theories of territoriality, the _sociocultural theorists'_ views emphasize the importance of (genetic/environmental) factors. They view territorial behavior as a function of social learning and cultural influences.

sociocultural   24. In addition, the _____ theorists maintain that human territoriality is very different from that displayed by other species.

25. Edney, for example, has listed several ways in which human and animal territoriality diverge. To become familiar with these differences, label the descriptions below with the words _animal_ or _human_.

human   _____ Uses territory for many purposes in a variety of ways.

human   _____ Does not necessarily use aggressive defense of territory.

human   _____ May maintain several territories rather than one.

human   _____ May use a territory only temporarily and for a brief time.

26. In a study conducted in a home for juvenile offenders, the most dominant boys

territories   were also the ones who used the most desirable _____ most frequently. Thus, as in the animal world, territoriality is related to

dominance   _____ .

27. By distributing space in a systematic manner, territoriality and dominance help

social

maintain a stable _____ order. The effectiveness of the system

dominant

in the boys' home became apparent after the two most _____ boys were released, following which there was a period of conflict and social reorganization.

Territoriality and Identity

28. Both my wife and I grew up in houses that were built before the turn of the century, as was the house we eventually bought. We subscribe to a magazine called the *Old House Journal*. We like old houses; but beyond mere liking it is

identity (self-image)

clear that our house is a part of our sense of _____.

29. In their choices of homes and selection of decorations and furnishings, people represent something about their personalities that is as clear to outsiders as to the individuals themselves. Thus, in one study students' ratings of the personality

agreed significantly

traits of homeowners (agreed significantly/disagreed) with the homeowners' self-ratings, despite the fact that the students and homeowners had not met. The students based their impressions on color photographs of the homeowners'

living rooms

_____ _____.

Learning Objectives

7. List the differences between the concepts of *personal space* and *territoriality*.

8. Name, describe, and give examples of the three types of human territories identified by Altman.

9. What is the role of defense and of heredity and environment in territoriality? Compare the views of the ethologists, sociobiologists, and sociocultural theorists.

10. List four differences between human and animal territoriality.

11. How is territoriality related to dominance? To a stable social order?

12. In what way is human territoriality, as represented in one's home, related to identity? Describe a study that supports this notion.

PRIVACY

The Nature of Privacy

withdrawal

control

30. Two key words are repeatedly mentioned in the text's discussion of privacy: the need for _____ from the company of others and the need to _____ access to oneself or to personal information. There are clear individual differences in the need for privacy, and the text describes six personality types that reflect variations in needs for withdrawal and control.

Development of the Individual's Concept of Privacy

withdrawal

controlling

31. A study of 900 children between the ages of five and seventeen revealed that children's concept of privacy changes with age. Children under eight are least likely to mention the _____ aspect of privacy, while children between the ages of eight and twelve are most likely to view privacy in terms of _____ access to a place.

withdrawal

control

32. The concept of privacy is more complex among adolescents, who are most likely to mention both the _____ or "being alone" aspect as well as the _____ of access to information.

Privacy and Self-Disclosure

self-

disclosure

nonverbal

33. One method of controlling privacy is to regulate _____-_____, the processes by which we tell others about ourselves. Self-disclosure is usually verbal but may also be _____, through eye contact, for example, or smiling.

reduce

34. There are several factors that affect the extent to which we self-disclose. The presence of a third person, for example, has been found to (reduce/increase) disclosure by an individual to an interviewer.

more

35. On the other hand, when we are assured *anonymity*, as in a discussion with a "stranger on a train," we are likely to be (less/more) self-disclosing than usual.

also

36. If the person we are talking to tends to be self-disclosing, then we are (also/not) likely to be self-disclosing. In other words, self-disclosure tends to be

reciprocal

_____.

37. If someone's self-disclosure threatens our privacy (due to pressure to reciprocate), we can avoid disclosing more intimate information by increasing the
breadth of our personal remarks (i.e., the number of topics) without increasing

depth   the _____ of our remarks.

Learning Objectives

13. List and describe the two key aspects of privacy presented.

14. How do children's concepts of privacy change as they develop?

15. Name and describe three factors that affect self-disclosure.

16. How may people respond to the pressure to reciprocate self-disclosure without revealing more intimate information?

CROWDING

The Nature of Crowding

density

38. While researchers used to define crowding in terms of _____,
the number of people in a given space, today they define it in terms of the

perception
is not

_____ of restricted space. Thus, while density is necessary for
crowding to occur, density by itself (is/is not) sufficient to produce crowding.

39. According to this definition, crowding may be alleviated either by acquiring

space/cognitions
  (perceptions)
less

more _____ or by changing one's _____ so
that the density is viewed as less unpleasant. It is also clear that people adapt to
high density. Residents of Hong Kong, for example, would feel (less/more)
crowded in a dense environment than would residents of an American suburb.

Crowding and Information Overload

40. Milgram has speculated that there are three aspects of urban living that produce

overload

information _____ : the large *numbers* of people living in cities,

density

the high _____ , and the *heterogeneity* of people's backgrounds.

41. People experience information overload when the amount of information they are exposed to exceeds their capacity to process it. To reduce this overload, city

norms   dwellers develop social _____ that diminish the intensity of social contacts. Reception of new information may be blocked, other people's needs may be ignored, and responsibilities may be shifted to others whenever possible.

42. One of the effects of this type of information overload is that individuals who experience overload appear to encode fewer aspects of their environments. For example, people sent into a department store during peak shopping hours remem-

less   bered (more/less) about the store's environment than did those who were sent to the store when it was uncrowded.

43. One of the most negative aspects of crowding may be that people who are placed

control   in high-density situations feel unable to _____ the information

less   input. Thus, shoppers told beforehand to expect certain physiological and psychological reactions to crowding reacted (more/less) negatively than did those who were not forewarned.

Learning Objectives

17. How do contemporary researchers define *crowding?* In what two ways may crowding be alleviated?

18. What aspects of urban living produce information overload, according to Milgram? How do city dwellers attempt to reduce this overload?

19. What is the effect of information overload on our encoding of certain aspects of our environment? Discuss the department-store study. How did forewarning affect negative reactions to crowding in the supermarket study?

Crowding and Social Withdrawal

44. One way to control the negative reaction to crowding is to

withdraw   _____ by avoiding social interactions. In one study, for example, students placed in a small, crowded room were much less willing to talk

intimate   about _____ topics than were students in a larger room.

45. Even the mere anticipation of being crowded may affect people's social behavior. Thus, students who expected to experience crowding had more

negative   (negative/positive) reactions both to the characteristics of a room and to its occupants than did those not expecting crowding.

46. Long-term crowding in living quarters appears to have a clear effect on the way people interact with others. Thus, students who lived in dormitories with seventeen double-occupancy rooms per lounge and bathroom behaved differently in interactions with others from those who lived in dormitories with only three double-occupancy rooms per lounge and bathroom: they sat

farther from/talked

(farther from/closer to) another person, _____ less, and

looked

_____ less at the other person.

47. In another study, a sudden influx of students led a college to assign three men to rooms designed for two. In comparison with students in rooms occupied by two, **negatively** students in the triples rated their roommates much more (negatively/positively)

control

and reported feeling much less _____ over almost every aspect of their situation.

Crowding and Altruism

48. As crowding increases, people become less inclined to help. Thus, students who asked if they could use people's telephones were more likely to be turned down **cities** by the residents of (small towns/cities).

49. While city dwellers may be more concerned about the possible criminal intent of **cannot** a stranger, that factor (may/cannot) entirely account for the reluctance of city **less** residents to help. In another study, city dwellers were (less/more) willing than were residents of small towns to provide information to a long-distance caller who had ostensibly dialed their number by mistake.

less

50. In general, then, the greater the density, the (less/greater) the likelihood that altruism will occur. When addressed and stamped envelopes were dropped (that is, supposedly lost) in either high-density, high-rise dormitories or in low-density dormitories, it was found that 100 percent of the letters were picked up and

low-density

mailed in the _____-_____ residences and that

high-

only 63 percent were mailed in the _____-

density

_____ residences.

less

51. An additional finding of the dormitory study was that the occupants of the high-density dorm trusted the other residents (less/more) than did the low-density residents, and more of them kept their doors locked.

Learning Objectives

20. Describe studies that indicate how people respond to crowding with regard to:
    a. the intimacy of topics discussed.
    b. interpersonal distance, amount of talking, and looking at the other person.
    c. liking for others in a crowded situation.

21. What is the effect of crowding on altruism? Describe the studies comparing:
    a. city dwellers versus small-town residents.
    b. high-density versus low-density dormitory residents.

MICROINTERPERSONAL BEHAVIOR

microinterpersonal

52. Irwin Altman has integrated the concepts of personal space, territoriality, privacy, and crowding into a larger concept which he refers to as

    _____ behavior.

privacy

53. The central aspect of microinterpersonal behavior is _____. It is to obtain the desired degree of privacy that one may change the size of the

personal space

    _____-_____ bubble or alter the vigilance with

territory

    which one defends a _____ .

54. While privacy results from manipulations of personal space and territory,

crowding

    _____ results from the failure to successfully control these factors.

DESIGN APPLICATIONS

55. By manipulating aspects of design, environmental psychologists maintain that they can change our use of personal space and territory and the feelings of privacy and crowding that result. In other words, they assert that changes in the

microinterpersonal

    physical environment affect what Altman refers to as _____ behavior.

56. For example, by changing the placement of chairs one can influence the use of personal space. In a study conducted in a mental health center it was found that the most successful initial interviews between patients and therapists occurred at

six

    a distance of _____ feet, within the closer range of

social

    _____ distance.

nine

three/personal

close

57. In that study patients felt that a distance of _____ feet, within the far social-distance zone, was too great and that a distance of

_____ feet, within the _____-distance zone, was too close. In this particular setting, then, conditions that encouraged communication at the (far/close) social-distance zone produced the greatest self-disclosure.

territoriality

58. In dealing with public housing projects Newman has proposed design changes that are influenced by the concept of _____. He suggested that crime levels in housing projects could be reduced by placing the buildings in clusters, so that some of the public areas (lobbies, grounds, and elevators) would provide natural opportunities for surveillance and would be perceived as

our

"_____ territory" rather than "nobody's territory."

isolation

59. With regard to design of the work place, at least one study has found that employees reported more job satisfaction in an office that provided them with visual and acoustic (isolation/accessibility). Thus, it may be that modifications of open-plan offices would improve both morale and job performance.

dormitory
increased
smaller

60. Crowding produces stress, and another recent study has found that a simple modification of a college _____ not only reduced stress but (increased/reduced) levels of social interaction. The plan involved converting three rooms on a long corridor to lounges in order to create two (smaller/larger) groups of residents.

Learning Objectives

22. What is microinterpersonal behavior? Discuss the four components of this concept and the central role of privacy.

23. Explain how the design of buildings and interior spaces may affect:
    a. communication in a clinical setting.
    b. territoriality and crime levels in public housing.
    c. stress in a college dormitory.